WITHDRAWN FROM
CANISIUS COLLEGE LIBRARY

Language Shift in the United States

Contributions to the Sociology of Language

34

Joshua A. Fishman
Editor

MOUTON PUBLISHERS · BERLIN · NEW YORK · AMSTERDAM

Language Shift
in the United States

Calvin Veltman

MOUTON PUBLISHERS · BERLIN · NEW YORK · AMSTERDAM

Library of Congress Cataloging in Publication Data

Veltman, Calvin.
  Language shift in the United States.

  (Contributions to the sociology of language ; 34)
  1. English language — United States — Social aspects.
  2. English language — Acquisition. 3. Children —
  United States — Language. I. Title. II. Series.
  PE2808.V44 1983   401'.9   83-13272

© Copyright 1983 by Walter de Gruyter & Co., Berlin. All rights reserved, including those of translation into foreign languages. No part of this book may be reproduced in any form – by photoprint, microfilm, or any other means – nor transmitted nor translated into a machine language without written permission from the publisher. Typesetting: Grestun Graphics, Abingdon – Printing: Druckerei Hildebrand, Berlin. – Binding: Lüderitz & Bauer Buchgewerbe GmbH, Berlin. – Cover design: K. Lothar Hildebrand, Berlin.

Printed In Germany

Contents

Presentation	ix
1. Introduction	1
2. Theory and Method in the Analysis of Language Shift	11

PART 1: THE STRUCTURE OF LANGUAGE SHIFT IN THE UNITED STATES — 39

3. The Anglicisation of Adults in Minority Language Groups	41
4. Intergenerational Anglicisation in the United States	91
5. The Context of Minority Language Use among American Adolescents	144
6. Reflections on the Process of Anglicisation	211

PART II: THE ROLE OF LANGUAGE CHARACTERISTICS IN THE ATTAINMENT PROCESS — 219

7. The Impact of Language Characteristics on Occupational and Income Attainments of American Adults	221
8. The Impact of Language Characteristics on the Educational Attainments of American Children	312
9. The Impact of Language Characteristics on the Educational Achievements of American Children	355
10. Reflections on the Role of Language Characteristics in the Attainment Process	385

PART III: LANGUAGE PLANNING IN THE CONTEXT OF IDENTIFIED NEEDS — 395

Appendix A: Source and Reliability of the SIE Estimates	403
Appendix B: Design Characteristics of High School and Beyond	417
Appendix C: Fidelity of Language Reports by HSB Students	424
References	429

Presentation

Every book is in a certain way a collective effort, even though it is the product of a single author. This book results from a number of influences on my style of conceptualizing and analyzing problems. It would not, however, have been possible to complete this book without the support, both financial and personal, of a number of persons. Without going into the details of which secretary typed which page (I generally do my own typing), I should like to thank those who have made the greatest contributions.

In terms of the influences which made this book possible, I have always been fascinated by the problem of immigrants and immigrant languages. Like so many others, my ancestors are relatively recent arrivals in the United States, the product of successive waves of Dutch Calvinists settling in the Chicago metropolitan area. It is perhaps the rapidity of the anglicisation of the Dutch, together with the intensity with which they retain their ethnic identity, which inspired my original interest in this topic. Unlike so many others of my compatriots, however, I found the Lithuanians, Poles, Irish, Mexicans, and others, as interesting as were we (if not more so). The opportunity to live and work in Brooklyn only whetted my interest in the cultural transformations affecting the Italians and Puerto Ricans among whom I lived.

However, my interest in linguistic and cultural assimilation never occupied a central place either in my sociological interests or in my teaching until I accepted a position at the State University of New York at Plattsburgh. Not wishing to live in a small town (the pretentious would say 'city'), I had the privilege instead of establishing residence in Montreal. Gasoline was cheaper then. Although I did not realize it at the time, nothing would have a greater impact on my professional interests. Characterized by the presence of a large English speaking minority in constant competition with the French speaking majority (for nearly everything and everyone), Montreal is a natural laboratory for the researcher interested in ethnic and linguistic processes.

The work which sparked my initial scientific interest in the demography of language shift was the publication of Charles Castonguay's 'l'anglicisation du Canada' in *Le Devoir* (our equivalent of the *New York Times* — not published, however, on Sunday, so you have no need to truck it home). Although the first to exploit the language data from the 1971 Census of Canada, Charles has continually contributed to the systematic development of the theory of language shift. I have made rather frequent references to his work in this book, not as many as I should have perhaps, since the quality and rigor of his own analyses merit much larger diffusion in the international community than they have received. Not only has Charles contributed much to the theoretical development of language shift analyses; he read frequent drafts of the earlier chapters of this book and provided personal encouragement.

There are others in Quebec who also made significant contributions to the development of the ideas presented in this book. Rejean Lachapelle, in addition to providing a trenchant criticism of an article I prepared using 1970 U.S. Census data, was quick to point out the importance of the distinction I have drawn between English monolingualism and English bilingualism as forms of anglicisation. His own book on language shift in Canada (with Jacques Henripin), while no more perfect than this one, is the definitive treatment of the topic and covers all aspects of the growth and decline of linguistic minorities in Canada. Other members of the *Association des démographes du Québec* have made contributions to this work, partly through their comments on some specific aspect of the analysis which we discussed, mostly because they have made me feel less an immigrant and more Québécois. Every immigrant needs some reassurance in this direction from time to time (if not constantly).

The second half of this book is largely inspired by sociological analyses of labor force activity. However, it seems that my interest in this area of human activity is not unrelated to the fact that I pursued a baccalaureate degree in economics. When I published my initial analysis of the relationship between language shift and income in Quebec (1976), two econometric analyses of the same type were published almost simultaneously. This fortuitous circumstance led to a period of relatively intense collaboration with the authors of the two studies, Jac-André Boulet and François Vaillancourt, both in terms of projects which we have jointly undertaken and in terms of their willingness to read and comment upon multiple regression analyses for this or that subject.

In many respects, then, my analysis of the American linguistic scene is largely Quebec-inspired. It should not be thought, however, that Quebec methods were preferred to American methods. The efforts of Joshua Fishman and David Lopez develop the same general logic as that used in the first part of this book; those of Marta Tienda, Steve Garcia, and Gilles Grenier that used in the second half of the book. It is rather the case that Quebec researchers have simply had more time, better data, and more experience developing

Presentation

the research tools by which language shift and its correlates may be assessed. This is particularly true with respect to the use of cross-sectional data to obtain longitudinal-type interpretations. If some of these analyses seem a bit foreign at first to English speaking readers I am confident that the logic of the analysis will become evident to those endowed with an ordinary dose of patience.

The number of persons who provided other types of support for my research is somewhat larger. I should like to thank first of all Leo Estrada who, while at the U.S. Census Bureau, saw the promise of my research project and suggested which agencies might be interested in sponsoring such research. Secondly, I should like to publicly acknowledge the contribution made by Les Silverman of the National Center for Education Statistics who saw immediately the possibilities inherent in the analysis of language shift. The funding of my earlier work by NCES freed me from the necessity of teaching for two years and laid the basis for what is now contained in this book. In addition, his personal encouragement and enthusiasm have in no small way persuaded me to carry on with this project. Thirdly, I should like to thank my former colleagues in the sociology faculty at SUNY-Plattsburgh, who supported and defended me in an institutional setting relatively inhospitable both to research and things Québécois. Others who provided assistance at important periods in the development of my initial research were Robert Moll, financial assistant to the Dean of Liberal Arts at SUNY-Plattsburgh, James Quinn, then computer analyst/programmer at SUNY-Albany and now with Digital Equipment Corporation, and Ron Pedone, my project officer at NCES.

Most assuredly, this book would not have been completed had I not joined the faculty of l'Université du Québec à Montréal. Not only has this event been the realization of a personal dream (working in a French language university); it made available computer services and support which were not provided in the previous institution with which I was associated. The verification and correction of data previously published and the addition of new analyses required large amounts of data processing which were provided as part of the regular institutional support to research activities. In addition, Jean-François Guédon and André Ostiguy found ways to read otherwise illegible data tapes and provided technical assistance to solve this or that particular problem. They also introduced me to the world of word processors, without which at least five of the chapters in this book would be less intelligible than they actually are. Once again, my professional colleagues (Départment d'études urbaines) played an important role in the completion of this book. On the one hand, they accepted with good grace my resistance to being over-burdened with administrative tasks. More importantly, they listened patiently to the description of some new problem or finding, a particularly onerous task for individuals more generally interested in city and regional planning. My department chairperson, Danielle Pilette, was the person most frequently victimized in this respect.

Finally, I should like to thank my editor, Joshua Fishman, for his encouragement and helpfulness. It was at his suggestion that I decided to expand my three NCES publications into a more integrated and more complete work. Parts of two chapters of this book have already been published in the *International Journal of the Sociology of Language*, of which he is editor. The two years which I have already dedicated to this project have been profitable ones, permitting me to integrate and refine certain of the analyses. Where there are still weaknesses, they are entirely my own.

Montréal
June, 1983

Chapter 1

Introduction

This is not the first book written about the process of language shift in the United States. However, it is unique in that it represents the first complete attempt to assess the macrosociological process by which minority language groups are assimilated to the English language majority. The single most important attempt to accomplish this task in the past was the seminal work by Fishman and his collaborators, *Language Loyalty in the United States* (1966). The earlier work relied only in part on data available from the national decennial census in the United States, since such data has not always been available and since such data as were available made reference only to the mother tongue of the minority language population. The existence of a single data item such as mother tongue is not alone sufficient to yield rates of minority language retention and loss. Consequently, the remainder of *Language Loyalty* is dedicated to the analysis of a series of indirect indicators of minority language retention and loss. Since no direct data were available to assess this problem, the Fishman team was forced to examine the presence of minority language media, educational institutions, parishes, social organizations, and the like.

In this book, however, we have the opportunity to directly asses the use of minority languages in the United States. Thus, we can compare the (declared) language practices of respondents at the time of the survey to their language origins, this latter being defined by the mother tongue of such individuals. If, then, we have reason to believe that persons in minority language groups can assess with relative accuracy their current language use patterns, we can construct measures of the extent to which they retain or lose the facility to speak their mother tongues. This direct comparison is extremely important, since it bypasses the tedious work involved in constructing indirect measures of relatively unknown quality.

The direct measurement of language shift has been most developed by Quebec-based researchers, who moved rapidly to exploit the availability of usual home language data from the 1971 Census of Canada. A variety of demographic and economic studies used the comparison between mother tongue and usual language to probe the correlates of language shift in Canada.

However, the type of methodology used by the Quebec researchers is not entirely unknown in the United States. Lopez (1975) has used a similar methodology in his analysis of Chicano language loyalty in East Los Angeles while Fishman and others have examined in detail the language practices of Puerto Ricans in Jersey City (1972, 1975). However, no national data have been available in the United States to permit such a methodology to be applied at the national level. This is the task set before us in this book: to examine in detail the current situation of minority language groups in the United States, to measure the structure, the extent and the pace of linguistic assimilation.

Since our book expands upon the American tradition of language research developed by Fishman, we shall make use of his data to prepare the terrain for our study. We begin our analysis with a brief examination of the mother tongue data made available in the 1940, 1960 and 1970 U.S. Census. The question asked of the so-called White population in the 1940 Census was the following: 'What language was spoken in this person's home when he was a child?' A similar question was asked of the foreign born in the 1960 Census, from which Fishman and Hofman have constructed population estimates for minority language groups. We have combined Danish, Finnish, Norwegian, and Swedish into a single 'Scandinavian' category so that we can compare the 1940-1960 figures to those derived from later reports. The relevant data for the French, German, Greek, Italian, Polish, Portuguese, Russian, Scandinavian, Spanish and Yiddish language groups are presented in Table 1.1.

As Fishman and Hofman have noted in their analysis of this data, the major language groups derived from the great immigrations of the 19th and early 20th centuries underwent a marked decline in the twenty year period. The Scandinavian group declined by 48.9 percent, the Yiddish by 44.9 percent, and the German by 36.4 percent. Other groups underwent lesser declines but only the Italian group remained more or less stable in size. Only two groups grew in size, the Greek language group and, most notably, the Spanish. Since in this study we shall have recourse to the examination of findings for the Spanish and non-Spanish groups taken as a whole, we have calculated separately the rate of decline for this latter group. The data reported in Table 1.1 indicated that the major non-Spanish language groups declined from 17.3 million members in 1940 to 12.9 million in 1960, a decline of 25.3 percent.

When we consider the factors which may have caused the decline of these language groups and the expansion of the Spanish group, it is quite evident that the level of international immigration probably played the greatest role. Cut off from continued immigration, the German, Scandinavian, and Yiddish language groups underwent rapid erosion as adults became English speaking

Table 1.1 *Estimated number of persons of selected mother tongues United States, 1940 and 1960*

Language group	Estimated population size 1940	1960	Change 1940–1960
French	1,412,060	1,043,220	−26.1%
German	4,949,780	3,145,770	−36.4%
Greek	273,520	292,030	+ 6.8%
Italian	3,766,820	3,674,140	− 2.5%
Polish	2,416,320	2,184,940	− 9.6%
Portuguese	215,660	181,110	−16.0%
Russian	585,080	464,830	−21.2%
Scandinavian	1,946,280	995,160	−48.9%
Spanish	1,861,400	3,335,960	+79.2%
Yiddish	1,751,100	964,410	−44.9%
Total non-Spanish	17,316,620	12,941,610	−25.3%

Source: Fishman, 1966
Note: Scandinavian = Danish, Finnish, Swedish, Norwegian

and raised English speaking children. Since these latter probably had English for their mother tongue, they no longer fit the Census definition of mother tongue. Consequently, the language groups which resulted from earlier immigrations were rapidly decimated between 1940 and 1960. Those which issued from more recent immigrations underwent somewhat less rapid declines, while those language groups continuing to receive large numbers of international immigrants increased in number. At the very least, their losses may have been masked by the impact of continued immigration.

Since these observations are based on mother tongue reports from the national censuses of 1940 and 1960, it would seem perfectly logical to continue this type of modified trend analysis to the 1970 Census. It is indeed the case that the U.S. Census Bureau published a series of 1970 Census data called 'mother tongue.' These data were based, however, on the following question: 'What language, other than English, was spoken in this person's home when he was a child?' This question differs markedly from that asked in the 1940 Census because it contains the phrase set off by commas, *'other than English'*. The 1940 Census required the respondent to furnish the language spoken in the person's home. The respondent was required to furnish the understanding that the question sollicited the identification of the principal home language. Thus, the 1940 question implied the existence of the word 'usually' to define 'spoken.' This implication is no longer required in the 1970 Census question, since the Bureau rendered the question more explicit. The term 'other than English' makes it clear that a minority language is being sollicited (Lachapelle, 1976). Consequently, the two language questions are no longer comparable, since the 1970 Census question may have been interpreted as meaning, 'Have you ever heard a language other than English spoken in your home when you were a child?'

The Bureau of the Census was not insensitive to this problem. To check the validity of the 1970 Census question, the Bureau proceeded to evaluate the manner in which respondents interpreted the question. During the Reinterview Study designed to verify (or clarify) a certain number of census questions, interviewers were asked to ascertain whether the respondent himself was in early childhood (1) monolingual in the minority language, (2) used the minority language most frequently but also spoke English, (3) used both languages with equal frequency, (4) usually spoke English but also used a minority language frequently, usually spoke English but also spoke the minority language (5) 'occasionally' or (6) 'seldom,' or (7) did not speak the minority language at all. The Census referred to these seven categories as 'levels' of minority language use. The results of the Reinterview study are reported in Table 1.2.

Table 1.2 *Reinterview classification of persons declaring a minority mother tongue in 1970 census, United States, 1971*

Reinterview classification	Number	Percent
Dominant minority language	809	48.9
Minority/English equally	38	2.3
Dominant English language	276	16.7
English almost exclusively	93	5.6
English only	439	26.5
Totals	1,655	100.0%

Source: Census, 1975

The Census Bureau found 1,655 individuals (of 11,202 reinterviewed) who had said in the 1970 Census that a minority language had been spoken in their homes when they were children. Of this number, 847 satisfied the

Introduction

criteria defining levels 1 and 2. That is, they had been either monolingual in the minority language in early childhood or they had used the minority language as their principal language of use. If we define mother tongue as the language spoken by the child when his parents first taught him to speak, it is almost certain that the persons found in levels 1 and 2 did in fact have a minority language for their mother tongue. Actually, they are the only people who unambiguously respond to this definition. In addition, another 38 persons (2.3 percent of the total) said that both languages were of equal importance in childhood (level 3). Given the direction of language shift in the United States, it is highly probable that such persons also had a minority mother tongue and subsequently learned English. This raises the total percentage of such persons to *51.2* percent who probably had a minority language as mother tongue.

On the other hand, 26.5 percent of the individuals interviewed said that they themselves had not spoken the minority langauge at all, while an additional 5.6 percent said that they had only spoken it occasionally or seldom. It is highly unlikely that these latter could have had the minority language for their mother tongue; it is more likely that they acquired some minimal competence in the minority language as a second language. Clearly, the English language was so dominant that it does not seem reasonable to presume that they had already abandoned their mother tongue. Thus, an estimated 31.5 percent of the sample almost certainly did not have a minority language for their mother tongue, in spite of the fact that the published 1970 Census tables said they did.

Having established relatively clearly which of the persons in levels 1 to 7 did (or did not) have a minority language for their mother tongue, we must now consider the linguistic origins of the 16.7 percent of the sample who said that they usually spoke English but also spoke a minority language with some regularity. Some of these people may indeed have had a minority mother tongue but most are likely to have had English for their first language. We should not presume that some reasonable facility in the minority language guarantees that that language was the first language learned by the child. Rather, in a context of language shift, the parents may still use the language with some frequency, i.e., adequate to impart some working knowledge of the language to the children. In any case, we can fix 67.9 percent (51.2 + 16.7 = 67.9%) as the maximum proportion of those identified in published 1970 Census reports as having minority 'mother tongue' who do in fact respond to the more normal understanding of the meaning of the term.

The authors of the Reinterview report realized the significance of the reinterview data. After having examined the findings, the analysts concluded:

'Census respondents tended to apply a literal interpretation to the mother tongue question and to report any foreign language usage in their childhood homes, regardless of degree or intensity of usage.' (Census, 1975: 9).

We might add, 'regardless of their actual mother tongue.' In view of the deviation of the Reinterview findings from the published 1970 Census tables, we can also admire the sense of humor of the Census analyists, their gift for understatement being matched only by their unwillingness to admit the magnitude of their error. That they should continue to use the term 'mother tongue' to refer to the data in the light of their own evidence to the contrary is certainly curious.

The data officially released by the Census Bureau indicated that 33,175,000 Americans reported the presence of a minority mother tongue in 1970. This figure represented 16.3 percent of the population. On the basis of the Reinterview study, it is clear that these estimates need to be revised downward to an important extent if they are to have any resemblance to a real definition of mother tongue. The Census analysts obligingly furnished the relevant statistics for the nation as a whole, although not for specific minority language groups. Taking as a definition of 'mother tongue' certain of the levels of language use previously defined the Census provided the following percentage estimates (Census, 1975: Table F). We have supplied the appropriate conversions to population estimates:

Level of use	Percent	Population
Levels 1-2	7.7%	15,647,000
Levels 1-3	8.1%	16,460,000
Levels 1-4	11.2%	22,760,000
Levels 1-6	12.5%	25,401,000

These data clearly show the reduced population sizes which result from successive definitions of mother tongue. The reported estimates of 33 million are evidently much too high in the light of the new evidence furnished by the Census itself. Even were occasional or infrequent usage admitted as evidence of the presence of a minority mother tongue, the Census estimate remains nearly 8 million persons lower than their published data reports. Given the analysis previously presented, we prefer the estimate of 8.1% and 16,460,000

Introduction

persons as representing the best estimate of the size of the population of minority mother tongue in 1970.

Fortunately, this interpretation is confirmed by a new national data set issued in 1977. This data set is known as the Survey of Income and Education and was based on a sample of more than 150,000 households. A more detailed description, together with reliability estimates, of the SIE data is presented in Appendix A. The SIE contained a number of language questions, among which was the following: 'What language was *usually* spoken in this person's home when he was a child?' This question has none of the ambiguity which characterized the 1970 Census question, and is even more rigorously defined than was the 1940 Census questions. The word 'usually' has been provided rather than simply implied. Since this question corresponds more closely to the common definition of mother tongue, the size of the minority language population should be considerably smaller than that presented in the 1970 Census. The relevant comparisons for the major language groups presented in Table 1.3.

Table 1.3 *Estimated number of persons of minority mother tongue, United States, 1970 and 1976*

Language group	Estimated population size	
	1970	1976
French	2,598,410	1,268,749
German	6,093,050	2,230,260
Greek	458,700	422,057
Italian	4,144,320	2,336,518
Polish	2,437,940	1,421,606
Portuguese	365,300	416,446
Russian	334,620	175,854
Scandinavian	1,647,590	595,933
Spanish	7,823,580	7,503,110
Yiddish	1,593,990	608,700
Major Non-Spanish	19,673,920	9,476,123
Total	27,497,500	16,979,233

Source: U.S. Census, 1970; Survey of Income and Education, 1976

An examination of Table 1.3 confirms that our expectations are correct. The SIE estimates are markedly lower than the 1970 Census estimates in nearly all cases. The French, German, Italian, Polish, Scandinavian, Russian, and Yiddish language groups are decimated by the application of a more adequate definition of mother tongue. On the other hand, the Portuguese language group is actually larger than it was in 1970, reflecting population growth resulting from continued immigration, while that of the Spanish language group is only marginally smaller. That it is smaller at all, however, suggests that the Spanish language group has also undergone some anglicisation.

When we examine the total number of persons estimated to belong to minority language as frequently as English), is quite close to that obtained different results. The SIE finds only 9.5 million persons in the major non-Spanish language groups as compared to 19.7 million for the same language groups according to the published Census results. The importance of adequately selecting a definition of mother tongue could not be more clearly underlined. Interestingly, the 1976 SIE yields a total estimate of approximately 17 million persons of minority mother tongues. When we apply the 8.1 percent estimate which we prefer as the 'true' estimate of the number of minority language persons to the 1970 Census, we obtained an estimated 16.5 million persons. This figure, which indicates the number of persons in levels one to three as defined by the Census (persons who minimally used a minority language as frequently as English), is quite close to that obtained from the SIE. This correspondence suggests that our preference for the 8.1 percent figure is relatively well-founded in empirical reality.

The impact of the decline of these language groups can be better assessed when the percentage of the decline is calculated. Two such calculations have been made, one representing the decline from 1960 to 1976 based on the Fishman-Hofman estimates for 1960, a second that from 1940 to 1976 based on data produced by the Census itself.

If we use the Fishman-Hofman estimates as the basis for the calculation of rates of decline, the data show that four groups have increased in size between 1960 and 1976, notably the Spanish and the Portuguese. That the Greek language group has increased is probably also quite likely. In the absence of heavy immigration and given the data presented later in this book, it would seem quite unlikely that the French language group did in fact increase in size during this period. It is rather more likely that the Fishman-Hofman estimates of the size of the French language group were too low. Other rates based on the 1960 data indicate sharp declines in the number of persons having German, Italian, Polish, Scandinavian, Russian and Yiddish mother tongue, i.e., members of those groups having their largest wave of immigration at or before the turn of the century. The global decline estimated for the non-Spanish groups presented in this table was 26.9 percent.

When we compare the 1976 data to the 1940 data, the rates of decline for

Table 1.4 *Percentage change in number of persons of minority mother tongue, United States, 1940-1976*

Language group	Percent change during the period	
	1960-1976	1940-1976
French	+ 21.6	− 10.1
German	− 29.1	− 54.9
Greek	+ 44.5	+ 54.3
Italian	− 36.4	− 38.0
Polish	− 34.9	− 41.2
Portuguese	+129.9	+ 93.1
Russian	− 61.9	− 70.0
Scandinavian	− 40.1	− 69.4
Spanish	+124.9	+303.1
Yiddish	− 36.9	− 65.2
Major non-Spanish	− 26.9	− 45.4

Source: Fishman-Hofman, 1966; SIE, 1976

most major groups are, of course, still sharper. This may be expected since these groups experienced relative decline in both the 1940-1960 and in the 1960-1976 periods. The German, Scandinavian, Russian and Yiddish language groups declined by more than fifty percent. The Italian and Polish language groups declined by approximately forty percent, while the decline of the French language group appears more limited. The Greek, Portuguese and Spanish language groups experienced relatively important growth during the period, the Spanish language group tripling in size during the thirty-six year period. When the non-Spanish groups are combined into a single group, the major non-Spanish languages examined in Table 1.4 declined by 45.4 percent. This is indeed one major characteristic of the post-war period. The Spanish language group has become the only large minority language group, whereas in the past there were a number of large, important minority language groups resulting from earlier periods of immigration.

While the analysis of the mother tongue data does provide long run data on the decline of the major non-Spanish languages and the rise of the Spanish language, the analysis of language shift based on mother tongue alone is methodologically unacceptable. Minority language groups may vary widely in terms of age structure, place of birth, period of immigration, as well as economic position. Since minority language groups may vary both in composition and in rates of language shift to English, the use of mother tongue alone as an indicator of retention is seriously deficient (see also McArthur, 1981). A better procedure is to examine current language practice in relationship to linguistic origin. That is to say, current use should be compared to mother tongue. Since the Survey of Income and Education also contains data on the current language use of the American population, it can be used to make such direct comparisons. It is for this reason that we have built the principal analyses contained in this work on the SIE. Not only is the mother tongue question more appropriately drawn; it provides the basis for a direct comparison between current practice and minority language origin.

In this book, then, we shall attempt to empirically establish the 'facts' of linguistic assimilation in the United States. While others may attempt to 'explain' why some groups have higher rates of assimilation than others (Grosjean [1982] lists some thirty factors), we think that the actual data are too poorly understood to support such broad theorizing. We do not accept at face value the assertions that some groups have been assimilated more rapidly than others. No national data base existed before the SIE which would permit such assertions to be grounded in empirical reality. Consequently, apparent differences in rates of assimilation or maintenance/retention may have their source in the composition of various minority language groups. Such differences have been uncontrolled in previous studies using SIE data (Grosjean, 1982; McArther, 1981; Waggoner, 1981). Before we can accept propositions that some group is more retentive than another, we need to establish clearly that such is in fact the case, i.e., once the appropriate compositional effects have been eliminated.

This book, then, is largely empirical in orientation. We shall attempt to carefully document the structure, the extent and the pace of language shift in the first half of the book. In this endeavor we see our work as a sequel to *Language Loyalty in the United States* with but a single exception — we have no need to rely on indirect measures of minority language retention. In the second half of the book, we shall attempt to explore the link between language characteristics and socioeconomic achievement. It is only after the empirical reality has been adequately examined that the task of theorizing can be undertaken. Too frequently, but understandably in the absence of data, theorizing about the causes of language shift and retention have preceded the analysis. Our objective is to correct this situation.

Chapter 2

Theory and Method in the Analysis of Language Shift

The Growth and Decline of Subpopulations. This is a book about subpopulations in the United States, specifically about subpopulations defined in terms of linguistic criteria. If we state our objective in its most polemic terms, we shall examine in this book the survival prospects of specific minority language groups in the United States; in more scientific terms, we shall examine the structure, the extent, and the pace of language shift from minority language groups to the dominant national language.

Such an enterprise requires first of all a conceptual framework to guide the analyst. The conceptual model which underlies the first half of the book is drawn directly from the population model proposed in courses in introductory demography. Some of the distinctions drawn by us in our discussion of the elementary population model serve to guide the analysis developed in the second half of the book, where we examine more closely the impact of language characteristics on socioeconomic attainment. The elementary population model proposes that the size of a given population at some future point is a function of a finite number of factors: its original size, the relation between the number of births and deaths which occur during the period being examined, and the relation between the number of immigrants and emigrants which enter and leave the territory during that period of time.

This population model can readily be applied to subpopulations with only minor modifications. It is most particularly the notion of 'immigration' and 'emigration' which requires adjustment. Two types of immigrants and emigrants may be defined. The first type consists of that defined by the act of crossing of an international border to establish residence in a country. Those who enter may be defined as 'international immigrants' while those who leave may be called 'international emigrants.' The second type of migration consists of internal migration between subpopulations. In terms of linguistic subpopulations, a person who takes up residence outside the area in which his linguistic group of origin resides may be considered to have left that group if he participates primarily in the life of some other language group. Similarly, when an adolescent or young adult leaves the parental home to establish his own residence, he may cease to participate actively in the life of the minority language group of origin and to participate only in the life of the English language group. It is not, however, necessary to establish a new residence in order to complete a linguistic migration. One or more members of a family or household may decide to reduce to a minimum his participation in the life of the minority language group and to maximize his participation in that of the English language group. In fact, the entire family may undertake such a process. Thus, linguistic emigrants are those who leave their language group of origin; linguistic immigrants those who enter a minority language group.

The relationship between these various aspects of the population model can be summarized in the following equation,

$$p1 = p0 + (b - d) + (i_i - e_i) + (i_l - e_l)$$

Where (p1) is the population at some subsequent time period, (p0) is the original population, (b) represents the number of births during the period and (d) the number of deaths. The term $(i_i - e_i)$ represents the net migratory balance for the linguistic subpopulation accruing from movements across international boundaries, while the $(i_l - e_l)$ term represents the net migratory balance due to linguistic migrations.

In this book we shall focus on only one aspect of this equation, the (e_l) term which refers to linguistic emigration. This choice may appear rather arbitrary to some and obviously merits further discussion. In the first place, we propose that the term (i_l) is always approximately equal to zero. There is almost no in-migration into minority language groups from the English language group. We are not here referring to the numbers of people from English language background who learn a minority language. Rather, when we speak of linguistic migration into a minority language group, we require that a person of English language origin adopt the minority language as his principal language of use. This is a rather stringent test, one which we shall justify later in this chapter. What is important to understand, however, is that in terms of this definition, there is virtually no linguistic in-migration into minority language groups. A high degree of bilingualism in a minority language does not constitute linguistic immigration. A linguistic immigrant to the Spanish language group is someone who 'becomes' Spanish-speaking in the full sense of the term. He is an active participant in the daily life of the Spanish language group, not someone who simply speaks Spanish, however well.

Since the number of such linguistic immigrants to minority language groups is nearly always equal to zero, it follows that the value of the term

($i_1 - e_1$) is always negative in the United States. Language minorities always lose more persons to the English language group than they receive from that group. Even persons who intermarry are likely to adopt the English language as the principal language of use. Those persons of English language background who come to adopt a minority language as principal language of use are exceedingly rare. Thus, we can safely dispense with the calculation of the (i_1) term.

Obviously, the same cannot be said of the remaining factors in the population equation. Let us consider first of all the problem of the relation between the number of births and deaths in a minority language group. In focussing our attention only on the (e_1) term, we have in fact decided to invoke the assumption that the fertility and mortality rates of minority language groups do not differ from those of the English language majority. For those familiar with the literature, it is evident that this assumption is not entirely correct. For example, in their analysis of household income Angel and Tienda (1981) find that the average household size of Hispanics of Mexican origin is approximately 17 percent larger than those of non-Hispanic whites. Those of other Hispanic groups are also somewhat larger than those of whites. Thus, the Hispanic group would appear to enjoy somewhat higher rates of natural increase than would the larger non-Hispanic population. Some of this advantage may be erased by higher mortality rates, particularly that of infant mortality.

Nonetheless, we are not required for the purposes of our analysis to investigate in detail the patterns of differential fertility and mortality. There are limits to the extent to which women of any minority group can be expected to maintain larger family sizes to offset the linguistic assimilation of their peers. Lachapelle and Henripin (1980) have calculated that the average woman must give birth to 4.5 children to assure the numeric stability of the group when the linguistic emigration rate is approximately fifty percent. Chicano women living in the households examined by Angel and Tienda had only 2.9 children, well below that which would be necessary to assure the long term replacement of anglicized persons at such a rate of anglicisation. Given the rates of anglicisation which we shall establish in this book, it is clear that differential fertility cannot arrest the decline of minority language groups.

Furthermore, while minority language women in the immigrant generation are more likely than native born women to have larger families, it is unrealistic to assume that (North) American women of whatever language group would willingly maintain fertility levels markedly higher than the societal norm. Thus, native born women in the different subpopulations tend to have family sizes which are rather similar. The only group of native born women which had markedly higher levels of fertility in 1976 were Black women, the different groups of women of Hispanic ancestry having between 2.0 and 2.5 children in that year. These findings suggest that we can minimize the problems associated with differential fertility. Fertility differentials, particularly among the native born, are not sufficiently important to compensate for the extremely high rates of linguistic emigration which characterize all American minority language groups.

While we can ignore the calculation of the (i_1) term and minimize the impact of differential rates of natural increase, we cannot ignore the problem of international migration. Since it is impossible to obtain accurate data on the extent of international emigration, we are obliged to focus our attention on the impact of international immigration. If, for example, the level of such immigration is relatively low, persons who leave the minority language group via linguistic emigration will cause the size of the group to decrease. The decline will be more or less rapid depending on the rate of such linguistic emigration.

On the other hand, if the level of international immigration is sufficiently high, a language group may experience absolute numeric growth even though it loses large numbers of its members through linguistic emigration. This is currently the situation of the Spanish language group in the United States. The SIE data reveal that in 1976 there were some 2.5 million persons aged 14 and over who were born in the United States and who had Spanish as their first language. Of these 2.5 million persons who originally spoke Spanish as their principal language, approximately 1.6 million reported that they usually spoke English as their principal language at the time of the survey. These are linguistic emigrants to the English language group. However, of the 3.2 million persons of Spanish mother tongue who were international immigrants, *only* 1.0 million no longer continued to speak Spanish as their principal language of use. The 2.2 million international immigrants who continued to make Spanish their principal language more than compensated for the 1.6 million persons of native birth lost to the English language group. In terms strictly of the number of persons who spoke Spanish as their usual language, the Spanish language group experienced an absolute growth from the 2.5 million persons born in the United States to 3.1 million persons at the time of the Survey (.9 + 2.2 = 3.1). This represents an increase of 26 percent in the number of persons speaking Spanish as their usual language, this in spite of a linguistic emigration rate of nearly 65 percent among the native born.

This absolute growth of the Spanish language group has not failed to have an impact on public consciousness. Large numbers of Americans have become aware of the increased presence of Spanish-speaking people, particularly in the larger American cities. To cater to this expanding Spanish language market, there has been a proliferation of publicity and advertising in the Spanish language, furthering the impression that the Spanish language group has arrived *en masse*. It is just this kind of accountant's mentality which has led to claims that the Spanish group is the most rapidly growing subpopulation in the United States.

While there is some truth to this perspective if we restrict our discussion to ethnic ancestry, this argument is largely false with reference to language. Had none of the Americans or international immigrants of Spanish mother tongue made English their usual language by 1976, the population of adults who usually speak Spanish would have been nearly 5.8 million persons instead of the 3.1 million persons observed. This would have represented an increase of 132 percent instead of the modest 26 percent increase actually observed. Consequently, the analyst must be exceedingly rigorous in defining the terms of the debate, a debate where some otherwise enlightened observers cannot distinguish English from Spanish speaking Hispanics. Not all Hispanic Americans are Spanish speaking, in addition to which large numbers of persons of Spanish mother tongue have adopted English as their preferred language of use.

As the preceding discussion has indicated, we are not unaware of the importance of international immigration for minority language groups. One may presume that the French, German, Italian, Polish, Scandinavian, and Yiddish language groups also experienced a period where their losses to the English language group were camouflaged by continued immigration. As we shall show in this book, these groups have been virtually eliminated as language groups in the United States, having replaced a linguistically defined identity by one based on a common ethnic origin. Consequently, by ignoring the problem of continued international arrivals, we permit ourselves to ask whether this or that specific minority language group could survive in the long run given the language behavior observed. This question in itself is entirely legitimate.

The typology of linguistic assimilation. Having clearly identified the orientation of our study, we shall now explore more fully the idea of language shift, particularly that form of language shift which we have called 'emigration.' Obviously, such emigration results from contact between people of one language group and those of another language group. Whenever two (or more) language groups cohabit a given territory, a limited number of outcomes will result from language contact between these groups. Two extremes are relatively well defined. At the one extreme, a language group may be characterized by what may be called language retention, a situation which has been defined by Fishman and his colleagues (1966) as 'language loyalty.' In principle, all members of the group continue to speak their mother tongue as their principal language of use throughout their entire lifetime. The English language group in Canada and in the United States approaches this ideal type of language retention. Nearly everyone of English mother tongue continues to speak English as his principal language of use. Moreover, this situation is thought by most English speaking people to be 'normal.'

At the other extreme, a language group may lose all of its members through linguistic assimilation (emigration) to another group, all persons of the given mother tongue coming to speak the language of some other group. Since in the United States linguistic emigration takes the direction of integration into the English language group, we shall call this phenomenon 'anglicisation.' Anglicisation may be considered to be one type of what Gordon (1964) has called Anglo-conformity: persons of minority language background flow into the dominant English language group.

It appears that some observers object to the term 'anglicisation' on the grounds that the term implies cultural as well as linguistic assimilation. Peng (1981) goes so far as to maintain that Chinese Americans have been anglicized in language but not in culture. While we would prefer to leave this domain to cultural anthropologists, it appears to us patently silly to maintain that Chinese Americans who are monolingual in English are culturally indistinguishable from Taiwanese or mainland Chinese. That Chinese constitute an American ethnic group with high levels of endogamy is perfectly plausible, as is the possibility that they share certain values not cherished by other Americans. It seems to us that those who wish to assert that linguistic anglicisation is not accompanied by cultural anglicisation should, however, bear the burden of proof. The relatively high degree of integration into American life and declining rates of exogamy of French, Italian, German, Polish, Scandinavian and Eastern European ancestry groups would seem to support the proposition that the two phenomena are related. Nonetheless, the definition retained in our analysis is *strictly linguistic*; no relation between linguistic and cultural anglicisation need be inferred.

Since the polar concepts of retention and anglicisation (assimilation) are 'ideal types' in the Weberian sense, empirical observations of the language shift process fall on the continuum defined by these two extremes. The problem which besets the analyst of the continuum is determining where to draw certain lines. When does the level of linguistic emigration become 'high,' 'important' or the like? These are indeed very difficult questions to answer when posed abstractly.

To respond to the difficulties inherent in such evaluations, we have developed some intermediate concepts which permit us to distinguish between different degrees of language shift, each type representing more extensive movement toward the English language. We begin by considering the situation of the person who is monolingual in a minority language. Let us propose that such a person is a child who was given this language as his or her first language (mother tongue). Such persons living in the United States are obliged to encounter situations where the English language is the only language used. Children must attend school, they watch television, they live in neighborhoods. Thus, they must live in what is largely an English language environment. This reality leads such persons to develop adequate verbal facilities in the English language. Consequently, the first type of language shift from minority language monolingualism consists in becoming bilingual in English. It is neither necessary (nor implied) that such persons become English speaking in the sense of accomplishing a linguistic migration to that group. Rather, we propose that 'simple bilingualism' describes the linguistic situation of persons who generally retain their mother tongue as their principal language of use but who also speak English.

Once persons of minority language background come to speak English with a relative high degree of fluency, a further choice is possible. They may either retain their mother tongue as their principal language of use, or they may make English their privileged vehicle of communication. The decision to adopt English as one's principal language of use is one which has grave consequences for the future of the minority language group. While persons who simply speak English well do not pose a threat *per se* to the survival of the minority language group, those who take the further step of making that language their principal language directly undermine the future of their group of origin. Such persons subordinate their mother tongue to the status of a second language, more or less frequently spoken according to the context or the situation in which the person finds himself. Since the English language has become the principal language of use, we refer in this book to this type of language shift as 'English bilingualism,' indicating the priority of the English language. The term 'bilingualism' indicates that the mother tongue has been retained as a second language.

This particular type of language shift does not, however, reduce the size of the population which speaks the minority language. English bilinguals still use the minority language with sufficient frequency that they may rightly be counted among those who currently maintain the use of the minority language. However, while they continue to participate in the minority language group on a more or less frequent basis, there has been a qualitative change in the nature of their linguistic behavior. The fact that they usually speak English means that persons with whom they frequently interact will normally be addressed in English. This feature of their linguistic practice becomes crucial for their children, since they will be exposed to a predominantly (although not exclusively) English language environment. Consequently, they may be expected to have the English language for their mother tongue. The principal language spoken by the parents should logically become the mother tongue of their children. The children of English bilinguals may also be expected, however, to develop some facility in what will become their second language but which was the mother tongue of their parents.

These observations make it clear that researchers cannot simply count the numbers of persons who declare that they speak a minority language with some regularity. Among those persons who do so, qualitatively different types of linguistic behavior can be distinguished, types of behavior which will determine the survival prospects of the minority language group. Those who continue, for example, to speak Spanish as their principal language of use may be expected to have children of Spanish mother tongue. Those who have become English bilinguals may be expected to have children of English mother tongue. Thus, although English bilinguals continue to contribute to the maintenance of the minority language, they have already accomplished a linguistic migration to the English language group. They will not contribute children to the minority language group, at least not in the sense of native speakers of the language. It is for this reason that we call such persons 'anglicized' and that we view this type of language shift as particularly crucial.

One further type of language shift still more definitive than English bilingualism can also be conceptualized. A certain number of persons may cease to speak their mother tongue on a regular basis. That is to say, they may continue to speak it in very specialized settings but they do so with less and less frequency. Some may not speak it at all. When such persons are asked whether or not they speak their mother tongue with some regularity, they respond in the negative. Such persons have become 'English monolinguals' to all intents and purposes. They have abandoned their mother tongue as a vehicle of communication.

English monolingualism has the same essential consequences as does English bilingualism. Children of such persons will have English for their mother tongue. Consequently, we refer to both English bilingualism and English monolingualism as constituting two forms of anglicisation. However, English monolingualism has two additional consequences. First of all, English monolinguals do not continue to actively participate in the life of the minority language group. Such persons are unambibuous migrants to the English language group. Secondly, their children will not be expected to have verbal skills in the minority language, since they are not exposed to contact with the language that was the mother tongue of their parents. Thus, both parents and children are lost to the minority language group, depriving it both of present and future support.

These four types of language behavior permit us to specify more clearly the range of language practice on the continuum between minority language retention and emigration. Each type is dependent on the previous type defined and represents a further degree of movement to the English language group. Those who do not speak English with reasonable facility correspond to the polar end of the continuum defining retention; those who have become bilingual in English have made some movement in the direction of becoming English speaking. Once one has learned English well, the possibility of making English one's usual language is offered. We define the making of English as one's usual language as 'anglicisation,' this process having a less extreme and a more extreme form. The less extreme form consists in the retention of the minority language as a second, subordinated language, while the more extreme form consists in an unambiguous emigration to the English language group. The minority language is no longer used with any great frequency, if at all.

Our discussion of types of language shift has been based on the experience of specific individuals in any given minority language group. However, only a short step separates us from the analysis of the language shift patterns of the entire group. Given an entire subpopulation of persons of a given mother tongue, we may describe their current language characteristics in terms of linguistic mobility. Just as sociologists derive rates of occupational mobility between social classes, we may establish rates of linguistic mobility from the minority language group to the English language. The various types of intermediate adaptations to the English language environment permit us to measure not only the degree of language shift but also its extent for any given minority language group.

The structure of linguistic emigration. Our presentation of the logic for measuring linguistic assimilation has tended to present the pattern of language shift as rather undifferentiated in nature. That is to say, the concepts developed can be used to construct general measures of language shift. However, previous analyses of the structure of language shift have revealed that this process is structured by the life experiences of the individual. When the mother tongue of the individual differs from the politically and economically dominant language of a given region, language shift from the minority to the majority language is observed. This language shift is characterised by an age structure which is grounded in the social experiences of the individual. When the child is very young, his mother tongue and subsequent language use are largely determined by the behavior of his parents. Consequently, little language shift is observed. That is to say, the child continues to speak his mother tongue as his principal language of use. However, when the child attends school, the linguistic behavior of his peers, together with the official language of instruction and school authorities, begins to play a role in the language capabilities and preferences of the child. During this period there is a notable increase in the percentage of persons who make the definite break with the language of daily use. A more definite break with the constraining authority of the parental home is associated with the entry of the young adult into the work force or institutions of higher learning and/or with the selection of a mate. There is accordingly a surge in the rates of language emigration in the late teens and early twenties. Since such choices are nearly always completed by the age of thirty or thirty-five, further language shift should be rather unexpected (Castonguay, 1976). This theoretic structure is graphically illustrated in Figure 2.1.

The line labelled 'a' in Figure 2.1 represents any given level of linguistic emigration which may prevail in any region for any specific minority language group. Since we are treating the problem of anglicisation in the United States, we have given the symbol 'a' to this line. The anglicisation rate is reported on the vertical axis and ranges from zero (0) to one hundred (100) percent. Findings from previous research suggest that differences in the levels of anglicisation are more likely reflected by differences in the location of the curve 'a' rather than by differences in the shape of the curve itself. That is to say, the process of language shift is presumed to be more or less invariate in Western societies, the age curve presented in Figure 2.1 being similar for all language groups and regions. What differs is the extent of language shift, that is, whether the curve is located nearer to the top or nearer the bottom of the figure.

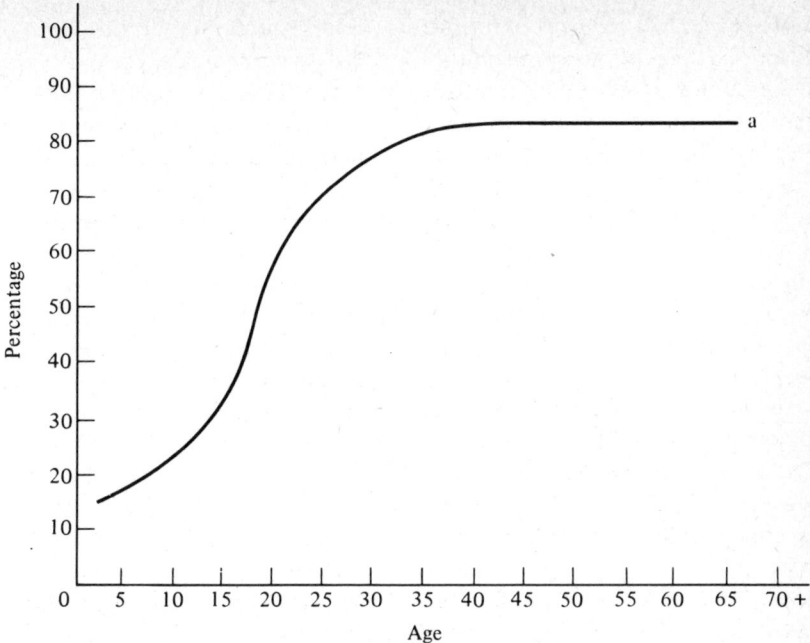

Figure 2.1 *Theoretic distribution of language shift by age*

Since the theoretical analysis which we have outlined suggests that linguistic emigration to another group is completed by the age of thirty or thirty-five, older age cohorts provide us with estimates of the extent to which they underwent language shift before they reached the age of thirty-five. That is to say, if we can postulate that there is no further linguistic mobility after the age of thirty-five, then the extent of anglicisation of the minority language population aged forty-five faithfully reflects the anglicisation rate which prevailed ten years earlier (that is, when they completed their language shift process). Similarly, that of the group aged fifty-five represents the extent to which they were anglicized twenty years earlier. Consequently, the language mobility rates of persons older than thirty-five years of age permit us to ascertain the secular evolution of the language shift process.

If anglicisation is an invariant process for a given language group, then each age group older than thirty-five years of age should contain similar proportions of anglicized persons. The appropriate curve for this condition is presented in Figure 2.2 by the curve labelled 'c' (for 'constant').

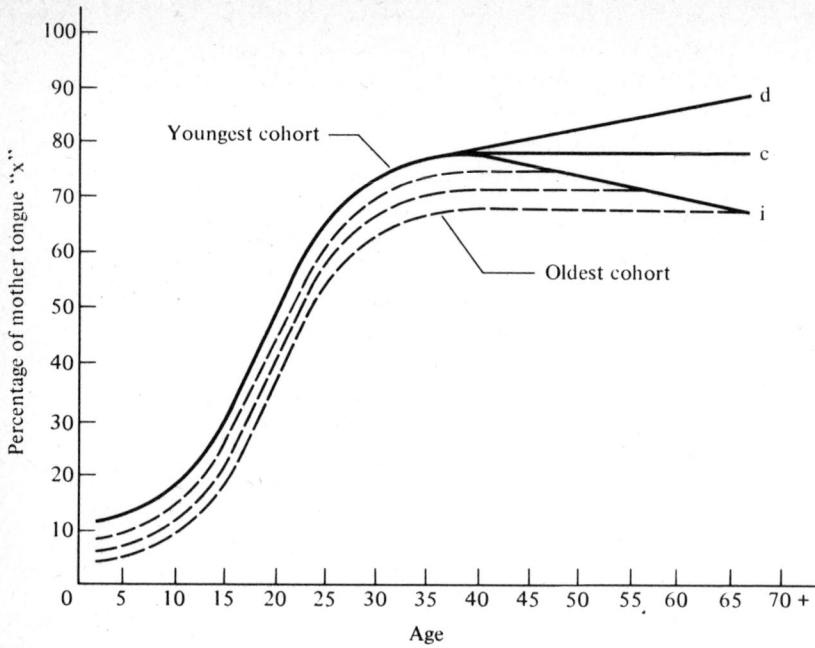

Figure 2.2 *Theoretic distribution of language transfers by age under conditions of changing rates of language shift*

If, on the other hand, anglicisation has been increasing in a secular manner over the past several decades, the 35-39 year old age group should have higher levels of anglicisation than should the 40-44 year old age group. This latter group in turn should have higher levels than those observed for the 45-49 year olds, etc. This situation is graphically illustrated by the curve labelled 'i' (for 'increasing'). The appropriate age-specific curves for certain of the age groups are represented by the broken lines. Since each older age cohort is somewhat less anglicized, the anglicisation curve as a whole descends to the right after the age of thirty-five. If, finally, the anglicisation rate has been declining over the past decades, then the anglicisation curve should be found to slant upwards as in the curve labelled 'd' (for 'decreasing'), each younger cohort being less anglicized than its predecessor.

Since the pattern of language shift generally observed conforms to the curve labelled 'i', some observers have proposed an alternative explanation. After the age of thirty-five, some members of minority language groups may 'return' to the predominant use of their mother tongue, this after a long period of time in which they used the dominant language. This line of argument does not make much sense. First of all, any such movement is likely to be nullified by the continuing anglicisation of other members of the group even after they have reached the age of thirty-five. Such a process is likely produced by continuing exposure to the American language environment. The fact that the percentage of immigrants who adopt the English language as principal language increases proportionally with length of residence in the United States tends to support this proposition. Thus, the best estimate of anglicisation rates for persons older than thirty-five years of age would appear to be those obtained from the data itself. Such differences as are obtained reflect secular, evolutionary changes in the rate of language shift rather than effects produced by maturation.

Furthermore, we should observe that even were such a maturational explanation retained, such linguistic returns to the mother tongue group are without importance for the future of the language group. The returning persons have already borne and in large part raised their children, having given them English mother tongue and English usual language. In reality, they have made their contribution to the anglicisation of their children, so that any such return is devoid of long term consequences. In addition, since all the data presented in this book indicate the strong, undirectional character of language shift (to the English language), this alternative interpretation of the 'i' curve is highly untenable.

Methodologically, the existence of an age structure to language shift indicates that a general rate of anglicisation (or language shift more generally) may not be an accurate estimate of current rates of anglicisation, that is the anglicisation being accomplished by those children and young adults in the process of emancipation from parental language constraints. Children who are still younger are subjected to parental language practices and wishes. Accordingly, their anglicisation rates do not reflect voluntary behavior. On the other hand, if anglicisation rates have been increasing over the past decades, the older age groups will have rates below those of the younger groups. When the older age groups are proportionately rather large and where the anglicisation rate has been rising rapidly, the failure to examine the age-specific rates of anglicisation may lead to serious underestimates of the current rates affecting the young adults in the group.

Two examples of the 'i' curve which we have depicted in Figure 2.2 have been presented by Castonguay (1981) using data from the 1971 Census of

Canada. In a single illustration he examines the anglicisation rates of the population of French mother tongue living outside the province of Quebec and the francisation rates of the population of English mother tongue living in Quebec City. These two curves are presented in Figure 2.3.

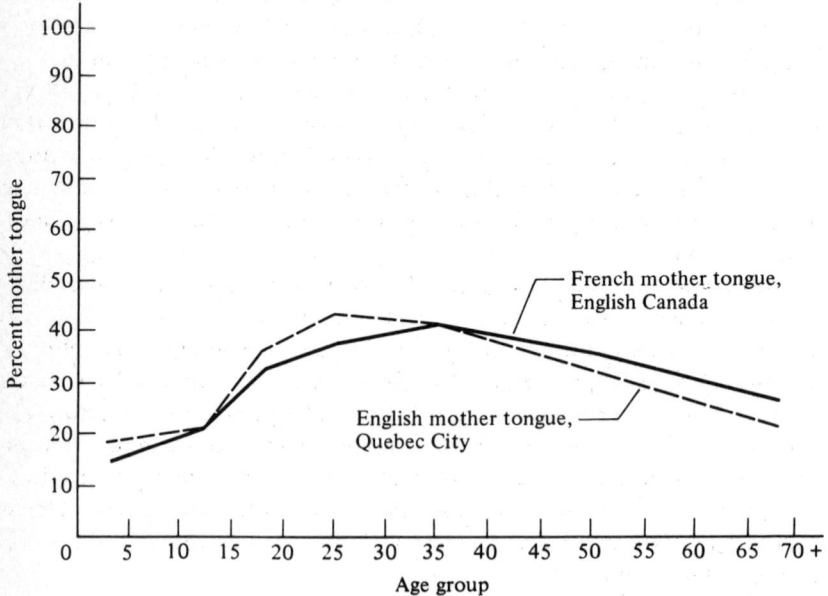

Figure 2.3 *Language shift of persons of French mother tongue in English Canada and of persons of English mother tongue in Quebec City, 1971*

This figure illustrates quite concisely the proposition that language shift curves may be expected to have the same shape for all groups. The two curves illustrate the upsurge in linguistic emigration which occurs during the teenage years, the pattern of levelling off which occurs during the period when persons attain thirty to thrity-five years of age, and the declining curve to the right with increasing age which indicates an upsurge in language shift rates over the past several decades. Furthermore, the data appear to indicate that the francisation of the English minority in Quebec City has risen more rapidly than has the anglicisation of the French minorities in English Canada. The older members of the English language group had lower rates of language shift than did their French language counterparts, while the younger members of the English language group already have higher rates of language shift than do their French language peers.

While this brief analysis of the Canadian data illustrates nicely the use to which age-specific language shift rates can be put, some observers will be certain to observe (see Estrada, 1981 for an example) that this type of analysis consists of making longitudinal affirmations from data which is merely cross-sectional in nature. This violates one of the elementary rules of the interpretation of data. This is in fact exactly what we are proposing to do. While this proposed methodology has become accepted in the Canadian literature (Lachapelle and Henripin, 1980), empirical verification does in fact require longitudinal comparisons. However, neither the 1971 Census of Canada (on which basis this methodology was developed) nor the 1976 Survey of Income and Education is a longitudinal study. Nonetheless, certain analyses seem to increase the empirical plausibility of the general model.

First of all, based upon an intercensal cohort analysis of the Finnish national census for the years 1950 and 1960, DeVries (1974) found that most language shift from Swedish mother tongue to Finnish usual language occurred before the age of thirty. DeVries concluded that the ages from ten to twenty-nine are the principal years during which such linguistic emigrations occurred and that the most important factors associated with such shifts were entry into high school and university, entry into the work force, and the contracting of marriage.

Secondly, Lieberson (1965) has shown that bilingualism in the region of Montreal is stable for any given cohort from one census to another. Nearly all second language learning occurred before the age of thirty-five. Since linguistic emigration to another group is predicted upon the learning of a second language, language shift should be expected to follow the same time schedule.

Thirdly, Castonguay (1979) has established that the age curves for anglicisation of French Canadian minorities parallel those of linguistic exogamy. Intercensal comparisons have established that linguistic exogamy has been increasing in English Canada throughout the twentieth century. Since the two age curves are so precisely parallel, it is reasonable to assume that common processes are involved. Since intercensal comparisons of the French language minority in Canada are semi-longitudinal in nature, these findings suggest that anglicisation rates have also been increasing in this century. This is precisely what the age-specific rates calculated from the 1971 Census of Canada suggest.

Fourthly, Castonguay (1979b) has shown that projections based on the anglicisation rates derived from the 1971 Census of Canada are confirmed by mother tongue data from the 1976 Census of Canada. Although the 1981 Census of Canada will permit the first complete intercensal analysis of language shift itself, the 1976 findings tend to support the longitudinal-type interpretations derived from the 1971 Census.

Fifthly, Bowman (1981) has observed similar patterns in the National Chicano study. He notes that one would normally expect that longer residence in the United States should be associated with higher rates of language shift to English. Consequently, among the native born we should expect to find that the older the age group, the higher the rates of anglicisation. The reverse is found, indicating that rates of anglicisation appear to be increasing.

The measurement of linguistic mobility. Having completed our description of the theoretical basis upon which language shift may be assessed, we are obliged to procede to the operationalization of the theory. It is, however, one task to create the theory which provides the basis for the measurement of a certain phenomenon; it is quite another to create the measures themselves. It is still more difficult to assess the extent to which the measures developed faithfully reflect that which we are attempting to measure. It is to this task that we now turn our attention.

The measures developed for any study, of course, depend to a large degree on the nature and type of the data available for analysis. The data upon which this book is based consist of the declarations of respondents to two nationwide surveys sponsored by the National Center for Education Statistics. The first survey, the Survey of Income and Education (SIE), reached over 150,000 households and was carried out by the U.S. Bureau of the Census in 1976. The second survey, High School and Beyond, is a national sample of more than 58,000 high school students and was carried out by the National Opinion Research Center of the University of Chicago. Both surveys asked respondents to furnish information regarding their language background and current behavior. The responses to these questions furnish the material for this book, declarations which we are obliged to accept at face value. To do otherwise is to refuse to acknowledge that social scientists can discover anything about the world in which we live by asking questions of ordinary people.

The measurement of any type of mobility requires two essential items of information: a point of departure and the point of arrival. More formally, we need to establish a clear starting-point to which the state of the person at the moment of the survey can be compared. In the case of social mobility, for example, we can examine the current class position of persons of working (manual) class origins. That is to say, we compare the current occupations of the son (daughter) to that of his (her) father or mother. The point of departure is the occupation of the parent; the point of arrival, that of the child (now adult).

In the analysis of linguistic mobility, there are a number of potential points of departure which have been proposed or which can be offered to establish the measurement of language shift. In the succeeding paragraphs, we shall discuss the use of ethnic origin, mother tongue, and current parental practice. The appropriate point of arrival for each of these concepts is, respectively, membership in a minority language group, current language practice, and the current language practice of the children.

1. *Measurement of linguistic mobility based on ethnic origin.* Ethnic origin has been widely used by Canadian researchers to estimate the extent to which the French language minority has been assimilated to the English language group in the various regions of that country. Since data on the mother tongue of Canadians provided the only clear indicator of language use prior to 1971, the percentage of persons of French mother tongue was compared to the percentage of persons of French ethnic origin. Such a comparison requires that we invoke the hypothesis that all persons of French ethnic origin had ancestors who at some point spoke French as their principal language of use, an hypothesis which is not devoid of face validity. The calculations of the decline in the number of persons having French mother tongue provides a gross measure of the linguistic assimilation which occurred *prior* to the current generation of persons of French mother tongue. That is to say, the language shift so measured was not accomplished by the persons of French ethnic origin responding to the Census; rather, it was carried out by their parents, grandparents, or even more distant ancestors. The actual group of people who made English their usual language cannot be ascertained. Consequently, the use of ethnic origin as the basis for the calculation of anglicisation rates lacks a clear time frame and yields an inherently weak measure of anglicisation. A certain part of the observed linguistic assimilation probably occurred in the recent past, the rest in some more distant generation of ancestors. For groups resident in the country for a long period of time, there is simply no way to disentangle these events.

This is not, however, the only problem associated with the use of ethnic origin as a point of departure in the analysis of language shift. Four further problems suggest that the calculation of rates of historic anglicisation (i.e., by past ancestors) will seriously underestimate the 'true' rates which actually occurred. First of all, there is considerable resistance in the United States to considering one's self an hyphenated member of the polity (Greek-American, Italian-American, etc.). There is, therefore, a tendency on the part of some persons to deny their ethnic origin when the interviewer asked for such a declaration, at least to deny what may be considered an accurate response.

Secondly, many anglicized persons in the United States have mixed ethnic origins, the father and the mother (and perhaps the grandparents as well) coming from different ethnic origin groups. Since such persons are unlikely to be able to satisfy the Census' need to select a single ethnic origin group, it is likely that all ethnic origin groups in the United States are substantially larger in size than the estimates derived from the SIE presented in this book. The large category of 'Another group not listed' suggests that many persons could not (or would not) satisfy the classification scheme devised by the Census.

Thirdly, in certain instances there may be a rather weak relationship between ethnic origin and a specific language group. Thus, members of what may be defined by the SIE as the 'Arab' language group may not declare an 'Arabic' ethnic origin. Rather, reference may be made to either national origin or to some sub-national unit. Similarly, a 'Russian' language origin might cover a range of Russian linguistic minorities, particularly since 'Ukranian' was not included in the list of languages offered to the respondents in the 1976 SIE. In addition, the Census created additional problems for the analyst by deciding to refuse certain answers. For example, 'Canadian' was not considered a legitimate response to the ethnic origin question. Persons who offered such a response were instructed to find some other more 'acceptable' response. This technical decision undoubtedly causes a serious underestimate of the size of the Franco-American population for many of whom 'Canadian' ('Canadien' in French) is in fact the appropriate ethnic identifier. Similarly, since the Census instructed interviewers to refuse a 'Jewish' ethnic origin, there is no appropriate ethnic referent for the 'Yiddish' language group.

Finally, ethnic origin declarations are variable over time. Castonguay (1978) has documented the existence of widespread changes in declarations of ethnic origin in the Canadian census, while Johnson (1974) has shown in a longitudinal analysis the instability of ethnic origin data in the United States. While the total number of persons in each ethnic group remains relatively stable, approximately one-fourth of American respondents did not declare the same ethnic origin from one year to another (i.e. at one year intervals). Thus, the specific responses of specific individuals to ethnic origin questions in the United States cannot be taken too seriously.

When we attempt to assess the impact of these various problems with using ethnic origin as the basis of the assessment of language shift, we should note first of all that the problem of which ancestors were anglicized cannot be remedied. Consequently, differences in the calculated rates of anglicisation cannot be taken as indicative of different rates of linguistic anglicisation for different groups. Such differences as are observed are likely to be related to time-of-arrival factors. Since, for example, the largest wave of German immigrants arrived before the First World War, a large proportion of the adults of German ethnic origin are probably the grandchildren or great grandchildren of the persons who made English their usual language. Consequently, rates of anglicisation based on ethnic origin may be expected to be relatively high. On the other hand, the wave of Hispanic immigration is largely recent. It would be extremely unlikely that we should find as high a percentage of persons of English language background in the Hispanic groups. As a result, comparisons based on ethnic origin have an extremely limited utility. They merely depict the extent to which persons of English language background are found in the various ethnic origin groups.

The remaining objections to the use of ethnic origin data do not seriously hamper the analysis. The failure to establish a clear correspondance between ethnic and linguistic origin does not appear to apply to most major U.S. language minorities. The single exception would appear to be that of persons of Yiddish language origins where no rate of historic anglicisation can be calculated. On the other hand, the underestimates of the size of minority groups simply causes the rates of historic anglicisation to be somewhat lower than a 'true' rate would find. Thus, the estimated rates are rather conservative. On the other hand, the instability of responses is relatively unimportant for obtaining estimates of the size of each ethnic origin group since this figure remains relatively constant. We should note, however, in passing that Johnson found that persons of Hispanic ethnic origin were more likely to report the same ethnic origin in subsequent time periods. This leads us to suggest that ethnic origin referents tend to become more fluid when the language group which gave birth to these sentiments has been anglicized. Since more Hispanic-Americans still speak Spanish than do Italian-Americans Italian, the former are more likely characterized by a clear sentiment of ethnic origin.

Given these very serious reservations about the quality of rates calculated when using ethnic origin data, we shall use this procedure at only one point in this study. A rate of 'historic anglicisation' may be developed by dividing the number of persons having no minority language background by the total number of persons belonging to the ethnic group associated with that particular language. Thus, the rate of historic anglicisation for the French group is obtained by dividing the number of English monolinguals by the total number of persons declaring French ethnic origin. This rate will be calculated using only those persons declaring that they were born in the United States, since the ancestors of immigrants cannot have already been subjected to the anglicisation process. While we have already indicated some of the limits inherent in the development of this rate, we shall use it simply to define the extent to which members of a specific minority language group were anglicized prior to the experience of the current generation. We can examine more directly the linguistic experience of members of ethnic groups who come from minority language backgrounds using more appropriate procedures. It is to this subject that we now turn.

2. *Measurement of linguistic mobility based on mother tongue.* If measures of language shift based on ethnic origin have extremely limited utility, the same cannot be said for measures based on mother tongue. The historic referent for such measures is extremely clear. Mother tongue refers to the first language spoken by the individual in early childhood. While we accept in principle the concept of multiple mother tongues, the incidence of such phenomena appears quite marginal in western societies. Most children are raised with a single first language.

The analysis of mother tongue data conducted in the follow-up study to the U.S. Census of 1970 reveals that language data are generally somewhat superior in reliability than are declarations of ethnic origin. The Census (1974) found less than six percent errors in language declarations among persons who had lived in homes where the minority language was actively spoken as the principal home language. This error factor is markedly lower than the error factor calculated for ethnic origin or for such other commonly used variables as occupation or income (Census, 1975).

The fact that declarations of mother tongue are more stable over time than are other types of declarations (except age, sex, and race) should not surprise the analyst. On the one hand, when we ask someone what language he spoke in early childhood, the question has a very clear referent. On the other, the respondent normally should be expected to have a clear idea of the accurate response. Since the question is both precise and salient, the respondent is unlikely to change the response when a second interviewer asks the same question at some subsequent point in time. Consequently, we have every reason to have confidence in the quality of the responses to a clearly formulated question regarding mother tongue.

This observation leads us to examine the mother tongue questions posed in the SIE and the HSB. Since the SIE data cover all age ranges, we shall pay somewhat greater attention to the results of this study than to that of the HSB. Furthermore, the questions asked in the SIE are somewhat less clear than those presented in the HSB, a fact which also requires somewhat greater discussion. The SIE question was phrased: 'What language was usually spoken in this person's home when he was a child?' The principal problem with this question is that it does not require that the person himself should have spoken that language in early childhood. While, generally speaking, we may expect that the child would have the principal household language for his mother tongue, one may readily imagine circumstances in which such would not be the case. Thus, in a three generation household the parents may willingly speak the minority language to the grandparents but make a conscious effort to raise their children in English. Such decisions would be motivated by the desire to facilitate the integration of the children in the neighborhood and school settings.

The extent to which similar situations are likely to occur probably varies with the extent to which a minority language group is undergoing assimilation. In relatively stable linguistic situations, the principal home language will undoubtedly be the mother tongue of the child; in less stable environments, such is less likely to be the case. In any case, the argument developed suggests that some children of English mother tongue are likely to have been erroneously classified as having had a minority mother tongue because of the way the SIE question was framed. Since persons of English mother tongue nearly always have maintained English as their principal language of use, this misclassification causes the calculated rates of language mobility to be somewhat higher than an optimal definition of the question would have produced. That is, some individuals are thought to have made a shift from a minority mother tongue to the English language, when in fact these persons had English for their first language. Thus, the calculated rates of language shift are likely to be slightly inflated above the 'true' rate of language shift.

To test the extent to which such misclassifications have occurred, we examined the mother tongues of 14-17 year old children living in homes where the parents usually spoke the minority language. The data suggest that some six percent of the children living in Spanish language homes were reportedly of English mother tongue. Comparable figures were eight percent for the German language group, nine percent for the Italian language group. Thus, we propose that the higher the rate of anglicisation which characterizes any given group, the greater the number of misclassifications of mother tongue. On the whole, however, such misclassifications appear to be limited to less than ten percent.

This observation does not mean, however, that the calculated rates of linguistic mobility may be approximately ten percent too high. Let us suppose an initial minority language population of 100,000 persons of whom 90,000 now usually speak English. The calculated anglicisation rate from the SIE would be 90.0 percent. If we subtract the 10,000 persons who may have been misclassified, we obtain a population base of 90,000, of whom 80,000 speak English as their usual language, yielding an anglicisation rate of 88.9 percent. This is an extremely marginal decline. Similarly, if only 40,000 of the original population had been anglicized and we apply a misclassification rate of six percent, we obtain a corrected anglicisation rate of 36.1 percent (34,000/94,000 = 36.1%). Thus, the higher the anglicisation rate, the greater the proportion of errors but the smaller the net effect; the lower the anglicisation rate, the fewer the proportion of misclassifications but the greater the effect. Nonetheless, in both instances the differences between a corrected rate and a calculated rate are relatively unimportant. Furthermore, we intend to demonstrate in this book that the trends are so clear that refinements of this nature are merely of academic interest to the researcher interested in such precision.

Having assured ourselves that the point of departure for the analysis of the language shift process is sufficiently solid, we turn our attention to the measurement of the point of arrival, i.e., the current language use of individuals of minority mother tongues. We have previously indicated that four current types of language practice can be defined, minority language retention, simple bilingualism, English bilingualism, and English monolingualism. The measurement of these concepts requires at least two questions, one to determine the language usually spoken by the respondent, the second to determine the presence or absence of a second language. The first question was phrased: 'What language does this person usually speak?' We observe first of all that this is an extremely direct and clear question. Castonguay (1981) has, however, observed that the question is not context-specific, and since we are principally concerned with the language that the respondent usually speaks at home, the question may sollicit responses which are unduly biased by the participation of the individual in the world of education or of work. Since the English language clearly dominates these two domains, the question may encourage individuals to answer 'English.' To the extent that this is true, the calculated anglicisation rate may be biased upwards for persons involved in formal English language institutional settings.

In response to this critique, we should note that the SIE was administered in the home setting of the respondents. Furthermore, the questions relating to personal language use were administered after the household language questions which were in fact context-specific. These questions asked what languages were usually spoken at home by the persons living in the household. This feature of the interview setting suggests that respondents may have imposed a context-specific interpretation on the personal language questions, minimizing the bias which may have been caused by the failure to specify the home context. The extent to which these factors may have affected the responses offered cannot be ascertained. Nonetheless, insofar as we restrict our analysis to the SIE data themselves, this problem may be presumed to have affected all groups to the same extent. Thus, intergroup comparisons of rates of language shift are not likely to be biased by the context problem.

The question designed to ascertain the presence of a second language was phrased: 'Does this person often speak another language?' If the response was affirmative, the specific language was ascertained. There is, rather obviously, some ambiguity attached to the meaning of the word 'often.' While a language which is judged by the respondent to be 'often' spoken must necessarily have greater importance to him than one which is not, we cannot assume the complete abandonment of the mother tongue if a negative answer is furnished to this question. The respondent may indeed still speak the language from time to time or with particular persons, but in his own judgment no longer speaks it with regularity, that is, as an important daily language. Such usage may be ceremonial, vestigal, or folkloric in character. Consequently, we understand a negative response to the second language question as indicating a functional pattern of English monolingualism for persons of minority mother tongue. They are by their own definition no longer active participants in the daily life of their minority language group.

The responses to these two language use questions permit us to establish our measures of current use. They define the point of arrival to be compared to the point of departure, mother tongue. They permit us to develop the general rates of language mobility necessary to our task. The two principal rates calculated in this study are the two general rates of anglicisation, the rate of English bilingualism and the rate of English monolingualism. Both are defined as the percentage of persons of a given mother tongue who have adopted the English language as their principal language of use, the English bilinguals having retained their mother tongue as a second, frequently-spoken language, the English monolinguals declaring that they have not. When the two rates are added together, they yield a general rate of anglicisation. Symbolically, these three rates can be represented as follows. Let 'mt' equal the total number of persons having a given mother tongue. Then,

the rate of English monolingualism = em / mt
the rate of English bilingualism = eb / mt
the rate of anglicisation = (em + eb) / mt

where 'em' represents the number of persons who usually speak English and who no longer speak their mother tongue frequently; and where 'eb' represents the number of persons who usually speak English but often speak their mother tongue as well. The rate of anglicisation defines the percentage of persons of a given mother tongue who have made English their principal language of use.

Two similar measures can be developed for persons who retain their mother tongue as their principal language of use, those who declare that they frequently speak English as a second language, those who say they do not. However, the analysis of the data indicates that the declaration of English as a second language frequently spoken (i.e., simple bilingualism) is nearly universal. Thus, this distinction has been discarded in favor of a further distinction based on declared ability to speak the English language. We have divided the retentive persons into two subgroups based on the following SIE question: 'How well does this person speak English?' We define as persons having 'high' competence those who reportedly speak English 'well' or 'very well'; as having 'low' competence those who reported 'not very well' or 'not at all.'

While this measure of competence is self-reported and while actual competence levels may be somewhat lower than perceived levels (Dubois, 1980), the distinction between high and low levels of competence is not unimportant. Lieberson (1970) has shown that the presence of persons who do not speak English well retards the language mobility of the group as a whole. The presence of such persons requires that other members of the group maintain minimal competence in the minority language in order to communicate with them. The rates of high and low competence in English for persons of minority mother tongue are not, however, major components of our analysis. We treat this distinction as being indicative of the extent to which members of any given language minority do not speak English well.

Our discussion of the manner in which general rates can be calculated makes it clear that age-specific rates can be obtained in the same manner. Similarly, we can establish rates specific to certain geographic regions or to given nativity groupings. However, the calculations of these additional rates is somewhat more risky in view of the increasingly smaller sample sizes on which we are forced to rely. As sample sizes decline the reliability of the estimates also falls.

Unfortunately, if we are to glean as much useful information as possible from the SIE, we have no choice but to accept this risk. We leave the interested reader with two observations which may provide some small reassurance. First of all, the SIE data base is markedly superior in quality to any data base ever collected in the United States. The 1980 Census contained only a single question on current language use, and the re-interview study included the 1970 question on mother tongue. No anglicisation rates can be calculated from the responses to a single question and the 1970 census question is hopelessly inadequate to the task. Thus, we have no choice but to extract all the useful information possible from the SIE. Secondly, the SIE national sample is extraordinarily large. It is extremely unlikely that still larger national samples will ever be drawn. Consequently, no national data base will ever exist which will be sufficiently large to permit us to calculate either age-specific, regional, or nativity rates of language shift in which we could have substantially greater confidence. We invite the reader who remains skeptical to consider such analyses as exploratory in nature.

Similar types of measures of language mobility can be readily developed from the High School and Beyond data set. The mother tongue question presented in this study does not share the problems raised by that used in the SIE. Respondents were asked to indicate the first language spoken by them in early childhood, i.e., before they started school. The usual language question is identical to that posed in the SIE, so that direct comparisons between principal language of use and mother tongue are readily made. No second language question as such was asked in the HSB. However, respondents were asked to indicate the extent of their competence to understand, speak, read, and write both the English language and the appropriate minority language. They were also asked to indicate the frequency with which the minority language was used in a variety of settings, permitting a much more in-depth analysis of current language use than can be obtained from the SIE. Since, however, the HSB is limited in age range to students enrolled in secondary education programs, we shall restrain most of our commentary on the construction of additional measures to the chapter in which this data will be presented.

3. *Measurement of linguistic mobility based on parental language use.* There is in the SIE one important limitation on our ability to use mother tongue as the basis for the calculations of rates of language shift. The question was not asked for children aged 0 to 13. Those who wrote the questionnaire assumed that the usual household language ('What language do the people in this household usually speak here at home?') would in fact be the mother tongue of the children living in the household. This is an extraordinarily naive assumption, since the language used by members of the household is likely to undergo some evolution as the personal language behavior of the individuals composing the household changes. Thus, for example, the entry of children into school may not only be associated with a rapid improvement of the English language skills of the children; it may also be associated with the development of a set of values such that they do not wish to speak the minority language at home. Frequently, the parents do not resist such a movement, or if they do, they abandon the conflict at some point in time as relatively fruitless (during the child's adolescence). Consequently, the principal language of the home may also change.

To obtain some idea of the extent to which such a process may occur, we examined the mother tongue of 14-17 year old children living in homes where English was the dominant household language but where Spanish was also spoken. We find that fully twenty-eight percent of children were reported to have Spanish as mother tongue, presumably because that language was the principal household language when they were born. These data suggest that joint parental-child linguistic mobility has occurred in a relatively high percentage of cases, the Spanish language having been dominant when the child was very young, the English language when the child was aged 14-17 (in 1976). Thus, the framers of the SIE questionnaire committed a serious error by failing to obtain adequate data on the mother tongue of younger children.

If then, we are to examine the current language behavior of young children, we need to establish some other point of departure which will permit us to calculate rates of movement. The most appropriate measure would appear to be that which compares the current language practices of children with those of their parents. Since the SIE contains data on both the usual and second languages of both parents and children, the two sets of language characteristics can be directly compared. For example, we suggested earlier that Eglish bilingual parents may be expected to have English bilingual children. This hypothesis can be directly examined by observing the language characteristics of children who have English bilingual parents. Similarly, we can examine the language characteristics of children living in homes where both parents usually speak the minority language. Such comparisons permit us to ascertain the degree of linguistic mobility which has occurred in situations where the children are still subjected to parental language constraints.

A somewhat similar but not identical procedure can be developed to treat data from High School and Beyond. Students were asked to indicate the frequency with which their parents spoke the minority language to them. Since they were also asked to indicate the extent to which they themselves used the minority language in a variety of settings, some indication of the extent of movement toward the English language can be ascertained.

These three general types of comparisons, ethnicity to language, current language to mother tongue, and parent to child usage provide the logic upon which the analysis of language shift is erected. If we cannot have much confidence in the first method, we can have much greater confidence in the results produced by the latter two types of comparisons. The analysis of the language shift process is presented in the first major section of the book. In the second section we shall use the language shift characteristics of children and adults (as developed in this chapter) to ascertain the impact of language on the attainment process.

Part One:

The Structure of Language Shift in the United States

Having presented both the logic and the method by which our measures of language shift have been developed, we are now prepared to undertake our first task, the examination of the language shift process in the United States. This section of the book examines the pattern, the pace, and the extent of language shift for minority language groups in the United States. In Chapter 3 we analyze the language shift process of American adults, this chapter presenting a much more complete analysis of the data from the Survey of Income and Education than that presented in the report previously published by the National Center for Education Statistics (Veltman, 1981b). We present in this chapter not only the rate of historic anglicisation for specific minority language groups; we also present the general rates of anglicisation for persons of minority mother tongue according to their place of birth. These data are then followed by the presentation of national age-specific rates of language shift for the Spanish and French language groups. These data are subsequently refined to the regional level.

In Chapter 4 we shall examine in great detail the structure of intergenerational language shift in the United States. Having reorganized the SIE data so that the language characteristics of children can be directly compared to those of their parents, we shall examine the contribution of a number of important factors to the explanation of language shift, notably parental language characteristics, parental place of birth, and parental socioeconomic status. After having presented the most important aspects of the data in cross-tabular form, we procede to a multivariate analysis of the determinants of English monolingualism of children living in minority language homes.

In Chapter 5 we present an in-depth analysis of the language characteristics of American adolescents who participated in High School and Beyond. Since the number of language questions posed during this study permits a much more refined analysis than was possible using the SIE, the relationship between declared ability to speak a language and reported use of that language can be examined. Furthermore, the impact of bilingual education programs on minority language retention and shift can be ascertained.

Our objective in the first part of this book is to provide answers to a number of questions which plague both researchers and the American public in general. The principal language-related question usually asked in American society is the following: 'Is the Spanish language group successfully resisting assimilation to the English language group?' Those who ask this question usually presume that the answer is 'yes.' A second question asked more generally only by researchers and scholars is the following: 'Are there important differences in the anglicisation process by language group?' A third question might be: 'Can a minority language survive as a second language once it has been subordinated to English?' These (and other more specific) questions have given shape to the presentation of the data in the first part of this book.

Chapter 3

The Anglicisation of Adults in Minority Language Groups

Introduction. Having presented the measures which we shall use in this chapter, we shall briefly examine the method by which respondents were assigned to language groups. A series of successive criteria were applied in sequence to permit such an assignment: mother tongue, usual language, and second language. If, for example, a respondent declared that his mother tongue was not English, he was assigned to the appropriate minority language group. Failing this test, the usual language spoken was used as the placement criterion. If the respondent was still unassigned, the second language was examined to detect a minority language background.

Once classified into minority language groups, such individuals were then subjected to a series of further tests, notably to ascertain the consistency of responses. Those few persons who indicated the presence of more than one minority language were eliminated from the analyses presented in this chapter. Since more than one minority language was indicated, it is difficult to know into which language group such persons should be placed. Furthermore, the direction of the movement is difficult to classify, some persons emigrating from one minority language group to another. In addition, since the mother tongue of persons failing to respond to the relevant question is unknown, these persons were also eliminated from the data analysis. There is simply no way of appropriately classifying such persons. In any case, the number of persons eliminated for these two reasons is extremely small.

The same cannot necessarily be said for two further groups of persons who had furnished valid responses to these three questions but who were nonetheless eliminated from most of the data analyses. We eliminated first of all those few persons who emigrated from the English language group to a minority language group. Since they bring so little support to these groups in the face of the massive anglicisation to which they are subjected, it did not seem worthwhile to examine their contribution. Furthermore, whatever findings may have been obtained would not attain statistical significance.

In addition, persons of English mother tongue who were bilingual in a minority language have generally not been included in the analysis. There are two principal reasons motivating this decision. The first is that the presence of such persons is also rather limited and is generally restricted to childhood. As people attain maturity, the presence of this pattern drops dramatically. The second is that the analysis presented in the following chapter indicates that this pattern is transitional and has no long term consequences. Consequently, the principal sample retained for analysis consists only of those persons having a valid minority mother tongue and for whom no second minority language was declared.

Once the classification of persons into minority language groups on the basis of the three personal language questions was completed, we were required to assign the remaining English monolinguals to some group. Two successive language criteria were applied to assign some English monolinguals to minority language groups. First of all, the presence of a minority language as usual household language was used as a selection parameter. This was followed by the application of the second home language as a further criterion for assignment. Those English monolinguals not assigned in this manner lived in English monolingual home settings. They were subsequently assigned to ethnic groups on the basis of their responses to the ethnic origin question.

The measurement of historic anglicisation. As we have indicated earlier, we can obtain a rough measure of the anglicisation of the ancestors of current adults by dividing the number of persons of minority language background in a given group by the total number of persons declaring the appropriate ethnic origin. This procedure is not, however, as simple as one would like, since persons of the 'wrong' ethnic background may be found in any given minority language group on the basis of the classification procedures previously explained. Since in our view language group membership is more salient than is ethnic group membership, we have accorded priority to this characteristic. As a result, the ethnic figures reported for any given group consist of two types of persons, those having the appropriate minority language associated with the group and those having an English monolingual language background who declared the appropriate ethnicity. For example, persons who declared both Irish ethnic and French language origin are classified with other members of the French language group. Most such persons declared an 'Other' (probably mixed) ethnic origin. As we have indicated, many persons of French Canadian origin have been classified as 'Other,' apparently because they did not see themselves as having 'French' (from France) origin. Since most of the persons added to the various ethnic groups came from the 'Other' ethnic category, the application of our classification procedures adds persons of minority language background to each group, thus suppressing still more the estimated rate of historic anglicisation. Since the rate is already underestimated for the reasons outlined in the previous chapter, the figures presented in Table 3.1 should be seen as extremely conservative estimates.

Table 3.1 *Percentage of English monolinguals in selected ethnolinguistic groups, native born persons aged 14 and over, United States, 1976*

Language Group	English monolingual	Population estimate	Percent monolingual
Arab	70,769	97,970	72.2
Chinese	556,699	126,287	44.8
Filipino	76,032	102,981	73.8
French	1,957,724	2,986,672	65.6
German	12,479,007	13,937,728	89.5
Greek	157,885	318,004	49.6
Italian	3,747,101	5,244,646	71.4
Japanese	218,711	402,528	54.3
Korean	4,387	6,604	66.4
Native American	691,199	899,809	76.8
Polish	2,017,100	3,116,314	64.7
Portuguese	233,951	392,211	59.6
Russian	1,072,269	1,155,274	92.8
Scandinavian	2,723,104	3,150,399	86.4
Chicano	704,749	2,989,306	23.6
Cuban	3,534	29,061	12.2
Puerto Rican	63,360	272,799	23.2
Other Hispanic	763,576	1,317,063	58.0
All Spanish	1,535,219	4,608,229	33.3

Source: 1976 Survey of Income and Education

The data presented in Table 3.1 indicate varying amounts of English monolingualism in the native born population aged 14 and over. Examining first of all the non-Hispanic groups, the data reveal that over eighty-five percent of the persons in the German, Scandinavian, and Russian origin groups were monolingual in English. Nearly all the groups listed in Table 3.1 contained more than fifty percent English monolinguals, the two exceptions being the Greek and Chinese ethnic origin groups. As we have previously indicated, these rates would appear to be extremely sensitive to time-of-arrival in the United States, the groups which arrived prior to World War I having very high proportions of English monolinguals, those arriving since that period having lower proportions. The further removed the anglicized ancestors from the adults furnishing the information contained in Table 3.1, the higher the proportion of English monolingual persons. Nonetheless, even among the more recently arrived groups, the presence of English monolingualism among the native born is already quite strong.

When we examine the proportion of English monolinguals in the Spanish language group, we note first of all that more than 1.5 million persons claiming Hispanic ethnic origin declared that they had no working knowledge of the Spanish language. This figure represents 33.3 percent of the native born, a percentage which should surprise those who think that all persons of Hispanic ancestry speak Spanish. As may have been anticipated, the extent of English monolingualism varies from one Hispanic group to another, depending once again on the recency of immigration. Thus, Cubans have the lowest percentage of English monolinguals among the native born (12.2%), while persons of 'Other Hispanic' origin (i.e., not Cuban, Chicano, or Puerto Rican) have the highest percentage, some 58.0 percent of the latter being monolingual in English. The rate of English monolingualism among the native born in the Puerto Rican and Chicano ethnic groups is slightly higher than twenty-three percent, a figure quite a bit lower than those found for the non-Hispanic groups.

Furthermore, when we examine the extent of English monolingualism by age group among persons of Hispanic ancestry (and in other groups as well), the data show that the percentage of English monolinguals has been steadily increasing. For example, approximately 22 to 24 percent of persons in the age groups 40 to 49, 50 to 59, and 60 and over reported that they were monolingual in English. The rate obtained for the 30 to 39 year olds is 30.0 percent, for the 20 to 29 year olds 36.1 percent, and for those under 20 years of age exceeds forty percent. These data show that increasing proportions of native born persons of Hispanic ancestry have an English monolingual language pattern, this in spite of continued heavy immigration over a long period of time. That is to say, the anglicisation of the native born and earlier immigrants appears to be sufficiently rapid that the percentage of English monolingual children continues to increase. In fact, not only has the percentage of English monolingual children increased over time; the percentage of all native born children having English as mother tongue has also risen. While only 28.0 percent of all 40 to 49 year olds of Hispanic ancestry had English for their first language (22.1% English monolingual + 5.9% English bilingual), 54.4

percent of the 15 to 19 year olds declared English for their mother tongue (40.1% English monolingual + 14.3% English bilingual). The rate is still higher for the 14 year olds. These data confirm what appears to be an 'inexorable' march to English monolingualism among the native born. At any rate, they suggest that the general rates reported in Table 3.1 underestimate the extent of English monolingualism present in younger age groups.

In general the data reported in Table 3.1 confirm what we may have expected. All language groups had undergone a good deal of anglicisation prior to the time of the 1976 SIE, a generalization which does not exclude the Spanish language group. It is not, however, those who responded to the SIE who had been anglicized, at least not as measured in this table; rather, their ancestors of whatever distance had accomplished this anglicisation. Nonetheless, in all cases there is already a substantial, if not overwhelming, presence of English monolingualism among the native born.

Given the extensive anglicisation of minority language groups which occurred at some undefined period in the past, it is not surprising that the samples of persons of minority mother tongue are markedly smaller. Indeed, it was for this reason that the SIE sample was planned to include such a large number of households. Nonetheless, the successive division of the minority language samples into increasingly smaller units does affect the accuracy of the estimates.

Nativity of persons of minority mother tongue. Having examined the anglicisation which affected the ancestors of the adults responding to the 1976 SIE, we are now prepared to examine directly the language shift process of these adults themselves. Since we have every reason to believe that the linguistic behavior of the foreign born differs from that of the native born, it is particularly important that we segregate our analysis of language shift along these lines. We examine first of all in Table 3.2 the distribution of place of birth for each minority language group.

Examining first of all the relative size of each minority language group (as classified by mother tongue), the data reveal that only five language groups contained more than one million persons aged 14 and over. The Spanish language group is by far the largest with nearly 5.8 million members, followed by the Italian and German groups with over two million persons each. The French and Polish language groups contain over 1.2 million persons of the appropriate mother tongue. The remaining groups are rather small in size,

Table 3.2 *Place of birth by mother tongue, persons aged 14 and over, United States, 1976*

Language group	Place of birth		Population estimate
	Foreign born	Native born	
Arab	74.8%	25.2%	122,516
Chinese	87.3	12.7	369,386
Filipino	94.3	5.7	326,912
French	27.4	72.6	1,207,789
German	44.7	55.3	2,087,440
Greek	63.2	36.8	366,476
Italian	40.1	59.9	2,232,256
Japanese	49.0	51.0	304,258
Korean	98.4	1.6	117,714
Navajo	0.0	100.0	93,108
Polish	23.8	76.2	1,266,393
Portuguese	59.0	41.0	346,566
Russian	51.0	49.0	174,610
Scandinavian	36.9	63.1	569,574
Vietnamese	100.0	0.0	82,637
Yiddish	54.5	45.5	594,180
All others	46.5	53.5	2,420,477
All non-Spanish	45.1	54.9	12,681,752
Chicano/Mexican	37.9	62.1	3,239,212
Cuban	95.7	4.3	539,871
Puerto Rican	79.0	21.0	907,832
Other Hispanic	68.2	31.8	1,074,959
All Spanish	55.5	44.5	5,761,874

Source: 1976 Survey of Income and Education
Note: When other native Americans are added to Navajo, the relevant figures are 0.8% foreign born, 99.2% native born, and a population estimate of 189,579.

the Scandinavian and Yiddish groups being reduced to under 600,000 persons each.

When we examine place of birth data for each minority language group, we find a wide variety of patterns. All of the persons of Vietnamese mother tongue were born outside the United States, as were nearly all those of Korean mother tongue. The data also reveal that 87.3 percent of the persons of Chinese mother tongue were foreign born, while almost three-fourths of those of Arab mother tongue were not born in the United States. More than half of those of Greek, Portuguese, Russian, and Yiddish mother tongues were not born in the United States. Given the large proportions of the foreign born in these particular groups, it would not be surprising to find that any rate of language retention that ignored nativity might be rather high. Thus, Grosjean's (1982) observation that the Vietnamese are characterised by extremely high rates of language maintenance is entirely explained by the composition of the group.

On the other hand, certain groups are characterized by relatively high proportions of the native born. The Navajo language group is nearly entirely composed of the native born and is unique in this respect. However, approximately three-quarters of the persons in the French and Polish groups are native born, a fact which may be expected to produce relatively high rates of anglicisation when nativity is ignored. The Italian group is also largely composed of the native born, although it is perhaps somewhat surprising that both the German and Italian language groups have such relatively high percentages of immigrants. Clearly, those adults who in 1976 said that they spoke these two languages as mother tongues were not even largely the children of previous immigrants. Both groups seem to have relied heavily on immigration to replenish their numbers. In spite of the great diversity which characterizes the non-Spanish group, we have calculated the percentage of native born persons in the entire group. The figure obtained indicates that 54.9 percent of the 12,681,752 persons of (non-Spanish) minority mother tongue were born in the United States.

This figure contrasts somewhat with that obtained for the Spanish language group. Only 44.5 percent of the 5.8 million persons of Spanish mother tongue were born in the United States, indicating the largely immigrant origins of this group. However, the percentage of native born Hispanics varies by ethnic origin group. Nearly all persons of Cuban ancestry were born outside the United States, while nearly four in five Puerto Ricans and two in three 'Other Hispanics' were also foreign born. Only the Chicano group contains a majority of native born persons of Spanish mother tongue, nearly five in eight persons having been born in the United States. These differences suggest once again that students of the Spanish language group should exercise caution before assuming too much homogeneity based on a common language.

Language shift among the foreign born. We begin our analysis of language shift by examining the language characteristics of the foreign born, a group which may be expected to have largely retained the use of their mother tongues. Since many of the foreign born came to the United States as adults, their language practice was already formed on arrival. Consequently, we have little reason to believe that major alterations in their linguistic behavior should occur upon immigration to the United States. The choice of a preferred language of use is, after all, relatively personal. The relevant data are presented in Table 3.3.

Table 3.3 *Language shift patterns of the foreign born by mother tongue, persons aged 14 and over, United States, 1976*

| Language group | English usual language | | | Non-English usual language | | | Weighted sample |
| | Mono-lingual | Bi-lingual | Total | English competence | | | |
				High	Low	Total	
Arab	9.0	59.5	68.5	20.0	11.5	31.5	91,664
Chinese	6.0	28.1	34.1	36.0	29.9	65.9	322,549
Filipino	15.3	46.4	61.7	31.8	6.5	38.3	308,129
French	33.6	40.1	73.7	20.9	5.4	26.3	330,838
German	49.7	42.6	92.3	6.3	1.4	7.7	932,697
Greek	9.9	36.8	46.7	30.2	23.2	53.4	231,746
Italian	27.5	37.7	65.2	18.4	16.4	34.8	894,142
Japanese	21.3	32.0	53.4	16.4	30.2	46.6	148,996
Korean	16.5	30.1	46.6	13.7	39.7	53.4	115,810
Polish	27.6	37.2	64.8	21.9	13.3	35.2	301,444
Portuguese	11.7	26.2	37.9	26.4	35.7	62.1	204,458
Russian	63.4	24.3	87.7	10.4	1.9	12.3	89,095
Scandinavian	65.2	29.7	94.9	4.4	0.7	5.1	210,432
Vietnamese	7.3	25.9	33.2	42.1	24.7	66.8	82,637
Yiddish	60.9	31.0	91.9	7.2	0.9	8.1	323,921
All other	30.2	39.9	70.1	20.5	9.4	29.9	1,124,774
All non-Spanish	31.7	32.3	64.0	18.6	17.4	36.0	5,713,332
Chicano	2.2	19.3	21.5	23.6	54.9	78.5	1,229,151
Cuban	1.3	26.2	27.5	34.5	38.0	72.5	516,408
Puerto Rican	3.5	28.6	32.1	35.5	32.4	67.9	716,916
Other Hispanic	7.3	32.8	40.1	23.3	36.6	59.9	732,775
All Spanish	3.5	25.5	29.0	28.0	43.0	71.0	3,195,250

Source: 1976 Survey of Income and Education

Beginning with the percentages of persons reporting 'low' competence in spoken English, it can readily be seen that the vast majority of immigrants believe that they speak English fairly well. No minority language group contains a majority of persons who declare difficulties with spoken English. However, some 39.7 percent of the persons of Korean mother tongue and 35.7 percent of those of Porguguese mother tongue reported such low competence in English. Relatively high proportions of persons in the Chinese, Greek, Japanese, and Vietnamese language groups also reported such difficulty. On the whole, however, the subtotals column indicates that only 17.4 percent of the foreign born reported difficulty with spoken English, indicating that immigrants on the whole make a rapid adaptation to the dominant English language environment.

The same table also shows, however, that high percentages of the foreign born not only speak English well; relatively high percentages take the additional step of making English their preferred usual language. More than eighty-five percent of the persons of German, Scandinavian, Russian and Yiddish mother tongues have been so anglicized. The mother tongue has generally been abandoned among the anglicized as an important daily language. On the other hand, Table 3.3 reveals that the Chinese, Portuguese, and Vietnamese language groups are characterized by the lowest degree of anglicisation. However, even in these three instances the anglicisation rates exceed thirty percent, indicating that a minimum of one in three persons born outside the United States already speaks English as his or her usual language. Under these circumstances, however, the rate of English monolingualism remains relatively low. The overall rate of anglicisation obtained for the non-Spanish groups is 64.0 percent, the type of anglicisation selected being almost evenly divided between English monolingualism (32.3%) and English bilingualism (31.7%). It would appear that there is a general relationship between the anglicisation rate as a whole and the rate of English monolingualism. The higher the rate of anglicisation, the more that anglicisation takes the form of English monolingualism. The lower the rate of anglicisation, the more that anglicisation takes the form of English bilingualism.

When we turn to the examination of the Spanish language group, the rates of anglicisation are markedly lower. Only 29.0 percent of the foreign born have made English their usual language, only 3.5 percent having effectively abandoned the use of Spanish as a daily language. Furthermore, the proportion of persons declaring 'low' competence in English is markedly higher, Some 43.0 percent of the foreign born persons of Spanish mother tongue said that they did not speak English well at the time of the survey. When we examine the Hispanic ethnic origin groups, the data indicate that the Chicano group is characterized by the lowest anglicisation rates and by the highest percentage of persons indicating low competence in spoken English. Only 21.5 percent of the foreign born of Chicano origin said they usually spoke English, while 54.9 percent said they had difficulty with that language. The anglicisation rates of the Cubans and Puerto Ricans born outside the continental United States are somewhat higher than those observed for Chicanos, approaching those observed for the Chinese, Vietnamese, and Portuguese groups. Only the 'Other Hispanic' group differs markedly within the Hispanic language group, the anglicisation rate surpassing forty percent (40.1%).

Some of the intergroup differences observed among the foreign born may, however, be attributed to different patterns of immigration. Some groups may have arrived more recently in the United States, others at a period in the more distant past. Consequently, to assume from the differences reported in Table 3.3 that different groups are characterized by different rates of language shift is not yet warranted. To address this problem, we have divided the foreign born into three components, those who arrived prior to 1960, those having arrived during the 1960's, and those who arrived during the period beginning with January, 1970 and ending at the time of the survey (Spring, 1976). While such differences as may persist may not be entirely attributable to intergroup differences in the rates of language shift, the probability that this is the case will be markedly improved. The distribution of reported period of arrival is presented in Table 3.4.

This table shows that there is a great deal of variation within the foreign born population in terms of the time of arrival of different groups within the United States. Nearly all of the Vietnamese and the marority of Koreans and Arabs arrived in the United States during the six years immediately preceding the survey. Nearly one-half of the persons of Filipino language origin also arrived in this most recent period. On the other hand, the German, Italian, Polish, Russian, Scandinavian, and Yiddish groups were early arrivals in the United States, large majorities of each group having arrived prior to 1960. The majority of persons of French, Greek, Japanese, and 'All Other' mother tongues also arrived in the earliest period. A third nativity pattern is also observable, the Portuguese and Chinese language groups having arrived in approximately equal proportions in each of the observed time periods. These differences in period of arrival appear to be related to differences in the general rates of anglicisation reported in Table 3.3, those arriving earliest having the highest rates, those later, the lower.

The Spanish language group as a whole has an immigration pattern very

Table 3.4 *Period of arrival of the foreign born by mother tongue, persons aged 14 and over, United States, 1976*

Language group	Period of arrival			Weighted sample
	Before 1960	1960–1969	1970–1976	
Arab	19.6	28.7	51.7	91,664
Chinese	29.1	34.1	36.8	322,549
Filipino	25.5	27.0	47.5	308,129
French	57.2	27.5	15.3	330,838
German	81.0	15.1	3.9	932,697
Greek	50.7	27.6	21.7	231,746
Italian	72.6	19.2	8.2	894,142
Japanese	55.8	17.7	26.5	148,996
Korean	4.6	20.3	75.3	115,810
Polish	81.9	14.3	3.8	301,444
Portuguese	35.8	33.3	30.9	204,548
Russian	91.7	7.0	1.3	89,095
Scandinavian	84.1	11.7	4.2	210,432
Vietnamese	0.7	3.9	95.9	82,637
Yiddish	97.5	1.9	0.6	323,921
All other	54.8	20.9	24.3	1,124,774
All non-Spanish	61.4	19.6	19.0	5,713,332
Chicano	38.5	30.7	30.8	1,229,151
Cuban	16.6	61.3	22.1	516,408
Puerto Rican	61.3	23.7	15.0	716,916
Other Hispanic	21.5	40.4	38.1	732,775
All Spanish	27.5	36.3	36.1*	3,195,250

Source: 1976 Survey of Income and Education
* 15.5% before 1950; 20.6% from 1950–1959

similar to that of the Chinese and Portuguese groups. Some 15.5 percent of the foreign born arrived prior to 1950, while 20.6 percent arrived during the 1950's. Thus, 27.5 percent of the foreign born arrived before 1960, while the remainder of the foreign born is equally divided between the two most recent periods. That is to say, approximately the same number of persons of Spanish language origins arrived in the first six years of the 1970's as had arrived during the entire preceding decade. These figures indicate the continuity and recency of the Spanish language immigration to the United States. Once again, there are important intergroup differences within the Hispanic group in terms of time-of-arrival. The majority of Puerto Ricans arrived prior to 1960 while the majority of Cubans arrived during the 1960's. The Chicano group is composed more heavily of earlier immigrants; the Other Hispanic of proportionately fewer earlier immigrants. It should be remembered that this survey predates the arrival of additional Cubans in the early 1980's.

Having examined the period of immigration of each of the minority language groups, we can now test for broad intergroup differences in the rates of anglicisation by examining data for each period. Thus, we have decomposed Table 3.3 into three components, one for each time period. The data relevant to those who arrived prior to 1960 are presented in Table 3.5.

When we examine the type of anglicisation accomplished by these earlier immigrants, the data show that the majority have become English monolingual after a minimum period of residence of sixteen years, nearly everyone comes to speak English fairly well. Only 6.6 percent of all the persons in the non-Spanish language groups said that they did not speak English well. The two most striking exceptions are the Chinese and Japanese language groups, where more than one-fourth of the persons interviewed said that they did not speak English well. On the other hand, the rates of anglicisation are extremely high. More than eighty-five percent of persons of Arabic, French, German, Russian, Scandinavian, and Yiddish mother tongue reported that they usually spoke English. The Italian and All Other groups have anglicisation rates in the seventy percent range, followed by the Portuguese, Greek, Polish, and Filipino groups in the sixty percent range. The Japanese have an anglicisation rate of exactly fifty percent, while only the Chinese have a rate inferior to that figure. *Only* 43.4 percent of the persons in this group were anglicized at the time of the survey.

When we examine the type of anglicisation accomplished by these earlier immigrants, the data show that the majority have become English monolingual in language practice. The percentage of English monolinguals is 7.3 points higher than the percentage of English bilinguals (43.7 - 36.4 = 7.3%). The rate of English monolingualism exceeds that of bilingualism in nearly all of the major minority language groups. It appears that those groups which have the highest percentage of persons reporting low competence in English are those which have the lowest rates of English monolingualism, confirming the general observation reported by Lieberson (1970). On the whole, these findings indicate the rapidity with which anglicisation takes place in the United States for the non-Spanish groups. In fact, if one looks at the subtotals for the non-Spanish group, 80.1 percent of the persons interviewed said that they

Table 3.5 *Language shift patterns by mother tongue of immigrants arriving before 1960, persons aged 14 and over, United States, 1976*

Language group	English usual language			Non-English usual language			Weighted sample
	Mono-lingual	Bi-lingual	Total	English competence High	Low	Total	
Arab	27.3	61.4	88.7	2.7	8.6	11.3	17,987
Chinese	11.5	32.9	43.4	29.9	25.7	55.6	93,682
Filipino	14.7	55.0	69.7	25.9	4.4	30.3	78,737
French	48.2	37.5	85.7	11.4	2.9	14.3	189,301
German	52.8	41.2	94.0	4.7	1.3	6.0	754,403
Greek	18.5	45.7	64.2	27.0	8.8	35.7	117,446
Italian	35.5	36.4	71.9	17.8	10.4	28.1	649,094
Japanese	23.0	27.0	50.0	11.8	38.2	50.0	83,193
Korean	82.7	3.3	86.0	0.0	14.0	14.0	5,057
Polish	31.9	37.1	69.0	21.0	9.9	31.0	252,103
Portuguese	27.3	37.0	64.3	23.0	12.7	35.7	73,290
Russian	66.5	21.6	88.1	10.1	1.8	11.9	81,714
Scandinavian	72.3	23.8	96.1	3.2	0.7	3.9	176,931
Yiddish*	62.4	29.5	91.9	7.1	1.0	8.1	315,703
All other	42.1	36.4	78.5	15.5	6.0	21.5	617,047
All non-Spanish	43.7	36.4	80.1	13.3	6.6	19.9	3,506,229
Chicano	4.2	31.3	35.5	25.1	39.4	64.5	473,482
Cuban	2.9	42.5	45.4	37.2	17.4	54.6	85,892
Puerto Rican	4.7	35.2	39.9	35.9	24.2	60.1	439,300
Other Hispanic	20.1	44.5	64.6	22.3	13.1	35.4	157,798
All Spanish	6.5	35.4	41.9	29.7	28.4	58.1	1,156,472
Before 1950	8.5	36.4	44.9	25.4	29.7	55.1	496,897
1950–1959	4.9	34.7	39.6	33.0	27.4	60.4	659,575

Source: 1976 Survey of Income and Education
* Population estimate for Vietnamese = 539

usually spoke English. The magnitude of this language shift needs to be appreciated. If we take as an example the anglicisation patterns of the Chinese, the most retentive of the non-Spanish groups, the data reveal that 43.4 percent usually spoke English while nearly one in eight (11.5%) declared that they no longer spoke Chinese on a regular basis. The rates for all other groups are correspondingly higher.

Turning to the examination of the Spanish language group, we observe that the percentages of those who declared difficulty with English are markedly higher (28.4 as opposed to 6.6%). Similarly, both the rate of anglicisation and that of English monolingualism are markedly lower. Only 41.9 percent of the persons of Spanish mother tongue reported that they usually spoke English at the time of the survey, while only 6.5 percent reported that they had abandoned the use of Spanish as an important daily language. Nonetheless, and this should be clearly underlined in the reader's mind, more than four in ten immigrants in the Spanish language group during this period voluntarily chose to make English the most important language they speak. This choice, we have emphasized, has important consequences for the mother tongue of their children and/or for retention of minority language skills. The data suggest that while Spanish language immigrants have lower levels of language shift to English, there is no evidence which would suggest that immigrants in this language group resist the adoption of the English language as the principal language of use. Once again, this process is rather clearly associated with exposure to the American environment, those having immigrated prior to 1950 being more anglicized than those who arrived during the 1950's.

The data examined in Table 3.5 permit us to conclude that there are some intergroup differences in anglicisation rates within both the non-Spanish and Spanish language groups. Most non-Spanish groups are markedly more anglicized than are the Spanish, although the Spanish group as a whole has a language profile which strongly resembles that of the Chinese. Within the Spanish language group, the Chicanos have once again the most retentive patterns, followed by the Puerto Ricans and the Cubans. The Other Hispanics have an anglicisation rate of nearly sixty-five percent, similar to that of the Greek, Polish, and Portuguese groups.

A similar set of data for immigrants of minority mother tongue who arrived in the United States during the 1960's is presented in Table 3.6. We should observe first of all that the overall rate of anglicisation is markedly lower than that observed in Table 3.5. The general rate of anglicisation for immigrants who arrived in the 1960's is 60.4 percent for the non-Spanish groups as a whole. Furthermore, English bilingualism is clearly the dominant form of anglicisation for more recent immigrants. In addition, the percentage of persons unable to speak English well has increased somewhat, although only 14.7 percent declared that this was a problem.

The examination of the language shift patterns of the various minority language groups reveals some sharp differences in patterns of language shift. For example, the German, Russian, Scandinavian, Vietnamese, and Yiddish

Table 3.6 *Language shift patterns by mother tongue of immigrants arriving during the 1960's, persons aged 14 and over, United States, 1976*

Language group	English usual language			Non-English usual language			Weighted sample
	Mono-lingual	Bi-lingual	Total	English competence High	Low	Total	
Arab	5.2	63.5	68.7	26.6	4.7	31.3	26,313
Chinese	4.1	22.2	26.3	37.2	36.5	73.9	118,770
Filipino	27.1	44.4	71.5	25.9	2.6	28.5	83,128
French	15.9	43.3	59.2	36.4	4.4	40.8	90,825
German	37.7	51.5	89.2	10.3	0.5	10.8	142,012
Greek	1.0	28.7	29.7	36.2	34.1	70.3	63,974
Italian	8.3	45.1	53.4	23.1	23.5	46.6	172,116
Japanese	24.3	54.5	78.8	16.2	5.0	21.2	26,325
Korean	33.2	36.1	69.3	24.3	6.3	30.6	23,526
Polish	4.8	42.6	47.4	25.8	26.8	52.6	37,954
Portuguese	3.1	26.8	29.9	25.7	44.4	70.1	68,000
Russian	33.8	53.2	87.0	9.7	3.3	13.0	6,239
Scandinavian	31.8	68.0	99.8	0.2	0.0	0.2	24,638
Vietnamese	2.3	97.7	100.0	0.0	0.0	0.0	3,217
Yiddish	0.0	91.9	91.9	8.1	0.0	8.1	6,270
All other	17.7	48.3	66.0	24.5	9.5	34.0	234,624
All non-Spanish	16.1	44.3	60.4	24.9	14.7	39.6	1,119,258
Chicano	1.8	19.4	21.2	27.2	51.6	78.8	377,689
Cuban	1.4	27.4	28.8	38.6	32.6	71.2	316,343
Puerto Rican	1.9	23.4	25.3	41.0	33.7	74.7	169,752
Other Hispanic	6.3	35.2	41.5	23.5	40.0	63.5	295,907
All Spanish	2.9	26.2	29.1	31.3	39.6	70.1	1,159,691

Source: 1976 Survey of Income and Education

language groups are characterized by anglicisation rates higher than eighty-five percent. On the other hand, the Chinese, Greek, and Portuguese language groups have anglicisation rates inferior to thirty percent and tend to be characterized by relatively high proportions of persons reporting difficulty with spoken English. In nearly all other cases, the anglicisation rates exceed fifty percent, indicating once again the relative rapidity with which immigrants adopt the English language as principal language of use. The data also indicate the presence of relatively high percentages of English monolinguals in the Filipino, German, Japanese, Korean, Russian, and Scandinavian language groups.

The Spanish language group is once again characterized by generally low rates of anglicisation, approximately one-half that prevailing among the non-Spanish groups taken as a whole. The percentages of persons reporting difficulty with English are markedly higher (39.6% vs. 14.7%), while the impact of English monolingualism is very weak. Only 2.9 percent of the immigrants of Spanish mother tongue in the 1960's abandoned the Spanish language as a daily language. On the whole, the language characteristics of the Spanish group strongly resemble those observed for the Chinese, Greek, and Portuguese language groups.

There are, once again, the usual intergroup differences in language shift within the Spanish group. The Chicanos are least anglicized, followed by the Puerto Ricans and Cubans. The Other Hispanics are the most anglicized, having language characteristic patterns which resemble those of the Polish language group.

Similar data are presented for the most recent immigrants to the United States in Table 3.7. It is perhaps worth underlining one more time that the maximum period of residence which these immigrants could have enjoyed was only *six years*. Thus, any language shift at all in the direction of English must be seen as extremely rapid.

Examining first of all the overall averages, the data reveal that 43.5 percent of the non-Spanish immigrants had already made English their usual language of use. While this is markedly lower than that observed for immigrants resident in the U.S. for a longer period of time, one cannot help but observe the rapidity with which such change occurs. Furthermore, 9.2 percent had already ceased to use their mother tongue as a frequently spoken second language. Only 27.3 percent reported that they had difficulty with English. On the whole, then, the data for the non-Spanish group indicate extremely rapid movement both to bilingualism in English and to the making of English one's principal language.

When we examine the rates of language shift for specific groups, the data reveal that more than fifty percent of the persons of Arabic, Filipino, French, German, Scandinavian, and All Other mother tongues had already made English their principal language of use. The rates of English monolingualism already exceed ten percent in all of these groups except the Filipino language group, attaining no less than 31.9 percent in the German group. We must conclude that this degree of language shift within a six year period is indeed extraordinary. On the other hand, the Chinese, Greek, Polish, and Portuguese

Table 3.7 *Language shift patterns by mother tongue of immigrants arriving during the 1970's, persons aged 14 and over, United States, 1976*

Language group	English usual language			Non-English usual language English competence			Weighted sample
	Mono-lingual	Bi-lingual	Total	High	Low	Total	
Arab	4.1	56.4	60.5	23.0	16.5	39.5	47,365
Chinese	4.1	22.2	26.3	37.2	36.5	73.7	118,770
Filipino	8.9	43.0	51.9	38.4	9.7	48.1	146,264
French	10.5	44.2	54.7	28.9	16.4	45.3	50,712
German	31.9	39.4	71.3	21.8	6.9	28.7	36,282
Greek	0.9	26.1	27.0	30.1	42.9	73.0	50,326
Italian	1.8	32.5	34.3	11.9	53.8	65.7	72,932
Japanese	15.9	27.7	43.6	26.2	30.2	56.4	39,478
Korean	8.2	30.1	38.3	11.6	50.1	61.7	87,227
Polish	7.3	21.5	28.8	26.8	44.4	71.2	11,386
Portuguese	2.7	13.1	15.8	31.2	53.0	84.2	63,168
Scandinavian*	18.2	41.3	59.5	40.5	0.0	40.5	8,863
Vietnamese*	7.6	23.2	30.8	44.0	25.2	69.2	78,880
All other	14.0	40.6	54.6	28.4	17.0	45.4	273,201
All non-Spanish	9.2	34.3	43.5	29.2	27.3	56.5	1,087,845
Chicano	0.0	4.1	4.1	18.1	77.8	95.9	377,980
Cuban	0.1	10.4	10.5	21.1	68.4	89.5	114,173
Puerto Rican	0.9	9.8	10.7	25.3	64.0	89.3	107,864
Other Hispanic	0.9	23.6	24.5	23.8	51.7	75.5	279,070
All Spanish	0.4	11.8	12.2	21.2	66.6	87.8	879,087

Source: 1976 Survey of Income and Education
* Estimated population sizes: Russian = 1,143; Yiddish = 1,948

language groups have anglicisation rates inferior to thirty percent, while the Italian, Korean, and Vietnamese groups have rates between thirty and forty percent. As expected the rates of English monolingualism tend to be relatively low in most minority language groups for these most recent immigrants.

As expected, the observed rates of language shift for the most recent Spanish immigrants are still lower. Approximately two-thirds (66.6%) reported that they could not speak English well, fixing a ceiling on the number of potential emigrants to English. Only 12.2 percent said that they usually spoke English, the bilingual form of anglicisation being nearly always the type selected. Nonetheless, we should not fail to observe that within the six year period covered in this table, nearly one in eight persons of Spanish mother tongue had selected English as his or her usual language. Needless to say, the extent to which this is true varied by ethnic group. The most recent Cuban arrivals were nearly as anglicized as the Other Hispanics, while the Chicanos and Puerto Ricans had much lower anglicisation rates. The pattern of percentages of persons not speaking English well is, of course, inversely related to the general rate of anglicisation.

Summarizing the analysis of the foreign born, we have found some evidence for intergroup differences in the language shift rates of the foreign born. Even after period of immigration has been controlled, the data tend to indicate that the Chinese, Portuguese, and Greek groups are among the most retentive groups in the non-Spanish group, while the German, Russian, Scandinavian, and Yiddish language groups are among the least retentive. The Spanish language group as a whole appears to have general anglicisation rates more or less comparable to those of the Chinese, Portuguese, and Greek language groups. That anglicisation, however, more frequently takes the form of English bilingualism than it does in the non-Spanish groups. Within the Spanish language group, the Other Hispanics undergo the most rapid language shift, whereas the Chicano group is clearly the most retentive. The data also show that Cubans appear more readily anglicized than do Puerto Ricans.

Given the rapidity, however, with which minority language groups engage in anglicisation, it may be that some of these observed differences are partly explained by within-period differences in time-of-arrival. It would appear that extensive anglicisation occurs within a period of time as short as six years, such that earlier or later arrival within a period could have some effect on the observed rate of anglicisation. It is not likely, however, that such differences could explain all the observed differences reported in Tables 3.5 to 3.7.

Language shift among the native born. If, then, the immigrant generation of minority language groups already has undergone some (frequently quite extensive) anglicisation, we may expect that the native born generation is exposed to still greater language shift. Unfortunately, we cannot divide the native born population into those persons who had foreign born parents and those who had native born parents. Given the extent of the anglicisation of persons in most foreign born groups, however, it would seem quite unlikely that a large majority of native born persons of minority mother tongue should have native born parents. That is to say, most of the native born are likely the children of the foreign born themselves. The relevant data are presented in Table 3.8.

Table 3.8 *Language shift patterns by mother tongue, native born persons aged 14 and over, United States, 1976*

Language group	English usual language			Non-English usual language English competence			Weighted sample
	Mono-lingual	Bi-lingual	Total	High	Low	Total	
Arab	70.0	27.7	97.7	2.3	0.0	2.3	30,852
Chinese	29.3	60.7	90.0	8.9	1.1	10.0	46,387
Filipino	67.9	29.5	97.4	2.1	0.5	2.6	18,783
French	54.3	32.7	87.0	9.6	3.4	13.0	876,951
German	85.4	11.0	96.4	3.5	0.1	3.6	1,154,743
Greek	48.2	49.3	97.5	2.5	0.0	2.5	134,730
Italian	75.4	23.2	98.6	1.1	0.3	1.4	1,338,114
Japanese*	54.9	35.4	90.3	4.1	5.6	9.7	155,262
Navajo	3.9	20.8	24.7	43.0	32.3	75.3	93,108
Polish	73.4	24.3	97.7	2.0	0.3	2.3	964,949
Portuguese	59.9	36.6	96.5	2.2	1.3	3.5	142,018
Russian	77.2	21.8	99.0	1.0	0.0	1.0	85,515
Scandinavian	87.7	11.9	99.6	0.4	0.0	0.4	359,142
Yiddish	79.1	17.6	96.7	3.3	0.0	3.3	270,259
All other	71.0	22.1	93.1	5.7	1.2	6.9	1,295,703
All non-Spanish	71.5	22.8	94.3	4.3	1.4	5.7	6,968,420
Chicano	12.1	50.6	62.7	28.6	8.7	37.3	2,010,061
Cuban	1.6	79.6	81.2	12.2	6.6	18.8	23,463
Puerto Rican	15.9	65.9	71.8	17.9	0.3	18.2	190,916
Other Hispanic	23.5	43.5	67.0	27.2	5.8	33.0	342,184
All Spanish	13.8	51.0	64.8	27.5	7.7	35.2	2,566,624

Source: 1976 Survey of Income and Education
* Estimated population for Korean = 1,904
Note: The adjusted figures for native Americans as a whole are: English monolingual = 19.0%, English bilingual = 26.3%, anglicisation = 45.3%, high competence = 42.5%, low competence = 32.0%, non-English usual language = 54.7%.

The first observation derived from this table suggests that the inability to speak English well appears to be relatively rare among the native born. Only 1.4 percent of the non-Spanish and 7.7 percent of the Spanish indicate difficulty with spoken English. Only among the Navajo language group is the rate sharply higher, 32.3 percent. As expected, the anglicisation rates of the native born are also sharply higher. Fully 94.3 percent of the non-Spanish taken as a whole and 64.8 percent of the Spanish indicated that they usually spoke English. In the non-Spanish group the vast majority of the anglicized adopted the English monolingual form of language shift, whereas in the Spanish language group English bilingualism was by far the most prevalent.

With respect to the specific minority language groups, nearly all non-Spanish groups had general anglicisation rates higher than ninety percent. Only the Navajo had a sharply lower rate. The distribution of English monolingualism and English bilingualism varies somewhat from group to group, although only the Chinese and Navajo groups had English monolingualism rates below fifty percent.

The situation is somewhat different in the Spanish language group where English bilingualism was by far the most common adaptation among all ethnic groups. However, the rates of anglicisation for the Cuban group attained 81.2 percent, while that of the Puerto Ricans attained 71.8 percent. Even the generally more retentive Chicanos had an anglicisation rate of 62.7 percent. With respect to English monolingualism, this type of adaptation was virtually absent in the Cuban group, more frequent in the remaining groups, attaining 23.5 percent for the Other Hispanics.

Summarizing our findings from the analysis of the language shift process, we have found that time-of-arrival is indeed related to the extent of language shift in every group. The native born are the most anglicized, followed by those who have lived for the longest period of time in the United States. The anglicisation rate, for example, of the native born in the non-Spanish groups taken as a whole was found to be 94.3 percent, that of immigrants who arrived in the United States before 1960, 80.1 percent; that of those who arrived in the 1960's, 60.4 percent; while that of the most recent immigrants already attained 43.5 percent. We can only characterize such movement as both extremely rapid and quite extensive. The rates of English monolingualism vary accordingly, 71.5%, 43.7%, 16.1%, and 9.2% respectively. In general, then, the English monolingualism rate accelerates still more rapidly as a result of longer residence than does the rate of anglicisation as a whole. The more recent arrivals adopt English as usual language relatively rapidly but they retain the use of their minority language in the vast majority of cases. However, after a decade of residence in the United States, the use of minority languages as second languages appears to decline to a great extent. Among the native born, only a tiny minority continue to speak their mother tongue as a second language.

The same general patterns can be observed for persons of Spanish mother tongue. The rates of language shift are, however, markedly lower. They are not, however, low. Among the most recent immigrants, the rate of anglicisation already stood at 12.2 percent in 1976 while it attained 64.8 percent among the native born. The actual rate for the native born is probably still higher, since a certain number of illegal residents quite probably misled the Census interviewer as to their place of birth (Lopez, 1981). Thus, while the Spanish language group seems at this point in time to be relatively successful in limiting its losses to English to the form of anglicisation which we have called English bilingualism, the rates of anglicisation rise with increased length of residence in the United States. Among the native born, nearly two-thirds will raise children of English mother tongue, i.e., on the assumption that they will give their children what has become their principal language of use. Thus, while these data do not indicate the complete elimination of the group of people who retain Spanish as their principal language of use, there clearly will not be many children of Spanish mother tongue born to the current generation of native born adults. The data indicate that 13.8 percent will have no exposure to Spanish. We shall examine the probability that the children of the English bilinguals will themselves retain this bilingualism in the next chapter.

Apart from these very broad trends, the data do indicate that certain language groups appear to be more retentive than others. This is particularly true among the foreign born, where the Chinese, the Greek, and the Portuguese language minorities appear to have lower rates of anglicisation than do most groups, while the German, Russian, Scandinavian, and Yiddish language groups have experienced somewhat greater anglicisation than other groups. The Spanish language group taken as a unit appears to have anglicisation rates rather similar to those of the most retentive non-Spanish groups. However, within the Spanish language group, persons of Chicano ancestry are the least anglicized in each time period. Puerto Ricans also tend to have anglicisation rates inferior to the general rate calculated for the language group as a whole. On the other hand, persons of Cuban ancestry tend to have anglicisation rates which lie very close to the language group mean, although they are generally marginally higher. Persons of 'Other Hispanic' origin tend to have the highest rates of anglicisation, rates which tend to surpass those observed for the more retentive non-Spanish groups.

While the data suggest that intergroup differences remain after the period of immigration has been taken into account, most such differences have disappeared among the native born. All non-Spanish language groups with the exception of the Navajo have extremely high anglicisation rates. In most cases English monolingualism is the prevalent form of that anglicisation, indicating that the minority language cannot be transmitted to the following generation as a second language. Only the language shift patterns of the Navajo and the Spanish language groups differ markedly from these observations. While the pattern of intergroup differences within the Spanish language group remain unaltered, the rates of anglicisàtion are relatively high. Nearly two-thirds of the persons of Spanish mother tongue have made English their principal language of use, indicating that two-thirds of the children born to these adults should have English for their mother tongue. In addition, nearly one in seven adults (13.8%) no longer speaks Spanish on a regular basis and may be expected to have English monolingual children. In the most retentive group, the Chicano ethnic group, the anglicisation rate stands at 62.7 percent, attaining 81.2 percent among the least retentive Cubans. For a language group which is thought by many to resist language shift to English, the rates of linguistic emigration appear to be exceptionally high. This can be most readily demonstrated by comparing the Spanish language shift pattern to that of the Navajo. Only 24.7 percent of the latter have made English their usual language, only 3.9 percent having adopted the English monolingual form of anglicisation. By comparison, the anglicisation of persons of Spanish mother tongue appears extremely advanced. At any rate, if the Navajo group may be viewed as being relatively unique and the Spanish as somewhat less unique, it is quite clear that most intergroup differences in anglicisation have disappeared among the native born.

Age-specific rates of anglicisation. While age-specific rates of language shift can in fact be constructed for all American minority language groups, we have imposed two limits on the presentation of the relevant data. First of all, when the anglicisation rate of the native born as a whole is higher than ninety percent, the decomposition of the general rate into age-specific rates does not contribute to our understanding of the process of anglicisation. To achieve an anglicisation rate of more than ninety percent, nearly all members of the group irrespective of age must be anglicized. In certain instances, notably in the Polish and Italian language groups, the anglicisaton curve dips slightly to the right for the group aged 70 and over, indicating a slightly lower rate of anglicisation for this group. Secondly, to achieve any reasonable degree of confidence in the estimates, a minority language group must have some sufficiently large number of members to permit an analysis, in addition to which they should be adequately distributed among the various age groups. This criterion by itself would not eliminate any groups not already eliminated by the first criterion. It does, however, provide an additional reason for not presenting such data. The imposition of these criteria restricts our subsequent analysis to only three language groups, French, Spanish, and Navajo. Since the Navajo language group is concentrated in a single region, we shall present our age-specific analysis for this group as part of our regional analyses.

As we have indicated in our chapter on theory and method in language shift analysis, the anglicisation process begins in early childhood. Consequently, some use of the data collected for children aged 4 to 13 is desirable, even though we have already indicated our dissatisfaction with the failure of the planners of the SIE to have collected data on the mother tongue of such children. If we would attempt to compare the approximate anglicisation rates of children to those of adults, we are obliged to follow the procedure recommended by NCES, imputing the usual household language as mother tongue of the child. This procedure is likely to cause very conservative estimates of anglicisation for these children, since the children of minority mother tongue who live in English language households are excluded from the analysis. These children are still more likely to have adopted English as their principal language of use. Nonetheless, children aged 4 to 13 have been included in the age-specific analysis. At the same time, the reader is advised to consider these data as relatively weak in quality.

The age-specific language shift rates for the French language group are presented in Figure 3.1. The data are divided by ten year age groups (20 to 29, 30 to 39, 40 to 49, 50 to 59, 60 to 69, 70 and over), except of course, for those under the age of twenty. Adults aged 14 to 19 and children aged 4 to 13 are presented separately.

Three curves are drawn in Figure 3.1, dividing the area of the figure into four distinct parts. Among persons who have retained French as the language they usually speak, the upper curve distinguishes persons with low competence in English from those with high competence in English. It is evident from Figure 3.1 that only a small percentage of the very oldest and very youngest persons reportedly do not speak English well. Nearly everyone between the ages of 14 and 60 speaks English well. The curve has, nonetheless, the 'i' configuration indicative of increasing anglicisation over the past several decades.

The middle curve distinguishes persons who have retained French as their usual language from those who have made English their usual language. This is the anglicisation curve as we have defined it: all persons falling below this

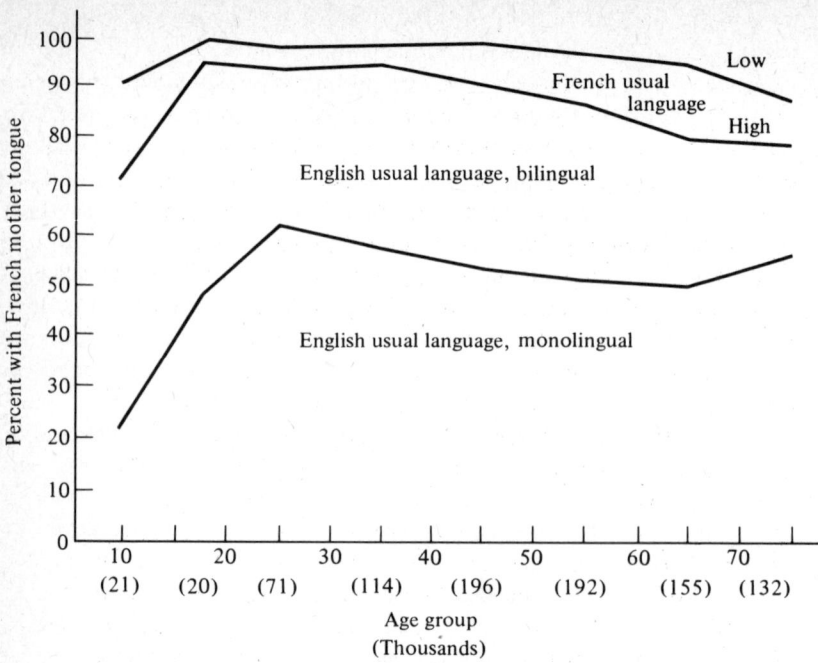

Source: 1976 Survey of Income and Education

Figure 3.1 *Percentage distribution of language shift by persons of French mother tongue by age group, native born, United States, 1976*

curve have adopted the English language as their preferred, most frequently spoken language. From figure 3.1 it can be readily seen that this curve also follows an 'i' configuration, confirming the hypothesis that younger cohorts have been increasingly anglicized over the past several decades. Once again, the younger children are less likely to have replaced their mother tongue with the English language. By the time, however, that they have reached their teenage years (or, by the time we have accurate data on the mother tongue of such children), the anglicisation rates exceed ninety (90) percent. Since the 15 to 19 and the 20 to 29 year olds have not yet completed their linguistic emigration, their final rates of anglicisation may be expected to be still higher than those currently indicated. As a result, the 'i' shape of the curve will be still more pronounced in the near future. By the year 2000, only those persons aged 60 and over should have an anglicisation curve where only the very tail of the curve dips off to the right. This curve will then resemble the current anglicisation curve of the Polish and Italian groups.

The lower curve in Figure 3.1 distinguishes between those who have retained the use of Fench as a frequently spoken, second language and those who no longer speak it 'often'. That is, it distinguishes between the English bilingual and English monolingual forms of anglicisation. This curve also tends to follow the expected 'i' shaped curve indicating increased language shift over the past several decades. The single exception to the 'i' shaped model is found for the oldest age group, an age group characterized by somewhat higher rates of English monolingualism than are several of the younger age groups. On the other hand, the lower curve demonstrates quite clearly the sharp increase in English monolingualism associated with the adolescent and early adult years, i.e., as these individuals leave the parental home. There is a sharp rise in the percentage of persons who stop speaking French as a second language.

Similar data are presented for the native born persons of Spanish mother tongue in Figure 3.2. We observe first of all that all three curves assume the familiar 'i' configuration which indicates increasing rates of language shift of all types. The upper curve indicates that there has been a sharp reduction in the percentage of persons declaring that they do not speak English well. While nearly one-half of those aged seventy or more reported such low competence in English, less than five percent of the group aged 30 to 39 declared that they did not speak English well. Evidently, younger cohorts have been increasingly exposed to social situations which require increasingly greater knowledge and use of the English language. This is quite clearly the case for the youngest adults where the capacity to speak English well is nearly universal. Even among the children of the Spanish language group, only seventeen percent said that they did not speak English well, a figure markedly lower than that obtained for the oldest adults. Consequently, there has been a rapid increase in the English language skills of the native born population over the past several decades.

Not only has the general ability to speak English well been increasing over the past decades; the adoption of English as one's usual language has also been increasing. While less than thirty-five percent of members of the two oldest groups made English their usual language, nearly seventy percent of the 30 to 39 year olds have done so. The 15 to 19 and 20 to 29 year olds are already characterized by equally high rates of anglicisation, a situation which presages still higher levels in the near future. Among adults aged 14 and over it is evident that the general anglicisation rate of 64.8 percent masks impor-

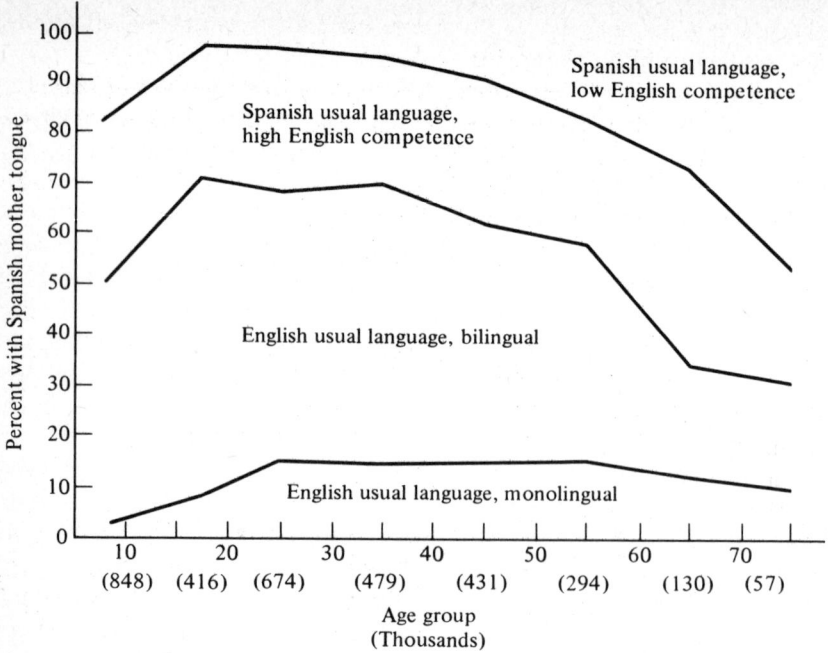

Source: 1976 Survey of Income and Education

Figure 3.2 *Percentage distribution of language shift by persons of Spanish mother tongue by age group, native born, United States, 1976*

tant differences in the age-specific rates of anglicisation. As expected, the anglicisation rates of the children are somewhat lower, although fifty-one percent have already made English their principal language.

The curve which distinguishes English monolingualism from English bilingualism appears to have been relatively stable over the past few decades. It is nearly flat between the ages of 20 and 60, the percentage of English monolinguals remaining virtually constant. As expected, there are relatively few children living in Spanish language homes who have dropped the use of Spanish as a second language. Nonetheless, the rate of English monolingualism increases rather sharply during the teenage and early adult years, underlining once again the importance of these ages for the understanding of the language shift process. There is also some evidence that the rate of English monolingualism was lower in the more distant past, the curve tailing off on the right for the two oldest age groups.

The examination of these curves reporting age-specific rates of language shift reveals that they conform in essential respects to the findings obtained from the 1971 Census of Canada. There is a relatively steep rise in language shift behavior as children enter the school system. In our data large percentages of children have already made English their usual language; still larger percentages speak it well. The rates increase still further in the young adult years represented in our figures by the groups aged 14 to 19 and 20 to 29 years of age. The rates for all types of language shift reach a peak for the group aged 30 to 39. All three curves then tail off to the right, indicating that older groups were more retentive than are those currently completing the language shift process. In other words, all types of language shift have undergone a secular increase over the past several decades.

Furthermore, the location of the curves on the respective figures for the French and Spanish language group leads to another observation. Since even the oldest age groups in the French language group are highly anglicized, the slope of the 'i' curve is not as marked as that found for the Spanish language group. Since the older age groups among the native born are less anglicized in this latter group, the increase in anglicisation rates appears much sharper. Interestingly, the higher anglicisation rates of the younger age groups do not appear to have peaked. Since the younger groups are already as anglicized as, for example, that aged 30 to 39, they may be expected to have final rates of anglicisation which are still higher.

We should also point out that this secular increase in the anglicisation of the native born has occurred during a period which was also characterized by high levels of international immigration. This replenishing of the population of Spanish usual language may have two effects on the observed rate of anglicisation. On the one hand, it may serve to restrain the anglicisation of the group as a whole, i.e., causing the curves to be placed somewhat lower on Figure 3.2 than they would have been in the absence of such immigration. Secondly, it may explain why the rate of English monolingualism has been relatively stable over the past several decades, continued immigration requiring the native born to maintain minimal levels of competence in the Spanish language. Such immigration has not, however, affected the secular trend of anglicisation itself, the percentage of the anglicized increasing with each younger age group.

Regional patterns of language shift. While the national trends are in themselves quite interesting, most minority language groups are concentrated in specific regions. Since it is reasonable to suppose that those living inside such regions are less anglicized than other members of the group, some attention to regional variation would seem useful. While the analysis of the data indicates that anglicisation rates are marginally lower in most areas of regional concentration, the regional patterns reflect very closely those already presented at the national level (see Veltman, 1981b for the relevant tables). Since the presence of anglicisation rates superior to ninety percent among the native born renders such an analysis superfluous, we shall restrict our presentation to the analysis of the three principal groups demonstrating the highest rates of retention among the native born, the French, the Navajo, and the Spanish. In the case of both the French and Spanish language groups, regional differences are also related to differences in ethnic and/or national origin.

The construction of regional samples was based on the analysis of raw case counts (not weighted) for each SMSA in the SIE sample. In some cases only parts of certain states were selected for analysis. There were, for example, no persons of French mother tongue in the Shreveport, Louisiana SMSA. In other cases certain states or parts of states were joined with others. Thus, the New York metropolitan area sample consists of two New York, two Connecticut, and two New Jersey SMSA's. The objective of such an *ad hoc* procedure was the construction of meaningful social units. However, the implementation of such an objective renders meaningless the estimates of population variances for the various States. The reader should understand that no scientific virtue is claimed for the analyses which follow, since there is no way to evaluate data which are organized in this way. In addition, the sample sizes frequently become rather small. Nonetheless, we present in Table 3.9 the parameters used to select the regional samples.

Having established the geographic limits of our regional samples, we shall first of all examine the nativity characteristics of persons in the minority language groups which inhabit these regions. The place of birth of adults for the relevant language groups and regions is presented in Table 3.10.

The examination of this table shows that there are relatively important differences in the nativity configuration of the French and Spanish language groups inhabiting the various regions. The French language group is largely composed of the native born in each region, less than twenty-five percent of the persons of French mother tongue having been born outside the United States in the two New England regions. The francophone population of

Table 3.9 Geographic parameters of the regional language samples

Region	Geographic units
Northern New England	Maine, Vermont, New Hampshire
Southern New England	Massachusetts, Rhode Island, Connecticut (except New Haven, Bridgeport)
Metropolitan New York	New York, Nassau-Suffolk, Newark, Patterson, Jersey City, New Haven, and Bridgeport SMSAs
North Central States	Illinois, Michigan, Indiana, Ohio, Wisconsin
Louisiana	Rural Louisiana, New Orleans, Baton Rouge, Beaumont (Texas)
Florida	Florida
Texas	Rural Texas, El Paso, Corpus Christi, San Antonio
New Mexico	New Mexico
Arizona	Arizona
Rocky Mountain States	Colorado, Wyoming, Idaho, Utah, Nevada, Montana
California	Rural California, Los Angeles, Anaheim, San Diego, San Bernadino, Oxnard-Ventura, Santa Barbara

Louisiana is nearly entirely native born, a pattern shared only by persons of the Navajo language group.

Persons of Spanish mother tongue are also largely native born in the regions of New Mexico, the Rocky Mountain States, Texas and Arizona. On the other hand, the Spanish language groups in New York and Florida are overwhelmingly composed of the foreign born, i.e., outside the continental United States. The Spanish language groups in California and the industrial midwest (North Central) tend to be more largely composed of the foreign born, although the percentage of native born is higher than that found in New York or Florida. Were we to ignore the impact of nativity, we should undoubtedly find higher rates of language retention in these latter areas than we should, for example, in the Rocky Mountain states.

Although the percentage of foreign born persons in certain of these regions is quite high, it does not seem prudent to decompose the language characteristics of the foreign born by period of immigration. The sample sizes are already much smaller than those presented in our national analysis of the Spanish language group. Since the regions identified in Table 3.9 contain the vast majority of persons in the Spanish language group, it is quite likely that

Table 3.10 *Nativity by region, persons of selected mother tongues aged 14 and over, United States, 1976*

Language group and region	Place of birth		Weighted sample
	Foreign born	Native born	
French:			
Northern New England	21.3%	78.7%	162,958
Southern New England	34.8	75.2	238,180
Louisiana	0.3	99.7	311,407
Spanish:			
New York Metropolitan	86.1	13.9	1,051,781
Florida	87.4	12.6	460,751
North Central States	63.5	36.5	344,278
Texas	27.7	72.3	1,168,477
New Mexico	8.5	91.5	217,790
Arizona	26.3	73.7	158,743
Rocky Mountain States	20.0	80.0	145,444
California	58.8	41.2	1,154,253
Navajo, New Mexico and Arizona	0.0	100.0	83,253

Source: 1976 Survey of Income and Education

regional findings would be similar in nature, i.e., that the extensiveness of anglicisation is a function of length of residence in the United States. Consequently, we shall focus primarily on the analysis of regional differences in the patterns of language shift. We present in the upper panel of Table 3.11 the data pertaining to the language characteristics of the foreign born.

Beginning our analysis with persons of French mother tongue, the data reveal that the anglicisation rates are markedly higher in southern New England, the region which has the largest percentage of the foreign born. Of the 81.0 percent of persons who made English their usual language, the majority retained French as a second language. However, 34.7 percent of these immigrants declared that they no longer spoke French 'frequently'. These percentages contrast clearly with those found in northern New England. Just over one-half of the persons of French mother tongue were anglicized, the rate of English monolingualism standing at 18.6 percent. In addition, some 16.0 percent stated that they did not speak English well, while a high level of competence in spoken English is nearly unversal in southern New England.

In spite of the major differences in the regional patterns of nativity of

Table 3.11 *Language shift patterns by place of birth and region, persons aged 14 and over, selected language groups, United States, 1976*

Language group	English usual language			Non-English usual language			Weighted sample
	Mono-lingual	Bi-lingual	Total	English competence High	Low	Total	
Foreign born:							
French:							
N. New England	18.6	32.2	50.8	33.2	16.0	49.2	34,786
S. New England	34.7	46.3	81.0	16.5	2.5	19.0	59,034
Spanish:							
New York	1.8	26.9	28.7	32.4	38.9	71.3	905,413
Florida	0.9	22.6	23.5	35.8	40.7	76.5	402,694
North Central	3.6	28.5	32.1	27.8	40.2	67.9	218.786
Texas	1.0	15.2	16.2	27.0	56.8	83.8	324,213
New Mexico	1.0	22.2	23.2	22.0	54.8	76.8	18,433
Arizona	4.4	24.8	29.2	32.8	38.0	70.8	41,766
Rocky Mountains	9.4	39.0	48.4	22.9	28.7	51.6	29,082
California	1.8	25.4	27.2	21.7	51.1	72.8	678,905
Native born:							
French:							
N. New England	40.8	43.3	84.1	14.5	1.4	15.9	179,146
S. New England	60.3	35.3	95.6	4.3	0.2	4.4	128,173
Louisiana	37.1	36.8	73.9	17.3	8.8	26.1	310,621
Spanish:							
New York	12.9	67.6	80.5	9.2	0.3	19.5	146,368
Florida	20.5	43.0	63.5	34.2	2.3	36.5	58,057
North Central	21.0	54.2	75.1	18.7	6.2	24.9	125,492
Texas	5.2	37.0	42.2	43.0	14.8	57.8	844,264
New Mexico	9.0	41.7	50.7	40.1	9.2	49.3	199,356
Arizona	7.5	56.1	63.6	33.2	3.2	36.4	116,977
Rocky Mountains	24.4	59.6	84.0	13.1	2.9	16.0	116,361
California	17.3	68.4	85.7	10.4	3.9	14.3	475,348
Navajo	2.2	21.1	23.3	41.9	34.8	76.7	83,253

Source: 1976 Survey of Income and Education

persons of Spanish mother tongue, the data reveal few differences in the process of language shift among the foreign born. There are only two exceptions to a picture of relatively constant anglicisation rates by region. Table

3.11 shows that 48.4 percent of the persons living in the Rocky Mountain states usually spoke English, a figure substantially higher than that found in the remaining regions. The rate of English monolingualism was also markedly higher. On the other hand, the anglicisation rates are lower in the Texas region than they are elsewhere. Only 16.2 percent of the foreign born have made English their usual language, less than one percent abandoning the frequent use of Spanish.

The size of the anglicisation rate of the foreign born persons of Spanish mother tongue in Texas should not be lost upon the reader. In the most retentive region of the United States, where the ties of the foreign born are both relatively recent and geographically close (to Mexico), sixteen percent of the foreign born in Texas have chosen to use English as the principal language of their daily lives. Since the anglicisation rates are still higher in other regions of Hispanic concentration, it is evident that Spanish immigrants accept the 'fact' of English language dominance in the United States. On arrival, even in Texas, they begin to make relatively rapid adjustments to this situation, not only learning English but making it their principal language.

Similar data for the native born are presented in the lower panel of Table 3.11. As expected the levels of both English bilingualism and English monolingualism are markedly higher. For example, the anglicisation of the native born population of French mother tongue in southern New England is nearly complete. Furthermore, more than sixty percent said that they no longer spoke French with sufficient frequency to have declared it as a second language. Similarly, the anglicisation rate in northern New England stands at 84.1 percent, although a slight majority of the anglicized retained French as a second language. Nonetheless, more than forty percent had abandoned its use, having become effective English monolinguals. For those interested in the retention of minority languages, the situation appears less bleak in Louisiana, the remaining Franco-American homeland. Even in Louisiana, however, nearly three of every four persons of French mother tongue have made English their usual language, half retaining French as a frequently spoken, second language, the other half having adopted an English monolingual pattern. In general, then, the examination of the regional rates of language shift for the French language group indicate a very serious erosion in the use of the language. Even in the traditional areas of settlement this erosion has undoubtedly passed the critical stage.

An examination of the language shift data for the native born persons of Spanish mother tongue also indicates that the rates of anglicisation of both types are sharply higher. The lowest rate of anglicisation is once again found in Texas, where *only* 42.2 percent of the native born have made English their usual language. The rate of English monolingualism was only 5.2 percent. The only other region with a relatively retentive pattern is that of New Mexico, where the anglicisation rate stood at 50.7 percent. These are, it should be noted, two regions where the population is largely native born, indicating that the presence of the foreign born does not in itself appear to constrain language shift to English. Rather, their appears to be some dynamic intrinsic to these regions (and to a lesser extent that of Arizona as well) which limits the extent of language shift to English. The regions with the highest anglicisation rates are those of New York, California, and the Rocky Mountain states, the two former regions characterized by large percentages of immigrants, the latter by a high percentage of the native born. It does not appear, then that regional differences in the extent of anglicisation are generally related to recency of immigration in the Spanish language group. The evidence suggests, rather, that there are inherent regional differences.

In spite of these rather high regional rates of anglicisation in the Spanish language group, the anglicized generally continue to retain the use of Spanish as a second language. English bilingualism is clearly the dominant pattern of accomodation to the American environment for both foreign and native born persons of Spanish mother tongue. This distinctive feature of the Spanish language group persists in all regions irrespective of the anglicisation rate.

The anglicisation rates of the Spanish language group are, however, exceptionally high when compared to those of the Navajo. While small language islands (Fishman, 1966) may continue to exist here and there for some of the other minority language groups, only the Navajo language groups manifests such low levels of anglicisation in the United States (insofar as we can ascertain from this survey). Only 23.3 percent of the persons of Navajo mother tongue, all of whom were native born, had made English their usual language. Less than three percent had abandoned the frequent use of Navajo as a second language, nearly all such persons residing in the urban areas of New Mexico and Arizona. Almost all of those living in the rural areas of these states, presumably on the Navajo reservation, continued to speak the Navajo language, the vast majority as their usual language. Furthermore, it would appear that such high levels of retention are not unrelated to the fact that more than one-third of the persons of Navajo mother tongue declared that they could not speak English well. Their presence undoubtedly exercises certain constraints on the linguistic behavior of the persons with whom they come into contact.

Age-specific and region-specific rates of anglicisation. Since the examination of the national data in Figures 3.1 and 3.2 indicate that the general rates of language shift tend to understate the current rates, we shall now procede to the presentation of age-specific rates of language shift for the native born. However, such rates will not be presented for persons of French mother tongue in southern New England since nearly everyone has been anglicized. In addition, since there are so few native born persons in the Spanish language group in Florida (in terms of unweighted cases), no further analysis will be presented for this group. The relevant data revealed that nearly two-thirds of the native born had already been anglicized, although most were so young that they cannot be presumed to have completed the language shift process. While these data predate the arrival of large numbers of additional Cuban refugees (1980), they suggest that the native born children have rapidly embraced English as their preferred, usual language.

We begin our analysis with the presentation of the language shift curves for persons of French mother tongue in northern New England. Once again, we have followed the recommended NCES procedure and assigned the usual household language as the mother tongue of children, thus obtaining anglicisation rates for children aged 4-13. The relevant data are presented in Figure 3.3.

While the sample sizes are too small in some cases to produce completely smooth curves, the 'i' shaped curve indicating increasing rates of anglicisation is unmistakeably present. The anglicisation curve falls sharply to the left, indicating the lower expected levels of anglicisation among the young. Again both the lower and upper curves tend to follow the 'i' configuration of the anglicisation curve inself. We conclude that all forms of language shift to English have been increasing among the native born French minority in this region, although according to these data very few persons in any age group do not speak English well. However, while some thirty percent of the oldest age group maintained French as their usual language, approximately five percent of the 25-34 year olds retained French as their usual language. Increasing percentages of people have also been moving to an English monolingual form of language use, approximately one-half of the 25-34 year old age group having abandoned the frequent use of French. The lower rates of anglicisation and English monolingualism observed for younger age groups should rise as they attain majority, such that their final language shift patterns should be characterized by somewhat higher rates of anglicisation in general and English monolingualism in particular than is the current 25-34 year old age group.

Methodologically, this figure illustrates once again the importance of

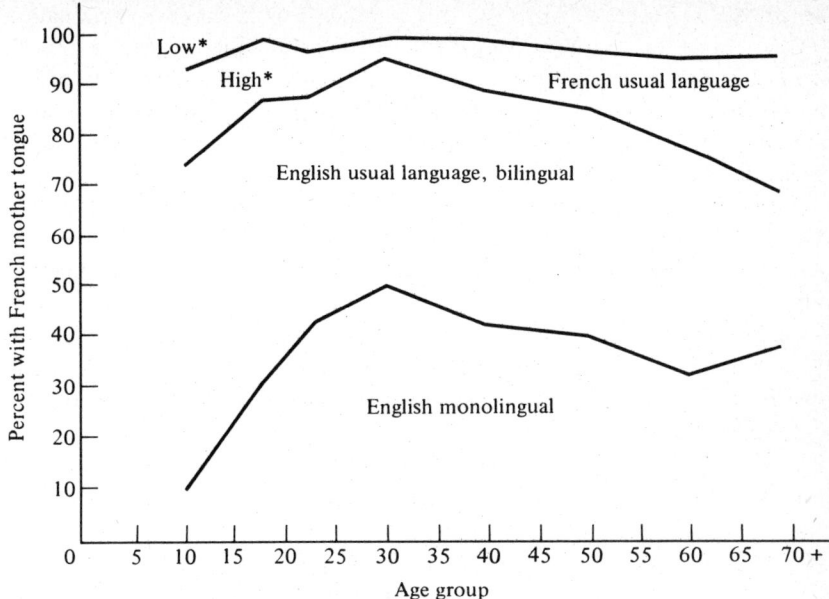

Source: 1976 Survey of Income and Education

Figure 3.3 *Percentage distribution of language shift by persons of French mother tongue by age group, native born, Northern New England, 1976*

comparing age-specific anglicisation and language shift rates with the general rate of anglicisation. From Table 3.11 we obtained a general anglicisation rate of 84.1 percent and a general rate of English monolingualism of 40.8 percent. However, the anglicisation rate for the 25-34 year olds completing the language shift process already attained 96 percent, while the rate of English monolingualism stood at 51 percent. The presence of less anglicized older (and younger cohorts) causes the general rate of both anglicisation and English monoligualism to seriously underestimate the rates which are affecting age groups currently attaining majority.

The language shift curves for Louisiana, presented in Figure 3.4 are rather erratic for the younger age groups, principally because of a precipitous decline in the number of persons of French mother tongue. Thus, while there are an estimated 26,400 (weighted) persons in the 25-34 year old age group, there are only 2,050 in the age group from 4-14 years of age. Nonetheless, certain patterns are clearly evident. First of all, the steepness with which the

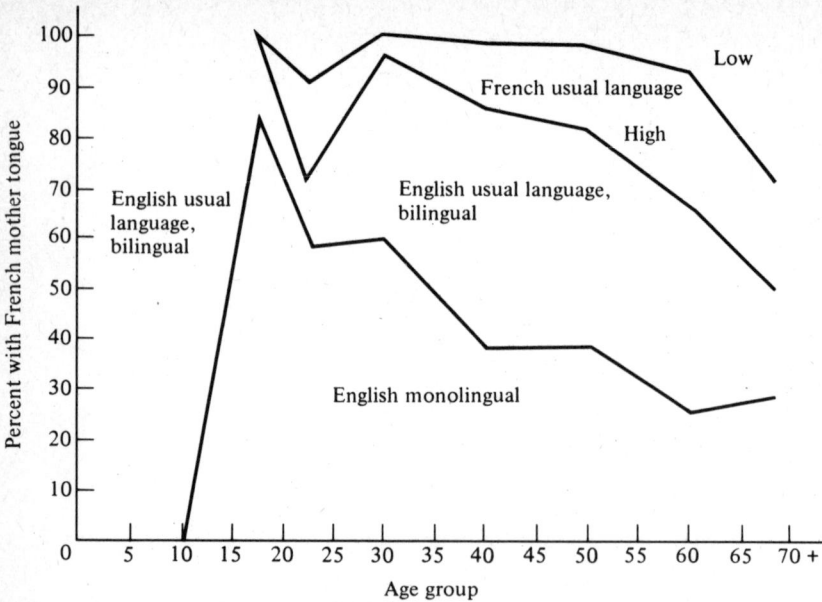

Source: 1976 Survey of Income and Education

Figure 3.4 *Percentage distribution of language shift by persons of French mother tongue by age group, native born, Louisiana, 1976*

anglicisation curve falls to the right for age groups over thirty-five years of age indicates that the French language has undergone a rapid decline in recent decades. While over fifty percent of the oldest age group retained French as their usual language, not a single person sampled under the age of twenty usually spoke French. One could almost say that hardly anyone under the age of thirty-five usually spoke French, the few remaining persons not having as yet completed their language shift process. Secondly, there has been a radical decline in recent decades in the use of French as a second language. The rates of English monolingualism have been climbing steadily. The 15-19 year olds already have higher rates of English monolingualism than do the 25-34 year olds, while the 20-24 year olds have a rate comparable to that of the 25-34 year old age group. These rates may be expected to increase still further. As in New England the general rates of anglicisation and English monolingualism seriously underestimate the current rates of language shift which the younger age groups are experiencing. The general anglicisation rate for

Louisiana was 74 percent; the rate for 25-34 year olds was 94 percent. The general rate of English monolingualism was found to be 37 percent; the rate for the 25-34 year old age group was 59 percent and that for the 15-19 year old cohort already over eighty percent.

The general rates of language shift clearly mislead us with respect to the relative situation of the French language in these two regions of the United States. The general rates lead us to suggest that the decline of the French language is more advanced in northern New England. The age-specific language curves suggest that the French language will be retained as a frequently spoken, second language by a large minority of the native born in northern New England for decades to come. The data we have examined cast serious doubt on even this limited possibility for continued French language use in Louisiana. The data suggest a recent, extremely rapid decline in the position of French both as the principal language of use and as a second, subordinated language.

Figure 3.5 presents partial data for the Spanish language group in the greater New York area, there being very few native born adults over the age of thirty-five. Although the rates of English monolingualism are quite modest when compared to those previously observed for the French language minorities, this is not surprising in view of the high proportion of the New York Hispanic population that is foreign born. The small native born population is probably largely composed of the children of the foreign born themselves, living in a context which is dominated by the more retentive language behavior of the foreign born. Nonetheless, the fragmentary evidence available from the SIE suggests that English monolingualism is following an 'i' type curve, the rate of the adoption of this type of language behavior by the 20-24 year olds being already higher than that found for the 25-34 year olds and higher than the general rate as a whole. In addition, the aglicisation rate as a whole is extremely high and also appears to follow the 'i' shaped curve. Over eighty percent of the 15-19 year olds have already made English their usual spoken language. Finally, the only native born persons who are reported to have low competence levels in Engish are the young children. We conclude that in spite of the overwhelming dominance of the foreign born component of the New York Spanish population, the native born population is experiencing high levels of language shift to English. This language shift is principally characterized by English bilingual patterns of language use, although the data also suggest increased rates of English monolingualism as well.

The age-specific language shift curves for native born persons of Spanish mother tongue living in the midwestern states of Ohio, Michigan, Indiana,

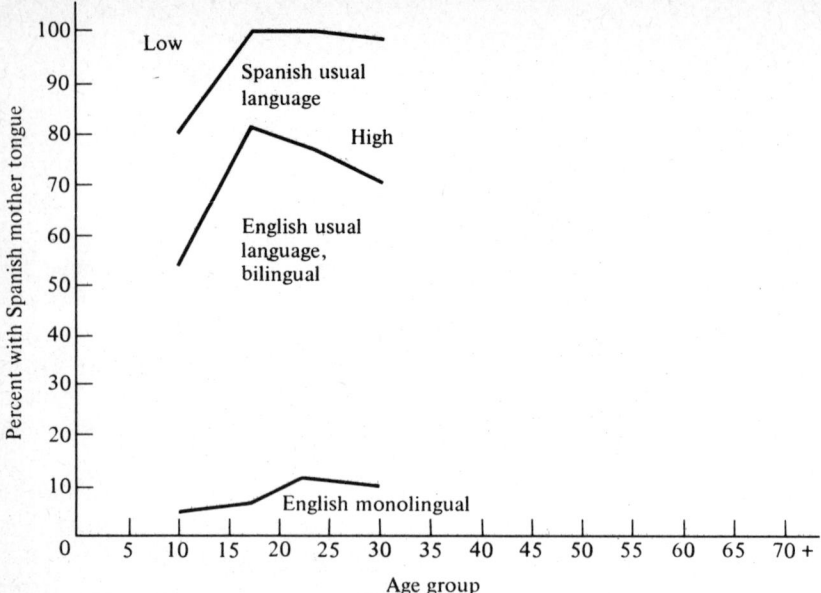

Source: 1976 Survey of Income and Education

Figure 3.5 *Percentage distribution of language shift by persons of Spanish mother tongue by age group, native born, metropolitan New York, 1976*

Illinois, and Wisconsin are presented in Figure 3.6. Again the 'i' shaped curve which indicates increasing rates of language shift in recent decades describes the shape of the two upper curves. The inability to speak English well appears to be something more than a childhood phenomenon in the Midwest. Approximately twenty percent of the 45-54 year olds reportedly had low levels of competence in spoken English. However, each younger cohort has proportionally fewer persons with low levels of English language competence. The anglicisation curve departs just a bit from the classic 'i' curve and tends to approach the 'c' curve of stability. However, the 20-24 year olds already have a level of anglicisation which is higher than that of the older cohorts, suggesting a closer resemblance to an 'i' than to a 'c' type curve.

The irregularity evidenced in the anglicisation curve by the slightly lowered anglicisation rate of the 25-34 year old age group is associated with a marked drop in the rate of English monolingualism for this age group. The drop is so severe that the curve of English monolingualism has a bimodal shape. We sug-

The Anglicisation of Adults in Minority Language Groups

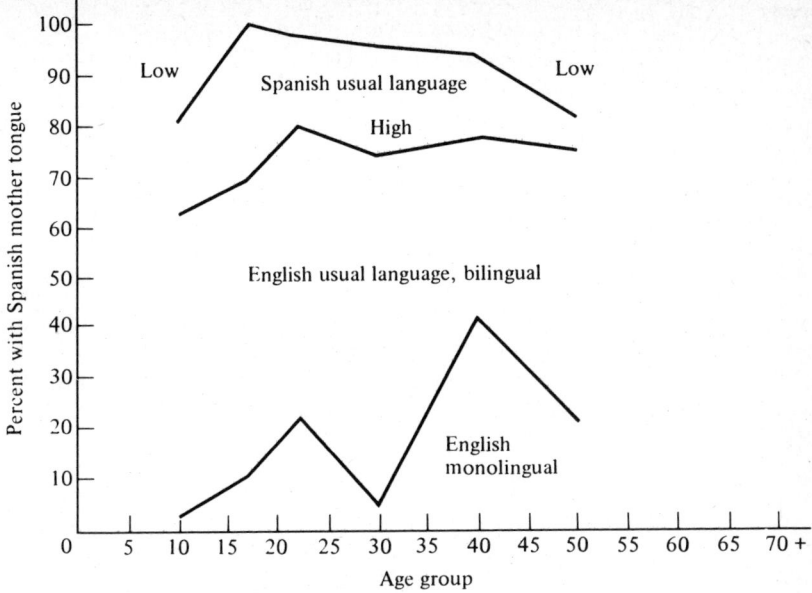

Source: 1976 Survey of Income and Education

Figure 3.6 *Percentage distribution of language shift by persons of Spanish mother tongue by age group, native born, Midwest, 1976*

gest that this anomaly is probably explained by changes in the composition of the Spanish population of the Midwest during the past decades. Cardenas (1976) suggests that midwestern Hispanics are derived from two separate waves of migration, the first having its source in Mexico itself and arriving before the Second World War, the second having its source in the American Southwest and arriving after the Second World War. We suggest that the native born persons older than thirty-five years of age represent the children of the first wave immigrants. Those under twenty-five years of age are either new interregional migrants themselves or the children of such migrants. The arrival of the new immigrants with their more retentive Southwestern language patterns may have created a larger pool of Spanish-speaking people. Such a situation would serve to depress the rate of English monolingualism for native born persons already resident in the Midwest. Since the interregional migrants were also likely to have been native born (in the Southwest), their presence also contributed to the low rate of English monolingualism observed for the

25-34 year old age group. The same process may account for the slightly lower than expected anglicisation rate for the same group. Irrespective of the exact explanation for this anomaly, it is evident that the anglicisation rate in the Midwest is approaching eighty percent for the 20-24 year old age group. The rate of English monolingualism for this age group is also rather high, indicating that the Spanish language is undergoing serious erosion in the Midwest.

There are certain affinities between the language shift curves of native born persons in the California and Rocky Mountain regions. These curves are presented in Figures 3.7 and 3.8. Nearly everyone in both regions speaks English well. The exceptions, as in the Midwest, are a small percentage of young children and a small percentage of the oldest age groups. Secondly, the anglicisation curves are similar in both shape and location. Over ninety percent of the 25-34 year olds are anglicized in each region. The anglicisation

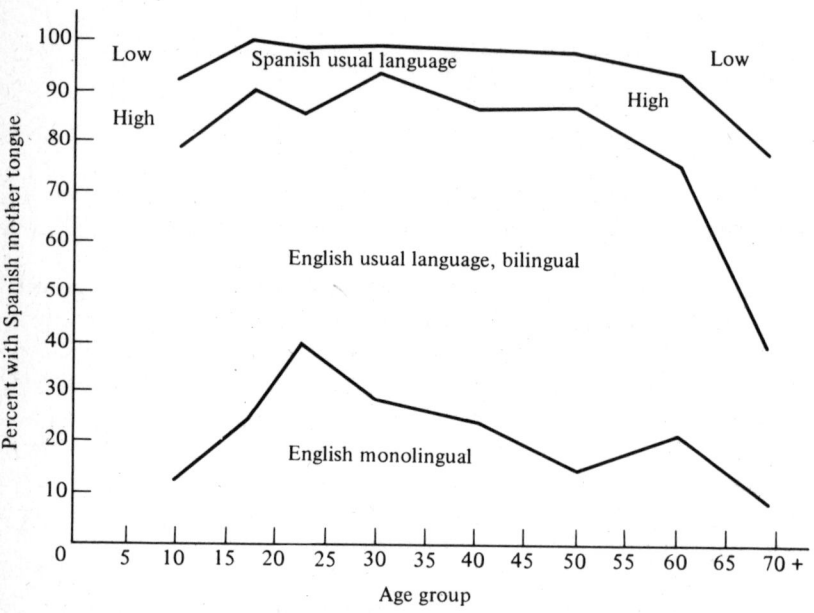

Source: 1976 Survey of Income and Education

Figure 3.7 *Percentage distribution of language shift by persons of Spanish mother tongue by age group, native born, Rocky Mountain States, 1976*

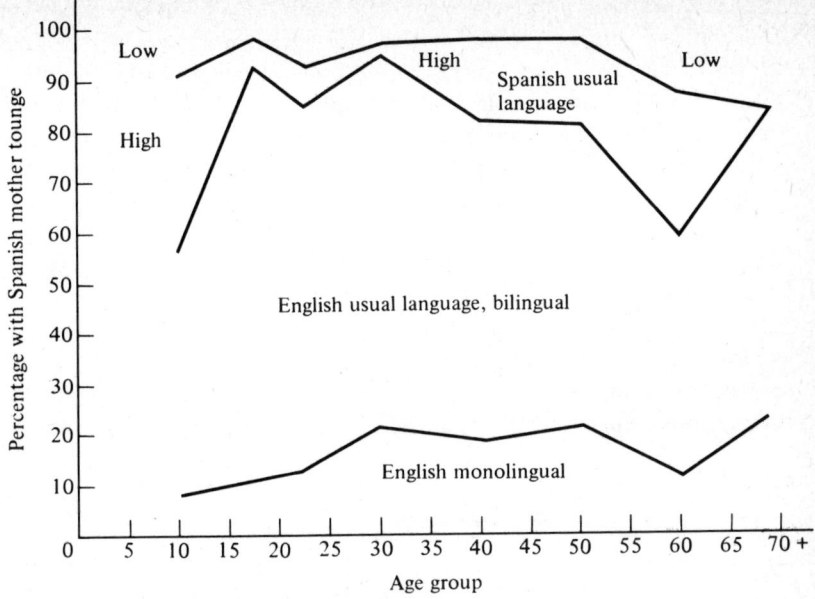

Source: 1976 Survey of Income and Education

Figure 3.8 *Percentage distribution of language shift by persons of Spanish mother tongue by age group, native born, California, 1976*

curve in both regions has a marked 'i' shape, indicating that the younger age groups are more heavily anglicized than the older age groups. There are, nonetheless, two relatively minor departures from this similarity. The younger children in California appear somewhat less anglicized than those in the Rocky Mountain region, and the oldest age cohort in California is more anglicized than the 55-64 year old cohort.

This relative similarity in the location and shape of the anglicisation curve in the two regions is somewhat surprising in the light of the composition of the two Spanish language populations. Table 3.9 showed that only 20.0 percent of the total Rocky Mountain Spanish language group of 145,444 persons were born in the United States. Of the 1,154,250 persons with Spanish mother tongue in California, 58.5 percent were born outside the United States. Under these circumstances we should expect to find higher levels of retention of Spanish in the California region. This is not, however, the case with respect to levels of anglicisation. It appears to be the case with respect to the rates of

English monolingualism. It seems that continuous immigration may affect the rates of English monolingualism of the native born, probably because the continued existence of a pool of persons with limited conversational skills in English requires a minimum level of Spanish language maintenance. This minimum level takes the form of English bilingualism. Where the effects of immigration are minimal, such as in the Rocky Mountain region, the English monolingualism curve takes the familiar 'i' shape as opposed to the 'c' shape evident in California.

The language shift curves for the Spanish mother tongue population of Arizona are presented in Figure 3.9. This figure reveals the presence of lower levels of anglicisation in Arizona than in the previous areas of Hispanic residence. Although a small proportion of the older cohorts reported a low competence level in English, virtually everyone under the age of thirty-five reportedly spoke English well. The anglicisation curve follows the expected 'i'

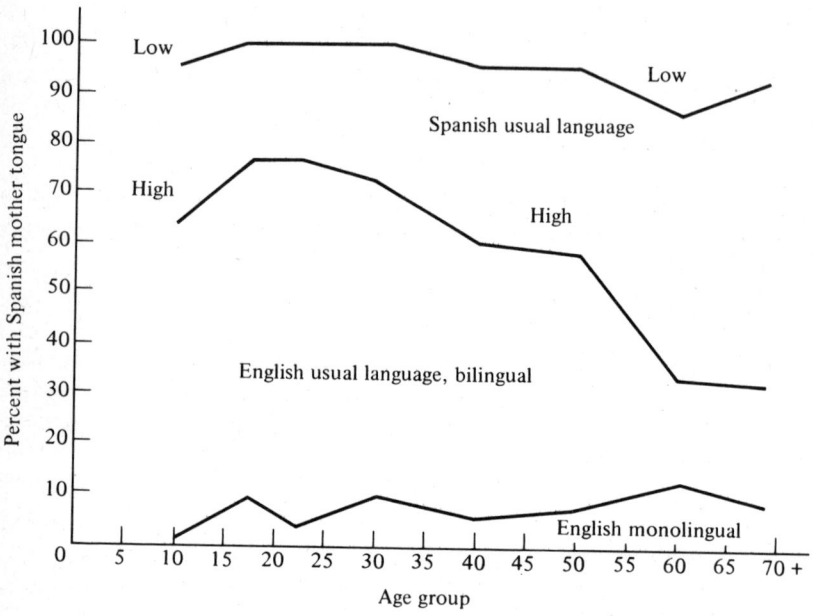

Source: 1976 Survey of Income and Education

Figure 3.9 *Percentage distribution of language shift by persons of Spanish mother tongue by age group, native born, Arizona, 1976*

shape and indicates a steep rise in the anglicisation rates over the past several decades. While approximately thirty percent of the two oldest age groups made English their usual spoken language, the 15-19 and 20-24 year old age groups are already characterized by anglicisation rates in excess of seventy-five percent. When these two age groups complete their language shift process, the rates are likly to be still higher. These findings indicate a marked decline in the status of Spanish in Arizona as the principal language spoken by persons of Spanish mother tongue. While over one-half of the two oldest cohorts usually spoke Spanish but also spoke English well, the frequency of this type of language shift has undergone a marked decline, giving way to an increasingly large proportion of persons who have selected an English bilingual language pattern. Interestingly, the rate of English monolingualism appears to be both low and relatively stable over time. This suggests that in spite of the high degree of anglicisation of the Spanish language group, Spanish is widely being retained as a second language in Arizona. This is true in spite of the fact that over three-fourths of the Spanish population is native born. Thus, the 'c' shaped curve of English monolingualism does not appear to be dependent in Arizona on continuous immigration; it appears that anglicisation in Arizona takes a somewhat unique form, more frequently bilingual and relatively stable than that observed elsewhere.

The New Mexico language shift curves resemble to a large extent those obtained for Arizona. Presented in Figure 3.10, the data show that the oldest cohort was both less anglicized and contained a relatively large proportion of persons who reported low levels of competence in spoken English. Approximately one-half of the native born persons aged sixty-five and older reported that they did not speak English well, while approximately ninenty percent continued to speak it as their usual language. There is a sharp decline in the percentages of persons who do not speak English well among persons aged 55-64, accompanied by a sharp increase in the anglicisation rate. However, comparing the anglicisation rates of the 20-24 year olds with those of the 55-64 year olds, the anglicisation rates have risen much more rapidly in Arizona than in New Mexico. This has occurred in spite of the fact that the proportion of immigrants is higher in Arizona than in New Mexico. Again, regional factors appear to play an independent role in both the level and rate of change in anglicisation rates.

This appears to hold true as well for the rate of English monolingualism. This rate appears to have been lower in New Mexico for the oldest cohorts. However, the rate of English monolingualism in New Mexico appears to conform to the 'i' type curve which indicates an increase in this phenomenon

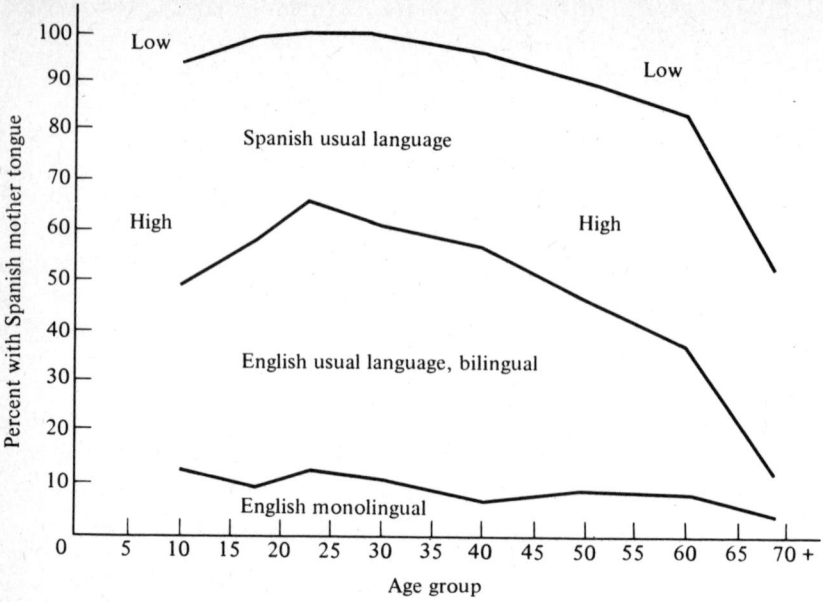

Source: 1976 Survey of Income and Education

Figure 3.10 *Percentage distribution of language shift by persons of Spanish mother tongue by age group, native born, New Mexico, 1976*

over the past decades. Thus, the 20-24 year olds already are characterized by the highest rate of English monolingualism. The lack of reliable data on the mother tongue of the 4-13 year olds does not permit us to affirm with confidence that their rate is already higher than those observed for the other age groups. Given the secular trend, however, this finding is possible, if not probable.

The age-specific language shift rates for the native born Spanish language population of Texas are presented in Figure 3.11. We have already indicated that this region is characterized by the lowest levels of language shift to the English language. From Table 3.11 we have obtained a general anglicisation rate of 42.4 percent and a general rate of English monolingualism of 5.2 percent. Some 14.8 percent of the 844, 264 native born persons of Spanish mother tongue said that they did not speak English well. The curves drawn in Figure 3.11 demonstrate as expected that these general rates do not adequately

The Anglicisation of Adults in Minority Language Groups

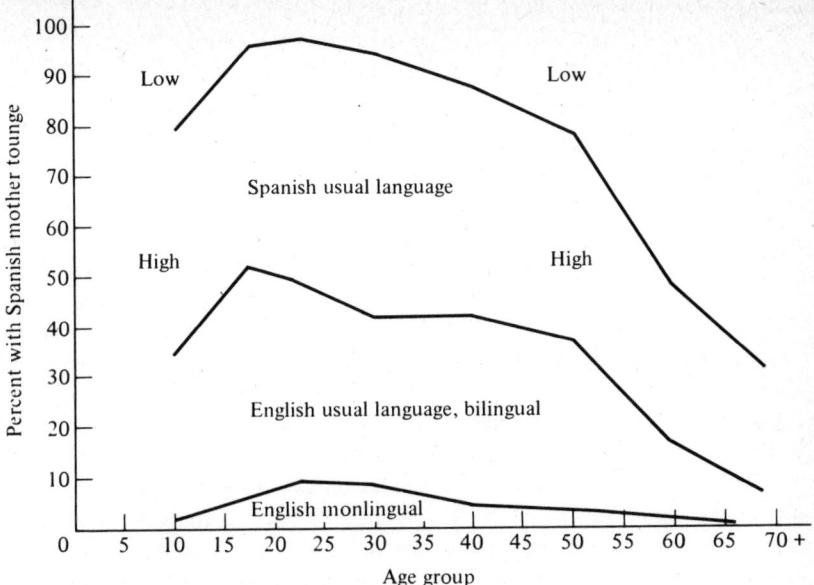

Source: 1976 Survey of Income and Education

Figure 3.11 *Percentage distribution of language shift by persons of Spanish mother tongue by age group, native born, Texas, 1976*

represent the current linguistic situation of the younger age groups now attaining majority..

Although there are very few young adults with low levels of competence in English, this situation did not prevail in the recent past. More than ten percent of the 35-44 year olds reported difficulty with spoken English. The comparable figure for persons aged 55-64 was more than fifty percent, while that for persons aged 65 or more was more than seventy percent. Obviously, there has been a rapid rise in the proportions of persons reporting high levels of English language competence over the past several decades. The appropriate curve has a very pronounced 'i' shape which conforms to this observation.

The anglicisation curve is also characterized by an 'i' shape of a rather pronounced type. While less than ten percent of the oldest cohort reported that they usually spoke English, the anglicisation rate of the 35-44 year old age group was approximately forty percent. However, both the 15-19 year and 20-24 year old age groups have already surpassed this figure. The 15-19 year olds have an anglicisation rate which even surpasses that of the 20-24 year olds, this in spite of the fact that they still have a longer period of time in which to complete their language shift process. We may expect that the final anglicisation rates of these age groups will be still higher than the current level of approximately fifty percent.

The curve depicting English monolingualism has a less pronounced 'i' type shape. While virtually none of the members of the older cohorts abandoned the use of Spanish as a daily language, some eight percent of the 20-24 and 25-24 year old age groups have adopted English monolingual language behavior. There has been a steady increase in the rates of English monolingualism over the time period examined.

On the whole the language shift curves which characterize the native born population of Texas resemble those previously described for the populations residing in Arizona and New Mexico. The examination of the age structure of language shift in Texas indicates that the same pattern is present. What appears to be different is the position of the curves on the relevant figures, each age group in Texas being relatively less anglicized than their New Mexico or Arizona counterparts. A similar observation applies to the observed rates of high levels of competence in the English language among persons who continue to use Spanish as their daily language. In all three regions, however, the rates of English monolingualism remain relatively low, indicating that nearly all native born persons of Spanish mother tongue in these regions retain the use of Spanish as a second language in the event that they have made English their first language.

The analysis of these age-specific rates of language shift in each region of Hispanic residence indicates the importance of regional analysis. Persons of Spanish mother tongue in the New York, California, Midwest, and Rocky Mountain regions are characterized by very high levels of anglicisation. Where these rates were somewhat lower in the past, they appear to have risen rapidly. The rates have also risen relatively rapidly in the Arizona, New Mexico, and Texas regions retained for analysis, but they were both lower to begin with and they remain somewhat lower than those found in the remaining regions examined. Nonetheless, the data indicate that the native born Spanish language population is undergoing relatively high levels of anglicisation in all regions of the country. What tends to remain lower in comparison with the French language minority is the rate of English monolingualism. This may at least be in part attributable to the effects of continuous immigration, although the data suggest that regional differences play a larger role.

The most retentive language group in the United States is not, however, one of the Spanish language groups. It is the Navajo language group which presumably inhabits the Navajo reservation in Arizona and New Mexico. The language shift curves for this group are presented in Figure 3.12. These curves conform to the 'i' type curve which indicate a pattern of increased language shift to English. There has been a rapid decline in the percentage of persons reporting difficulty with the English language. While seventy percent or more of the oldest age groups reported an inability to speak English well, little more than ten percent of the 20-29 year old age group reported such a language pattern.

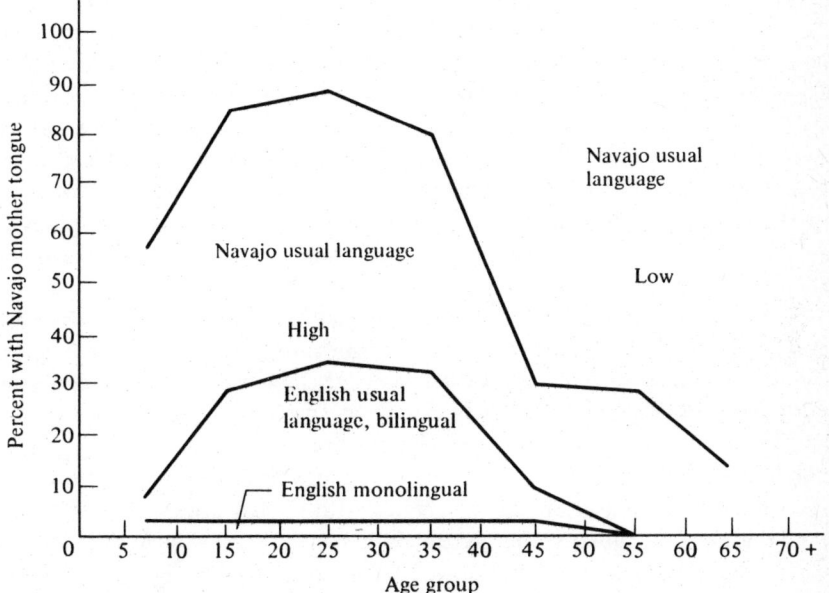

Source: 1976 Survey of Income and Education

Figure 3.12 *Percentage distribution of language shift by persons of Navajo mother tongue by age group, native born, New Mexico and Arizona, 1976*

While the anglicisation curve also has an 'i' shape, it does not rise as steeply as does the English language competence curve. Although none of the Navajo aged fifty or more reported that they usually spoke English, the figures have exceeded thirty percent for the age groups 20-29 and 30-39. This represents nonetheless a rather sharp increase in a relatively short time period. However, the anglicisation rate still remains quite a bit lower than that found for the Spanish language group in Texas. In addition, the rate of English monolingualism appears to be relatively constant over time. One must conclude that the English monolingualism curve conforms to the 'c' type curve of stability.

These regional analyses of age-specific rates of language shift conform in the essentials to the findings obtained for the French and Spanish language groups at the national level. While there are important regional differences in the general levels of language shift, and while the slope of the anglicisation curve varies by region (and language group), the 'i'-type curve of anglicisation is unmistakeably present in all minority language regions. Given the hypothesis that most language shift ceases when individuals attain thirty to thirty-five years of age, these findings indicate that language shift has been increasing in all regions and for all minority language groups since the Second World War. The younger age groups in each and every case are characterized by higher rates of language shift of virtually every type than are the older age groups. This is clearly true for the decline of the percentage of persons with low competence in English and for the rise of anglicisation. It is generally true as well for the rise in the rate of English monolingualism, although in some regions it appears that this rate is relatively constant over time.

Since the younger age cohorts have higher rates of language shift than the older age groups, including these latter in the calculation of the general rates of langauge shift creates an underestimate of the current levels of language shift affecting persons in the process of accomplishing the decisions most associated with definitive language choice. Among these decisions are those connected with child-bearing and child-rearing. Consequently, the future of any language group is intimately associated with the language shift patterns of young adults and those in the immediately younger age groups, because it is the language practices of these groups which will determine both the mother tongue and the language skills of their children. Since most child-bearing in the West is completed by the age of thirty-five, the language shift patterns of older age groups are relatively unimportant from the perspective of the future reproduction of the minority language group. On the other hand, their language practices are quite important for providing estimates of the language shift history of the group.

The imputation of the household language as the mother tongue of children reveals once again the affinity of the American and Canadian data. In all but one of the regional figures the 4-14 year olds are markedly less anglicized than the 15-19 and 20-24 year old age groups. The single exception is found in Louisiana where there are virtually no children of French mother tongue in this age range, and where rampant anglicisation in the language group as a whole is reflected in the complete anglicisation of everyone under the age of twenty and nearly everyone under the age of thirty-five. In general, however, each curve follows that observed in Figure 2.3 for persons of French mother tongue in English Canada and for persons of English mother tongue in Quebec City. Since this increase has been widely documented in Canada for the French, the English, and for other minority language groups, we may have some greater confidence that the American findings are not accidental. They conform to the sociological theory which we have described which anchors language shift in the maturational process of the child.

Since the regional findings also conform to the Canadian findings for persons older than thirty-five years of age, we may have somewhat greater confidence in the validity of these data as well. It appears that everywhere in North America, minority language groups have been subjected to increasingly greater pressures to adopt the language of the dominant group. The younger age groups are more anglicized than the older age groups everywhere in both the United States and in English Canada. Given the consistency of these age-specific patterns, we may have greater confidence in the reliability of the SIE estimates than the sample sizes themselves would permit us to expect.

Conclusion. The presentation of these national and regional data already permit us to assess the extent to which American language groups approach the ideal types of language retention or assimilation. The analysis of the data leaves no serious doubt. All American language minorities in all regions of the country exhibit high levels of anglicisation, the sole possible exception being the Navajo language group. This conclusion was already presaged in the table presenting the historic measure of anglicisation, a table which showed that substantial numbers of persons in the major ethno-linguistic groups were English monolinguals. We subsequently showed that foreign born persons of minority mother tongue engaged in rapid movement to the English language. Even the most recent arrivals in the United States, particularly those in the non-Spanish language groups, exhibited a strong tendency to adopt the English language as their principal language of use. This tendency increased markedly as a function of length of residence in the United States. We conclude that immigrant language groups manifest a strong willingness to accomodate their language behavior to that of the American environment. They are not only disposed to learning the English language, and to learning to speak it well;

they are disposed to making English their principal language of use, while many go still further and abandon the use of their mother tongue as a language frequently spoken.

If this widespread disposition to adopt English as the prinicipal language of use is evident among the foreign born, the data reveal that the native born are still more anglicized. Even the Spanish language group, widely thought to be exhibiting a high degree of language retention, does not escape this generalization. When the age-specific rates of anglicisation are examined, they indicate that the general rate of anglicisation seriously underestimates the extent of language shift characterizing those groups currently engaged in the process of establishing their language use patterns. Furthermore, the analysis indicated that the rates of anglicisation have been increasing in an evolutionary way over the past decades. Even the continued addition of new Spanish speaking immigrants does not appear to have markedly affected this process. For example, in the most retentive region of those Spanish regions examined, the rate of anglicisation achieved by young adults already exceeds fifty percent.

The examination of these data does not indicate a rosy future for American language minorities. The continued survival of all groups in all regions depends on continued immigration. When the foreign born are not completely anglicized themselves, the first generation of the native born completes the task, the majority of the latter in most groups establishing an English monolingual pattern of language use. While the Navajo language group constitutes the principal exception to this rule, the Spanish language group in certain restricted regions, Arizona, New Mexico, and Texas, appears to offer some greater resistance to the complete anglicisation of the native born.

On the whole, however, that which most distinguishes the Spanish language group from the other non-Navajo groups is not the lower rates of anglicisation which have been found; it is the fact that anglicisation more frequently takes the form of English bilingualism in the Spanish language group. This may in fact constitute the one way in which continued immigration acts upon the language shift process, although we have already observed that the proportion of the foreign born is relatively low in the most retentive regions. At any rate, while these findings indicate that Spanish will not survive as the principal language of use among the native born, it may be able to survive in an English bilingual framework, that is, in subordination to English. This prospect requires that English bilingualism be successfully transmitted from one generation to another. This is one of the principal topics of the next chapter.

Chapter Four

Intergenerational Anglicisation in the United States

Introduction. The data presented in chapter three led us to conclude that all minority language groups in the United States are ultimately required to depend on continued immigration to assure the presence of persons who usually speak the minority language. The extent to which this is true varies somewhat by language group and region of the country, but no immigrant group appears to be able to retain its language as the principal language of its members in the generation of the native born. The same data show us, nonetheless, that many of the foreign born opt for an English bilingual form of language use, a form of anglicisation which at least permits the possible transmission of the language as a second language. Moreover, English bilingualism is clearly the dominant form of the language shift process affecting the Spanish language group in the United States at the present time, the rates of English monolingualism being relatively low in most regions.

What are the linguistic consequences of English bilingualism? As a general rule we have assumed that children will have the same language characteristics as do their parents. For example, we expect that the usual language spoken by the parents should be the mother tongue of the children. Thus, we expect that parents impose the language structure of the household, children learning the languages which are frequently spoken by the parents. Accordingly, the children of English bilinguals may also be expected to be English bilinguals.

As soon as this issue is raised, however, the larger issue of the intergenerational transmission of language characteristics is joined. It need not be accepted as a foregone conclusion that persons who usually speak Spanish will raise children who usually speak Spanish. In a context where the parents themselves have adopted anglicized language behavior, they may promote still more anglicized behavior for their children. They may consciously avoid speaking Spanish with their children, making every effort to see to it that the children have a solid grounding in the dominant American language. Children themselves may resist learning or speaking a minority language which they see as symbolizing low social status, their 'foreign' origins, or both. While we have no data at our disposal which permit us to assess the language shift characteristics of children under the age of fourteen, we can assess the current language practices of children. These current patterns can then be compared to the language patterns which prevail in the household context.

The procedure normally used by Federal government analysts with the SIE consists in comparing the current language practices of children with the language most often spoken in the household unit (Silverman, 1978; McArthur, 1979; and Brown et al., 1980). The household unit is selected as the appropriate comparative unit because the necessary data processing procedures which permit the construction of such data are relatively simple. We have not adopted the common procedure, although in certain respects some of our tables are similar in nature. This approach was not adopted because recent Canadian findings suggest that parental nativity plays an important role in the explanation of language shift and retention. DeVries and Vallée (1979) note that apparent between-group differences in the language retention rates of children are largely explained by differences in parental origin. Children who continue to speak Ukranian or Italian as a usual language, for example, are most likely to have parents who were born in the Ukraine or in Italy. These findings suggest that differences in the apparent anglicisation rates of native born children are likely to be spurious, being instead functions of the composition of the parental group with respect to place of birth.

Methodology. The Canadian findings make it apparent that an adequate data file must contain not only data on the language use of children; it must set these characteristics in their appropriate parental context. Household language characteristics, while undoubtedly related in part to parental nativity, cannot be considered to have the same reliability as direct data on parental nativity and language practice. Consequently, we have reorganized the SIE data in such a way that data from both child and adult records were placed in the same file. The child was matched to the head of the household, defined in 1976 as the male in households characterized by the presence of a husband and a wife. If both a husband and wife were present, the wife's characteristics were also retained for analysis. We shall refer in this study to these persons as 'parents', even though in some cases this is not the case. Single parents have been integrated into the sample by assuming that the absent parent would have had identical characteristics. The low proportions of single parent families and the similarity of the responses of children to similar linguistic settings indicate that separate treatment of biparental and monoparental families is not imperative. The reorganization of the SIE data file permits us to place the child in his household setting, a setting defined not only by the household language characteristics but by a variety of parental language, nativity, and socioecomomic characteristics.

In order to obtain as large a sample as possible and to more clearly examine the effects of age on language shift, we have selected all children aged 4 to 17 for analysis. However, we have excluded those adolescents who were already married. We then tested the data for the presence of a minority language by applying ten language parameters, the two household language questions, the mother tongue, usual language and second language of each parent, and the usual and second languages of the child himself. When no minority language was detected using these criteria, children were excluded from the minority language sample. Such children and their parents came from (and maintained) homes which were exclusively monolingual in English.

The remaining children were then divided into two groups, the active and inactive minority language samples. The active minority sample was defined by one of two characteristics: either children lived in homes where a minority language was actively spoken as the usual or second household language, or they themselves reported that they usually spoke a minority language as usual or second language. Needless to say, the relationship between the two sets of criteria is extremely close. The inactive minority sample is composed of children living in English monolingual households where one or more of the parents came from a minority language background. Although in some cases the parent(s) continued to speak this language on a regular basis, it apparently was not frequently used in the home. Such households were detected by applying the three language parameters for each parent. Usually, of course, the presence of a minority mother tongue was the characteristic defining parents (and their children) into this sample.

To classify children into specific minority language groups, we first of all applied the criterion of usual language and subsequently that of the second language of the child. Since many children remained unclassified as a result of the presence of an English monolingual language pattern, the parental characteristics were used to permit assignment to a specific group. Each adult was assigned to a language group by applying in order the criteria of usual language, second language, and mother tongue. The languages currently spoken by the parents were given precedence over mother tongue since the basis of comparison is the current use of languages by both parents and children. The language shift of parents themselves has already been assessed in the previous chapter.

Once parents had been classified into a language group, we proceeded to classify their children. If both parents belonged to the same minority language group, that language group was assigned to the child. If one of the parents belonged to the English language group, the child was assigned to the language group of the other parent. If each belonged to a different language group, the child was assigned to a residual category of mixed language origin. A total of 441 unweighted cases representing an estimated 171,000 American children were found to have such origins. Since no minority language was spoken in these homes and since the children themselves were English monolinguals, they have been omitted from subsequent analyses. Their absence causes estimated rates of language shift for specific groups to be somewhat lower than they would have been had these children been randomly assigned to one group or another.

The percentages of children living in active and inactive minority language settings are presented in Table 4.1. The percentages of children living in inactive minority language settings can be used to estimate the extent of the English monolingualism of their parents. This rate differs somewhat from those previously estimated since parental nativity is not taken into account, since not all adults at any given age level have children aged 4-17, and since some adults have intermarried into the English language population. Nonethe-

Table 4.1 *Type of language maintenance for parents of children aged 4-17, United States, 1976*

Language group	Active minority language	Inactive minority language	Estimated sample
Spanish	88.1%	11.9%	3,680,286
Italian	33.4	66.6	905,494
German	30.6	69.4	886,770
French	43.4	56.6	692,338
Polish	19.6	80.4	415,871
Japanese	27.9	72.1	154,129
Filipino	73.5	26.5	153,960
Scandinavian	16.2	83.8	151,715
Greek	55.4	44.6	151,125
Chinese	78.0	22.0	119,083
Portuguese	59.6	40.4	121,962
Navajo	88.5	11.5	62,154
Yiddish	49.4	50.6	114,068
All other	49.5	50.5	1,092,890

Source: 1976 Survey of Income and Education

less, the percentages of such parents indicate the extent to which English monolingual households are maintained by persons from each language group.

The four groups with the lowest such rates of inactivity are the Navajo, Spanish, Chinese, and Filipino language groups, ranging from the low rate of 11.5 percent for the Navajo language group to 26.5 percent for the Filipino language group. The rate for the Spanish language group approximates that of the Navajo language group, a finding probably explained by the nativity composition of the Spanish language group. Only three other groups are found to have inactivity rates below fifty percent, the Greek, Chinese, and Portuguese groups, three groups which we have already shown to have relatively high percentages of the foreign born. In all other minority language groups the percentage of children living in English monolingual households surpasses fifty percent, attaining over eighty percent for the Polish and Scandinavian language groups. Thus, in most groups at least one-half of the parents who have minority language backgrounds (normally defined by mother tongue) maintain English monolingual households.

Language characteristics and the nativity of the child. The issue which most directly concerns us in this chapter is not, however, the extent of parental abandonment of minority languages but the effects of parental retention. These effects can be obtained by examining the children of the active minority language sample. We begin by presenting their nativity characteristics in Table 4.2.

The first observation which we derive from Table 4.2 is the overwhelming importance of the Spanish language group. Some 3.2 million children live in homes where the Spanish language is frequently spoken. This figure is markedly higher than that of all the remaining language groups taken together. Of the great waves of Italian, German, French, and Scandinavian immigrants who came to the United States in the late 19th and early 20th centuries, only small numbers of children remain in contact with the ancestral languages. And we have not even begun to explore their own personal language use, which we may expect to be of a still greater anglicized pattern than that of their parents.

The second observation which derives from Table 4.2 is the extent to which children in minority language groups are native born. Over eighty percent of the children in the Spanish, Italian, German, French, Polish, and Scandinavian language groups are native born. The Navajo and Yiddish language groups are the most indigenous, virtually all of the children being native born. The highest percentages of foreign born children are found in the Portuguese and

Table 4.2 *Nativity of children aged 4-17 in minority language groups, United States, 1976*

Language group	Foreign born	Native born	Total
Chinese	45.3%	54.7%	92,877
Filipino	39.7	60.3	113,199
French	7.1	92.9	300,608
German	13.5	86.5	271,088
Greek	29.7	70.3	83,718
Italian	15.2	84.8	302,600
Japanese	34.1	65.9	42,968
Navajo	0.0	100.0	54,978
Polish	2.3	97.7	81,719
Portuguese	46.1	53.9	72,740
Scandinavian	10.1	89.9	24,541
Spanish	19.4	81.6	3,241,670
Yiddish	0.4	99.6	56,304
All other	30.9	69.1	541,437

Source: 1976 Survey of Income and Education

Chinese language groups, where 46.1 and 45.3 percent respectively of the children were not born in the United States. The Filipino and Japanese language groups are also characterized by relatively high percentages of the foreign born.

Since the nativity of adults is related to their language use characteristics, it is quite likely that similar differences should be observed for children. The language characteristics of children not born in the United States are presented in Table 4.3. Children are divided into three language behavior groups, English monolingual, English bilingual, and children who usually speak a minority language. Since these children were not born in the United States, it is highly probable that English was not their mother tongue. If this is true, as the observation of the mother tongue of 14-17 year olds confirms, Table 4.3 reveals extensive anglicisation of foreign born children. Although the sample sizes are extremely small outside the Spanish language group, it appears that the German, Japanese, and Filipino language children are characterized by relatively extensive monolingualism in English. In most of the other groups the rates of English monolingualism are very low, indicating that children born outside the United States continue to speak their mother tongue on a frequent basis.

Table 4.3 *Language characteristics of foreign born children aged 4–17, active minority language households, United States, 1976*

Language group	English monolingual	English bilingual	Usually non-English	Estimated sample
Spanish	4.0%	45.5%	50.4%	594,887
Italian	3.4	59.2	37.4	45,925
German	36.3	56.7	7.0	36,567
French	5.4	80.3	14.3	21,242
Polish	0.0	100.0	0.0	1,905
Japanese	29.0	50.6	20.4	14,656
Filipino	30.6	59.0	10.4	44,972
Greek	0.0	78.6	21.4	24,830
Scandinavian	0.0	88.5	11.5	3,469
Chinese	5.5	52.3	42.1	42,114
Portuguese	1.8	42.8	55.4	33,545
Yiddish*		100.0		217
All other	17.7	40.5	41.8	167,877

* There were no foreign born children in the Navajo group
Source: 1976 Survey of Income and Education

However, Table 4.3 also indicates that in only two instances, those of the Spanish and Portuguese children, do a majority of the children in any group usually speak the minority language which presumably they spoke on their arrival in the United States. Even in the case of the Spanish and Portuguese children the rates of retention of the minority language as the usual language spoken barely exceed fifty percent. The retention rates for the other groups are still lower, 42.1 percent for the Chinese, 37.4 percent for the Italian. All other language groups (with the exception of the undefined group of 'all others') are characterized by retention rates of under twenty-five percent. Thus, the estimated anglicisation rates for these children are quite high, particularly in view of the fact that they are so young. Most of these children face two additional decades of living in the American English language environment before they will complete their language shift experiences.

As expected, the native born children in each respective group are even more anglicized than the foreign born children. These data are presented in Table 4.4. They indicate that approximately eighty percent or more of the children in each language group do not usually speak the minority language as their principal language. The single exception to this rule is the Navajo

Table 4.4 *Language characteristics of native born children aged 4-17, active minority language households, United States, 1976*

Language group	English monolingual	English bilingual	Usually non-English	Estimated sample
Spanish	30.9%	48.9%	20.2%	2,646,783
Italian	57.4	37.6	5.0	256,675
German	62.4	25.2	12.4	234,521
French	76.9	20.2	2.8	279,366
Polish	72.9	26.2	0.9	79,814
Japanese	72.4	25.9	1.7	28,312
Filipino	84.9	11.0	4.1	68,227
Greek	45.3	42.3	12.4	58,888
Scandinavian	76.8	18.9	4.4	21,072
Chinese	12.9	75.7	11.4	50,763
Portuguese	39.3	44.1	16.6	39,195
Navajo	9.5	23.4	67.1	54,978
Yiddish	58.1	25.6	16.3	56,087
All other	56.8	32.1	11.0	374,560

Source: 1976 Survey of Income and Education

language group where more than two-thirds of the children speak Navajo as their usual language. In the Spanish language group, considered by many Americans to be highly retentive, only 20.2 percent of the native born children speak Spanish as their principal language. In nearly all other minority language groups, including the Portuguese and Chinese, the percentages of children who usually speak the minority language are exceedingly low.

In addition to the higher percentages of children who usually speak English, the percentages of native born children having English monolingual language use are also sharply higher. Over seventy percent of the children living in households where the French, Polish, Japanese, Filipino, or Scandinavian languages are spoken do not themselves often speak the appropriate minority language (if at all). The comparable figures exceed fifty percent in the Italian and German language groups as well. Even in the Portuguese and Spanish language groups, which we found to have relatively retentive characteristics among foreign born children, 39.3 percent and 30.9 percent respectively of the children had English monolingual language behavior. The only groups with very low percentages of English monolingual children were the Chinese and Navajo language groups.

These findings indicate that English monolingualism is not unambiguously the dominant form of anglicisation among native born children. While English monolingualism is the dominant pattern in the Italian, German, French, Polish, Japanese, Filipino, Scandinavian and Yiddish language groups, English bilingualism is equally dominant in the Navajo and Chinese language groups. The English bilingual pattern is also more frequently found in the Spanish and Portuguese language groups, while the English monolingual pattern is only slightly more dominant in the Greek language group.

While these are the current patterns for the native born, we may expect that continued anglicisation of the minority language children will produce higher percentages of English bilingualism and of English monolingualism as they grow older. In our description of Table 4.4 we have avoided labelling the observed language patterns with the term 'rates.' We prefer the term 'observed patterns' since we cannot be certain that the native born children in these minority language homes did in fact have a minority language as mother tongue. The basis of such language shift as we may be observing in this table being relatively unclear (dominant vs. second household language), we prefer to speak of the extent to which a specific pattern is present.

Parental nativity and the language characteristics of children. The data presented in Tables 4.2 to 4.4 suggest that some language groups appear to be somewhat more retentive than others. Generally, the Chinese, Navajo, Portuguese and Spanish language groups are characterized by somewhat more retentive language patterns. Children were both more likely to speak the minority language as their usual language, and were less likely to have an English monolingual language pattern. However, the analysis of these tables is subject precisely to the criticism offered by DeVries and Vallée. We have obtained differences in the apparent distribution of minority language usage for native and foreign born children, but these differences may be caused by the nativity and language characteristics of the parental generation. Unless the composition of the parental generation is examined, observed differences in the behavior of children cannot be assumed to represent real differences in rates of retention and assimilation. If children in the Chinese group are constrained by the language characteristics of their foreign born parents, we should not assume that the children themselves manifest more retentive language patterns.

The examination of parental nativity for its effects on language shift requires that the data analysis be approached from a somewhat different perspective. The nativity of parents is quite likely related to decisions to establish an English monolingual household in the same manner in which it is related to anglicisation in general. Since many children in the active language sample have English monolingual language characteristics, there is no explicit reason to exclude children in the inactive language sample from the analysis of parental nativity effects. Combining the active and inactive language samples, the parental nativity characteristics are presented in Table 4.5. Three categories of parental nativity are defined, mixed ancestry as having one foreign born and one native born parent.

Table 4.5 *Nativity of parents of children aged 4-17 by minority language background, United States, 1976*

Language group	Native born	Mixed ancestry	Foreign born	Total*
Spanish	45.0%	18.0%	37.0%	100.0%
Italian	66.9	12.7	20.4	100.0
German	50.3	35.7	14.0	100.0
French	80.3	10.1	9.6	100.0
Polish	84.4	8.9	6.7	100.0
Japanese	49.0	40.4	10.5	100.0
Filipino	10.2	23.2	66.7	100.0
Greek	47.2	22.8	30.0	100.0
Scandinavian	70.4	22.1	7.5	100.0
Chinese	4.8	16.0	79.2	100.0
Portuguese	45.5	11.7	42.8	100.0
Navajo	100.0			100.0
Yiddish	62.8	22.5	14.7	100.0
All other	55.7	15.5	29.1	100.0

* Totals approximately the same as those reported in Table 4.1
Source: 1976 Survey of Income and Education

Table 4.5 reveals considerable variation in the patterns of parental nativity. On the one hand, in the only indigenous minority language group, the Navajo, all of the parents of the SIE children were themselves native born. On the other, few of the parents of the Chinese or Filipino language children were born in the United States. This latter finding explains why so few children in these latter groups were found in the inactive minority language sample (Table 4.1). Since so many parents were not born in the United States, it is highly unlikely that English monolingual households would have been established. Furthermore, the data reported in chapter 3 indicate that the parents of these children are more than likely relatively recent immigrants to the United States. Such immigrants are relatively unlikely to abandon the use of their mother tongue.

The data reported in Table 4.5 also suggest an explanation for the findings that children in the different language groups have more or less retentive patterns of language behavior. For example, we found in Table 4.3 that children in the Chinese, Portuguese, and Spanish groups were more likely to speak a minority language as their usual language than were other foreign born children. In Table 4.4 we found that these same groups had relatively lower rates of English monolingualism than did other native born groups. The data reported in Table 4.5 seem to suggest that the presence of larger numbers of foreign born parents in these groups is related to these findings. Although there is no one-to-one relationship between parental nativity and childhood language use, the data unmistakeably suggest the presence of such a relationship.

This explanation, however, presupposes uniformity in the language use patterns based on the distribution of parental nativity. To assess the extent to which such uniformity exists, we present in Table 4.6 the percentage of

Table 4.6 *Percentage of children with parents who usually speak English by parental nativity and language group, United States, 1976**

Language group	Native born	Mixed ancestry	Foreign born
Spanish	64.4%	44.1%	17.3%
Italian	99.4	92.2	46.9
German	93.4	99.0	89.7
French	92.6	95.2	57.4
Polish	99.3	91.7	59.3
Japanese	99.5	90.2	56.3
Filipino	100.0	94.6	68.3
Greek	99.8	83.7	19.6
Scandinavian	100.0	100.0	79.7
Chinese	100.0	93.9	28.0
Portuguese	100.0	72.8	3.8
Navajo	26.3		
Yiddish	93.0	89.2	82.3
All other	91.3	95.2	49.1

* Includes children living in homes with English only household language and those living in homes with an active minority language where the parents usually speak English
Source: 1976 Survey of Income and Education

children in each language group having native born, foreign born, or mixed ancestry parents who usually speak English.

Parents who usually speak English are defined as including those who maintain English monolingual households (parents of children in the inactive sample) and those who live in households where the minority language is spoken but who themselves usually speak English. Not included in the percentages of children having parents who usually speak English are those children who have one parent who usually speaks English and another parent who usually speaks a minority language.

Table 4.6 shows that the assumption of uniform language behavior among the native born parents is generally supported. With but two exceptions, the Spanish and the Navajo, over ninety percent of the native born parents maintain homes where both parents usually speak English. In the Spanish language group 64.4 percent of the native born parents maintain English language homes, a figure just slightly below that found for second generation Chicanos in Los Angeles (Lopez, 1978). It is the Navajo, however, which again constitute the major exception to the rule, nearly three-fourths of the entirely native born sample continuing to maintain Navajo as the language they usually speak.

Interestingly, the presence of a single foreign born parent does not seem to have much effect on the language patterns selected by the couple. Generally, the percentage of children with parents who usually speak English is nearly as high for those with parents of mixed ancestry as it is for those with native born parents. The presence of a Greek, Portuguese, or Spanish parent born outside the United States does tend to depress somewhat the extent of English language use in mixed ancestry homes. Nonetheless, the percentage of children in the Greek and Portuguese language groups who live in such homes where English is usually spoken remains very high. Only in the Spanish language group do less than fifty percent of the mixed ancestry children have parents who usually speak English.

The greatest differences in terms of retentive language behavior is found when both parents are foreign born. Three groups stand out as being very retentive, the Portuguese, Spanish and Greek groups (in that order). Three groups stand out as being very anglicized, the German, Scandinavian, and Yiddish groups. The French, Polish, Japanese, Filipino, and the Residual language groups are all characterized by relatively high rates of the formation of English language homes. These findings conform quite well to those presented in the preceding chapter, the Italians being somewhat more retentive than those members of other major language groups, the Chinese tending to fall near the retentive end of the continuum.

The examination of these data generally tend to show a great deal of uniformity in the extent to which parents in each nativity group form English language homes. This is particularly true when at least one of the parents is native born. These data tend to indicate that between-group differences in the language retention characteristics of children are principally caused by differences in the nativity patterns of the respective parental groups. Two exceptions seem noteworthy, both the Navajo and Spanish language groups exhibiting relatively unique characteristics. Consequently, for the remainder of the analysis of intergenerational language shift, we shall consider each of these groups separately.

On the other hand, we shall combine all of the remaining minority language groups into a single language group which we shall name the 'Residual' language group. However, such a procedure creates difficulties insofar as we have already observed differential behavior when both parents are foreign born. Thus, using only the category 'foreign born' in the analysis would tend to mask these differences. Such is not, however, the case since we have also included the language characteristics of parents as important explanatory variables. These characteristics are considered at the same time as are parental nativity effects. In fact, when we constructed separate parental language use matrices for the Chinese, Filipino, and Portuguese language groups, the findings did not differ in any appreciable way from those which we shall present for the Residual language group as a whole. While we shall later examine the effects of membership in a specific language group on the frequency of English monolingualism, the combination of the remaining minority language groups into a single group also permits us to augment considerably the sample size and hence the reliability of our analysis.

The parental language matrix and the language use of children. While the data presented in Table 4.6 permit us to explain observed differences in the English language behavior of children in different language groups, they do not permit us to draw a distinction between the absence or presence of a frequently spoken minority language. Neither do they permit us to examine directly the impact of specific language patterns on the language behavior of children. Since children living in English monolingual homes are presumably monolingual in English, no variation exists which can be studied. Consequently, the parental language use matrix is constructed only for children living in settings where a minority language is actively spoken. The parental language matrix serves as the tool by which children's language usage is placed in its appropriate setting.

The parental language matrix consists of a nine cell table which is defined by the joint distribution of father's and mother's language characteristics. The three language characteristic categories are defined as previously, English monolingual, English bilingual, and non-English usual language. Interestingly, a certain (small) proportion of the parents report a joint distribution of English monolingual language use in spite of the fact that they have been defined into the active language sample (albeit generally by the presence of a second household language which was often spoken). This finding suggests that the word 'often' used in the questionnaires created classificational problems for some respondents. Thus, a certain fluidity must have prevailed in situations where the respondent was called upon to judge between 'often' and 'quite often' and where the linguistic reality being evaluated was not itself very clear.

Two cells in the parental language matrix are particularly important for our analysis. They are the cells defined by consistent English bilingual behavior and by consistent non-English usual language behavior. When both parents practice an English bilingual language behavior, we can examine the extent to which their children retain such English bilingualism or, conversely, the extent to which such children have adopted English monolingual language use. When both parents usually speak a minority language, we can examine the extent to which children usually speak that language. In addition, we can distinguish the extent to which those who usually speak English have opted for English monolingual rather than English bilingual behavior. These two cells are, then, crucial for an analysis of intergenerational language shift, because they permit unambiguous interpretations of the behavior of both parents and children.

The parental language use matrix for the Navajo language group is presented in Table 4.7. An examination of this Table reveals that it is divided into three panels, each of which is a nine cell table based on the joint distribution of parental language use. In the first panel (titled, 'Parental language use') the percentages of children living in each type of language setting are presented. Thus, 3.1 percent of the children live in homes where both parents are declared to be English monolinguals, 10.9 percent where the parents are English bilinguals, and 78.0 percent where both parents usually speak Navajo.

The second panel presents the percentage of English monolingual children living in each type of home setting. For example, only 1.6 percent of the children living in homes where both parents usually spoke Navajo were

Table 4.7 *Language characteristics of children aged 4–17 by the language use characteristics of parents, Navajo language group, all parental origins, United States, 1976*

All origins*	Parental language use Father			Percent children English monolingual Father			Percent children with English usual language Father		
	E_m	E_b	NE	E_m	E_b	NE	E_m	E_b	NE
Mother									
E_m**	3.1%	1.2%	3.4%	84.0%	100.0%	80.4%	94.9%	100.0%	100.0%
E_b	1.2	10.9	0.9	5.6	10.1	0.0	100.0	83.8	100.0
NE	0.0	1.3	78.0	–	0.0	1.6	–	53.0	17.3
Total	N = 53,493								

* An estimated 87 children did not have two native born parents
** Notation: E_m = English monolingual, E_b = English bilingual, NE = Non-English usual language

Source: 1976 Survey of Income and Education

declared to have an English monolingual language use pattern, and only 10.1 percent of the children living in English bilingual homes were reportedly English monolinguals, while 100.0 percent of the children with an English bilingual father and an English monolingual mother were English monolinguals. When the mother is an English monolingual and the father usually speaks Navajo, the children are nonetheless quite frequently English monolinguals as well.

The third panel presents the percentages of children who usually speak English. This includes children who are English bilinguals as well as English monolinguals. Considering children who live in homes where both parents usually speak Navajo, the third panel shows that 17.3 percent of the children usually speak English. Since only 1.6 percent of them are English monolinguals, it follows that 15.7 percent are English bilinguals. The third panel makes it clear that virtually all of the children who have one English-speaking parent (bilingual or monolingual) usually speak English themselves. The single exception appears when the mother usually speaks Navajo, only 53.0 percent of the children speaking English when the father is an English bilingual.

On the whole the second and third panels provide some evidence for the proposition that children are more anglicized than their parents. This proposition is principally suported by the 10.1 percent rate of English monolingualism for children in English bilingual households and by the 17.3 percent rate of anglicisation in settings where both parents usually speak Navajo. On the other hand, we find that some groups of children have less anglicized language behavior than the parental language characteristics would lead us to expect. Thus, 5.1 percent of the children living in English monolingual settings usually spoke Navajo (100 − 94.9 = 5.1). Similarly, 16.2 percent of the children living in English bilingual settings usually spoke Navajo (100.0 − 83.8 = 16.2).

Consequently, the data from the Navajo parental language matrix indicates that there is some back-and-forth movement between Navajo and English. Some parents are more anglicized than their children, others less. Evidently, there is sufficient contact with Navajo-speaking children, institutional settings, or extended-family patterns not discerned in our analysis to permit some children to use Navajo with greater frequency than their parents. However, since the sample sizes are quite small, it is prudent not to push our explanations or hypotheses too far. The data are most interesting, nonetheless, since they present by far the most balanced linguistic situation currently found in the United States.

A somewhat similar table for the Residual language is presented in Table 4.8 in the category entitled 'All origins.' In addition, Table 4.8 is cross-classified

Table 4.8 Language characteristics of children aged 4–17 by the language use characteristics of parents and by parental origin, residual language group, United States, 1976

Mother	Parental language use Father			Percent children English monolingual Father			Percent children with English usual language Father		
	E_m	E_b	NE	E_m	E_b	NE	E_m	E_b	NE
All origins									
E_m	12.5%	7.0%	0.7%	88.2%	87.8%	97.4%	99.4%	99.0%	100.0%
E_b	12.5	32.3	2.5	70.8	60.1	62.0	99.1	98.7	90.2
NE	0.4	6.6	25.5	12.6	15.8	10.6	88.4	85.3	53.4
N = 1,887,277									
Native born of native parents									
E_m	24.2	11.7	1.3	93.5	92.5	100.0	100.0	100.0	100.0
E_b	13.9	31.5	3.2	77.4	74.4	72.7	100.0	99.9	93.7
NE	0.1	1.3	12.7	37.9	13.5	14.6	100.0	37.4	36.2
N = 694,738 (36.8%)									
Mixed ancestry									
E_m	11.0	8.5	1.3	73.3	86.1	93.5	96.1	100.0	100.0
E_b	38.8	27.0	2.1	64.4	62.4	87.3	98.3	98.3	87.3
NE	2.1	4.5	4.8	11.4	40.2	12.4	86.2	96.8	59.6
N = 325,797 (17.3%)									
Native born of foreign parents									
E_m	4.9	3.6	0.2	91.6	73.5	0.0	100.0	100.0	100.0
E_b	2.0	46.1	2.6	80.4	55.6	31.0	100.0	99.6	90.1
NE	0.1	11.8	28.8	–	11.6	18.3	–	91.4	74.0
N = 524,942 (27.8%)									
Foreign born of foreign parents									
E_m	1.7	1.2	0.0	10.5	63.0	–	100.0	100.0	–
E_b	0.7	18.0	1.0	100.0	24.1	65.0	100.0	91.5	73.8
NE	0.0	11.2	66.1	–	13.9	3.6	–	82.9	45.9
N = 341,800 (18.1%)									

by a certain number of parental and child nativity characteristics. Four such nativity categories are presented. Most children in the 'Mixed ancestry' category are native born, there being so few children who were not born in the United States that it was not further subdivided. There were also some children who were born outside the United States to American-born parents. Their numbers were so small that they have been simply omitted from the analysis.

Examining first of all the parental language use patterns for the group as a whole, only 25.5 percent of the Residual language children lived in homes where the parents usually spoke a minority language. Another 32.3 percent of the children lived in English bilingual homes, while about the same proportion lived in English language homes where at least one parent was an English monolingual (12.5 + 12.5 + 7.0). Surprisingly, one-eighth of the parents in the active Residual language sample reported a joint distribution of English monolingualism, although this figure also includes single parent families where the head is an English monolingual. The remaining children had one parent who usually spoke English and one parent who usually spoke a minority language. The mother is more frequently the person who speaks the minority language (0.4 + 6.6 = 7.0) than is the father (0.7 + 2.5 = 3.2).

As may have been anticipated this pattern varies according to the nativity categories which we have constructed. Two-thirds (66.1%) of the foreign born children of foreign born parents live in homes where the parents usually speak a minority language. Another 18.0 percent of the children live in English bilingual homes, while very few children live in English language homes where (at least) one parent has adopted an English monolingual language use pattern (1.7 + 1.2 + 0.7 = 3.6). The remaining children live in a home setting where one parent, overwhelmingly the mother, usually speaks a minority language and the other parent is an English bilingual.

A rapid shift in the linguistic behavior of foreign born parents is already evident among those whose children are native born. Our analysis of the effects of length of residence in the preceding chapter leads us to expect such a shift. Only 28.8 percent of children live in homes where the parents usually speak a minority language. Nearly one-half (46.1%) live in English bilingual homes and the presence of (at least) one English monolingual parent is found in 10.5 percent of the cases (4.9 + 3.6 + 2.0). The data again reveal that women have retained the use of the minority language as a principal language to a greater extent than have their male counterparts.

This movement to the formation of English language homes is evidenced with even greater force when one of the parents is native born. Only 4.8 percent of the children with mixed ancestry parents lived in a setting where both parents usually spoke the minority language. An additional 6.6 percent (2.1 + 4.5) lived in homes where the mother usually spoke the minority language and the father usually spoke English, while another 3.4 percent (1.3 + 2.1) lived in homes where the opposite pattern prevailed. Fully 85.3 percent of the children of mixed ancestry parentage lived in households where both parents usually spoke English, 11.0 percent in English monolingual settings and 27.0 percent in English bilingual contexts. The remaining 47.3 percent (38.8 + 8.5) had one parent who usually spoke only English, overwhelmingly the father, and one parent who maintained an English bilingual pattern.

When both parents are native born, the distribution of the parental language use indices differs somewhat from that observed for the parents of mixed ancestry. The percentage of children living in homes where a minority language is usually spoken actually rises to 12.7 percent. On the other hand, the percentage of children living in English monolingual language homes also rises to 24.2 percent. No longer are women characterized by more retentive language patterns. While more women than men have maintained an English bilingual language pattern (13.9 + 31.5 + 3.2 = 48.6% versus 11.7 + 31.5 + 1.3 = 44.5%), more men than women have retained a minority language as the principal language of use. The percentage of English monolinguals is approximately the same for the two sexes.

With respect to the language characteristics of children the data presented in Table 4.8 indicate the presence of extensively anglicized language use. The data presented for children of all origins can be directly compared to that already examined for the Navajo language children. These data reveal first of all that English monolingualism varies in accord with the language use characteristics of the mother. Even when the father is an English monolingual, only 12.6 percent of the children who have a mother who usually speaks a minority language are reported to be English monolinguals. By way of contrast, when the mother is an English monolingual and the father usually speaks a minority language, 97.4 percent of the children are reportedly English monolinguals. While the 97.4 percent figure is probably not very reliable in view of the 88.2 percent and 87.8 percent incidence of English monolingualism when the father himself also speaks English, Table 4.8 leaves us with little doubt as to the importance of the language behavior of the mother in the determination of childhood language use.

Nonetheless, the examination of the children living in English bilingual homes reveals that 60.1 percent are characterized by English monolingual language behavior. The importance of this figure should not be underestimated.

While only ten percent of the Navajo children living in such situations were reportedly English monolinguals, more than six in ten children living in homes where the parents frequently speak a minority language other than Spanish do not themselves frequently speak that language (if at all). Similar observations apply to children living in settings where the parents usually speak a minority language. More than one-half (53.4%) of these children usually speak English, although as may be expected such children are usually English bilinguals. Nonetheless, that 10.6 percent of the children living in homes where a minority language is spoken with such frequency should be reported to be practicing English monolinguals is somewhat startling. These figures testify to the rapidity of the anglicisation process in the United States, a rapidity which witnesses to the power and attractiveness of the English language to children in minority language groups.

Before passing to the examination of the possible effects of nativity on the language characteristics of children, we should note that the sex effects observed in the explanation of English monolingualism largely disappear when the variable being analyzed is the percentage of children who normally speak English. Thus, 88.4 percent of the children with an English monolingual father and a mother who usually speaks a minority language are reported to usually speak English. The role of the mother in the language retention process consists in maintaining the minority language as a language frequently spoken by the child. Nonetheless, the minority language is relegated to the status of a second, frequently spoken language. Few children in the absence of two parents who usually speak a minority language retain that langauge as their usually spoken language.

Examining first of all the percentage of children who usually speak English, the data in each of the four nativity categories indicates that nearly all children usually speak English when one of their parents does so, irrespective of the language characteristics of the other parent. The figures are everywhere superior to eighty percent with one exception. Native born children of native born parents who have an English bilingual father and a mother who usually speaks a minority language maintain the use of the minority language as principal language in all but 37.4 percent of the cases. Since only 1.3 percent of the children in this nativity category live in such settings, we could relatively easily dismiss the importance of this finding.

However, the examination of the language use characteristics of children living in homes where the parents usually speak a minority language tends to confirm the findings. The children living in the homes of native born parents have less anglicized language characteristics than children having parents with some other nativity pattern. Only 36.2 percent of the children of native born parents usually speak English. This figure is lower than that prevailing for the foreign born children of foreign parentage and less than one-half of that obtained for native born children of foreign parentage. These findings suggest that the greatest losses to minority language groups occur very early in the immigration process. When the adults themselves do not adopt anglicized language practice, their native born children do. In the event that a small number of persons survive this very rapid process of anglicisation, they appear to be better prepared to resist further anglicisation, perhaps through the maintenance of 'language islands' (Fishman, 1966).

Considering the impact of nativity categories on the distribution of English monolingualism, the two principal categories which retain our attention are the two largest, the children living in English bilingual homes and those living in homes where the parents usually speak a minority language. The findings generally show that foreign born children of foreign born parents are least likely to have English monolingual language characterisitics, while native born children of native born parents are most likely to have such language characteristics. For example, while 'only' 24.1 percent of the foreign born children who have foreign born, English bilingual parents are English monolinguals, the figure rises to 74.4 percent of the children who have native born parents. And while only 3.6 percent of the foreign born children who have foreign born parents who usually speak a minority language are themselves English monolinguals, the comparable figure among children with native born parents is 14.6 percent. The highest figure is found for native born children of foreign born parents, again illustrating the extraordinary rapidity of the anglicisation process and perhaps once again contributing to the 'language island' theory. In all nativity categories the important retentive role played by the mother is evident, the children being much less frequently monolingual in English when the mother is the parent who usually speaks the minority language.

Summarizing the principal findings for the intergenerational language shift process of the non-Spanish minority language groups as revealed in Table 4.8, we find that parental language use patterns are strongly associated with childhood language use. The presence of one parent who usually speaks English leads in general to English as the usual language of the children, irrespective of the other parent's language behavior. Even when both parents usually speak a minority language, the presence of English as usual language is relatively high among the children. Nonetheless, the presence of a mother who usually speaks a minority language tends to constrain the language use of children, anglicisation taking the form of English bilingualism rather than that of English monolingualism. These findings tend to hold true for all nativity categories, leading us to conclude that parental language usage has a relatively uniform effect on the language behavior of children. Nativity does, however, appear to play two separate roles. On the one hand, length of residence in the United States appears to determine to a certain extent the distribution of parental language skills. Native born parents have more anglicized language practices than do the foreign born parents. On the other, in the two crucial cells where the language behavior of children can easily be compared to the language setting of the home, children of native born parents exhibit more anglicized language characteristics than do children of foreign born parents. Nonetheless, the data also suggest the possibility of the existence of selected language islands.

A similar data set is presented in Table 4.9 for the Spanish language group. Examining first of all the data for children of all origins, Table 4.9 shows that 51.2 percent of the children in the Spanish language group live in homes where the parents usually speak Spanish. Another 23.8 percent live in English bilingual households, while 11.7 percent (5.9 + 5.8) of the children have one parent who usually speaks Spanish while the other is an English bilingual. Only 12.3 percent of the children live in English language homes where one parent is an English monolingual (4.4 + 2.8 + 5.1). There are virtually no households where one partner usually speaks Spanish and the other is an English monolingual. Thus, in general the Spanish language parents have much less anglicized language use patterns than do the Residual language parents. This is true in spite of the fact that fewer of the Spanish language parents are foreign born (26.4 + 15.8 = 42.2% for the Spanish language group as opposed to 27.8 + 18.1 = 45.9% for the Residual language group). In addition, a higher percentage of the Spanish language parents are both native born (41.9% versus 36.8%). These data once again confirm the findings that the Spanish language parents generally manifest more retentive language behavior.

As expected the distribution of parental language characteristics is affected by nativity and time-of-arrival characteristics. Thus, 87.9 percent of the foreign born children (having foreign born parents) live in homes where the parents usually speak the Spanish language. The figure drops to 68.7 percent when the foreign born parents have resided in the United States for a period sufficiently long that their children are native born. Only 42.7 percent of the children of mixed ancestry parents live in homes where the Spanish language is usually spoken by both parents, and the figure drops to 29.4 percent for the children of native born parents.

The corollary of this pattern is obviously an observed increase in the

Table 4.9 Language characteristics of children aged 4–17 by the language use characteristics of parents and by parental origin, Spanish language group, United States, 1976

Mother	Parental language use Father			Percent children English monolingual Father			Percent children with English usual language Father		
	E_m	E_b	NE	E_m	E_b	NE	E_m	E_b	NE
All origins									
E_m	4.4%	2.8%	0.4%	78.0%	77.4%	18.5%	99.9%	100.0%	75.5%
E_b	5.1	23.8	5.8	71.1	49.2	28.3	99.1	98.8	92.5
NE	0.6	5.9	51.2	46.1	5.2	5.4	99.1	84.2	52.4
N = 3,135,287									
Native born of native parents									
E_m	9.2	5.4	0.7	79.9	79.6	2.1	99.9	100.0	63.4
E_b	7.8	34.4	8.7	70.8	55.4	28.9	98.6	98.6	94.0
NE	0.5	3.9	29.4	91.8	11.5	11.0	97.7	82.1	60.4
N = 1,314,198 (41.9%)									
Mixed ancestry									
E_m	1.2	3.5	0.5	59.6	67.7	83.9	100.0	100.0	100.0
E_b	11.2	19.9	9.4	71.4	42.4	35.7	100.0	100.0	88.4
NE	1.7	9.9	42.7	16.5	4.0	5.8	100.0	82.2	55.8
N = 496,408 (15.8%)									
Native born of foreign parents									
E_m	1.2	0.0	0.2	65.2	—	0.0	100.0	—	100.0
E_b	0.4	20.8	1.5	71.4	39.7	12.4	100.0	98.3	89.6
NE	0.2	7.1	68.7	41.1	2.4	4.2	100.0	85.0	55.0
N = 828,363 (26.4%)									
Foreign born of foreign parents									
E_m	0.0	0.1	0.0	—	—	—	—	—	—
E_b	0.1	4.5	1.6	—	25.4	0.0	—	99.7	100.0
NE	0.3	5.6	87.9	1.5	1.8	1.6	100.0	89.7	40.5
N = 496,678 (15.8%)									

formation of English language households of all types. While only 4.5 percent of the foreign born children of foreign born parents live in English bilingual households, the figure rises to approximately twenty percent for the children of mixed ancestry parentage and for the native born children having foreign born parents. However, 34.4 percent of the children who have native born parents live in English bilingual settings.

The percentage of children having at least one English monolingual parent vary in the same direction. Less than 0.5 percent of the foreign born children of foreign born parents have one English monolingual parent. The figure increases to two percent when the foreign born parents have native born children. It attains 18.1 percent for the children of mixed parental ancestry and 23.6 percent for those who have native born parents.

While the all origins matrix does not show major sex differences in the distribution of language characteristics, the analysis of the nativity groupings suggests the presence of such sex effects. The percentage of mothers who usually speak Spanish exceeds the percentage of fathers who do so by 4.3 percent $((0.3 + 5.6) - (0.0 + 1.6))$ when both parents and children are foreign born. When foreign born parents have native born children, the difference climbs to 5.6 percent $((0.2 + 7.1) - (0.2 + 1.5))$. However, among native born parents it appears that the fathers have the more retentive language characteristics, five percent more of the fathers reportedly speaking Spanish as their usual language $((8.7 + 0.7) - (0.5 + 3.9)$. At the same time there are fewer English monolingual women among the native born parents, a finding which is also visible among parents of mixed ancestry. Thus, while the data seem to indicate the existence of some sex effects in the distribution of language characteristics, the data do not lend themselves to the unambiguous conclusion that women have more retentive patterns than do men.

Examining the percentages of children who have English monolingual language patterns, the data are remarkably similar in most respects to those obtained for Residual language children. The principal difference appears to be the absence of clear sex effects on the language behavior of the Spanish language children. Considering children of all origins, when the father is an English monolingual and the mother usually speaks Spanish, 46.1 percent of the children are reportedly monolingual in English. When, on the other hand, the mother is an English monolingual and the father usually speaks Spanish, only 18.5 percent of the children are monolingual in English. These are, however, the two categories which contain the fewest children and are accordingly not very important. Looking at the other two sets of comparisons, the data support the proposition that the mother exercises greater retentive influence on the language behavior of the children. When one parent is an English monolingual and the other an English bilingual, 6.3 percent less of the children are monolingual in English when the mother is the bilingual parent (77.4 - 71.1 = 6.3%). When one parent is an English bilingual and the other usually speaks Spanish, 23.1 percent less of the children are monolingual in English when the mother is the parent who usually speaks Spanish (28.3 - 5.2 = 23.1%). This pattern, while less pronounced than that observed for the Residual language group, tends to persist across nativity groupings and is also observable when the dependent variable is the percentage of children who usually speak English.

Table 4.9 again demonstrates the importance of intergenerational language shift. In English bilingual homes 49.2 percent of the children of all origins reportedly are monolingual in English. In addition, 5.4 percent of children living in homes where the parents usually speak Spanish reportedly do not often speak the language. These findings vary in the expected direction by nativity groupings. While only 1.6 percent of the foreign born children living in homes where the Spanish language is spoken by both parents are declared to be English monolinguals, the figure is successively higher for the native born children of foreign parentage, for children of mixed parentage, and for children of native born parents. The same process is observable for the percentages of English monolingual children living in English bilingual settings.

When the total percentages of children who usually speak English are examined, the data again tend to indicate that the presence of a single English-speaking parent is adequate to produce nearly complete anglicisation of the children living in such a setting. When one of the parents usually speaks Spanish, a small percentage of the children do not usually speak English. Again, there is very little observable variation from one nativity category to another. The effects of parental language characteristics are relatively independent of nativity grouping.

The single exception to this rule concerns children living in homes where both parents speak Spanish as their usual language. Under these circumstances the familiar pattern is observed, the children of native born parents more frequently having adopted the English language as their usual language than have the foreign born children of foreign born parentage. The other two nativity groupings have the expected intermediate levels of language shift. Nonetheless, the percentages of children who usually speak English in settings where the parents usually speak Spanish are relatively high. The figure is 52.4 percent for children of all origins, ranging from the low of 40.5 percent for the foreign born children of foreign born parents to 60.4 percent for the children of native born parents. The extent of this shift is quite striking. Even when we examine the language behavior of those children whose parents reported that they either did not speak English well or did not speak it 'often', 32 percent of the children reportedly speak English as their usual language, although it is not surprising that nearly all still spoke Spanish with sufficient frequency to be classified as English bilinguals (data not presented in tabular form).

Only one finding suggests that the anglicisation of Spanish language children is not as advanced as these data suggest. The data show that 22.0 percent of the children living in English monolingual language settings are not themselves monolingual in English (100.0 - 78.0 = 22.0). This figure is higher than the comparable figures obtained for the Navajo and Residual language groups. This finding indicates that there must be a large number of parents whose language behavior must be rather evenly divided between English and Spanish. When faced with an evaluation of their own behavior in terms of the word 'often,' they opt for the English monolingual response. Again, the children may have slightly more contact with persons who usually speak Spanish, perhaps grandparents or other children. Or perhaps the anglicisation of the parents is outstripping the pace of the anglicisation of their children. Whatever the cause of these findings, parents do agree that these children do indeed usually speak English, indicating that the English language is relatively well fixed as the dominant language.

In general, then, we conclude that there are strong resemblances in the intergenerational language shift processes of the Spanish and Residual language groups. There are broad similarities in the effects of sex, nativity grouping, and parental language use characteristics on the language use of children. That which most distinguishes the two groups is the language shift choices of the parental groups. In each parental nativity category the Spanish language parents have maintained greater usage of the minority language, both as the usual language spoken and in the English bilingual form of anglicisation. These language choices are in turn affected by parental nativity and exposure to the American environment, native born parents forming more anglicized households than do foreign born parents in both groups. Once these language choices are accomplished, their effects on the children are relatively similar.

A second factor which distinguishes the Spanish from the Residual language group resides in the language behavior of the children themselves. This can be more clearly seen by isolating the two cells which we have identified as permitting clear analysis. These data are presented in Table 4.10. Examining first of all the percentage of children who usually speak English, we find nearly

Table 4.10 *Summary Table: Language shift by parental setting, Navajo, Spanish, and residual language children aged 4–17, United States, 1976*

	Children's language use	
Type of parental language use	Percent English monolingual	Percent English usual language
English Bilingual:		
Navajo	10.1	83.8
Spanish	49.2	98.8
Residual	60.1	98.7
Non-English usual language:		
Navajo	1.6	17.3
Spanish	5.4	52.4
Residual	10.6	53.4

Source: Tables 4.7, 4.8, and 4.9

identical percentages of children living in English bilingual home settings who usually speak English. Most interesting is the degree of correspondence in the percentage of children who usually speak English when the parents usually speak a minority language. The data indicate that just over one-half of the children in such settings usually speak English. The contrast with the Navajo language children is indeed striking.

However, Table 4.10 also shows that the Spanish language children have lower levels of English monolingualism than do the Residual children in similar settings. Thus, in English bilingual settings 10.9 percent more Residual language children have English monolingual characteristics (60.1 - 49.2 = 10.9%). In settings where the parents usually speak a minority language the percentage of children who are reportedly monolingual in English is nearly twice as high in the Residual language group (10.6 versus 5.4 percent). Thus, it appears that English bilingualism more often characterizes the adaptation of Spanish language children than it does that of the Residual language group. The Navajo language group again stands apart in this comparison.

The determinants of English monolingualism. While the parental language matrices presented in Table 4.7 to 4.9 permitted us to examine the effects of a number of factors simultaneously, there are still other interesting aspects of the language shift process which we should like to examine. However, any further subdivision of the parental language matrices would render interpretation virtually impossible. Consequently, we shall present the results of a multivariate analysis to explain the observed differences in the rates of English monolingualism. In addition to the variables already examined, we shall include a set of variables which represent the specific language groups in the non-Spanish minority language sample. A similar set of variables representing the principal ethnic groups in the Spanish language group will be examined. More importantly, however, we should like to examine the effects of socioeconomic status on language retention and shift. Finally, we shall examine the independent effect of age on observed language shift.

The principal variables retained for the explanation of anglicisation are the parental language index, parental nativity, and parental education. The parental language index has been collapsed into six categories, the off-diagonal cells being joined with the opposing pair. Thus, in this analysis it makes no difference whether the father or mother is the English bilingual or the English monolingual. The child is classified as having one English bilingual parent and one English monolingual parent. We have also modified the parental nativity categories, distinguishing which parent was foreign born in mixed ancestry pairs. This decision was reached as a result of the analysis of the parental language matrices. We have also added a new variable, parental education, which is defined as the higher year of education completed by either the mother or the father.

A variety of other indicators were also tested for their relationship to anglicisation. Household income and the occupational status of the head of the household were rejected after preliminary analysis showed that parental education was clearly the most powerful predictor of anglicisation. The three variables are intercorrelated in such a way that the simultaneous use of these variables renders interpretation extremely difficult. Two other variables were rejected because of the high degree of collinearily with the parental language index. These were defined by the number of adults who spoke a minority language to the children of the household and the language which a child spoke to his siblings. While highly correlated both to anglicisation and the parental language index, these variables were also rather imperfect in coverage since not all adults in the sample we are using were asked the first question; on the other hand, not all children have siblings.

The characteristics of the Spanish and Residual language samples with respect to the retained variables are presented in Table 4.11. Since we have defined the dependent variable by the most extreme form of anglicisation, English monolingualism, Table 4.11 reveals that the incidence of English monolingualism is markedly lower in the Spanish language group. Only 26 percent of the Spanish language children were monolingual in English as opposed to more than 52 percent of the non-Spanish children. What is perhaps most surprising is not that it is lower, since this was expected from our previous analysis. What is surprising is that the figure is so high, indicating rather starkly that one in four children living in Spanish language homes does not speak that language with some frequency (if at all). For a language group where many profess to see very little anglicisation, this figure is in fact quite remarkable.

As we have previously noted, the parents of children in the Spanish language group are more frequently native born. More interestingly, the sex decomposition of the mixed ancestry parents reveals that more than twice as many native born women as men have married foreign born partners in the Spanish language group. Among the mixed ancestry parents in the Residual language group the native born men have more frequently chosen foreign born women for partners than have native born women chosen foreign born men. If indeed it can be shown that the presence of retentive women has a retentive impact on the language behavior of the children, the non-Spanish group should have higher retentive levels since so many more of the mixed ancestry women are foreign born.

The reclassification of the parental language indices follows closely the patterns observed in Tables 4.8 and 4.9. The categories which represent consistent parental language behavior tend to include the largest percentages of persons in both groups. The category which represents the counter-diagonal cells in Table 4.11 is very small in both groups, the pattern of English monolingual – usual minority language being both theoretically unlikely and empirically unpopular. On the other hand, the English bilingual – English monolingual category contains a large percentage of the Residual language parents, while the English bilingual – Spanish usual language category characterizes nearly one in eight Spanish language homes (11.64%).

The mean educational attainments of the Spanish language parents are markedly lower than those of the non-Spanish parents. The mean educational attainment of the Spanish language parents is only 10.45 years of education, this figure representing the educational attainment of the best educated parent. This figure is nearly two and one-half years lower than that of the Residual language group parents, whose mean educational attainment level is less than one year lower than that of the remaining White population.

The distribution of the parental language indices in conjunction with this lowered educational attainment may lead some to believe that the lowered

Table 4.11 *Background characteristics of minority language children aged 4–17, United States, 1976*

Variable name	Mean or percent of language group in category	
	Spanish	Residual
Childhood English monolingualism	25.89%	51.17%
Parental nativity:		
Both native born	42.54%	37.27%
Father native born	8.88	12.56
Mother native born	19.72	10.60
Both foreign-born	28.86	39.57
Parental language index:		
Both Eng. mono. (1)	4.54%	12.85%
Eng. mono.; Eng. bil.	8.06	19.44
Both Eng. bil.	23.73	32.26
Eng. mono.; NEL	.98	1.16
Eng. bil.; NEL	11.64	8.98
Both NEL	51.05	25.39
Parental education:	10.45	12.88
Ethnicity:		
Chicano	60.07%	
Puerto Rican	15.56	
Cuban	5.22	
Other	19.15	
Language group:		
Chinese		4.89%
Filipino		5.86
French		15.26
German		13.24
Greek		4.18
Italian		15.34
Japanese		2.23
Polish		3.96
Portuguese		3.82
Scandinavian		1.22
Yiddish		2.96
Other		27.06

Table 4.11 *continued on next page*

Table 4.11 continued

	Mean or percent of language group in category	
Variable name	Spanish	Residual
Nativity of child:		
Native born		77.68%
Foreign born		22.32
Sample size, raw	4,722	4,468
Sample size, weighted	3,170,494	1,901,237
(1) Eng. mono. = English monolingual		
Eng. bil. = English bilingual		
NEL = Non-English ususal language		

Source: 1976 Survey of Income and Education

educational attainment is a function of these more retentive language characteristics. In this view the reason that parental education is so relatively low is a function of the retentive characteristics of the group. Thus, both the Spanish language and the retentive characteristics of the Spanish language parents are seen as associated with lowered social status. That some children in the Spanish language group might wish to dissociate themselves from such stigmatized evaluations by engaging in anglicized behavior is not surprising. While we do not have the data to adequately assess the role of language characteristics in the educational attainment process of adults, we shall address this issue by examining the educational attainments of children in the second section of this book. Suffice it to say for the moment that immigrants from Europe or Asia are probably more likely to have higher educational attainments than those from Latin America, principally because of greater ease in satisfying immigration criteria which favor better educated immigrants. Children of better educated immigrants are also likely to be better educated, this being the logical outcome of the American class system.

Table 4.11 also reveals that the Spanish language sample is overwhelmingly of Chicano ethnic origin. Only fifteen percent of the children are declared to have Puerto Rican ancestry, less than six percent Cuban ancestry, while some twenty percent were declared to belong to other ethnic groups. Most of these latter children belonged to other Hispanic groups, Dominican, Ecuadorian, etc., but a small percentage have non-Hispanic backgrounds. These children probably come from mixed marriages between Hispanics and persons from other ethnic groups.

In the non-Spanish sample, the French, Italian, and German language groups together contribute nearly fifty percent of the children, most of the remaining groups contributing less than six percent each to the sample. The single exception is, of course, a group of which we know very little. It is the group of children coming from language groups still smaller than those listed in the Table or from groups whose languages were considered by the Census to be sufficiently unimportant that they were not listed on the questionnaire. This 'Other' language group contributes over one-fourth of the children to the Residual sample and at the very least constitutes something of a standard against which the anglicisation of the other groups may be assessed.

Finally, Table 4.11 reveals once again the very large sample sizes on which this analysis is based. We found 4,722 children in the Spanish language group who responded to the imposed sampling parameters. We required that children be aged 4-17, be unmarried, have parents with clearly defined language characteristics, and have clearly defined language characteristics themselves. When weighted to reflect the estimated number of such children in the population, the 4,722 cases represent 3,170,494 children. This figure differs slightly from that reported in Table 4.9 because of sampling parameter differences, most notably the omission in Table 4.9 of foreign born children who had native born parents. Comparable sample sizes for the Residual language group are 4,468 cases and an estimated population total of 1,901,237 children. The importance of these very large samples should not be minimized. Most public opinion polls in the United States are frequently less than one-half of the size of each of our language samples.

The data were treated by estimating ordinary least squares equations. The parental language index, language group, ethnic group, and the parental nativity variables were entered as binary (dummy) variables, all variables from a single set being entered on the same step. Three other variables were tested which yield interesting results, parental education, nativity of the child, and the age of the child and its square. Age^2 was entered to permit the examination of a possible non-linear relationship between the age of the child and English monolingualism. The results of the regression of each variable or variable set on anglicisation are reported in Table 4.12.

The most powerful set of variables for predicting the rate of English monolingualism in both groups is the parental language indices. The coefficient of determination (r-square) for each language group indicates that knowledge of the parental language index alone permits us to reduce our errors in predicting

Table 4.12 *Regression of English monolingualism on selected variables by language group, children aged 4-17, United States, 1976*

Predictor variables and regression statistics	Language group	
	Spanish	Residual
Parental language index:		
Regression coefficients:		
Both Eng. mon. (1)	.700*	.745*
Eng. mono.; Eng. bil.	.664*	.663*
Both Eng. bil.	.440*	.493*
Eng. mono.; NEL	.292*	.561*
Eng. bil.; NEL	.112*	.178*
Both NEL	#	#
Constant (Intercept)	.053	.106
R-squared	.332	.307
Parental nativity:		
Regression coefficients:		
Both native born	.349*	.463*
Father native born	.198*	.364*
Mother native born	.095*	.330*
Both foreign born	#	#
Constant	.074	.259
R-squared	.119	.175
Ethnicity:		
Regression coefficients:		
Chicano	-.099	
Cuban	-.187*	
Puerto Rican	-.284	
Other	#	
Constant	.362	
R-squared	.025	
Language group:		
Regression coefficients:		
Chinese		-.341*
Filipino		.204*
French		.291*
German		.152*
Greek		-.144*
Italian		.059*
Japanese		.138*
Polish		.255*

Table 4.12 *continued on next page*

Table 4.12 continued

Predictor variables and regression statistics	Language group	
	Spanish	Residual
Portuguese		−.217*
Scandinavian		.228*
Yiddish		.142*
All other		#
Constant		.437
R-squared		.104
Nativity of the child:		
Regression coefficient,		
Native born	.271*	.464*
Foreign born	#	#
Constant	.037	.151
R-squared	.057	.150
Age:		
Regression coefficient,		
Age of the child	.003	.015*
Constant	.228	.356
R-squared	.001	.014
*Age * Age:*		
Regression coefficient,		
Age-squared	$.012^{10^{-2}}$	$.068^{10^{-2}}$*
Constant	.244	.424
R-squared	.001	.014
Parental education:		
Regression coefficient,		
Parental education	.032*	.016*
Constant	−.079	.305
R-squared	.092	.017

Notes:
(1) Eng. mono. = English monolingualism
    Eng. bil.   = English bilingualism
    NEL   = Non-English usual language
\#   Reference characteristic, omitted category in the estimation of regression equations
* $p < .05$ (statistically significant)

Source: 1976 Survey of Income and Education

monolingualism in English by over thirty percent. No other set of predictors is nearly as important in the determination of English monolingualism. In addition, there is a high degree of similarity between the regression equations estimated for the two language groups. The coefficients of determination are nearly identical. The constants, which represent the extent of English monolingualism in households where both parents usually speak the minority language, are also similar. The rate of English monolingualism in such homes is five percent higher in the Residual language group (which conforms to our observations from Table 4.10). The regression coefficients in the two equations are also very similar, in most instances being approximately .05 (five percent) lower in the Spanish language group. Since the single exception to this observation (one English monolingual parent and one parent who usually speaks a minority language) represents only one percent of the parents, the differences in the regression coefficients can be safely ignored.

The meaning of the regression coefficients is easily understood. In the Residual language group the regression coefficient for children of English monolingual parents is .745. This figure indicates the proportion of children having English monolingual language use over and above the proportion of children having such language patterns and living in homes where both parents usually speak a minority language (the reference category). Since this latter figure is represented by the intercept, the estimated proportion of English monolingual children in English monolingual homes is 85.1 percent (10.6 + 74.5 = 85.1). The comparable figure for children in the Spanish language group is 75.3 percent (70.0 + 5.3 = 75.3). Since the difference in intercepts remains constant and since the regression coefficients for the principal parental language categories are approximately five percent lower in the Spanish language group, we may conclude that for equivalent parental language characteristics when at least one parent speaks English as his usual language, the rate of monolingualism in English is approximately ten percent lower in the Spanish language group.

In addition to the striking similarity of the two equations, the pattern of the regression coefficients is also expected. The data reveal quite clearly that more anglicized parents have more anglicized children. While only 5.3 percent of the children of parents who usually speak Spanish are reportedly monolingual in English, 75.3 percent of the children having English monolingual parents are reportedly English monolinguals themselves. Children with one English monolingual parent and one English bilingual parent have higher rates of English monolingualism than children with two English bilingual parents. The same expected pattern is observed in both language groups.

While these findings generally suggest that parental language use exercises the most important control on the language use of children, they also indicate an important weakening of the language groups. If children had language characteristics identical to those of their parents, children of Spanish-speaking parents should have a rate of English monolingualism of zero (intercept = 0.0). Children of English bilinguals should have a regression coefficient equal to zero as well. Nonetheless, English monolingualism is predicted in varying degrees for every single set of parental language characteristics, including those where the parents normally speak the minority language. While children abandon the minority language with much less frequency when both parents usually speak it, the rate of English monolingualism jumps markedly when one of the parents becomes an English bilingual. The rate rises by 11.2 percent in the Spanish language group and 17.8 percent in the Residual language group (the respective regression coefficients expressed in percentages). As expected, when both parents adopt the English language as their usual personal language, the rate of English monolingualism reaches epidemic proportions. When both parents are English bilinguals in the Spanish language group, approximately fifty percent of the children in the Spanish language group and sixty percent of the children in the Residual language group are English monolinguals. The rate is still higher when one of the parents is an English monolingual. Thus, parental control is only one aspect of the process of English monolingualism (and anglicisation as a whole). It interacts with the American environment in such a way that the anglicisation of the children exceeds to a great extent that of their parents.

The second most important set of predictor variables as judged by the coefficients of determination is the nativity patterns of the parents. Parental nativity alone permits us to reduce our errors in the prediction of English monolingualism by 17.5 percent in the Residual language group and by 11.9 percent in the Spanish language group. The equations themselves do not resemble each other as strongly as did the equations based on the parental language index. The intercepts indicate that 25.9 percent of the children of foreign born parents in the Residual language group were reported to have English monolingual language patterns, whereas only 7.4 percent of the comparable children in the Spanish language group reportedly had such a pattern. In addition, the regression coefficients for most of the remaining nativity categories are markedly higher in the Residual language group. In both instances the presence of a native born mother in the mixed nativity couples is associated with a lower rate of English monolingualism, markedly so in the case of the Spanish language group. Since, however, it is likely that parental nativity affects the rate of English monolingualism via the language shift process of the parents themselves, a multivariate analysis is necessary to isolate the independent effects of parental nativity.

The remaining variables appear to have little overall relationship to the extent of English monolingualism in the two language groups. The coefficient of determination for the ethnic origins of the Spanish language population is only .025. The data indicate that while 36.2 percent of the children in the 'Other' Hispanic ancestry group had English monolingual language use patterns, the figure was only 7.8 percent among Puerto Rican children (36.2 - 28.4 = 7.8), 17.5 percent among Cuban children (36.2 - 18.7 = 17.5), and 26.3 percent among children of Chicano ancestry (36.2 - 9.9 = 26.3). Again, these estimates are gross estimates and need to be examined in the light of parental nativity and language characteristics. The coefficient of determination when the predictor variables are the specific language groups in the Residual language group is somewhat higher, .104. Given the diversity in the nativity and language characteristics of the parents in each specific language group, it is not surprising that the coefficient of determination is larger than that found for the Hispanic ethnic groups. The intercept indicates that 43.7 percent of the children in the 'Other' language groups had English monolingual language patterns. As expected, the rate of English monolingualism varies from a low of 9.6 percent for children in the Chinese language group (43.7 - 34.1 = 9.6) to 72.8 percent for children in the French language group (43.7 + 29.1 = 72.8).

The nativity of the child appears to play a more important role in the process of English monolingualisation than do the language group or ethnic group variables. The coefficient of determination is, however, much higher in the Residual language group than it is in the Spanish language group. Not only is the nativity of the child more closely associated with English monolingualism in the Residual language group, the equation estimates that while only 15.1 percent of the foreign born children are English monolinguals, the figure is 61.5 percent for the native born children (15.1 + 46.4 = 61.5). The difference between foreign and native born children in the Spanish language group is less. While only 3.7 percent of the foreign born children are English monolinguals, the figure is 30.8 percent for the native born. The lower coefficient of determination for the Spanish language equation leads us to suggest that the language behavior of the Spanish language children is more closely controlled by other predictor variables.

The two age variables reported in Table 4.12, a linear and a nonlinear form of the age of the child, do not appear to have an important association with

English monolingualism. The coefficients of determination are extremely low in all four equations. The regression coefficients for the two age equations in the Spanish language group are not statistically significant at the .05 level. They are, however, significant in both equations estimated for the Residual language group, although the nonlinear equation fits the data better than the linear equation. This suggests a geometric increase in the incidence of English monolingualism with increasing age.

Finally, socioeconomic attainments do not appear to play a major role in English monolingualism. The coefficient of determination when the predictor variable is parental educational attainment is also very low in the Residual language equation. The regression coefficient is also small in size, indicating that an additional 1.6 percent of the children have English monolingual language use when parental educational attainment rises one year. By way of contrast both the coefficient of determination and the regression coefficient are somewhat higher in the Spanish language group. Each additional year of parental education is associated with an increase of 3.2 percent in the rate of English monolingualism, exactly double that observed in the Residual language group. In addition, parental education could explain 9.2 percent of the variation in English monolingualism in the Spanish language group, while it could explain no more than 1.7 percent of the variation in the Residual language group. Nonetheless, on the whole we must conclude that the socioeconomic status of the parents appears to be less strongly related to English monolingualism than the demographic factors previously examined.

However, while the data appear to indicate that higher parental socioeconomic status is related to higher anglicisation rates, this observation no longer obtains when both parental education and the parental language indices are examined simultaneously. The appropriate multiple regression results are reported in Table 4.13. Examining first of all the coefficient of determination in the Spanish language group, our ability to explain English monolingualism is but very slightly improved in comparison with the equation where only the parental language index is used as a predictor set. The coefficient of determination is only improved .001 when the parental education variable is added. This is due to the fact that parental education is intimately associated with the parental language index in the Spanish language group. The most anglicized members of the Spanish language group, for example, are also the best educated, while those who speak Spanish as their usual language have the lowest educational attainments. Thus, once the parental language index is entered into an equation with parental education, the independent contribution of parental education is markedly reduced. Nonetheless, the regression

Table 4.13 *Regression of English monolingualism on parental education and parental language indices of minority language children aged 4-17, United States, 1976*

	Language group	
Predictor variables and regression statistics	Spanish	Residual
Parental language index:		
Both Eng. mono. (1)	.684*	.787*
Eng. mono.; Eng. bil.	.644*	.713*
Both Eng. bil.	.426*	.537*
Eng. mono.; NEL	.280*	.604*
Eng. bil.; NEL	.102*	.207*
Both NEL	#	#
Parental education:	.003*	-.012*
Constant	.024	.226
R-squared	.333	.315

Notes:
(1) See Table 4.11
\# Reference characteristics
* $p < .05$

Source: 1976 Survey of Income and Education

coefficient remains both statistically significant at the .05 level and positively signed. Net (independently) of the language characteristics of the parents, each additional year of parental education is associated with higher rates of English monolingualism in the Spanish language group. The effect is not, however, very important. Only 3.5 percent more of the children having one parent with a doctoral degree (twenty years of education) are estimated to be English monolinguals than similar children whose best educated parent has a tenth grade education.

The results obtained from the comparable equation for the Residual language group are markedly different. First of all, although the regression of parental education on English monolingualism revealed a very low coefficient of determination, the contribution of parental education when added to an equation which already contains the parental language index is considerably greater than that obtained for the Spanish language group. The coefficient of determination is .008 higher than that estimated for the parental language index alone. This finding suggests that parental education is relatively independent of the parental language index in the Residual language group. Secondly, the sign of the regression coefficient is negative, indicating that as parental education increases, the rate of English monolingualism declines. Significant at the .001 level, this finding indicates that each additional year of parental education is associated with a decline of 1.2 percent in the rate of English monolingualism, independently of the language characteristics of the parents. Using the same example, the children of the parent with the doctorate have an estimated rate of English monolingualism 12.0 percent lower than the children of the person with the tenth grade education.

As we have previously shown, the language characteristics of the parents are correlated with their place of birth. Consequently, the introduction of the nativity variables into an analysis of English monolingualism with the parental language index produces interesting results. The relevant equations are presented in Table 4.14. We begin our analysis by noting that the proportion of the variance explained by the two variable sets is identical in the two equa-

Table 4.14 *Regression of English monolingualism on parental nativity and parental language index of minority language children aged 4-17, United States, 1976*

Predictor variables and regression statistics	Language group	
	Spanish	Residual
Parental language index:		
Both English mono (1)	.629*	.619*
Eng. mono.; Eng. bil.	.608*	.581*
Both English bil.	.399*	.440*
Eng. mono.; NEL	.257*	.469*
Eng. bil.; NEL	.088*	.187*
Both NEL	#	#
Parental nativity:		
Both native born	.124*	.225*
Father native born	.050*	.052*
Mother native born	.037*	.205*
Both foreign born	#	#
Constant	.009	.043
R-squared	.344	.344

Symbols (1, #, *): See Table 4.13

Source: 1976 Survey of Income and Education

tions. However, since the coefficient of determination when the parental language index is used as predictor was already higher in the Spanish language group, the addition of the parental nativity variables is more important in the equation estimated for the Residual language children.

Also worthy of attention is the similarity in the intercepts of the two equations. While only .009 (0.9%) of the foreign born children who had foreign born parents in the Spanish language group were reported to have English monolingual parents, the figure is also quite low in the Residual language group. Only 4.3 percent of such children were declared to be English monolinguals. Of equal interest are the regression coefficients for the parental language categories. Ignoring the smallest category of parents where one parent is an English monolingual and the other usually speaks a minority language, the estimated effects of the remaining parental language categories on the percentages of English monolingual children are quite similar. Only in the situation where at least one parent usually speaks a minority language do the Spanish parents appear to exercise greater control over the language behavior of their children.

The greatest differences observed in these two equations are the effects of having one or more native born parents. Actually, we can isolate the source of these differences still further. In the first place, the data indicate that having a foreign born mother has approximately the same effect in both language groups. Children with a foreign born mother in mixed ancestry couples have a rate of English monolingualism which is approximately five percent higher than that of children who have two foreign born parents. However, the presence of a native born mother in the Residual language group is associated with a rate of English monolingualism almost as high as that observed when both parents are native born. This sex effect is not observed in the Spanish language group, where the children who have a native born mother in mixed ancestry couples have a slightly lower (net) rate of anglicisation than children who have a foreign born mother and a native born father. Secondly, the regression coefficient when both parents are native born is markedly higher in the Residual language group. Net of the impact of parental language characteristics, ten percent more children are reportedly monolingual in English in the Residual language group when both parent are native born (.225 - .124 = .101 * 100 = 10.1). The figure is still higher when the mother is native born in mixed ancestry couples. Thirdly, in the absence of the sex effect observed in the Residual language group, the Spanish language group is characterized by a pattern of English monolingualism associated with length of residence. Thus, the children of the foreign born are but slightly anglicized, net of parental language characteristics. Those with parents of mized nativity patterns are more anglicized, while those who have native born parents have the highest rates of English monolingualism.

These findings suggest that one of the principal differences in parental language behavior is that of native born women in the minority language groups. It appears that native born women in the Residual language group facilitate the monolingualisation of their children, the statistics indicating few other differences in the behavior of foreign born women or in the impact of the parental language indices. Thus, it appears that in the Residual language group the role of the woman is indeed crucial. It is the woman who apparently exercises greater control over the language behavior of her children. When she is foreign born and usually speaks a minority language, her children retain the use of the minority language to approximately the same extent as do the children of similar Spanish language women. However, in the native born generation it appears that Residual women have opted for conformity to the English monolingual mores so omnipresent in the United States, either encouraging or permitting the English monolingualism which so characterizes their children when compared to similar children in the Spanish language group.

We shall now procede to add the ethnic and language group variables to an equation containing each of the three variables already examined. These data are presented in Table 4.15. First of all, we note that the three-factor model differs very little from the two two-factor models already presented. The differences in the constants (intercepts) and regression coefficients from those observed in the regression of parental nativity and parental language characteristics on English monolingualism are explained by the opposing signs of the parental education regression coefficient. However, net of other factors parental education is more strongly related to English monolingualism in the Spanish language group when the effects of parental nativity are also controlled. Thus, each additional year of parental education is associated with a .5 percent increase in the rate of English monolingualism, an increase over that observed in Table 4.13. On the other hand, the effect of parental education appears to be somewhat less in the Residual language group, although higher parental education continues to be related to lower levels of English monolingualism.

Adding the ethnic origin variables to the Spanish language equation increases only marginally the coefficient of determination. In addition, the regression coefficients for Chicano and Puerto Rican origin are close to zero and do not differ significantly from the rate of English monolingualism which characterizes children in the Other ancestry group (that is, in the reference

Table 4.15 *Regression of English monolingualism on selected background characteristics of minority language children aged 4-17, United States, 1976*

	Regression coefficients			
	Language group			
Predictor variables	Spanish		Residual	
Parental nativity:				
Both native born	.132*	.126*	.216*	.207*
Father native born	.061*	.057*	.051*	.055*
Mother native born	.048*	.040*	.191*	.187*
Both foreign born	#	#	#	#
Parental language index:				
Both Eng. mono. (1)	.602*	.600*	.653*	.621*
Eng. mono.; Eng. bil.	.573*	.572*	.619*	.591*
Both Eng. bil.	.376*	.373*	.473*	.434*
Eng. mono.; NEL	.237*	.245*	.503*	.465*
Eng. bil.; NEL	.073*	.072*	.207*	.190*
Both NEL	#	#	#	#
Parental education:	.005*	.006*	-.008*	-.008*
Ethnicity:				
Chicano		.003		
Puerto Rican		.015		
Cuban		-.059*		
Other		#		
Language group:				
Chinese				-.070*
Filipino				.250*
French				.119*
German				.035
Greek				-.085*
Italian				.040*
Japanese				.089*
Polish				.097*
Portuguese				-.058
Scandinavian				.071
Yiddish				.002
All other				#
Constant	-.043	-.045	.129	.116
R-squared	.344	.345	.347	.369

Symbols: see Table 4.13

Source: 1976 Survey of Income and Education

group). Moreover, when a t-test is applied to determine whether the coefficients differ significantly from one another, the data show that Cuban children have significantly lower levels of English monolingualism than do children in the Puerto Rican and Chicano groups. Nonetheless, the observed differences between the ethnic groups are relatively small, only 7.4 percent less of the Cuban children having English monolingual language patterns than children in the Puerto Rican origin group. Thus, differences in the mean rates of English monolingualism beteween the various Hispanic ancestry groups are largely explained by parental nativity and language characteristics. In addition, the more retentive patterns of the Cuban children are easily explained. Since nearly all Cuban parents are foreign born, this type of extreme anglicisation is not expected. Rather, in these circumstances we should expect to find English bilingualism as the dominant form of anglicisation.

The introduction of the language group variables into the equation of the Residual language group has somewhat greater impact. The coefficient of determination is 2.2 percent higher, indicating that the language variables do indeed make a small but independent contribution to the explanation of English monolingualism. In addition, the magnitude of the regression coefficients for each of the parental language index variables decreases by two to four percent. This reduction is attributable to the fact that the largest language groups in the Residual language group are also the groups characterized by the highest rates of net English monolingualism. Consequently, the failure to control for the effects of group membership in the three-factor model leads to somewhat stronger estimates of the impact of the parental language indices.

Nonetheless, when we examine the regression coefficients for specific minority language groups, the only group with a regression coefficient which departs markedly from the others is the Filipino language group. Membership in the Filipino language group is associated with a rate of English monolingualism 25.0 percent higher than that observed in the Other language group, independently of the effects of parental education, nativity, and language characteristics. The remaining coefficients are all relatively close to zero, that is, to the (net) rate of English monolingualism which characterizes the Other language group. The Japanese, Scandinavian, French, and Polish language groups tend to be characterized by somewhat higher levels of English monolingualism; the Chinese, Greek, and Portuguese language groups by somewhat lower levels. The lower levels of the incidence of English monolingualism in these latter groups can be readily explained by the presence of large numbers of foreign born parents in these three groups, an explanation already invoked for Cuban children.

However, since the French, German, Italian, and Other language groups constitute such an overwhelming percentage of the sample, their relative rates of English monolingualism warrant some greater attention. Using the t-test comparison of regression coefficients, the data indicate that the French language group is characterized by higher rates of English monolingualism than are the Italian, German, and Other language groups. Once again, the differences are not very large, some eight to twelve percent more of the French language children having English monolingual language usage than children in the remaining groups. There are not statistically supportable differences between the rates of English monolingualism in the Italian, German, and Other language groups. We are obliged to conclude that in general the specific minority language associated with a given group has very little impact on the development of English monolingualism among children in the Residual language group, just as ethnic origin was found to affect very little the rates of English monolingualism in the Spanish language group.

We have repeatedly observed that there is an age structure to the process of language shift. The examination of an equation which regressed English monolingualism on age showed disappointingly low coefficients of determination and one regression coefficient which was not statistically significant. Since, however, anglicisation takes place within specific linguistic contexts, the effects of parental language use, parental nativity, and other variables may need to be eliminated in order to permit the hypothesized effect to appear. The rates of English monolingualism by age group are presented in Table 4.16. The data have been grouped to eliminate erratic variations by specific year of age. These erratic variations are probably caused by excessively small sample sizes and they do in fact inhibit our ability to estimate entirely satisfactory equations. Nonetheless, the examination of Table 4.16 reveals a generally consistent increase in the percentage of English monolingual children between the ages of four and seventeen in the Residual language group. While an estimated 40.7 percent of the 4-5 year old children were reportedly monolingual in English, sixty percent of the 16-17 year old children had these language characteristics. The figures in the Spanish language group are both generally lower and increase much more slowly with age. There does, however, seem to be some preliminary evidence which suggests that the hypothesized increase in English monolingualism is observable in this sample.

Since this appears to be the case, we have added an age variable to the four-factor equations estimated in Table 4.15. In neither instance does the

Table 4.16 *Incidence of English monolingualism by age group, minority language children, United States, 1976*

Age group	Language group	
	Spanish	Residual
4-5	24.2%	40.7%
6-7	23.6	49.4
8-9	24.2	46.4
10-11	27.8	49.9
12-13	25.8	51.8
14-15	31.3	58.5
16-17	24.3	60.0

Source: 1976 Survey of Income and Education

addition of the age variable increase the coefficient of determination by an important amount, although the increase is statistically significant in both cases. Also statistically significant at the .01 level are two regression coefficients for age, .0049 for the Spanish language group and .0069 for the Residual language group. Over the fourteen year age span covered by our samples, these figures suggest that an additional 6.37 percent (.0049 × 14 (× 100)) of the Spanish language children have become English monolinguals, net of the other variables included in the equation. The comparable figure is 8.97 percent for the Residual language children.

These figures differ rather markedly from those estimated in the regresssion of English monolingualism on age (Table 4.12). The estimated effect of age in the Spanish language group only indicated a 3.83 percent increase in English monolingualism when comparing four to seventeen year old children. Yet the net effects of age are 2.54 percentage points higher, indicating that the older children have parents with more retentive language and nativity characteristics. An examination of the interaction between the age of the child and parental characteristics shows that in fact the older children are slightly more likely to have native born parents but that their parents have nonetheless somewhat more retentive language characteristics. Given the more retentive language characteristics of their parents, they may have been expected to have been still less anglicized than they in fact are.

The situation is entirely the reverse in the Residual language group. The estimated effect of children's age on English monolingualism in Table 4.12 indicated a 20.48 percent increase in English monolingualism over this age range. While a linear model of age effects appears to quite satisfactorily fit the data for the Spanish language group, a nonlinear model indicating a geometric rise in English monolingualism by age appears to better describe the anglicisation pattern of the Residual language group. According to this curvilinear relationship the gross rate of English monolingualism is 18.82 percent higher for the seventeen year olds than it is for the four year olds. The net increase in English monolingualism, independent of language group, parental education, parental nativity, and parental language characteristics is estimated to be 9.53 percent. While the gap between gross and net rates of increase in English monolingualism is reduced in the nonlinear model, it remains to be explained.

As may have been anticipated, the parents of the older children in the Residual language group are more likely to have been native born than are the parents of the younger children. The parents of 46.1 percent of the 16-17 year old children were themselves born in the United States. The comparable figure is 25.2 percent for 4-5 year old children and 33.8 percent for 6-7 year old children. Since native born parents have more anglicized children, the older children should be expected to be more anglicized, independently of the net effect of age. The effects of differential parental nativity by age account for approximately one-half of the nine percent gap between gross and net rates of English monolingualism.

Since the regression coefficients for the ethnic and parental education variables are so small, it is unlikely that differences in these variables by age could explain an important part of the remainder of this gap. Consequently, we may attribute the remainder to changes in the distribution of parental language characteristics. Since changes in the distribution of parental nativity cannot explain the entire increase in gross as opposed to net rates of English monolingualism by age, it appears that the parents themselves have accomplished some further language shift toward English during the same period. That is to say, to a certain extent the anglicisation of the parents has accompanied the anglicisation of their children. Most likely, as children enter into school and begin to learn English well enough to speak it as their usual language, this progressively larger use of English has repercussions on the language use of the parents. The parents of the older children are consequently somewhat more anglicized than their nativity characteristics would lead us to expect. This simultaneous and joint evolution of anglicisation by both parents and children probably accounts for the remainder of the gap between gross and net rates of English monolingualism by age. Thus, the 9.53 percent net increase in English monolingualism between the ages of four and seventeen should be understood as a minimum estimate, there being still further increases in anglicisation which are associated with joint parental-child movement toward increased use of English.

Only one other predictor variable can be used to substantially refine our model of the English monolingualisation of children, and that variable does not have the same importance for each language group. When the nativity of the child himself is added to the model which already contains parental nativity, parental language index, ethnicity or language group, and age of the child, the coefficient of determination in the Spanish language group rises by less than .003. The regression coefficients for the remaining variables are only slightly affected, but the constant is lowered, indicating that the nativity effect is relatively independent of the previously estimated variables. The regression coefficient indicates that independently of other factors 6.9 percent more native born children are English monolinguals. Perhaps of still greater interest, the greater retentiveness of Cuban children is explained by this variable, there being no remaining net differences in the rates of English monolingualism between the Hispanic ethnic groups.

The addition of the nativity variable to the model of the Residual language group has somewhat greater impact. The coefficient of determination rises by .022, a much greater increase than that observed for the Spanish language group. The regression coefficient indicates that net of other factors included in the model 21.1 percent more native than foreign born children have English monolingual language use patterns. This coefficient is triple that obtained for the Spanish language group, indicating that parental characteristics have much less impact on the language behavior of children in the Residual language group. The introduction of the nativity variable also reduces the impact of some of the other variables included in the model. The regression coefficients for the parental language indices are each reduced by .03-.05, indicating that each index predicts somewhat less anglicisation than previously, the nativity of the child being a better predictor to this extent. The coefficients for specific language groups are also somewhat reduced, although the patterns observed are unchanged. The greatest change, however, is produced in the parental nativity coefficients. The effect of having a native born mother is sharply reduced. Over and above the effects of the nativity of the child, the children of native born mothers have a net rate of English monolingualism only fourteen percent higher than the children of foreign born mothers. The introduction of the nativity of the child reduces this effect from the eighteen to twenty percent rate previously estimated.

Summary. In this chapter we have broadly pursued two goals, an assessment of the intergenerational stability of language behavior and an analysis of the factors associated with the process of anglicisation. We began by asking whether English bilingual parental behavior, or more generally any form of minority language behavior, was being effectively transmitted to the children. The analysis of the parental language matrices provide clear answers to this question. In the case of the Navajo language group there is evidence of significant linguistic stability. While the data indicate trends toward greater degrees of English bilingualism and to a lesser extent English monolingualism, the data also reveal that children are sometimes less anglicized than their parents. In view of the small sample sizes we cannot be certain as to the extent of such intergenerational stability or shift, but there is no doubt whatever that the Navajo language group as a whole is characterized by much higher stability than the Spanish or other minority language groups.

With respect to the other minority language groups we have shown that apparent differences in the retention of minority languages by native born children or by children living in minority language households are largely spurious. Such apparent differences are readily explained by differences in the nativity origins of the parents of children in the diverse language groups. While the data do indicate that foreign born parents in the Portuguese, Chinese, and Greek language groups have retained the use of their respective languages to a greater extent than parents in other minority language groups, these differences are not observed among parents of mixed nativity or among the parents who are native born. Thus, the greater retention exhibited by the Chinese, Portuguese, and Greek children are explained by the nativity patterns and language shift behavior of their parents.

It is only in the Spanish language group that a certain percentage of mixed ancestry parents and native born parents continue to maintain Spanish language homes. Even in this instance the evidence for language shift is impressive. While at least one parent usually speaks Spanish in 82.7 percent of the couples where both partners are foreign born, the figure drops to 44.1 percent of the mixed ancestry parents and to 35.6 percent of the native born parents (Table 4.9). Still, children who do not have foreign born parents in the Spanish language group are more likely to encounter the continued usage of the Spanish language as one's principle language than are children in the remaining language groups.

However, in both the Residual and Spanish language matrices, the data indicate an important interaction between parental nativity category and parental language use. In both cases native born parents exhibit more anglicized language use patterns than do parents in other nativity categories. The most recent arrivals, the foreign born parents of foreign born children, have the least anglicized parental language characteristics. Nonetheless, the data reveal an important difference in the language behavior of the parents in the two groups. In each category of parental nativity the Spanish language group has markedly less anglicized patterns of parental language use.

Once these parental choices have been accomplished, there is broad similarity in the responses of children to their language environment. First of all, there is a strong and consistent impact of the American language environment. English monolingual children are even found in homes where both parents usually speak Spanish, and where both parents have English bilingual forms of language use approximately sixty percent of the children in the Residual language group and fify percent in the Spanish language group have English monolingual language use patterns. Thus, while only 25.88 percent of the Spanish language children were reportedly English monolinguals, and while the comparable figure was 51.17 percent in the Residual language group, most of this difference is caused by the language choices of the parents themselves. When both parents usually speak a minority language, the rate of English monolingualism is only 5.4 percent higher in the Residual language group (Table 4.10). As mentioned, it is approximately ten percent higher when both parents are English bilinguals. And even these small differences disappear when the total rate of anglicisation is used as the dependent variable. Thus, 52.4 percent of the Spanish children and 53.4 percent of the Residual children are reported to usually speak English in spite of the fact that both parents usually speak a minority language.

These findings oblige us to conclude that there is a great deal of intergenerational language shift. Not only is English bilingualism unstable; all forms of minority language use appear to be unstable in the United States. The data everywhere suggest that children are more anglicized than their parents. These findings indicate that children in all minority language groups (except, of course, the Navajo) are moving inexorably toward English monolingualism. The rate is very rapid, particularly in view of the fact that the only type of adaptation which seemed possible from the previous chapter was one in which English bilingualism was successfully transmitted to the succeeding generation. The data in this chapter make it clear that no form of minority language use is so transmitted.

When we began to examine the factors associated with language shift, we observed that the parental language indices had strong and consistent effects for children in both groups, particularly when anglicisation as a whole was examined. The data also tended to support the proposition that children of native born parents had somewhat higher rates of anglicisation in both forms than children of foreign born parents. In other words, there was a small parental nativity effect such that the 'more' native born parents had more anglicized children. We also observed that the data may suggest the existence of tiny language islands among native born Residual parents. And while the mother in the Residual language group appears to exercise an important restraint on the development of English monolingualism, no such sex effects are evident for the Spanish language group and even the observed sex effect disappears when the dependent variable is the percentage of children who usually speak English.

The multivariate analysis of English monolingualism makes it clear that the parental language index is the single most important factor which determines the language behavior of children. The best two-factor model of English monolingualism included the parental language index and parental nativity. These two variable sets together explain 34.4 percent of the incidence of English monolingualism. The addition of four other factors, parental education, ethnicity or language group, age of the child, and nativity of the child, increased the proportion of the variance explained by 0.8 percent in the Spanish language group and by 5.1 percent in the Residual language group. Since even in this latter case the regresssion coefficients for most of the parental language and nativity categories were only marginally affected, we may be relatively well-assured that the parental language matrices adequately represent the most important aspects of the intergenerational language shift process.

In addition to the effects observed in the language matrices, the multivariate analysis permits us to draw a certain number of further conclusions. First of all, there does not appear to be an important socioeconomic effect on English monolingualism. While the parental education variable is positively related to English monolingualism, when the effects of the parental language indices are removed, somewhat different findings are obtained. It appears that a more nuanced theory of the relationship between socioeconomic attainment and English monolingualism is required. Let us propose that when a specific language is associated with a group that has a relatively low social status, children frequently desire to disabuse themselves of the language which symbolizes membership in the group. The social status of the group is generally fixed upon the entry of that group into the United States, any advantages or disadvantages being transmitted via the class structure to subsequent generations. This model describes the small positive regression coefficient associated with parental education in the Spanish language group.

On the other hand, when a minority language group enjoys relatively high social status, a certain proportion of the members of this group will consider the retention of English bilingual language use to be important. This is likely to be particularly true for minority language groups whose language is associated with international activity. Since the members of these minority language groups are relatively priviliged, they can afford to support cultural organizations devoted to language maintenance (Maison Française, Goethe Institute, etc.). This theory would explain the small negative regression coefficient associated with parental education in the Residual language group.

Nonetheless, on the whole we must conclude that socioeconomic factors do not appear to have much impact on intergenerational anglicisation. In both language groups the net impact of each year of parental education on the rate of English monolingualism is less than one percent. We are obliged to conclude that a demographic model of language shift appears to best explain the data. This is even more clearly evident when we observe that the differences in net rates of English monolingualism between Spanish ethnic groups and between specific minority language groups in the Residual sample are relatively small. The only other variable which significantly affects the coefficient of determination for English monolingualism is the nativity of the child, and this is only true in the Residual language group. Thus, the most important factors which can be invoked to explain English monolingualism are the parental language index, parental nativity, and nativity of the child. These are factors which are presumably related to length of exposure to the American environment on the one hand, and to the size, concentration, and institutional structure of the specific minority language group on the other.

In addition, at least two of these factors may be considered 'causal' rather than merely 'correlated.' That is to say, that parental language index and parental nativity are clearly temporally antecedent to the language behavior of the child. This is also true for parental education and the specific ethnic or linguistic group to which the child belongs. Logically, the same should hold true for the nativity of the child, since place of birth precedes the development of speech. Thus, the factors examined in this intergenerational analysis are not generally impeded by time sequence problems. While it is difficult in most analyses to segregate, for example, the temporal sequence whereby the best educated Hispanics also came to be the most anglicized, this problem is largely avoided in this analysis. All the events measured in this chapter, with the possible exception of joint parental-child anglicisation, generally may be assumed to have occurred prior to the development of the child's language behavior.

The multivariate analysis revealed one other effect which merits discussion. We have repeatedly emphasized the importance of the maturational process for the analysis of language shift. The examination of the multivariate equations has permitted us to isolate the independent effects of age. The analysis does indeed reveal the expected increases in the rate of English monolingualism for both language groups as children get older. A linear association between age and English monolingualism best describes the pattern observed for the Spanish language children; a geometric increase in the rate of English monolingualism by age is observed in the Residual language group. Further examination reveals that this pattern is also statistically significant at the .001 level in the Spanish language group, although the linear model still provides the best fit. Nonetheless, the data analysis tends to confirm not only increased rates of English monolingualism with increased age but of rising rates of English monolingualism as children approach the age of seventeen. Again, this age analysis is grounded in a sociological explanation of the evolution of the child's reality.

The verification of the expected age findings suggests once again that these children have not yet completed their language shift process. Thus, the extensiveness of the anglicized behavior which we have documented in this chapter must be understood as a minimum estimate of what the final language characteristics of these children will be. If fifty percent of the children of English bilinguals are already monolingual in English while they are living in the parental home where Spanish is frequently spoken, what will happen to these rates when the remaining children leave home to attend university, to accept employment, to get married? The data suggest substantially higher figures. If fifty percent of the children still living in homes where both parents usually speak Spanish have already adopted the English language as their usual personal language, how high will their rates of anglicisation be when they leave the parental home? If 5.4 percent have already adopted English monolingual behavior, how many more will do so? While only a longitudinal study will permit a definitive answer to these questions, the data examined to date suggest that the final language shift rates will be substantially higher than the extensive anglicisation documented in this chapter.

Chapter 5

The Context of Minority Language Use among American Adolescents

While the data in the previous chapters permit us to clearly establish the broad parameters of anglicisation in the United States, they do not permit us to conduct a refined analysis of the context in which minority languages are used, least of all during the critical periods of language shift during the teenage and early adult years. Such an analysis is, of course, impossible when using the Survey of Income and Education due to the limited number of language questions which were included. The most important aspects of our previous analyses are based on the responses to only three questions, mother tongue, usual language, and second language. Since the SIE represented the first federally-sponsored attempt to obtain language data at the national level, it is not surprising that a larger number of questions were not asked. As we have already suggested, this initial Federal effort is markedly superior in conception to that practiced by Statistics Canada, an organization with a long tradition of interest in the language question in a country beset by language conflict for more than two centuries.

However, interest in the language findings from the SIE led the National Center for Education Statistics to incorporate a larger number of language questions in a subsequent survey entitled High School and Beyond. The base year data for a national longitudinal study of the sophomore and senior high school classes of 1980 was collected in the spring of that year from 58,270 students in 1,015 high schools in the United States. Since this study is a national longitudinal study comparable to that of the NLS of the high school class of 1972, NCES intends to conduct periodic resurveys of subsamples of the students interviewed in 1980. The multi-wave, multi-cohort study design should make possible more powerful analyses of the relationship between background, educational attainment, entry into the work force and related problems. A more detailed analysis of the sampling design and characteristics is presented in Appendix B.

The data retained for analysis in this chapter are those obtained from the 11,303 students who indicated the presence of a minority language in response to one or more of the following five screening questions: mother tongue, a second language spoken in early childhood, current usual language, the language usually spoken in the student's home at the moment of the survey, or a second language frequently spoken in the student's home. Students were then subjected to a battery of language questions designed to ascertain perceived levels of competence in both the English language and in the principal minority language indicated. These questions follow rather closely the suggestions formulated by Fishman, Cooper, and Ma (1975) and are similar to those used in the national Chicano study conducted by the University of Michigan (1979). The HSB students were then asked to evaluate the frequency with which the minority language was used in a variety of settings. The answers to these questions furnish the data on which this chapter is based.

We should be remiss if we did not point out that the High School and Beyond data are limited to a very specific age group, an age group which we have already shown is particularly important to a theory of language shift. Our previous analyses have shown that a maturational pattern is associated with the language shift process, such that adolescence represents the beginning of a rapid emancipation from parental constraints. The adolescents represented in this study are by and large submitted to such parental constraints, since they range largely from fourteen to sixteen years of age. Nonetheless, this group is particularly prone to revise the linguistic behavior imposed by their home settings, a proposition amply demonstrated in previous chapters. Consequently, the data analysis presented in this chapter should be seen as a much closer examination of the language behavior of this specific group, an attempt to specify the context and extent of minority language usage among children of minority language background. For the same reasons indicated in our analysis of the SIE data, we have divided our sample into two principal groups, the Spanish and the non-Spanish or Residual groups.

Since the analysis of the data from the standpoint of language requires a certain logic and continuity, further preparation of the data was found to be necessary. Children were first of all classified into specific language groups by applying successively a number of selection criteria. The first such criterion imposed was the mother tongue of the child, which was followed by second childhood language, the language usually spoken by the child, the language usually spoken in his home, and the second language of the home (if present). Some 446 cases were then removed from the samples either because their patterns of responses indicated the presence of multiple responses to certain questions or because the presence of multiple minority languages rendered interpretation impossible. Consequently, the basic samples retained for analysis in this chapter consist of 6,417 students of Spanish language background and 4,440 students of non-Spanish language backgrounds. All data presented in this chapter have been weighted to reflect population values.

The distribution of mother tongues and usual languages. As has been customary in our analyses of language shift, we begin our analysis by examining the patterns of childhood language use reported by the respondents to the High School and Beyond questionnaire. Conceptually, four major patterns are discernable from the data. A student may have either English or some non-English (minority) language for his or her mother tongue, after which he or she may have acquired (or may not have acquired) some other language in early childhood. Mother tongue was defined in this study by the question, 'what was the first language you spoke when you were a child?' When we compare this question to the question asked in the SIE, we cannot fail to observe the lack of ambiguity which characterizes the question used in the High School and Beyond survey.

The mother tongue question was immediately followed in the survey by a question phrased as follows, 'What other language did you speak when you were a child — before you started school?' While this question does not permit us to ascertain the degree of competence in this second langauge nor to determine the frequency with which this language was spoken, it does nonetheless permit us to determine whether or not the child was already bilingual before he or she started school. The relevant mother tongue and second childhood language data for both the Spanish and Residual language groups are presented in Table 5.1.

A brief examination of the data presented in this table shows first of all that larger proportions of children in the Residual language group declared that English was their mother tongue, a finding not surprising in view of our previous SIE analyses. Some 74.1 percent of the Residual children reported that English was their first language as oppposed to 55.9 percent of the children of the Spanish language group. The percentage of children having English for their mother tongue is, of course, the result of the linguistic mobility accomplished by their parents. Given the prevalent anglicisation already documented for the United States, it would seem likely that the parents themselves were not of English language background but that they had some minority language for their mother tongue. Consequently, the proportion of children having English mother tongue provides us with an initial measure of the extent of the anglicisation undergone by their parents.

The distribution of early childhood bilingualism also follows the pattern

Table 5.1 *Distribution of mother tongue and second childhood language by language group, United States, 1980*

Mother tongue and early childhood language	Language group			
	Spanish		Residual	
English only	135,949	(32.7%)	282,773	(52.0%)
English bilingual	96,595	(23.2)	120,508	(22.1)
English mother tongue	232,544	(55.9)	403,281	(74.1)
Non-English only	75,981	(18.3)	70,680	(13.0)
Non-English bilingual	107,308	(25.8)	70,098	(12.9)
Non-English mother tongue	183,289	(44.1)	140,778	(25.9)
Total	415,833	(100.0)	544,059	(100.0)

Source: High School and Beyond

whereby the Residual children have higher rates of anglicisation. The data show that 70.2 percent of the Residual language children having English for their mother tongue reportedly did not speak the minority language associated with their backgrounds (52.0 / 74.1 = 70.2%). Only 58.5 percent of the children in the Spanish language group having English as first language reported that they did not speak Spanish in early childhood (32.7 / 55.9 = 58.5%). These findings lead us to propose that once parents have decided to give their children English for their mother tongue, only a minority of parents also decide to inculcate a working knowledge of the minority language. That the percentage of parents facilitating childhood bilingualism among children of English mother tongue should be somewhat higher in the Spanish language group is not surprising in the light of our previous analyses. These analyses have consistently shown that the Spanish language group is characterized by somewhat higher rates of bilingualism. Nonetheless, it is worth emphasizing that the presence of an English mother tongue is generally associated with English monolingualism in both language groups.

If we examine only those children of minority mother tongue, the data show that approximately one-half of the children in the Residual language group were monolingual in the appropriate minority language before they started school. On the other hand, well over one-half of the children of Spanish mother tongue were already bilingual in English before they started school (25.8 / 44.1 = 58.5%). Thus, the Spanish children were more anglicized in early childhood (in terms of percentages) than were the children of the Residual language group. This finding is principally explained by differences in the nativity patterns of the two groups. More than one-half of the children of Residual mother tongue were born outside the United States, while only one-third (approximately) of the children of Spanish mother tongue were foreign born. More generally, one of the more striking features of Table 5.1 is the observation that so few children were in fact monolingual in a language other than English before they started school. Only 18.3 percent of the children of Residual mother tongues did not speak English before beginning school.

Having completed our examination of the distribution of mother tongue and early childhood language use, we now turn our attention to an examination of the usual language spoken by these adolescents. The usual language question was phrased, 'what language do you usually speak now?' The data which permit us to compare childhood language use with current language use are presented in Table 5.2.

Table 5.2 *Distribution of English usual langauge by mother tongue and language group, United States, 1980*

Mother tongue and early childhood language	Language group	
	Spanish	Residual
English only	92.8%	97.2%
English bilingual	93.4	96.7
English mother tongue	93.0	97.0
Non-English only	67.0	78.3
Non-English bilingual	81.2	94.7
Non-English mother tongue	75.2	86.5
Estimated population	415,833	544,059

Source: High School and Beyond

We begin our discussion of Table 5.2 by observing that the children of English monolingual language use in early childhood have not necessarily remained (if indeed they really were) monolingual in English. Only 92.8 percent of the children in the Spanish sample and 97.2 percent of the children in the Residual language sample reported that they usually spoke English at the time of the survey. These percentages are very similar to those reported by the children who declared that although English was their mother tongue, they were bilingual in a minority language in early childhood. Apparently, the presence (or absence) of a minority language as a second childhood language does not affect the retention of English as the language usually spoken by these teenagers.

The fact that some of the children of English mother tongue have not remained monolingual in English suggests that there is a certain fluidity in the linguistic reality of minority language households and in that of children living in such settings. These children were presumably exposed to at least a minimal amount of conversation in the minority language, but not enough, apparently, that they felt that they could have declared that language as a second language frequently spoken in early childhood. Since the data analyzed thus far in this book point unambiguously to the unidirectional nature of language shift in the United States, it would seem rather unlikely that these children secured a working knowledge of the minority language after they had begun school. Again, it would seem still less likely that the learning of the minority language at a later date would lead to its adoption as the principal language of use. Consequently, we must assume that the minority language was in fact learned in early childhood, even though these children have not declared so. In spite of these cautious remarks, we should not fail to observe the great stabilty which characterize these data: children of English mother tongue nearly always have retained English as their principal language of use.

We now turn to the examination of the children of minority mother tongues. As we have previously done, we shall define the rate of anglicisation for these children. Anglicisation is defined once again by the proportion of children of minority mother tongue who declared that they usually spoke English at the time of the survey. The data presented in Table 5.2 demonstrate that the anglicisation rate of the Spanish monolingual children had already attained 67.0 percent at the time of the survey, while that of the bilingual children was found to be 81.2 percent. Taking both groups of Spanish mother tongue children together, this yields an anglicisation rate of 75.2 percent. This figure compares favorably with that presented in Figure 1 of this book. In fact, the anglicisation rate obtained from the self-reports of these high school students is just marginally higher than that calculated from the SIE data, the SIE data having been furnished by one of the adults in the family. As expected, a similar pattern is observed for the Residual language children except that the rates are still higher than those observed for the Spanish mother tongue children. The anglicisation rate of the monolingual children was 78.3 percent while that of the bilingual children was 94.7 percent, yielding a total anglicisation rate of 86.5 percent.

When we examine the anglicisaition rates of the Spanish and Residual language children taken as a whole, it is clear that we cannot study anglicisation *per se*. The English language is the language of use for 85.2 percent of the Spanish language children and for 94.3 percent of the Residual language children. Even among those children of minority mother tongue, the proportion of children who usually speak English is exceptionally high. The use of English as principal language is, therefore, nearly universal. The knowledge, however, of the minority language is not. And since we have not had an oportunity to directly examine the use of the minority language by the respondents to the SIE, it is this subject which will retain our attention in this chapter. We begin our analysis by examining the distribution of minority language skills in the two groups of children of minority language background. Later, as in the first part of the book, we shall turn our attention to the analysis of the abandonment of the minority language by these children.

The language skills of minority language children. The principal question upon which our initial analysis is based is the following, 'How well do you speak *that* language?' The word 'that' refers to the non-English language previously indicated by the respondent. The appropriate answers provided were 'very well,' 'pretty well,' 'not very well,' and 'not at all.' A residual category of 'not applicable' was also included and was presumably selected by persons who did not have a working knowledge of the language. For example, some six percent of the persons in the Spanish language group did not respond to this question. Neither did more than seven percent of the children in the Residual language group. It would appear that those who failed to respond to this question were children of English mother tongue and English usual language. Consequently, when using the responses to this question as the object of study, we should recognize that the sampling parameters are somewhat changed from those previously reported in Table 5.1 and 5.2. The resulting changes in sample composition are reported in Table 5.3.

While 55.9 percent of the children in the Spanish language group declared English as their mother tongue, only 54.2 percent of those who furnished a valid response to the question ascertaining spoken competence in Spanish reported that they had English as first language. Thus, the evidence suggests that higher proportions of the children of minority mother tongue furnished valid responses to this question. Similar findings are obtained for the children

Table 5.3 *Percentage of children of English mother tongue according to sampling parameters, by language group, United States, 1980*

Sampling characteristics	Language group	
	Spanish	Residual
Total sample	55.9%	74.1%
Valid response, speaking minority language	54.2%	73.3%

Source: High School and Beyond

of the Residual language group. These slight changes in sampling parameters suggest, nonetheless, that our analysis of the distribution of minority language skills will be slightly biased toward finding less anglicisation than actually exists. We will underestimate the extent of the shift to English and overestimate the retention of the minority language. Thus, the figures reported in the following pages are somewhat conservative estimates of the extent of anglicisation among high school students of minority language origin.

Our analysis of the response to the question regarding spoken competence of the minority language will take two principal forms. While we shall initially present the declared distribution of competence in the minority language in terms of a frequency distribution for selected groups, we shall also derive an index from the responses so furnished. This index is compiled by treating each increasing value of spoken competence as equidistant in value from each of the preceding values. Formally, we shall take the liberty of transforming an ordinal measure into an interval measure. To operationalize this procedure, we have assigned the value of three (3) to the response 'very well,' two (2) to the response 'pretty well,' one (1) to 'not very well' and zero (0) to 'not at all.' While it is perfectly logical to assign a maximum score to those who selected the maximal response and a minimal score to those who chose the minimal response, it is not at all clear that 'not (speaking the minority language) very well' lies one-third of the way up the continuum ranging from the minimal to the maximal scores. The same observation applies to the score assigned to 'pretty well.' While this assumption cannot be empirically justified in any specific way, the construction of the index does facilitate the analysis of the relationship between this specific measure of spoken competence in the minority language and a number of other variables which would (and could) have been derived from more cumbersome cross-tabular analyses.

Since we consider membership in a language community as being primarily defined by the ability to speak a specific language, we present in Table 5.4 both the distribution of declared competence and the index developed as a summary measure.

Table 5.4 *Reported ability to speak the minority language by language group, United States, 1980*

Reported speaking ability	Language group	
	Spanish	Residual
Very well	26.3%	15.2%
Pretty well	40.5	27.9
Not very well	27.6	35.8
Not at all	5.7	21.1
Total	100.0%	100.0%
Index	1.87	1.37

Source: High School and Beyond

As can be readily seen, children from the Spanish language group declare higher levels of oral competence in the minority language than do children from the Residual language group. Nonetheless, only 26.3 percent of the Spanish language teenagers and 15.2 percent of the Residual teenagers declared that they spoke the minority language 'very well'. And while only 21.1 percent of the Residual group said that they did not speak the minority language at all, only 5.7 percent of the Spanish language children declared that they did not speak Spanish at all. However, an additional 35.8 percent of the Residual children and 27.6 percent of the Spanish teenagers admitted that their minority language skills were not very good ('not very well'). On the whole then, the data indicate surprisingly low levels of spoken competence in the minority language for American teenagers of minority language backgrounds. This somber conclusion applies to both groups of minority language children, although evidently the picture is not as bleak in the Spanish language group.

The index score which we have developed has a value of 1.87 for the children of the Spanish language group, a figure which is just slightly below that represented by the evaluation 'pretty well.' The index score for the Residual group is only 1.37, approaching the 1.0 level which indicates that the respondents as a whole do not speak the minority language very well. This score is fully one-half (1.87 − 1.37 = 0.50) point below that of the children of the Spanish group on a scale which has a range of only three points.

Obviously, the index value which we have constructed is affected by the distribution of English and minority mother tongues among the children of minority language background. If the parents are themselves highly anglicized, it should not be surprising to find that their children (particularly those of English mother tongue) do not speak the minority language very well. In Table 5.5 we decompose the two language groups into their respective minority and English mother tongue subgroups.

Table 5.5 *Declared ability to speak the minority language by language group and mother tongue, United States, 1980*

Declared competence, minority language	Language group	
	Spanish	Residual
English mother tongue:		
Very well	12.5%	6.7%
Pretty well	37.0	25.4
Not very well	40.9	41.1
Not at all	9.6	26.7
Index	1.52	1.12
Minority mother tongue:		
Very well	42.6%	38.5%
Pretty well	44.5	34.5
Not very well	11.8	21.1
Not at all	1.1	5.8
Index	2.28	2.06

Source: High School and Beyond

We observe first of all that for both mother tongue groupings, the children of the Spanish language group manifest greater retentiveness of minority language skills. Considering first of all the distribution of responses offered by the children of English mother tongue, 12.5 percent reported being able to speak Spanish 'very well', while another 37.0 percent said they spoke it 'pretty well.' These figures are substantially higher than the 6.7 percent and 25.4

percent of the Residual children who offered comparable evaluations. Thus, 49.5 percent of these children in the Spanish group declared that they spoke Spanish at least 'pretty well'. Only 32.1 percent of the Residual language children declared equivalent competence in their languages. On the other hand, only 9.6 percent of the Spanish children said that they did not speak Spanish very well, a figure which attains 26.7 percent with respect to the Residual languages.

This greater retentiveness of the Spanish language children can also be found among children of minority mother tongue. While 42.6 percent of the Spanish children declared that they spoke the Spanish language 'very well,' only 35.8 percent of the Residual children reported that they spoke their appropriate minority language that well. Similarly, an additional 44.5 percent of the Spanish children said that they spoke Spanish 'pretty well,' yielding a cumulative total of 87.1 percent who said that they spoke Spanish with a (presumably) relatively high degree of competence. The comparable figure is only 73.0 percent of the Residual language children. Furthermore, only 1.1 percent of the Spanish children said that they did not speak Spanish at all, a figure which attains 5.8 percent among the children of the Residual language group.

Table 5.5 also makes it clear that the mother tongue of the child plays an important role in determining his or her competence in speaking the minority language. Thus, the percentage of children who maintain high levels of competence is much greater among children of minority mother tongue. These observations can be readily demonstrated by examining the use of the index of retentiveness which we have constructed. For children of English mother tongue the index value is only 1.52 in the Spanish language sample and only 1.12 for their counterparts in the Residual group. This latter score indicates that the average child of English mother tongue in the Residual language group does 'not (speak the minority language) very well.' The comparable child in the Spanish language group has a competence in spoken Spanish which falls half-way between 'not (speaking Spanish) very well' and between speaking it 'pretty well.' Thus, the children in the Spanish language group seem somewhat more likely to have acquired some minimal facility in the minority language than have the children of the Residual group, enjoying a net advantage of 0.40 points.

Although the Spanish language children have greater facility in the minority language among the children of minority mother tongue, the advantage is less pronounced than that observed among children of English mother tongue. The index values differ by only .22 points (2.28 − 2.06 = 0.22). However, in both cases the index values exceed the 2.0 level which indicates that the average child speaks the minority language 'pretty well.'

Having presented the logic of our index construction and shown its relationship to the frequency distributions of minority language competence, we shall now procede to transform a number of other language variables using the same technique. Seven such variables from High School and Beyond may be operationalized in the same manner: the ability to understand the minority language, the ability to read it, the ability to write it, and similar abilities with respect to the English language.

Continuing our practice of presenting the data first of all for each sample as a whole and later dividing it according to mother tongue subgroups, we present in Table 5.6 the relevant scores for the different types of minority language competence.

Table 5.6 *Declared competence indices for minority language use, by language group, United States, 1980*

Areas of minority language competence	Language group	
	Spanish	Residual
Understanding	2.21	1.71
Speaking	1.87	1.37
Reading	1.67	1.08
Writing	1.43	0.91

Source: High School and Beyond

It is first of all quite evident from Table 5.6 that children are more likely to understand the minority language than to speak it. In the case of both the Spanish and Residual language groups, the measured index gap between the understanding and speaking scores is 0.34 points (2.21 - 1.87 = 0.34) and (1.71 - 1.37 = 0.34). The data also show that the ability to speak is more developed than are the literate abilities of reading and writing. That is to say, personal competence in the minority language is more likely verbal than literate. What is perhaps most striking in this table is the marked decline in competence scores for both groups as one moves from understanding through speaking and reading to writing minority language. Since, as we have previously shown, the verbal competence of the children of the Residual language group is lower than that of the Spanish children, it is not surprising to find that their competence in other areas of minority language skills is also lower.

We present in Table 5.7 the same data decomposed by mother tongue subgroup.

Table 5.7 *Declared competence indices for minority language use by language group and mother tongue, United States, 1980*

Areas of minority language competence	Language group	
	Spanish	Residual
English mother tongue:		
Understanding	1.89	1.45
Speaking	1.52	1.12
Reading	1.44	0.90
Writing	1.19	0.74
Non-English mother tongue:		
Understanding	2.59	2.41
Speaking	2.28	2.06
Reading	1.94	1.56
Writing	1.71	1.37

Source: High School and Beyond

As may have been anticipated from our analysis of Table 5.5, the children of the Spanish language group demonstrate higher levels of competence in all aspects of minority language use, irrespective of their mother tongue. For example, among children of English mother tongue, the Spanish children have an index of 'understanding' the minority language of 1.89, that is, just below the 2.0 score representing 'pretty well'. This compares rather favorably with the 1.45 index score reported by the children of the Residual language group. The Spanish language children also have index scores which demonstrate greater facility in the reading and writing of the minority language than do children in the Residual language group. Nonetheless, the index scores for speaking and reading the Spanish language indicates competence levels halfway between 'not very good (well)' and 'pretty good (well).' The scores for Residual children approximate the judgment 'not very good (well)'. This is also the judgment reported by the Spanish children with respect to their ability to write the Spanish language. Thus, the first part of Table 5.7 makes it clear that there is a consistent decline in the abilities of children of English mother tongue to use the minority language as we move from comprehension to speech to the literate skills. The drop in the reported indices is approximately 0.7 points of the three point scale (for the Spanish: 1.89 - 1,19 = 0.70; for the Residuals: 1.45 - 0.74 = 0.71).

When we turn our attention to the children of minority mother tongue, the data reveal (as expected) that the reported competence levels in all aspects of minority language use are markedly higher than those found for children of English mother tongue. Once again, the children of the Spanish language group are found to have higher levels of competence. The data also reveal the same pattern of marked decline in competence levels as we move from cognitive to verbal to literate skills. Of somewhat greater interest is the respective distribution of verbal and literate skills. The mean index scores for comprehension and speaking in the two groups are rather similar, the differences in mean scores being only 0.18 points for understanding (2.59 - 2.41 = 0.18) and only 0.22 points for the ability to speak the minority language. However, the Spanish language children manifest much higher levels of literate skills, enjoying net advantages of 0.38 points for reading (1.94 - 1.56 = 0.38) and 0.34 points for writing (1.71 - 1.37 = 10.34).

Aside from some of these already familiar patterns observed in the data, we should emphasize quite strongly the relatively low levels of skill in minority language use of all types manifested by the children of minority language origin. This is true as well for the children of minority mother tongue, whether Spanish or other. The mean scores do not approach the 3.0 level which would indicate a high level of competence in the minority language. Furthermore, the ability to understand a minority language is in itself of relatively little consequence for the future if that language is not in fact frequently used. When one begins to examine more substantive criteria, the mean scores for speaking are just slightly higher than the figure indicating a self-evaluation of having a 'pretty good (well)' ability to speak the language, this among children of minority mother tongue. The abilities to read and write the language are still lower. The total measured drop in skill levels as we move from understanding the language to writing it is 0.88 points (2.59 - 1.71 = 0.88) for the children of Spanish mother tongue and 1.04 points (2.41 - 1.37 = 1.04) for the children of Residual mother tongue, this on a three point scale. This drop is somewhat greater than that observed among the children of English mother tongue, obviously because these latter have such low skill levels for both understanding and speaking the minority language.

A similar set of data with respect to declared competence in the English language is presented in Table 5.8 for the children of the two language groups.

Table 5.8 *Declared competence indices for English language use, by language group, United States, 1980*

Area of competence	Language group	
	Spanish	Residual
Understanding	2.83	2.87
Speaking	2.72	2.80
Reading	2.71	2.79
Writing	2.67	2.73

Source: High School and Beyond

Once again, the interpretation of the indices is the same as that previously indicated, the value of 3.0 indicating a declared ability to accomplish the task 'very well,' that of 0.0 indicating an inability to do so. An examination of the mean scores shows that both groups of children report uniformly high levels of competence in all aspects of English language skills. Those reported by the non-Spanish children are just slightly higher than those reported by the Spanish children. That these latter children declared such high levels of competence in English is in itself somewhat surprising, since these same children reported markedly higher levels of competence in the minority language. Obviously, they do not see competence in one language as interfering with their competence in another, in this case English.

Further inspection of Table 5.8 reveals the same pattern of declining competence levels as we move from verbal to literate skills as that observed for minority language skills. The ability to understand a language is more developed than the ability to speak it, which is in turn more developed than the ability to read it. In turn, the ability to read is more developed than the ability to write. These children seem to share the perception that there is a natural hierarchy of language skills. However, it is also clear from Table 5.8 that children in both groups evaluate all four types of their English language skills more similarly than they do their minority language skills. The reported decline in English language skills from understading through writing is only 0.16 points (2.83 - 2.67 = 0.16) among children of the Spanish group and 0.14 points (2.87 - 2.73 = 0.14) among those of the Residual group. The small decline observed, 0.16 points and 0.14 points, is relatively insignificant when compared to that previously observed with respect to minority language skills.

One further point seems worth observing with respect to Table 5.8. The mean scores reported by children of both groups tend to approach the value of 3.0, indicating that most children, for example, think that their English language skills are 'very good (well).' For example, the average score for the ability to read and write English varies from 2.67 to 2.79 points, that is, substantially above the 2.0 figure indicating a perceived level of 'pretty good' competence and much closer to that indicating 'very good' competence. This judgment is not likely to be shared by American teachers, who generally seem not unduly impressed by the reading and writing skills of American adolescents, let alone those of minority language origins. If the average minority language child thinks his or her reading and verbal skills are 'very good (well)', one has to wonder openly how poorly one would need to speak Engish in order to rate one's skills as 'pretty good (well).' Obviously, the same comment applies to the ratings of one's minority language skills. The rating of one's minority language skills as 'pretty good (well)' may not indicate a very high degree of competence in the minority language, particularly if the data suggest that these children are relatively uncritical in the formulation of such judgments. There is, nonetheless, little doubt that children in both minority language groups think that their English language skills are markedly superior to their minority language skills.

Turning to the analysis of reported competence in English by mother tongue subgroup, we present the relevant data in Table 5.9. We observe first of all that there appear to be no important differences in the reported skill

Table 5.9 *Declared competence in English language use by language group and mother tongue, United States, 1980*

Area of competence	Language group	
	Spanish	Residual
English mother tongue:		
Understanding	2.92	2.93
Speaking	2.85	2.87
Reading	2.83	2.85
Writing	2.81	2.80
Non-English mother tongue:		
Understanding	2.72	2.72
Speaking	2.57	2.62
Reading	2.57	2.62
Writing	2.51	2.55

Source: High School and Beyond

levels of children of English mother tongue in the Spanish and Residual language groups. The reported skill levels are very high and the decline observed from verbal to literate skills is very limited.

As expected, the reported skill levels of the children of English mother tongue are higher than those reported by the children of minority mother tongue. With respect to the understanding of English, for example, the index score is 0.20 to 0.21 points lower for the children of minority mother tongue (2.92 - 2.72 = 0.20 for the Spanish; 2.93 - 2.72 = 0.21 for the Residuals). Similarly, the scores for speaking, reading, and writing are lower than those of children of English mother tongue. The observed decline in skill levels as we move from verbal to literate skills is, however, somewhat sharper than that observed for the children of English mother tongue. With respect to written skills, for example, the index scores for both groups of children hover near the 2.5 mark indicating the middle of the continuum represented by writing 'very well' and writing 'pretty well.' This is a rather sharp decline from the index scores reported by the same children for understanding English. Still, the observed decline is much weaker than that declared by these same children with respect to their minority language skills.

Table 5.9 also suggests that the children of Spanish mother tongue have slightly lower competence levels in these three areas than do their Residual peers. Nonetheless, given the methodological problems involved in the construction of these indices, we should conclude that there are no important differences in the reported competence in English language skills between the two groups of children.

The analysis reported thus far in this section of the chapter leads us to a number of relatively clear conclusions. First of all, minority language children report that they have much higher levels of competence in the English language than they do in the minority language. Secondly, this finding holds true for children of either English or some minority mother tongue. Thirdly, knowledge of the minority language is exceedingly low among children of English mother tongue. Fourthly, the decline in minority language skills as we move from verbal to literate skills is very sharp when compared to that observed for similar English language skills. Finally, the data consistently show that the Spanish language children have higher levels of skill in the minority language than do Residual children. Their reported skill levels in the English language do not, however, tend to differ.

The language environment of minority language children. As we have consistently indicated throughout this book, we place much greater emphasis on the spoken language than on other aspects of minority language use. This emphasis is based on the fact that a living language is maintained by social interaction and will persist in a minority language context only so long as it is effectively transmitted to the coming generation. Thus, those children who understand a minority language but do not speak it will make no contribution to the future of their language group. Consequently, we shall turn our attention to the examination of the language environment which affects the development of minority language skills. Subsequently, we shall examine the use to which these skills are put by the children of High School and Beyond.

One aspect of the linguistic environment to which children are subjected is the language which the people in the household usually speak. The High School and Beyond students were asked to respond to the following question, 'What language do the people in your household *usually* speak?' From this question we may obtain the percentage of households where English is the principal household language. Other aspects of the language environment in which the child lived were obtained from a series of other language use questions. The relevant questions attempted to ascertain the context in which minority language use was most prevalent, that is actual patterns of use rather than the reports of general competence levels contained in the previous tables. To be sure, the responses to these language context questions are also self-reports but the fact that the questions demand context-specific evaluations should reduce much of the ambiguity contained in more general assessments of language use.

The language context questions attempted to ascertain the frequency with which various persons addressed the child in the minority language. For example, children were asked, 'How often does your mother speak (the minority) language to you?' Similar questions sollicited data regarding the frequency of minority language use by the father, by the parents when interacting with one another, and by relatives of the child in his or her presence ('around you'). Since the answers provided in the questionnaire constitute another series of ordinal level variables, the responses were recoded in the following manner: 'Always or almost always' = 4, 'mostly' = 3, 'about half of the time' = 2, 'sometimes' = 1, and 'never' = 0. Thus, the index scores developed have a minimum value of zero (0) and a maximum value of four (4). The relevant index scores for these language context variables are presented for the two sampled groups in Table 5.10.

We begin our analysis of this table with the observation that 56.4 percent

Table 5.10 *Language environment indices, by language group, United States, 1980*

Language environment indices	Language group	
	Spanish	Residual
Home language	56.38%	77.59%
By parents	2.40	1.47
By mother	2.21	1.38
By father	2.00	1.22
By relatives	2.06	1.70

Source: High School and Beyond

of the Spanish children and 77.6 percent of the Residual children declared that English was the principal language spoken in their home. This figure should probably be considered a minimal estimate of the percentage of English language households. In direct parent-child comparisons, the parents were more likely to indicate the presence of English as the principal household language than were their children (see Appendix C). These two figures may, accordingly, be taken as indicators of the seriousness with which parents are attempting to impose (or are succeeding at imposing) a minority language household environment.

If we compare these two figures to the data previously reported in Table 5.1, the general correspondence between the percentage of households of English usual language and the percentages of children having English as mother tongue is quite evident. Thus, methodologically, the percentage of English language households may serve as a loose measure of the percentages of children having English for their first language in any specific minority language group (as in the SIE). Still more interesting, however, is the comparison of the percentages of English language households with the current language practices of minority language children. From Table 5.2 we observe that 85.2 percent of the Spanish language children and 94.3 percent of the Residual language children usually spoke English. Both of these figures are substantially higher than the percentage of children living in homes where English is the principal household language, indicating once again that the children as a whole are substantially more anglicized than their general household environment.

When we turn to the analysis of the index measures developed for the language context variables, we observe that the mean scores for the Spanish language children range from 2.00 to 2.40. If we recall that the value 2.0 indicates the use of Spanish in approximately one-half of the interactions which are directed to the child, it can be readily seen that the English language is accorded approximately the same importance in family interactions as is Spanish. There are only two exceptions to this general rule: the parents are somewhat more likely to use the Spanish language in their personal interactions, and the mother is slightly more likely than the father to use Spanish in her interactions with the HSB respondent. Nonetheless, these findings indicate that the English language is used with a great deal of frequency even in the home setting.

As may have been anticipated from the percentages of English language homes in the Residual language group, the minority language is used much less frequently in family interactions. Once again, the parents are more likely to use the minority language in their interactions with one another than they are in their interactions with the child. Even so, the index value indicates that the parents use English in their personal interactions with greater frequency than they use the minority language. And while the data indicate once again that the mother is more likley than the father to use the minority language in interactions with the child, the data show that it is relatives who make the greatest use of the minority language. Since it is unlikely that the siblings of the HSB child would use the language more frequently than their parents, it would appear that it is the grandparents who are most likely to exercise a retentive influence in the Residual language group. Even in this case, they are still more likely to use the English language than the minority language.

These comparisons can, of course, be refined in the usual manner. The relevant data for the mother tongue subgroups are presented in Table 5.11. If we begin our analysis with the children of English mother tongue, the data show that a small percentage of these children live in households characterized by the use of the minority language as the principal language of the home. Only 83.5 percent of the Spanish children and 91.2 percent of the Residual children live in households where the English language is dominant. These findings suggest one of several interpretations. Either the family language environment has undergone some alteration since the children were born, such that a certain percentage of formerly English language households have become households where the minority language is now most frequently used; the household context is so thoroughly bilingual that the child could have answered the usual household language question in either of two logical ways; the child was unable to correctly report his or her mother tongue; or

Table 5.11 *Language environment indices by language group and mother tongue, United States, 1980*

Language environment indices	Language group	
	Spanish	Residual
English mother tongue:		
Home language	83.50%	91.18%
By parents	1.63	0.96
By mother	1.37	0.87
By father	1.21	0.76
By relatives	1.61	1.47
Non-English tongue:		
Home language	24.29%	40.49%
By parents	3.30	2.82
By mother	3.17	2.72
By father	2.94	2.44
By relatives	2.58	2.32

Source: High School and Beyond

the parents deliberately chose to raise the child as an English speaking child (that is, of English mother tongue), while at the same time maintaining a minority language household context. The first possibility seems intrinsically unlikely, there being little evidence that English speaking people undergo language mobility into a minority language group. Any or all of the three latter explanations seem intuitively plausible.

When we examine the scores developed to measure the frequency of the use of the minority language in different household settings, the data indicate that the children of English mother tongue are not exposed to a great deal of minority language use. In their interactions with one another and individually with the child, the parents of the Residual language children use the minority language with a frequency inferior to 'sometimes,' the latter being represented by the value one (1.0). Only relatives speak the minority language with a greater degree of frequency than 'sometimes,' although the mean score indicates that the frequency is closer to 'sometimes' than to 'about half the time'.

Interestingly, while the scores reported by the Spanish children of English mother tongue are higher, not a single one of the four scores is relatively close to the 2.0 value which would indicate that Spanish was used approximately one one-half of the time. Generally, the directions of the findings are similar to those previously observed. The parents speak the language more frequently to one another than they do with their children. The mother uses the language more frequently than does the father. However, the data also tend to suggest that for children of English mother tongue, the role of relatives outside the family (probably especially that of the grandparents) tends to be rather important. As in the case of the Residual children, however, even the relatives tend to use English as a general rule. Taken as a whole, this table leaves little doubt that the children of English mother tongue in both groups are principally exposed to the English language in all of their interactions with members of the family.

This is not the case for the children of minority mother tongue, since the findings indicate much higher levels of minority language use. However, it is also clear that the English language has made some inroads into the family language context. Some 24.3 percent of the children of Spanish mother tongue and 40.5 percent of the children of other mother tongues reported that the English language was the principal language of use in their respective households. While it can be argued (and is undoubtedly the case in a certain number of instances) that the parents gave the child a minority mother tongue and yet maintained an English language home environment so that childhood bilingualism might be assured, it is rather more likely that the presence of English language homes indicates that both parents and children have undergone a process of joint anglicisation. Some of this movement is likely to be coincident with the child's enrollment in school; another part of it is due to the adoption of the national language subsequent to immigration to the United States (as was shown in chapter three). In any case, there appears to have been some parental language shift in the direction of the English language since these children were born (and presumably given the principal household language for their mother tongue).

The index scores presented in Table 5.11 also indicate that the English language has made extensive inroads into the family language context for children of minority mother tongues. The index scores are substantially lower than the 4.0 score which would indicate the nearly exclusive use of the minority language. In the Spanish language group, for example, the highest index score is that defining the interactions of parents with one another. This score, 3.30, indicates that the parents speak the language to each other somewhat more frequently than 'most of the time' but not nearly 'all or almost all of the time.' The mother uses the language still less with the children but slightly more frequently than does the father. The relatives of children of Spanish mother tongue are still less likely to use Spanish than are the parents, the index score indicating that they do so substantially less than 'most of the time' but generally more than 'about half of the time.'

This pattern of language use is replicated in the Residual language group, the relatives no longer playing a conservative role as was found for the Residual children of English mother tongue. Rather, as for the children of Spanish mother tongue, the family itself bears the principal responsibility for teaching and using the minority language. In all cases, the parents use English more frequently with their children than they do with each other, the father more so than the mother. Nonetheless, it is also clear that the minority language is generally used with greater frequency than is the English language in the families of children of minority mother tongue.

In spite of generally retentive home settings, the children of minority mother tongue claim that they usually speak English. The relevant figures obtained from Table 5.2 indicate that 75.2 percent of the Spanish children and 86.5 percent of the Residual children reported that they usually speak English. It would appear, then, that even in this relatively retentive environment, the children experience extensive linguistic mobility toward the English language. Since this is the case, it may be that the home setting provides the only setting in which the minority language is used by the child of minority mother tongue. It is to this subject that we now turn.

Language practices of minority language children. Not only did the designers of the High School and Beyond survey attempt to ascertain the language contexts to which the student was exposed; they also attempted to ascertain in which contexts the minority language student used the minority language. Six such contexts were defined: in conversation directed to the father, in conversation directed to the mother, in conversation with the student's best friends, in conversation with other students, in the stores in which the students most often shopped, and in the workplace. Once again, the question sollicited responses concerning the frequency of use. Since the responses are identical to those presented in the preceding section of this chapter, they have been coded in precisely the same manner. The score four (4) indicates the nearly exclusive use of the minority language, that of zero (0) the exclusive use of English. The relevant data for the children of the two sampled groups are presented in Table 5.12.

Examining first of all the findings for the children of the Spanish language group, the highest index value is obtained for the frequency with which the child addresses his or her mother in the minority language (Spanish). This

Table 5.12 *Adolescent language use by language group, United States, 1980*

	Language group	
Language use area	Spanish	Residual
To mother	1.95	1.10
To father	1.71	0.98
To friends	1.19	0.51
To students	1.13	0.53
At work	0.94	0.35
In stores	0.85	0.29

Source: High School and Beyond

figure, 1.95, indicates that the child addresses his mother in Spanish approximately (just slightly less) one-half of the time. When we compare this figure to that presented in Table 5.10, we note that the mother is more likely to address the child in Spanish than the child to respond in that language. The difference is 0.26 points on our four point scale (2.21 - 1.95 = 0.26). Similarly, the father is more likely to address conversation to the child in Spanish than is the child to respond, the observed gap being approximately the same (2.00 - 1.71 = 0.29). Thus, it is quite clear from these data that the child is more frequently addressed by both parents in Spanish, while the child responds more frequently in English. In fact, the mean values of the relevant indices indicate that the child uses Spanish somewhat less than one-half the time in his conversation with his parents, even though his parents use Spanish more than half of the time in their conversations with him.

When we examine the data reported in Table 5.12 for the children of the Residual language group, we observe a similar phenomenon. The extent of the gap in language behavior is approximately the same as that observed in the Spanish language group. The extent to which the mother is more likely to use the minority language than the child in their mutual conversation is measured at 0.28 (1.38 - 1.10 = 0.28); in the case of the father, the gap is 0.24 (1.22 - 0.98 = 0.24). This pattern of asymmetric responses is consequently characteristic of minority language households. Children tend to prefer the English language still more than do their parents, these latter having themselves undergone extensive language shift to English (given the assumption that the parents themselves had a minority language for their mother tongue).

Once, however, we leave the family context, the minority language is still less frequently used, markedly so in fact. Among the children of the

Spanish language group, for example, the average student speaks Spanish to his best friends and to other students just slightly more often than 'sometimes;' at work and in his favorite stores, slightly less than 'sometimes.' The figures are still lower among the children of the Residual language group, the index values tending toward zero, indicating that the language is rarely if ever used outside the home.

When we control for the effects of the mother tongue of the Spanish and Residual children, only slight nuances are required to complete this generalization. The relevant data are presented in Table 5.13.

Table 5.13 *Adolescent language use by language group and mother tongue, United States, 1980*

	Language group	
Language use area	Spanish	Residual
English mother tongue:		
To mother	1.10	0.65
To father	0.90	0.58
To friends	0.81	0.35
To students	0.85	0.49
At work	0.60	0.26
In stores	0.50	0.22
Non-English mother tongue:		
To mother	2.92	2.28
To father	2.67	2.11
To friends	1.63	0.89
To students	1.45	0.65
At work	1.42	0.62
In stores	1.25	0.48

Source: High School and Beyond

Considering first of all the findings for the children of English mother tongue, we find that both the Spanish and Residual language children use the minority language but rarely. The fact that the Spanish language children use it slightly more frequently would not appear to have important consequences. For example, the mean score for the use of Spanish in conversation with one's mother is only 1.10. This value indicates that the child barely speaks the language more often than 'sometimes.' In all other cases, the child uses Spanish less frequently than 'sometimes,' a finding which is still more true of the

Residual children. Not only is the minority language of little consequence in the home setting; it is used still less frequently outside the home. We can safely conclude that children of English mother tongue rarely use a minority language in any setting.

When we examine the findings for the children of minority mother tongue, we discover a sharp distinction between use of the minority language in the home setting and use outside that setting, a distinction already presaged by our discussion of the relationship between usual household language and the usual language spoken by children of minority mother tongue. We find, for example, that Spanish language children have an index of 2.92 points for the use of Spanish in conversation with their mothers, a score which approximates the value indicating that the language is 'mostly' used for these interactions ('mostly' = 3.0). This figure is, to be sure, lower than that which measures the frequency with which the mother addresses the child in Spanish (3.17 - 2.92 = 0.25). Nonetheless, the figure remains quite high. The child also directs more than half of the conversations with his father in the Spanish language, although once again the father uses more Spanish than the child.

Nonetheless, once one leaves the family environment, the highest index score for frequency of use is 1.63 points, that obtained for the use of Spanish in conversation with the student's best friends. This is more than one point lower (on our four point scale) than the score indicating the frequency with which Spanish is spoken by the student to his father. The score itself suggests that the student speaks Spanish to his best friends considerably less than one-half the time. He speaks the language still less to other students, still less in the workplace, and still less in his favorite stores. For these latter three areas of interaction, the indices indicate that the proportion of use tends more toward 'sometimes' than toward 'about half the time.' Thus, there is markedly less use of Spanish even among close friends than that found in the family, and still less in the more formal settings of employment and commercial activity.

The same patterns are evident among the HSB students of Residual mother tongue, except of course that all of the frequency of use indices are lower than those observed in the comparable Spanish group. The minority language is used by the student in slightly more than one-half of the conversation directed to either his father or mother, although once again the parents use the minority language still more frequently in their conversations with the child. Whereas the frequency of use gap was approximately 0.25 points in the case of the Spanish language group, it is higher in the Residual language group. The index score which measures father-to-child use is 0.33 points higher than that which measures child-to-father use (2.44 - 2.11 = 0.33); a similar comparison for mother and child yields a gap of 0.44 points (2.72 - 2.28 = 0.44). In short, when the child of Residual mother tongue is addressed by his parents in the minority language, he is still more likely than the Spanish child to respond to his parents in English.

Outside the home, the use of the minority language is exceedingly rare for the children of Residual mother tongue. The same pattern of decreasing usage as one moves from informal to more formal settings is observed. Nonetheless, in all four settings the average child of minority (non-Spanish) mother tongue uses that language less frequently than 'sometimes.'

The examination of the HSB data has permitted us to refine considerably the analysis of the process of anglicisation by specifying the language environment and language use patterns of minority language children. If, however, we were to predict the future of minority language groups based on the data presented in Tables 5.1 to 5.13, the picture would be quite bleak indeed for those who would defend the retention of minority languages in the United States. Furthermore, the data from this second nation-wide study carried out by the U.S. Government confirm once again the extensiveness of the anglicisation of the Spanish language group. Not only were 55.9 percent of these children of English mother tongue; 75.2 percent of the remainder had made English their principal language of use. It is quite clear that the home setting is the only one in which the minority language is effectively spoken. Even in the home setting itself, children use the minority language considerably less than do their parents in conversation with one another or in conversation with the children. Children of English mother tongue use minority languages relatively little, even in conversations with their parents. Children of minority mother tongue also have index scores which indicate very low levels of minority language use outside the home setting.

These data may also be used to support the hypothesis that still higher levels of anglicisation will be attained as the children of minority mother tongue leave the parental home. There is no other context in which children of minority mother tongue speak the minority language as much as half the time. As they leave the parental home, their verbal skills in the minority language should deteriorate as they use that language with decreasing frequency. The peer group does not provide sufficient linguistic support to maintain minority language skills at a high level. If, for example, we were to use the index value of the variable which measures the frequency of minority language use in conversation directed to best friends as an indicator of the maximum possible skill level in the future, then we must compare at the very minimum this indicator with an indicator which measures parental language use. If we measure parental language use by the index value of the frequency with which they address one another in the minority language, then we can compare the two indices. Joint parental language use may then be taken as representing a more or less equivalent measure of peer usage in the parental generation.

This comparison shows that the frequency of use index has dropped by 1.68 points (3.30 - 1.63 = 1.67) for the children of Spanish mother tongue. It has dropped by 1.93 points for the children of Residual mother tongue (2.82 - 0.89 = 1.93). Furthermore, this is a minimalist approach to the measure of language shift. Current parental usage is likely to underestimate the extent to which parents spoke the minority language in the past, since it is likely that many parents either were monolingual in their mother tongue and have undergone some anglicisation themselves. In addition, some of the parents are not included in this comparison because they gave English to their children as mother tongue, a function no doubt of their own anglicisation. And finally, these children have not as yet left the parental home, when they will be still less constrained to speak the minority language. Consequently, a true intergenerational comparison must wait until they have completed their language shift experience, that is, when they have attained the same age as their parents. In spite of these important reservations regarding the parent-child comparison, these data indicate a very sharp drop in the use of the minority language as a principal personal language among parents and children of minority mother tongue. And since neither the children of Spanish mother tongue nor those of other mother tongues use the minority language as much as half of the time with their peers, it would seem indeed unlikely that many of these children would establish minority language homes in the future.

Determinants of the ability to speak the minority language. Having explored a variety of language use and context indices, we are now prepared to focus our analysis on the correlates of the decline in minority language skills observed among the HSB students. The variable which we shall examine in greater detail is that which indicates the reported ability to speak the minority language, irrespective of whether or not that language is frequently used. One of the more traditional ways of measuring the impact of a series of variables which is not measured at the interval level is to treat such a variable as a binary or dummy variable. The appropriate transformation consists in giving the variable one of two possible values, the value one (1) if certain conditions are met, the value zero (0) if they are not. In the case of the variable indicating spoken competence in the minority language, we have assigned the value one (1) to the inability to speak the language, the value zero (0) to an ability to do so. Consequently, the closer to which the mean value of the dependent variable approximates the value one (1), the higher the proportion of children who declared themselves unable to speak the minority language. In short, the rate of anglicisation (as we shall define it) is higher.

That which now needs to be determined is the point at which we shall divide our minority language children into those who can and those who cannot speak the minority language. Our previous analysis suggests an unambiguous answer: we should consider only those children who said that they did not speak it 'at all' as the appropriate group of children to whom the value one (1) should be assigned. These children are, after all, the only ones who are completely anglicized, if indeed they ever spoke the minority language. There is, however, an important empirical obstacle to adopting such a clear-cut strategy. We have already determined in Table 5.5 that only 1.1 percent of the children of Spanish mother tongue declared that they did not speak Spanish 'at all.' Consequently, were we to draw the dividing line between ability to speak and inability to speak at this level of competence, we should find knowledge of the Spanish language nearly universal. We would then have nothing left to study, at least for children of Spanish mother tongue. At the risk of being accused of having drawn our line elsewhere in order to find more anglicisation than actually exists, we are obliged to adopt a somewhat less stringent criterion. Since, however, our objective is no longer to demonstrate the extent of anglicisation but rather to determine its correlates, this accusation has little relevance.

In order to examine more carefully the grounds upon which a less stringent definition of the inability to speak the minority language could be safely adopted, we should remember that the actual use of the minority language outside the home context is extremely limited. We have, in fact, every reason to believe that children who report, for example, that they do not speak the minority language 'very well' do not in fact use it with much frequency. Our objective, then, is to determine whether we can combine those children who said that they did 'not (speak the minority language) very well' with those who said that they did not speak it 'at all' in order to form a relatively homogeneous group of children who may be defined as having poor minority language skills. At the very least the word 'poor' may be defined in terms of extremely infrequent usage. We present in Table 5.14 data relevant to such an assessment.

Table 5.14 *Language use indices by declared competence in the minority language, by language group, United States, 1980*

Spoken competence	Frequency of use indices					
	To Mother	To Father	To Friends	To Students	At Work	In Stores
Spanish:						
High	3.25	3.02	1.98	1.77	1.75	1.49
Medium	2.06	1.82	1.23	1.22	1.01	0.84
Low	0.82	0.63	0.49	0.55	0.33	0.27
None	0.09	0.07	0.10	0.08	0.06	0.06
Residual:						
High	2.91	2.71	1.46	1.11	1.01	0.87
Medium	1.50	1.33	0.70	0.76	0.53	0.38
Low	0.58	0.47	0.26	0.28	0.14	0.10
None	0.06	0.07	0.03	0.03	0.01	0.02

Note: High = speaks 'very well'; Medium = 'pretty well'; Low = 'not very well'; None = 'not at all'

Source: High School and Beyond

An examination of Table 5.14 confirms in large measure this premise. When we examine the language use patterns of children in the Spanish language group who said that they did not speak the language very well ('not very well'), we find that the mean scores are everywhere inferior to the 1.0 score, the score which would indicate that the language is not spoken very often. On the other hand, those children who reported that they spoke Spanish 'pretty well' reported that they used the language somewhat more frequently than 'not very often', even though the usage of the language is clearly affected by the context being evaluated. Consequently, there is some evidence that a line could be drawn to separate children who speak Spanish 'pretty well' from those who report the inability to do so. Clearly, those who said that they did not speak the language 'pretty well' do not use it very often. How infrequently must a language be spoken in order to be classified as being used 'not very often'?

As might have been expected, mean usage levels at any given declared level of spoken competence are still lower for the children of the Residual language group. Even those children who speak the language 'very well' use it less frequently than do comparable children in the Spanish language group. As a result, those children who claimed to speak the minority language 'pretty well' have usage scores which in absolute terms are very low, particularly outside the home context. Nonetheless, there remains an imporant gap between the usage scores of such children and those who said they did not speak the minority language very well, a gap which empirically sustains our decision to group together those children who said they did 'not (speak the minority language) very well' and those who said they did not speak it 'at all.'

Substantively, the fact that at any given level of declared competence the Spanish language children have higher declared levels of use should not be ignored. At any given level of facility, the Spanish language children employ the language more frequently than do the children of the Residual language group. Since the actual use of a minority language is in fact related to its survival prospects, the Residual languages are in fact closer to extinction than the percentage of children declaring a relative inability to speak the language would seem to indicate. Since those who can speak the minority language do so with less frequency, the actual situation of the Residual languages is worse than the percentages of children combined into our category of 'inability' may indicate.

Since the data have indicated all along the importance of the mother tongue of the child for language retention and shift, we should be remiss did we not decompose Table 5.14 by mother tongue. The relevant language use indices for children of English mother tongue are presented in Table 5.15. While the data presented in this table continue to demonstrate the higher use levels of minority languages by children in the Spanish language group, they also reveal that children who speak the language 'pretty well' (defined as 'medium' in the table) use the language very infrequently. For example, the children in the Spanish language group use Spanish slightly more frequently than 'sometimes' in conversation with their parents, the language use means not beginning to approach the figure which would indicate that the language was used even one-half of the time. The Spanish language is used outside of the home even less, particularly in the more formal settings of work and shopping. Needless to say, the use of minority languages by children of English mother tongue who reported low levels of competence is extremely limited, all mean scores falling well below the 1.0 level which would indicate infrequent use of the language.

A similar set of data for the children of minority mother tongues is presented in Table 5.16. A rapid comparison of Tables 5.15 and 5.16 reveals that at any given of declared competence, the children of minority mother tongues use minority languages with greater frequency than do the children

Table 5.15 *Language use indices by declared competence in the minority language, by language group, children of English mother tongue, United States, 1980*

Spoken competence	Frequency of use indices					
	To Mother	To Father	To Friends	To Students	At Work	In Stores
Spanish:						
High	2.71	2.35	2.17	2.13	2.07	1.89
Medium	1.29	1.09	0.94	1.04	0.69	0.50
Low	0.64	0.51	0.42	0.48	0.29	0.19
None	0.05	0.02	0.06	0.03	0.02	0.00
Residual:						
High	2.33	2.04	1.76	1.71	1.65	1.49
Medium	1.10	0.95	0.68	0.83	0.43	0.34
Low	0.48	0.39	0.23	0.28	0.10	0.06
None	0.05	0.07	0.03	0.03	0.02	0.03

Note: See Table 14 for definitions

Source: High School and Beyond

of English mother tongue. As a matter of fact, the children of minority mother tongues who reported low levels of competence also said that they used these languages more than did children of English mother tongue who declared medium levels of competence. For example, children of Spanish mother tongue declaring low competence in Spanish had a mean language use index of 1.61 for conversations directed to their mothers, while their peers of English mother tongue and medium competence in Spanish had an index of only 1.29. Thus, it is quite evident that the mother tongue of the child is related to self-evaluations of minority language competence and use. Children of English mother tongue tend to perceive that their competence is higher than would seem to be indicated by their actual use of the language. Those of minority mother tongue appear to compare themselves to native speakers of the language and perceive their competence levels as relatively low. The two groups of children appear to be relating to different reference groups to establish their perceived competence in the minority language.

Since, however, the meaning of 'low' competence is not the same for the two groups of children, we cannot easily conduct an analysis of the correlates

Table 5.16 *Language use indices by declared competence in the minority language, by language group, children of minority mother tongue, United States, 1980*

Spoken competence	Frequency of use indices					
	To Mother	To Father	To Friends	To Students	At Work	In Stores
Spanish:						
High	3.45	3.25	1.99	1.69	1.72	1.45
Medium	2.81	2.52	1.53	1.41	1.40	1.22
Low	1.61	1.24	0.77	0.84	0.68	0.62
None	0.54	0.88	0.74	0.68	0.45	0.82
Residual:						
High	3.18	3.02	1.39	0.90	0.80	0.65
Medium	2.30	2.10	0.80	0.68	0.75	0.50
Low	1.09	0.90	0.38	0.34	0.33	0.28
None	0.11	0.09	0.03	0.00	0.00	0.00

Note: See Table 14 for definitions

Source: High School and Beyond

of low competence unless the two groups are segregated. Even in this situation, we must remember that the meaning of 'low' competence differs from one group to another. Low competence for children of minority mother tongue appears to imply greater actual competence than does medium competence for children of English mother tongue. Nonetheless, we shall analyze separately the correlates of the relative inability to speak the minority language for both groups of children, first for those of English mother tongue, subsequently for those of minority mother tongues. When we have completed these analyses, we shall assess the importance of mother tongue in the process of retaining a minimal ability to speak the minority language.

1. *Factors examined for their effects on the inability to speak the minority language.* A number of factors have already been shown to be related to the anglicisation process in the previous chapters. It is not surprising, therefore, that these or similar variables be retained for analysis in connection with the High School and Beyond data. For example, we have retained an index of socioeconomic status which was developed by the HSB researchers at the

National Opinion Research Center, the principal contractor for the NCES research. The socioeconomic status index represents the combined impact of father's occupation, father's education, mother's education, family income, and an index of the family's material possessions. The value of the SES index has been adjusted in this report to have a minimum value of zero (0), a maximum value of one hundred (100), and a mean of fifty (50). As may have been anticipated, we have eliminated from further study respondents for whom the SES score was not calculated due to missing information.

We have also retained for analysis a set of regional variables. Since there were so few cases in certain regions, either for one or the other of the minority language groups, the Census regions have been collapsed into six categories. For example, in the Spanish language sample there were very few children living in the New England, East-South Central or the western Midwest states. The New England region has been added to the Middle Atlantic region, the East-South Central to the West-South Central region, and the western Midwest to the eastern Midwest states. As expected, the South Atlantic, Rocky Mountain and Pacific Coast regions are also represented in our analysis.

We also have retained a set of variables to examine the effects of nativity on the language characteristics of the sampled children. Originally, both parental nativity characteristics and those of the children were entered into the analysis separately. However, it is quite evident that the nativity of the child tends to be determined by the nativity of the parents. In addition, the simultaneous consideration of both factors taken together leads to the estimation of more satisfactory equations than when both factors are considered separately. Consequently, the two sets of nativity characteristics were combined into a single set of nativity variables. Parental nativity was first of all divided into three categories, that where both parents are native born, where one was native born and the other not (mixed ancestry), and where both were foreign born. The children were divided into those who were native born and those who were born outside the United States. When combined into a single set of nativity characteristics, six parent-child nativity combinations are produced for analysis.

A new variable has also been added to the analysis, one which attempts to estimate the importance of the type of education obtained by the child. A rather intricate series of transformations were necessary to develop a global measure of the estimated number of years of education which were completed in a minority language, that is, where the minority language was used as the medium of instruction. The question which served as the basis upon which the measure was constructed was phrased, 'Thinking about *all* the courses you had in each of those grades listed below, how much of the teaching was done in *that language?*' The word *that* refers to a minority language previously identified by the student. The words 'in each of the grades listed below' refer to grades 1 through 6, 7 through 9, and 10 through 12. The pre-coded responses to this question were the following: 'all or almost all of the teaching was done in that language,' 'most was in that language,' 'about half was in that language,' 'some was in that language,' 'none was in that language,' or 'was not in school in the U.S. then.' This latter response was furnished only for the two questions referring to the experience of the respondent in elementary and in junior high school. It was not available for the question referring to senior high school.

The answers to these questions were then assigned a numerical value. 'All or almost all' was assigned the value of 1.00 (that is, 100%), while 'none' was assigned the value of 0.00. Since it seems reasonable to assign the value of 0.50 to the response 'about half was in that language,' it did not seem incompatible to assign the values 0.75 to the response 'most' and 0.25 to the response 'some was in that language.' Children not in the United States during one or more of the earlier periods were assigned the value of 1.00 on the theory that most of them probably obtained their education in a minority language. Once each question had been coded accordingly, a global measure required some evaluation of the relative importance of each of the three questions. The numerical score assigned to the question regarding elementary school experience was multiplied by six. Similarly, the response to the question for grades 7-9 was multiplied by three. Finally, the response to the same question for grades 10-12 was multiplied by two, since the sophomores in the study were just completing their tenth year of school while the seniors were completing their twelfth, that is, the first and third years respectively in this category. The three figures thus weighted were then added together to obtain a total score, the total score representing an estimate of the number of cumulated years of minority language education.

Two language variables were also used in the initial analyses of the data, that referring to mother tongue and early childhood language use and that based on the principal household language. With respect to the former variable, the data analyses consistently showed that the presence or absence of early childhood bilingualism had little effect on the relative inability to speak the minority language at the time of the survey. That is to say, among children of English mother tongue, the presence or absence of early childhood bilingualism in the minority language had little or no effect on current spoken competence in the minority language. The effects consistently failed to attain statistical significance. A similar finding was obtained among the children of minority mother tongue, the presence or absence of second language bilingualism in English having no statistically important effects. Consequently, this distinction was discarded and children are classified only according to their mother tongue.

The initial data analyses also tested the effect of the principal home language on the inability to speak the minority language. The preliminary testing revealed on the one hand that the home language variable ('What language do the people in your home *usually* speak?') was among the most important determinants of current ability to speak the minority language, on the other that this variable is highly correlated with the mother tongue of the children. This latter finding is not unexpected, children being expected to have the dominant home language for their mother tongue. However, under situations of language shift some of this expected behavior is no longer found. To examine more carefully the combined relationship of mother tongue and home language with respect to current minority language competence, we created an interactive set of language variables. This set of interactive variables will be used to examine the importance of mother tongue in the process of language retention, i.e., after we have completed the analysis of the retention process for children in each mother tongue group.

Certain other variables which may have been thought to be important to the retention of oral competence in the minority language were examined for such effects and subsequently eliminated. This was, for example, the case for the language use variables (to father, to mother, to friends, to students, at work, in stores) and for the language context variables (by parents, by mother, by father, by relatives). A variety of indices were also constructed to measure the combined impact of these use and context items. In general, these variables are intrinsically related to the mother tongue and home language variables. Since these latter have consistently stronger effects on the dependent variable (relative ability/inability to speak the minority language), the net effects of the language use and language context variables, whether considered separately or in index form, were marginal. That is to say, they did not attain statistical significance. While this may seem disappointing to some, we should observe that it simplifies the analysis of language shift, since the results obtained from the home language and mother tongue questions seem adequate to the explanation of minority language competence. The information obtained from additional (and more refined) questions does not improve the explanatory power of the analysis.

2. *Characteristics of the minority language samples.* Having described in some detail the set of predictor variables retained for the analysis of the relative inability to speak the minority language, we shall now procede to examine the distribution of these characteristics in the two sampled groups. Since we shall present two sets of analyses, one for the retention of the minority language among the children of English mother tongue and one for its retention among only those children of minority mother tongue, we shall present the distribution of background characteristics in two steps as well. We begin by presenting in Table 5.17 the distribution of the various independent variables for the children of English mother tongue.

Considering first of all the dependent variable in our analysis, Table 5.17 reveals that 50.76 percent of the Spanish children and 67.85 percent of the Residual children of English mother tongue said that they did not have a good working knowledge of the minority language. Since, however, we have already described the extent of this anglicisation in the earlier sections of this chapter, we shall focus our attention on the distribution of the remaining (independent) variables.

The socioeconomic status of the parents of the children of English mother tongue tend to approach the national mean. Nonetheless, the Residual language children come from homes of higher than average socioeconomic standing (3.63 points) while those of the Spanish language group come from homes of lower than average status (3.04 points). Both groups of children live in highly anglicized settings. Some 83.23 percent of the Spanish households and 91.39 percent of the Residual households were characterized by the presence of English as the principal household language. Thus, the presence of the English language and higher socioeconomic status would appear to go hand-in-hand.

The distribution of both anglicisation (the relative inability to speak the minority language) and the presence of an English home language are rendered still more interesting when the nativity patterns of the two sampled groups are considered. Although characterized by more retentive language patterns, the children of the Spanish language group are more likely to come from thoroughly native backgrounds. Fully 76.01 percent of these children were both native born and had two native born parents. An additional 11.20 percent had one native and foreign born parent, while 7.45 percent had two foreign born parents, bringing to 94.66 percent the number of native born children. The percentage of native born children in the Residual language group is not much lower (89.88%), although more of them have either one or two foreign born parents, a feature which should nonetheless be associated

Table 5.17 *Background characteristics of children in the minority language samples, children of English mother tongue, United States, 1980*

Background characteristics	Language group	
	Spanish	Residual
Inability to speak the		
minority language	50.76%	67.85%
Mean socioeconomic status	46.96	53.63
English home language	83.23%	91.39%
Minority language education, years	2.08	1.47
Nativity: Parent/Child		
Native/Native	76.01%	63.72%
Mixed/Native	11.20	16.04
Foreign/Native	7.45	10.22
Native/Foreign	1.48	2.49
Mixed/Foreign	0.86	1.69
Foreign/Foreign	3.00	5.94
Region		
Northeast	13.38%	33.58%
South Atlantic	8.95	8.86
South Central	20.82	10.25
Midwest	15.73	26.96
Rocky Moutains	18.18	3.64
Pacific Coast	22.94	16.71
Ethnic Origin		
Chicano/Mexican	39.32%	
Cuban	1.29	
Puerto Rican	4.70	
Other Hispanic	9.53	
Other/U.S. only	54.84	
Language group		
Chinese		1.54%
Filipino		2.08
French		22.64
German		24.55
Greek		2.85
Italian		16.34
Polish		6.35
Portuguese		1.78
All others		21.85
Sample size	(2,919)	(2,730)

Source: High School and Beyond

with greater retention. As we have previously shown, the anglicisation of parents in the Residual language group being higher, the presence of higher percentages of foreign-born parents need not necessarily be related to higher retention of minority language skills.

As may have been anticipated from our previous chapter, the regional concentrations of the two minority language samples are quite different. The Spanish language group tends to be well represented in all of the regions retained for analysis. This is not, however, the case for the children of the Residual language group which is heavily concentrated in the Northeastern and Midwestern states. A smaller but sizeable concentration is found in the Pacific region.

When we examine the (declared) ethnic ancestry of the Spanish language adolescents, we find that the majority (54.84%) declared either a non-Hispanic or a 'U.S. only' ancestry. Very few teenagers who reported English as mother tongue also reported Cuban or Puerto Rican ancestry, probably because of the recency of immigration in these groups. On the other hand, 39.32 percent of the children of English mother tongue reported a Chicano ancestry, indicating the inroads of the English language in the parental (and earlier) generations. The presence of so many children declaring a 'U.S. only' ancestry suggests, of course, that they are more assimilated to American culture (of which language is one sign) than are those who selected a Spanish origin group.

Among the children of the Residual language group, there is once again a wide diversity of declared linguistic origins. The following groups were retained for analysis, composing the indicated percentages of the sample: Chinese (1.54%), Filipino (2.08%), French (22.64%), German (24.55%), Greek (2.85%), Italian (16.34%), Polish (6.35%), and Portuguese (1.78%). The residual category of 'all other groups' accounts for 21.85 percent of the Residual language sample. This category, it should be remembered, is defined linguistically rather than ethnically and contains all children not defined into the major groups listed.

Given the fact that the Residual language children were more likely to have been born outside the United States, we should expect that these children have had greater exposure to minority language education. Such is not, in fact, the case. Table 5.17 reveals that the Residual language children had obtained an average of only 1.47 years of MLE while the children of Spanish language group had obtained 2.08 years. Given the high proportions of children in both groups born in the United States, these findings suggest that much of this MLE took the form of what has been popularly called 'bilingual eduation.' Furthermore, the findings suggest that the Spanish language children, i.e., those of English mother tongue, received a larger share of the educational effort expended in such programs.

Having completed our examination of the characteristics of the children of English mother tongue, we present a similar set of data for the children of minority mother tongue in Table 5.18. We find first of all from Table 5.18 that the anglicisation rates (as defined) are markedly lower. Only 12.26 percent of the children of Spanish mother tongue and 27.38 percent of those of Residual mother tongue reported that they did not speak the minority language passably well. This is, of course, not surprising unless viewed from the opposite standpoint. That some of these children should report an effective monolingualism in English after having spoken a minority language for their mother tongue may in fact be surprising. This was the case for one in eight children in the Spanish language group and for one in four in the Residual language group, this in a situation where these children were still subjected to parental language constraints.

With respect to socioeconomic achievement, the mean scores are markedly lower than those observed for the parents of children of English mother tongue were included, most notably so for the Spanish language group. Mean SES is nearly fifteen points lower than that observed for the parents of children of Residual mother tongues (47.11 - 32.65 = 14.46). Since the mean SES score for all parents included in the HSB sample is 50.00 points, the unfavorable socioeconomic position of the parents of children of Spanish mother tongue can be clearly underlined.

With respect to the presence of an English home language, Table 5.18 shows that 24.43 percent of the Spanish children lived in English language homes, while 40.69 percent of the Residual children did so. Once again the parents of the Residual language children appear to have made fewer efforts to retain a minority language home environment than have the parents of the children of Spanish mother tongue.

When we examine the nativity patterns of the two groups, the data reveal once again that the Residual language parents and children are more likely to have non-native origins. For example, only 17.88 percent of the children in the Residual language sample were native born to parents of native birth; the comparable figure in the Spanish language group was 34.14 percent. Again, 39.46 percent of the Residual children were born outside the United States to parents of foreign birth; the comparison figure is only 23.76 percent in the Spanish language group. These comparisons are much more conclusive than those obtained when comparing the two groups of children of English mother tongue. The children of Spanish mother tongue are much more likely to be

Table 5.18 *Background characteristics of children in the minority language samples, children of minority mother tongue, United States, 1980*

Background characteristics	Language group	
	Spanish	Residual
Inability to speak the		
minority language	12.26%	27.38%
Socioeconomic status	32.65	47.11
English home language	24.43%	40.69%
Minority language education	2.99	2.92
Nativity: Parent/Child		
Native/Native	34.14%	17.88%
Mixed/Native	9.38	7.88
Foreign/Native	23.73	21.06
Native/Foreign	5.65	8.12
Mixed/Foreign	3.34	5.60
Foreign/Foreign	23.76	39.46
Region		
Northeast	21.46%	35.60%
South Atlantic	11.70	8.12
South Central	25.86	5.15
Midwest	8.24	17.37
Rocky Moutains	9.12	6.26
Pacific Coast	23.62	27.52
Ethnic group		
Chicano	48.09%	
Cuban	10.46	
Puerto Rican	17.83	
Other Hispanic	11.74	
Other/U.S. only	11.88	
Language group		
Chinese		9.49%
Filipino		6.32
French		9.32
German		13.63
Greek		7.09
Italian		8.44
Polish		2.87
Portuguese		3.90
All others		38.95
Sample size	(2,434)	(1,027)

Source: High School and Beyond

of native birth and native origins than are those of Residual mother tongue. Nonetheless, the latter live in more anglicized home settings and are themselves more anglicized.

While there do not appear to be major differences with respect to the number of mean years of minority language education attained by the two groups, there are some interesting changes in the geographic distribution of the two samples. Children of Spanish mother tongue are more likely to be found in the Northeast, the South Atlantic, and the South Central regions than are children of English mother tongue in the Spanish language group. This observation is related to differential regional patterns of anglicisation as already documented from the SIE in earlier chapters. Similarly, the children of Residual mother tongue are less likely to be found in the Midwest and more likely to be found in the Pacific Coast states than were their peers of English mother tongue.

The ethnic and linguistic composition of the two samples is markedly affected by the mother tongue of the children examined. When compared to children of English mother tongue, for example, the proportion of children declaring Chicano ethnic origin rises by 8.77 percent (48.09 − 39.32 = 8.77%), while that of Cuban origin increases by 9.17 percent (10.46 − 1.29 = 9.17%). Similarly, children of Puerto Rican origin increase by 13.13 percent (17.83 − 4.70 = 13.13%) and those of Other Hispanics by slightly more than two percent (11.70 − 9.53 = 2.17%). Needless to say, the percentage of children not declaring a major Spanish origin group declines markedly from 54.84 to 11.88 percent, a fall of 42.96 percent. The relationship between English mother tongue and "U.S. only" ethnic ancestry could not be more clearly illustrated.

Similar changes are observed in the composition of the Residual language group. The German, French (French Canadian/Québécois), Italian and Polish language groups are markedly less important in the sample of children of minority mother tongue than they were in the Residual sample of English mother tongue. On the other hand, all of the smaller, more recently arrived minority language groups are more heavily represented in the minority mother tongue sample, notably the Chinese (+7.95%), the Filipino (+4.24%), the Greek (+4.24%), and Portuguese (+2.12%) language groups. Furthermore, the presence of other unidentified (smaller) language groups is also revealed to be more important in this sample, the share of 'All other groups' rising by 17.10 percent (38.95 − 21.85 = 17.10%). These findings quite obviously correspond to those previously presented, indicating the rapid dissolution of the major language groups which arrived in the United States prior to the Second World

War. They also indicate the increased importance of the new wave of immigration for the Residual language group, although the same data indicate the rapid anglicisation of these groups as well.

3. *The multivariate analysis of the inability to speak the minority language.* We begin our multivariate analysis of the principal determinants of anglicisation (defined as the relative inability to speak the minority language) by examining the relationship between each independent variable (or variable set) and the dependent variable. Each relationship is treated in a single regression equation where anglicisation is the dependent variable. The relevant equations for children of English mother tongue are presented in Table 5.19. Standard errors are indicated in parentheses throughout this analysis.

Our analysis begins with the examination of the relative impact of each variable or variable set on anglicisation, impact being measured by the proportion of the variance explained by such variables. First of all, Table 5.19 shows that no variable or variable set succeeds in explaining a high proportion of the variability in anglicisation. This suggests that anglicisation is not determined to an important extent by any of the factors retained for analysis. In the Spanish language group the most powerful predictive factor is that of minority language education which succeeds in explaining only 3.3 percent of the variance in anglicisation (r-squared = 0.033). This variable is also important in the determination of anglicisation among the children of the Residual language group, the proportion of the variance explained attaining .045. In both cases, the relationship between MLE and anglicisation is negative. As the number of years of MLE increases, the percentage of persons unable to speak the minority language decreases. The effect is stronger in the Residual language group, statistically significant for both groups.

A second factor which seems to have a consistent effect on anglicisation is the principal language spoken in the child's home. When English is the dominant household language, an additional twenty-three percent of the children in both groups (.225 for the Spanish, .232 for the Residual children) declare that they are unable to speak the minority language with some facility. Once again, the effect is relatively indeterminate although statistically significant, the proportion of the variance explained being less than three percent in the Spanish language group, less than two percent in the Residual language group.

The impact of the remaining variables examined in Table 5.19 seem to vary according to the group of children being studied. For example, membership group appears to be relatively important in the Residual language group

Table 5.19 *Regression of selected variables on the inability to speak the minority language, by language group, children of English mother tongue, United States, 1980*

	Language group	
Independent variables	Spanish	Residual
Socioeconomic status	.0010 (.0005)*	−.0017 (.0005)*
Constant	.461	.769
R-squared	.001	.004
English home language	.225 (.024)*	.231 (.003)*
Constant	.320	.467
R-squared	.028	.019
Minority language education	−.028 (.003)*	−.035 (.003)*
Constant	.565	.730
R-squared	.033	.045
Nativity: Parent/Child:		
Mixed/Native	−.141 (.029)*	.002 (.025)
Foreign/Native	−.188 (.035)*	−.107 (.003)*
Native/Foreign	−.005 (.076)	−.066 (.058)
Mixed/Foreign	−.157 (.100)	−.188 (.069)*
Foreign/Foreign	−.147 (.054)*	−.063 (.038)
Constant (Native/Native)	.543	.698
R-squared	.018	.008
Region:		
Northeast	−.009 (.032)	−.023 (.027)
South Atlantic	−.122 (.036)*	−.120 (.037)*
South Central	−.022 (.028)	.007 (.035)
Midwest	−.070 (.030)*	.016 (.028)
Rocky Moutain	.058 (.029)*	.043 (.052)
Constant		
(Pacific Coast)	.525	.694
R-squared	.010	.006
Ethnic group:		
Chicano	−.001 (.020)	
Cuban	−.287 (.082)*	
Puerto Rican	−.237 (.045)*	
Other Hispanic	−.017 (.033)	
Constant		
(Other/U.S. only)	.524	
R-squared	.014	

Continued on next page

Table 5.19 Continued

Independent variables	Language group	
	Spanish	Residual
Language group:		
Chinese		−.017 (.072)
Filipino		−.029 (.063)
French		−.254 (.025)*
German		−.127 (.026)*
Greek		−.097 (.054)
Italian		−.001 (.028)
Polish		.111 (.039)*
Portuguese		−.041 (.067)
Constant		
(All others)		.763
R-squared		.058

* p < .05

Source: High School and Beyond

(r-squared = .058), the French and German groups being somewhat less anglicized than expected, the Polish group more anglicized. On the other hand, membership group appears to be less important in the Spanish language group, the proportion of the variance in the rate of anglicisation explained being only .014. Still, the data show that Cubans and Puerto Ricans are significantly less anglicized than are members of the remaining groups. Similarly, the effects of socioeconomic status, while weak, are not consistent from one group to another. SES is positively related to anglicisation among the Spanish language children, negatively related among the Residual language children.

Turning to the analysis of the impact of the nativity variables on the inability to speak the minority language, the intercept term in the equations estimated indicate that 54.3 percent of the native of native Spanish children were unable to speak the minority language with reasonable facility. This figure is markedly higher than the figure reported by children in most of the other nativity categories. Only foreign born children to two native born parents are anglicized to an equivalent extent, children in most of the remaining categories being significantly less anglicized than children in these two groups. Thus, the data tend to suggest that when both parents are not native born, the presence of the foreign born partner tends to inhibit the anglicisation of the children, this to the extent of decreasing the anglicisation rate by approximately fifteen percent (-.141 to -.188). This effect is not observed with equal consistency in the Residual language group. Rather, only two groups of children have significantly lower anglicisation rates than do the native of native children. Even foreign born children of foreign ancestry have anglicisation rates which do not differ significantly from those of the native born children. As suggested by the proportion of the variance explained (.008), nativity appears to play a lesser role in the anglicisation of the Residual children of English mother tongue.

Finally, the impact of regional variables appears to be more important in the Spanish group as well. The proportion of the variance explained is somewhat higher (although very low at .010), and the data indicate that children in the South Atlantic and Midwest regions are somewhat less anglicized than those in most other regions, while those in the Rocky Mountain region are somewhat more anglicized. Only children living in the South Atlantic region are significantly less anglicized than those living in other regions in the Residual language group.

All of the preceding observations based on Table 5.19 are, of course, derived solely from differences in the mean anglicisation rates observed for each category. Thus, the differences which we have been examining are gross differences rather than those which may persist after other relevant factors have been taken into account. To estimate the net impact of a number of various factors on anglicisation, we have once again calculated a series of multiple regression equations. In the course of our preliminary testing of the variables most affecting the anglicisation process, we discovered rather rapidly that equations using only the language characteristic, nativity, socioeconomic status, and MLE variables were nearly as effective as those which added ethnic or linguistic origin, region, and/or a variety of other factors. By 'nearly as effective', we mean, of course, that the proportion of the variance explained by these four factors was nearly as high as that explained when additional factors were introduced. Consequently, we shall restrain our presentation of the data in the following pages to that of these 'baseline equations.' reserving our comments on ethnic, language, or regional variables to the text itself. That is to say, we shall not formally present the additional data.

We present in Table 5.20 the two baseline equations which serve to explain the inability to speak the minority language in the Spanish and Residual language samples.

Table 5.20 reveals that the proportion of the variance explained by these baseline equations in each language group is approsimately the same (r-squared = .07), a rather disappointingly low figure. As expected, the intercept

Table 5.20 *Baseline regression on the inability to speak the minority language, by language group, children of English mother tongue, United States, 1980*

Baseline variables	Language group	
	Spanish	Residual
Socioeconomic status	−.0001 (.0005)	−.0021 (.0005)*
English home language	.189 (.025)*	.203 (.031)*
Minority language education	−.027 (.003)*	−.034 (.003)*
Nativity: Parent/Child:		
Mixed/Native	−.132 (.029)*	−.009 (.024)
Foreign/Native	−.160 (.035)*	−.082 (.030)*
Native/Foreign	.041 (.074)	−.022 (.056)
Mixed/Foreign	−.132 (.097)	−.163 (.067)*
Foreign/Foreign	−.138 (.054)*	.008 (.037)
Constant	.441	.667
R-squared	.072	.072
Sample size	(2,919)	(2,730)

* p < .05

Source: High School and Beyond

(constant) for the two equations presented in this table shows that the anglicisation rate is generally higher in the Residual language group, that is, for certain equivalent characteristics. These equivalent characteristics are defined by the reference group (omitted category) for nativity and language characteristics and by an estimated score of zero for parental SES and for the number of years of MLE. Accordingly, when both parents and children are native born, when the minority language is the principal household language, and when both SES and MLE are set equal to zero, 66.7 percent of the Residual children and 44.1 percent of the Spanish children are found unable to speak the minority language. It is with respect to the children having these characteristics that the regression coefficients refer.

Examining first of all the net impact of the set of language characteristic variables on anglicisation, we find that an additional 18.9 percent of the children living in English language homes are unable to speak the minority language in the Spanish language group. This figure represents the net impact of this characteristic, that is, net of nativity, socioeconomic status, and MLE factors. A similar figure is obtained for this characteristic among the Residual language children (20.3%). Thus, for children of English mother tongue, the maintainance of a minority language home is associated with a net decrease in anglicisation of approximately twenty percent. Needless to say, both of these estimated coefficients differ significantly from the constant estimated for the equation.

Turning to the examination of the impact of socioeconomic status, Table 5.20 reveals that it plays no independent role in the explanation of anglicisation in the Spanish language group. Its gross effects (from Table 5.19) are better (or more consistently) explained by the remaining variables included in the equation. That is to say, since SES is related to both nativity and language characteristics, its net independent effect is not statistically significant. We cannot, accordingly, conclude that higher or lower socioeconomic status is associated with the inability to speak the minority languge. On the other hand, the data indicate that the negative relationship between SES and anglicisation previously observed among the Residual language children has been strengthened by the introduction of the remaining variables. As we have found in the previous analysis of the SIE data, the data show that the higher the socioeconomic status of the parents, the lower the rate of anglicisation. That is to say, the higher the parental SES score, the greater the percentage of children able to speak the minority language passably well. The observed effect is, however, relatively slight. Each additional point of SES is associated with a net decrease of 0.21 percent (.0021) in the anglicisation rate. Thus, an increase of ten SES points will produce a decrease in the anglicisation rate of only 2.1 percent.

The examination of the coefficients for the different nativity patterns reveals that differences in nativity are relatively unimportant on the whole. Once again, the patterns observed are similar to those observed in Table 5.19. In the Spanish language group, for example, any combination of characteristics such that at least one parent is foreign born produces essentially identical results. These children are significantly less anglicized than are the native born children of native born ancestry. The net rates of anglicisation are approximately thirteen to sixteen percent lower than those observed for the native children of native ancestry. In certain respects the nativity patterns of the Residual children appear to be still less important to the explanation of anglicisation than previously estimated. First of all, three of the estimated coefficients (-.009, -.022, and .008) do not differ significantly from the constant term which is associated with the native born children of native ancestry. The remaining effects are not as strong as those estimated for children in the Spanish language group.

Finally, the data continue to indicate that the number of years of minority language education plays a significant role in the retention of minority language skills. The net effects of additional MLE are only slightly less once the impact of the remaining variables has been taken into account, each additional year of minority language education being associated with a net decline of 2.7 percent in the anglicisation rate of the Spanish language children and a 3.4 percent decline in that of the Residual language children. These findings, which have already eliminated the effects of nativity, mother tongue, home language, and SES, suggest that MLE programs could play a still more significant role in the retention of minority language skills. Obviously, they could not eliminate the anglicisation of these children as such. For example, had a group of children completed all eleven years in the MLE programs, the anglicisation rate of the Spanish children may be estimated at being 24.3 percent lower than that currently obtained (i.e., 9 X 2.7% = 24.3%). Since the average child has already obtained two years of MLE, the 2.7% figure need be increased by only nine years. A 24.3 percent decline would cut the current rate of anglicisation (50.8%) in half. A similar comparison would find a decline in the anglicisation rate of Residual children from 67.9 percent to 37.1 percent (9 X 3.4% = 30.6%). These are indeed important changes in the estimated percentages of children unable to speak minority languages with reasonable facility. Nonetheless, they remain quite high when compared to the expenditure which would be necessary to implement a complete system of minority language education, unless, of course, the presence of such a system would produce qualitative changes in the process of learning and retaining minority languages.

When we added the ethnic origin variables to the equation for the Spanish language children, the proportion of the variance explained rose by only .006 (to .078), indicating the relative unimportance of this factor. The pattern of the regression coefficients indicates that Puerto Rican and Cuban children of English mother tongue are significantly less anglicized than are other children in the remaining Spanish groups. The estimated anglicisation rates, net of other variables controlled in the equation, range from fifteen to twenty percent lower than those estimated for other groups. The addition of the regional variables to the analysis increases the proportion of the variance explained to .090, an increase of 1.2 percent. The pattern of the coefficients indicates that children in the Northeast and Rocky Mountain states are more anglicized than children in other regions, those living in the Midwest and South Central regions being less anglicized than other groups of children. The patterns of the remaining coefficients are but marginally altered by the addition of the ethnic and/or regional variables. While these findings do not conform in all respects to those obtained in our SIE analysis, they generally support the same observations. Children in the region which includes Texas are found to be less anglicized, as are children in the region which includes Florida. Given the previous findings, these results are not surprising.

When the membership group variables are added to the baseline equation for the Residual language children of English mother tongue, the proportion of the variance explained rises from .072 to .129, a rather sizeable increase. While only marginal changes are noted in the regression coefficients for the variables previously examined, the data do indicate rather important intergroup differences in observed net rates of anglicisation, that is, after nativity, language characteristics, SES and MLE have been controlled. Children in the Filipino language group are by far the most anglicized, having an anglicisation rate which exceeds that of the German children, for example, by some twenty-five percent. The rates of anglicisation of the Italian, Polish, and 'all other' groups also exceed by some ten to twenty percent those observed for children in the remaining groups. Only children in the French language group are somewhat less anglicized than expected, the net rate being fifteen to nearly forty percent lower than those observed in other groups of children of English mother tongue. The addition of the regional variables increases the proportion of the variance explained to .136, children living in the South Atlantic region being somewhat less anglicized than other children, those living in the South Central region being somewhat more anglicized than others. On the whole, however, the region of residence does not appear to play an important role in the anglicisation process.

Having examined the process of anglicisation as found among the children of English mother tongue, we shall now procede to an analysis of the anglicisation process among those children of minority mother tongue, that is, those who are most likely to have retained minority language competence. That these children should have lost the ability to speak the minority language with minimal fluency is somewhat more surprising. We begin by presenting the results of the first stage regression equations for the children of the two language groups (Table 5.21).

We begin our analysis of Table 5.21 by observing that most of the independent variables seem to play a more important role in the determination of the inability to speak the minority language. With the exception of the socioeconomic status of the parents, the proportion of the variance explained (as measured by r-squared) by the remaining independent variables is generally higher in these equations than was found for the children of English mother

Table 5.21 *Regression of selected variables on the inability to speak the minority language, by language group, children of minority mother tongue, United States, 1980*

Independent variables	Language group	
	Spanish	Residual
Socioeconomic status	.0013 (.0004)*	.0019 (.0007)*
Constant	.008	.186
R-squared	.005	.007
English home language	.162 (.002)*	.379 (.026)*
Constant (Non-English)	.083	.120
R-squared	.045	.174
Minority language education	-.004 (.002)	-.030 (.004)*
Constant	.135	.361
R-squared	.002	.059
Nativity: Parent/Child:		
Mixed/Native	-.090 (.024)*	-.031 (.058)
Foreign/Native	-.150 (.017)*	-.179 (.043)*
Native/Foreign	-.167 (.029)*	-.215 (.057)*
Mixed/Foreign	-.136 (.037)*	-.001 (.065)
Foreign/Foreign	-.169 (.017)*	-.278 (.038)*
Constant (Native/Native)	.220	.441
R-squared	.050	.066
Region:		
Northeast	-.031 (.020)	-.034 (.035)
South Atlantic	-.072 (.024)*	.014 (.056)
South Central	.010 (.019)	.101 (.067)
Midwest	.022 (.027)	-.025 (.043)
Rocky Mountains	.024 (.026)	.010 (.062)
Constant (Pacific Coast)	.131	.283
R-squared	.008	.005
Ethnic group:		
Chicano	-.063 (.021)*	
Cuban	-.158 (.028)*	
Puerto Rican	-.063 (.025)*	
Other Hispanic	-.084 (.027)*	
Constant (Other/U.S. only)	.190	
R-squared	.014	

Continued on next page

Table 5.21 Continued

Independent variables	Language group	
	Spanish	Residual
Language group:		
Chinese		.002 (.049)
Filipino		.188 (.059)*
French		.079 (.050)
German		.174 (.043)*
Greek		−.135 (.056)*
Italian		−.028 (.052)
Polish		−.066 (.084)
Portuguese		−.171 (.073)*
Constant (Other groups)		.251
R-squared		.045

* $p < .05$

Source: High School and Beyond

tongue. The impact of an English home language is stronger for children in both groups, but particularly so for the children of Residual mother tongue. The impact of parental and child nativity characteristics is also markedly stronger than that observed for the children of English mother tongue, and the role of minority language education in language retention is stronger among children of Spanish mother tongue than that observed previously. These observations suggest that the inability to speak the minority language is more strongly determined by the variables retained for analysis among the children of minority mother tongue than is the case for children of English mother tongue.

As can be readily seen from Table 5.21, the impact of socioeconomic status is extremely weak (r-squared = .005 and .007). While the estimated coefficients are statistically significant, the effects are not strong. A ten point rise in SES is associated with a gross increase of 1.3 percent in the anglicisation rate of the children of Spanish mother tongue, with a 1.9 percent increase for the children of Residual mother tongue.

Turning to the examination of the impact of an English household language on the distribution of minority language skills, Table 5.21 reveals that only 8.3 percent of the Spanish children and 12.0 percent of the Residual language children living in minority language homes declared that they were unable to speak the minority language, i.e., 'not very well' or 'not at all.' However, the presence of an English home language has a markedly different impact in the two groups. The anglicisation rate of the Spanish children rises by 16.2 percent when English is the principal home language; it rises by 37.9% for the children of Residual mother tongue. These findings suggest that the minority language is much more frequently used (as a second language) in the homes of the Spanish children than in those of the Residual children. In the latter group it appears that both parents and children move much more rapidly to the nearly exclusive use of English at home. Such an interpretation seems consistent with the data presented both in the first part of this chapter and with those presented in chapter three.

The nativity coefficients observed in Table 5.21 resemble very strongly those previously presented in Table 5.19 for the children of English mother tongue. In the Spanish language group, for example, any combination of foreign birth either for parent or child is associated with significantly lower rates of anglicisation. These children have anglicisation rates approximately fifteen percent lower than similar native born children of native born parents. A somewhat different situation prevails in the Residual language group, where the data appear to indicate that stronger concentrations of foreign origin are necessary to depress the observed rate of anglicisation.

Table 5.21 continues to demonstrate the role of minority language eduation in the retention of minority language skills. The relationship is extremely weak in the Spanish language group, each additional year of MLE being associated with a 0.4 percent decrease in the percentages of children unable to speak the minority language passably well. Thus, children having ten years of MLE would have an anglicisation rate approximately 4.0 percent lower than those who had none. On the other hand, the impact of MLE is substantially stronger for the children of Residual mother tongue. Each additional year of MLE is associated with a 3.0 percent decline in the anglicisation rate, children with ten years of MLE having an anglicisation rate 30.0 percent lower than those who had none. In addition, the higher r-squared in the equation for the Residual language children indicates the relative importance of this variable for the retention of minority language skills.

As previously suggested, the regional variables do not appear to play an important role in the anglicisation process, the proportion of the variance explained being extremely low. Only one coefficient in the two equations attains statistical significance, Spanish language children in the South Atlantic region being less anglicized than those living in most other regions. This finding is likely explained either by nativity or ethnic origin factors, the Cuban population in this region being of extremely recent origin.

As we have observed for the children of English mother tongue, group membership appears to play but a small role in explaining differences in anglicisation rates in the Spanish language group. While all groups have lower anglicisation rates than do those of 'Other/U.S. only' origins, the proportion of the variance explained is very low (r-squared = .014). The data also show that the Cuban group has an anglicisation rate significantly lower than those of the other major Hispanic groups. It appears, however, that group membership plays a more important role in the Residual language group where the proportion of the variance explained attains .045. The pattern of coefficients suggests that the Filipino and German language groups are more anglicized than other groups, while the children of Greek and Portuguese mother tongues are less anglicized than others. Whether these differences remain after other factors have been controlled remains, of course, to be examined.

To assess the independent (net) effects of the principal variables of interest, we have calculated the appropriate baseline equations. The results are reported in Table 5.22. As expected, the proportion of the variance explained in the equation estimated for the children of Residual mother tongue is markedly higher than that obtained for the children of Spanish mother tongue. This

Table 5.22 *Baseline regression on the inability to speak the minority language, by language group, children of minority mother tongue, United States, 1980*

Baseline variables	Language group	
	Spanish	Residual
Socioeconomic status	.001 (.000)*	.000 (.001)
English home language	.128 (.016)*	.309 (.029)*
Nativity: Parent/Child:		
Mixed/Native	-.115 (.024)*	-.088 (.054)
Foreign/Native	-.139 (.017)*	-.134 (.042)*
Native/Foreign	-.144 (.029)*	-.112 (.054)*
Mixed/Foreign	-.146 (.037)*	-.099 (.066)
Foreign/Foreign	-.141 (.017)*	-.168 (.037)*
Minority language education	-.004 (.002)*	-.017 (.004)*
Constant	.162	.306
R-squared	.085	.209
Sample size	2,434	1,027

* $p < .05$

Source: High School and Beyond

finding is undoubtedly attributable to the much stronger impact of English home language on the inability to speak the minority language among the Residual language children. Children living in English language homes have an anglicisation rate which is 30.9 percent higher than that of those living in Residual language homes, net of nativity, SES and MLE differences. The comparable figure is only 12.8 percent in the Spanish language group. These findings underscore once again the apparently greater importance of mother tongue in determining minority language skills in the Spanish language group, while home language exercises a more important role in the Residual language group.

Table 5.22 also reveals the relative unimportance of socioeconomic factors in the explanation of anglicisation. Each additional point of SES is associated with a net increase of 0.1 percent in the anglicisation rate of the children of Spanish mother tongue. The estimated effect of SES on the anglicisation of the Residual language children is not significant. We may conclude that socioeconomic status does not appear to play any important role in the maintenance (or loss) of minority language skills.

Contrary to our previous analyses, the data presented in Table 5.22 indicate that the impact of nativity is roughly similar in the two language groups. The coefficients estimated in the two equations are more or less of the same size, even though two of the coefficients in the Residual language equation fail to differ significantly from the constant (representing native children of native ancestry). The extremely small sample size would appear to play a major role in this respect. On the whole, however, it appears that the presence of at least one foreign born person, either parent or child, retards the anglicisation rate by approximately ten to fifteen percent in both minority language groups. The effect is somewhat stronger in the Spanish language group, somewhat weaker in the Residual language group.

The final variable to be examined in the baseline equation is minority language education. The net impact of minority language education in the Spanish language group is unchanged from the estimate of its gross impact. Each additional year of MLE is associated with a net decline of 0.4 percent in the anglicisation rate. The net impact of MLE in the Residual language group is somewhat less than its gross impact. Net of other background variables, each year of MLE is associated with a 1.7 percent decrease in the anglicisation rate. This figure remains, nonetheless, markedly stronger than that observed for the children of Spanish mother tongue. In neither case, however, does it appear that a complete system of minority language education (11 years) would be sufficient to eliminate the anglicisation observed. For example, an additional eight years of MLE at a net rate of 1.7 percent less anglicisation would reduce the observed rate by 13.6 percent in the Residual language group. The rate observed in Table 5.18 was 27.4 percent, indicating that even in the presence of a complete system of MLE, some 13.8 percent of the Residual children of minority mother tongue would be unable to speak the minority language with some facility. A similar procedure leads to an estimated 9.1 percent of the children of Spanish mother tongue who would be unable to speak Spanish with minimal fluency.

When the ethnic origin variables are added to the Spanish language equation, the proportion of the variance explained rises by .007 to .092. The coefficients indicate that the Chicano, Cuban, and 'Other Hispanic' children have anglicisation rates approximately five to seven percent lower than do children in the Puerto Rican and 'Other/U.S. only' groups, that is, after the other variables have been taken into account. When the regional variables are added to the equation, none attain statistical significance, indicating that regional differences in gross anglicisation rates are adequately explained by other compositional differences.

Adding the membership group variables to the Residual language equation improves the proportion of the variance explained by .030 (to .239). The pattern of the coefficients tends to confirm the findings obtained from Table 5.21, the Filipino language group having an anglicisation rate approximately twenty percent higher than most other language groups. The Greek and Portuguese children have a net anglicisation rate some ten to fifteen percent lower than those of children in most other groups. All other groups have anglicisation rates similar to those of children in the large 'Other' group. Once again, regional factors do not play a significant role in differential anglicisation.

On the whole, then, the multivariate analysis of the inability to speak the minority language leads us to relatively similar conclusions to those derived from the SIE. A relatively small number of largely demographic variables seems adequate to predict the rate of the relative inability to speak the minority language, at least to the extent to which such anglicisation appears structured rather than random. However, the proportion of the variance explained in the baseline equations estimated thus far seems to indicate that the anglicisation process is largely indeterminate. Such is not in fact the case. Rather, the choice to isolate mother tongue groupings does not permit us to examine the relative importance of mother tongue itself. Since the mother tongue of the child structures to an important extent the knowledge and use of the minority language, the impact of this factor needs to be directly examined.

Furthermore, the effect of mother tongue on anglicisation interacts with the effect of home language, such that the net impact of the home language variable may have been underestimated in the previous baseline equations.

To remedy this problem we have estimated two new baseline equations for the entire sample of minority language children. Since, however, the data presented in Tables 5.15 and 5.16 suggest that children of English mother tongue who declared that they spoke the minority language 'pretty well' had lower use levels than children of minority mother tongue who declared that they spoke the language 'not very well,' we have grouped these English mother tongue children into the category of children unable to speak the minority language fairly well. To a certain extent, then, the dependent variable in Table 5.23 represents a declaration of the extent of use of the minority language rather than a simple declaration of competence. It is, at the very least, redefined.

We begin our analysis of Table 5.23 by observing the high proportion of the variance in anglicisation explained by the two equations. The baseline

Table 5.23 *Baseline regression on the inability to speak the minority language, by language group, United States, 1980*

Baseline variables	Language group	
	Spanish	Residual
Mother tongue/home language (a):		
English/English	.102 (.016)*	.085 (.020)*
Non-English/English	-.497 (.019)*	-.331 (.024)*
Non-English/Non-English	-.616 (.017)*	-.658 (.023)*
Socioeconomic status	.0011 (.0002)*	.0001 (.0003)
Nativity: Parent/Child: (a):		
Mixed/Native	-.074 (.015)*	-.018 (.014)
Foreign/Native	-.153 (.013)*	-.048 (.015)*
Native/Foreign	-.122 (.024)*	-.067 (.025)*
Mixed/Foreign	-.156 (.031)*	-.050 (.030)
Foreign/Foreign	-.134 (.015)*	-.088 (.016)*
Minority language education	-.013 (.013)*	-.016 (.002)*
Constant	.798	.892
R-squared	.611	.550

(a) reference characteristics: Non-English/English and Native/Native
* $p < .05$

Source: High School and Beyond

equation succeeds in explaining 61.1 percent of the variability in anglicisation in the Spanish language group and 55.0 percent of that in the Residual language group. Furthermore, the analysis of the first step equations reveals that the single most important variable set is by far that of the mother tongue and home language characteristics of the child. When we examine the pattern of the language coefficients, the data reveal that 10.2 percent more of the Spanish language children of English mother tongue who lived in English language homes were anglicized when compared to similar children living in Spanish language homes. Similarly, 11.9 percent more of the children of Spanish mother tongue living in English language homes were anglicized when compared to those living in Spanish language homes ((-.616) - (-.497) = .119). Thus, the net impact of living in an English language home can be estimated at causing an increase of slightly more than ten percent in the anglicisation rate. The figure is approximately the same for children of English mother tongue in the Residual language group (8.5%), substantially higher for those of minority mother tongue ((-.658) - (-.331) = .327 or 32.7%).

The impact of mother tongue *per se* appears to be much stronger than that of home language, particularly in the Spanish language group. For example, the children of Spanish mother tongue and English home language have an anglicisation rate which is nearly fifty percent lower (.497) than those of the children having the reverse pattern. The figure is 33.1 percent in the Residual language group, indicating the exceptional importance of mother tongue in the determination of minority language competence in both groups.

Table 5.23 also reveals that the nativity variables continue to play a statistically significant role in the anglicisation process. In the Spanish language group, for example, the presence of a single person of foreign birth tends to appreciably reduce the anglicisation observed (from a minimum of 7.4 percent to a maximum of 15.6 percent). The effects are weaker in the Residual language group, the coefficients observed indicating that the presence of one or more foreign born persons does not reduce the anglicisation rate to the same extent as that observed among the Spanish language children.

The findings in Table 5.23 also indicate that minority language education continues to play a role in the retention of minority language skills. The effect is, nonetheless, relatively weak. Each additional year of MLE is associated with a net decline of 1.3 percent in the anglicisation rate of the Spanish language children, with a decline of 1.6 percent in that of the Residual language children. The data also indicate a weak relationship between SES and anglicisation in the Spanish language group, although no relationship is found in the Residual language group. Finally, although the data are not presented in

Table 5.23, subsequent equations reveal that regional factors have little or no importance, while children in the Cuban, Other Hispanic, and Greek groups have lower rates of anglicisation than their respective peers, only Filipino children having higher than expected anglicisation rates than their backgrounds would lead us to expect.

These findings suggest that mother tongue, home language, and nativity characteristics play important roles in the determination of the inability to speak the minority language, Furthermore, it seems plausible to postulate that the American environment as a whole, particularly the need of immigrants to communicate with neighbors and associates and to participate in American institutions is itself adequate to ensure linguistic mobility to the English language. Some children living in the most retentive settings cease to have a working knowledge of the minority language. For example with no MLE and a value of fifty (50) for parental SES, native born children of foreign parentage who have both minority mother tongue and home language have an estimated anglicisation rate of 8.4 percent in the Spanish language group. A similar comparison yields an estimated anglicisation rate of 19.1 percent for the children of the Residual language group, indicating the power of the American environment to stimulate language shift. Once again, we cannot segregate the extent to which such immigrants feel pressured to conform to the English language norm. The demographic variables of nativity and language characteristics serve merely to indicate the strength of the minority language in the home setting, which is in turn reflected in the ability of children to speak that language. As always, there appears to be willingness on the part of immigrants to use the English language, and there appears to be still greater willingness on the part of their children to do so, even in the home setting.

4. *The contribution of minority language education to the retention of minority language skills.* While language and nativity variables are clearly the salient variables in the explanation of language shift, the preceding analysis has revealed that minority language education consistently affects the ability to speak the minority language. In all of the equations estimated, this variable was negatively associated with anglicisation, even after other important factors were controlled. In this section we shall examine still more closely the contribution of this factor to the maintenance of minority language skills. In particular, we should like to ascertain the relationship between such language maintenance and the existence of bilingual education programs in the United

States. This seems to be one area in which there is a great deal of controversy and where public policy initiatives could be developed.

In order to examine this question, we must restrict our analysis only to those children who are native born. Some of the foreign born children probably attended school for a number of years in their country of birth, after which a certain percentage probably participated in some form of bilingual education programs in the United States. Since it is impossible to segregate these two components of minority language education, we are obliged to consider the relationship between this factor and language maintenance only for the native born children. We have previously suggested that the MLE scores for such children are likely to represent the cumulative number of years to which children were exposed to a minority language as the medium of instruction. Since we are once again interested only in the net effects of bilingual education, we shall control for the remaining baseline variables. The definition of the inability to speak the minority language is the same for both groups of children, i.e., only those children reporting no knowledge or poor knowledge of the minority language are considered anglicized. The appropriate equations for the two groups of Spanish language children are presented in Table 5.24.

As one may have expected from our previous analyses, there are marked compositional differences between the children of English mother tongue and those of Spanish mother tongue. Over eighty percent (80.29%) of the former were born to native born parents, while just over one-half of the latter (50.78%) had two parents born in the United States. The children of English mother tongue come overwhelmingly from English language households, whereas only 29.18 percent of the children of Spanish mother tongue lived in English language homes. The children of English mother tongue come from higher status families, mean SES being just over fourteen points higher than that of the children of Spanish mother tongue. Those of Spanish mother tongue have had greater exposure to MLE programs. Given the distribution of background characteristics, it is not surprising that 51.18 percent of the English language children reported that they did not speak the minority language. This figure compares to that of 15.51 percent for the children of Spanish mother tongue.

In spite of these major compositional differences, the coefficients obtained in the two regression equations are strikingly similar. Evidently there are important differences in the intercept term, an additional 29.5 percent of the children of English mother tongue being unable to speak the minority language when compared with children of Spanish mother tongue having equivalent

Table 5.24 *Baseline regressions on the inability to speak the minority language, by mother tongue, Spanish language children of native birth, United States, 1980*

	Mother tongue			
	English		Spanish	
Baseline variables	Value	Regression coefficient	Value	Regression Coefficient
Inability to speak the minority language	51.18%		15.52%	
English home language	82.93%	.194 (.026)*	29.18%	.154 (.020)*
Socioeconomic status	46.42	.000 (.001)	32.24	.001 (.001)*
Nativity: Parent/Child (a)				
Mixed ancestry	11.84%	-.131 (.029)*	13.94%	-.122 (.026)*
Foreign ancestry	7.87%	-.158 (.035)*	35.28%	-.138 (.020)*
Bilingual education	2.02	-.027 (.003)*	2.55	-.005 (.003)
Constant		.438		.143
R-squared		.070		.086
Sample size		(2,763)		(1,637)

(a) reference characteristic: Native/Native
Source: High School and Beyond

(English mother tongue) in the anglicisation rate. The effects of SES are very limited in both equations, while the presence of one or more foreign born parents suppresses the anglicisation rate by twelve (-.122) to sixteen percent (-.158).

The single factor which differs most significantly in the two equations is the minority language education variable. Each additional year of bilingual education is associated with a net decline of 2.7 percent in the anglicisation rate of the children of English mother tongue; it is only associated with a net decline of 0.5 percent in that of the children of Spanish mother tongue. While this latter coefficient fails to attain statistical significance, it does in equations estimated using ethnic and/or regional variables. Thus, bilingual education appears to make a greater contribution to the maintenance of minority language skills among the children of English mother tongue, children who are nonetheless much more highly anglicized than are those of Spanish mother tongue. Apparently these latter are adequately protected by their natural linguistic environment, at least to the extent that bilingual education programs do not reduce in any appreciable way the percentage of children unable to speak the minority language.

A similar set of equations is presented for the children of the Residual language group in Table 5.25.

Table 5.25 *Baseline regressions on the inability to speak the minority language, by mother tongue, Residual language children of native birth, United States, 1980*

	\multicolumn{4}{c}{Mother tongue}			
	English			Minority		
Baseline variables	Value	Regression coefficient		Value	Regression coefficient	
Inability to speak the minority language	68.58%			35.53%		
English home language	91.39%	.181	(.033)*	48.14%	.339	(.044)*
Socioeconomic status	53.06	−.002	(.001)*	46.12	.000	(.001)
Nativity: Parent/Child (a)						
Mixed ancestry	17.84%	−.009	(.024)*	16.82%	−.093	(.061)*
Foreign ancestry	11.37%	−.086	(.029)*	44.98%	−.125	(.049)*
Bilingual education	1.34	−.034	(.003)*	1.92	−.013	(.007)*
Constant		.690			.245	
R-squared		.066			.175	
Sample size		(2,453)			(481)	

(a) reference characteristics: Native/Native
Source: High School and Beyond

The compositional differences between the two groups of Residual language children conform to those already observed for the Spanish language children, except of course that the level of anglicisation is higher. There are, however, some differences in the pattern of the regression coefficients which indicate differences in the process of anglicisation between the two language groups. The findings indicate for example, that the presence of a single foreign born parent does not depress the anglicisation rate of children, although the presence of two foreign born parents does have such an effect. Socioeconomic status has once again a weak effect on the inability to speak the minority language, although there is a negative (and statistically significant) relationship between SES and anglicisation for the children of English mother tongue.

There are, nonetheless, two important differences in the equations estimated for these two groups of children. On the one hand, the impact of an English home language is more strongly associated with anglicisation among the children of Residual mother tongue. This finding appears to be derived from the fact that anglicisation of the children of English mother tongue is nearly universal. The children of native ancestry living in English language homes (SES and MLE set equal to zero) have an anglicisation rate of 87.1 percent (.181 + .690 = .871). It would be logically impossible for the regression coefficient to be as strong as that observed for the children of minority mother tongue because the anglicisation rate would surpass 100 percent.

Secondly, we find once again that bilingual education plays a more important role in language maintenance among the children of English mother tongue. Each additional year of bilingual education is associated with a net decline of 3.4 percent in the anglicisation rate of children of English mother tongue; with a 1.3 percent decline in that of children of Residual mother tongues. In both cases, these values are stronger than those obtained for the children of Spanish language origin.

These findings suggest that bilingual education programs do in fact play a role in reducing the percentage of children who cannot speak the minority language with reasonable facility. That role is, however, particularly important among those groups who are the least able to speak the minority language. The higher the mean rate of inability to speak the minority language, the greater the retentive impact of bilingual education. Viewed from the standpoint of program evaluation, this would not appear to be a very efficient use of resources. It would seem more desirable to intervene at the point where the minority language is clearly a living, frequently-used language to attempt to preserve minimum levels of oral competence than to intervene when the competence levels are already dangerously low. Furthermore, the actual use patterns of the minority language are even lower than are the reported competence levels, suggesting that the purported retentive effects of bilingual education for daily practice are likely exaggerated.

5. *The relative levels of anglicisation among minority language children.* One further topic which may be pursued using the data already presented in this chapter is that of the comparison of Spanish and Residual levels of anglicisation. What level of anglicisation should we expect if the Spanish language group were anglicized in accordance with the process observed among Residual language children? Two such comparisons are presented, one for the children of English mother tongue, a second for the children of minority mother tongue. The relevant data are presented in Table 5.26.

When the mean SES and MLE scores and the percentage distribution of language and nativity characteristics of the Spanish language children are

Table 5.26 *Expected inability of Spanish language children to speak Spanish according to the baseline equation estimated for Residual language children, United States, 1980*

	Mother tongue	
	English	Minority
Expected	.800	.242
Observed	*.508*	*.123*
Observed – Expected	–.292	–.118
Observed / Expected	.635	.510

Source: High School and Beyond

inserted into the baseline equation estimated for the Residual children of English mother tongue, the expected anglicisation rate is estimated at 80.0 percent. The observed rate (Table 5.17) was found to be 50.8 percent, only 63.5 percent of that expected. In other words, when the characteristics of the Spanish children are rewarded according to the equation estimated for the Residual children, the observed anglicisation rate for the Spanish language children is 36.5 percent lower than anticipated.

The second comparison concerns only the children of minority mother tongue. Using the same procedure, we obtained an expected anglicisation rate of 24.2 percent; the actual rate was only 12.3 percent, 51.0 percent of that expected. In short, the observed anglicisation rate was only one-half that predicted, at least if we consider the anglicisation process of the children of Residual mother tongue as normative. To a certain extent these findings are not surprising, since we have already shown that at any given level of declared competence, the Spanish language was actually used more frequently. In addition, we have also shown that anglicisation more generally takes the form of English bilingualism in the Spanish language group. Nonetheless, within the limits of the equations estimated in this chapter, the data do indicate that the Spanish language is more frequently retained than other minority languages, all other things being equal.

We should, however, observe that these comparisons tend to be relatively conservative ones. The data presented earlier in this chapter showed that at any given level of declared minority language competence, the Spanish language children declared that they used the minority language more frequently than did the Residual language children. In terms, then, of their contribution to the maintenance of their language group, the Spanish children are less anglicized than these comparisons would indicate. Even so, the data suggest that they are markedly less anglicized than their characteristics would lead us to expect.

Conclusion. The data contained in the High School and Beyond study permit us to examine more closely the nature of the anglicisation process in the United States, particularly as it effects this relatively crucial age group. The first part of the analysis presented in this chapter confirm the findings already derived from the SIE, namely that the anglicisation of minority language children in the United States is quite extensive and that children are everywhere more anglicized than are their parents.

Subsequent to this general confirmation, we were able to use data from the large number of language questions contained in the HSB study to construct indices of the language environment in which children live and to examine the frequency with which the minority language is used in a variety of contexts. The data analysis revealed that children live in language environments in which the use of English has already occupied an important place. In addition, however, the children themselves are less likely to use the minority language in their home setting than are their parents. Once the child leaves the home setting, the use of the minority language diminishes markedly. In fact, for children of English mother tongue, use of the minority language outside the home is virtually non-existent. For those of minority mother tongue, such use is more frequent. Nonetheless, when we compare the index of minority language use in the peer context to the index of parental language use (with each other), the data indicate a very sharp drop in minority language use from one generation to another. This measured drop does not even represent the full extent of intergenerational loss of minority language use. On the one hand, many of the children were given English rather than minority mother tongues and were not included in this comparison; on the other, the HSB children have not yet left the family household environment which alone sustains minority language skills. Thus, the measured drop in language use is rather less than that which will be attained when the children of minority mother tongue attain the age of their parents, i.e., when a 'true' generation will have been completed.

We should also observe that since the actual use of the minority language is more important in the long run than are reported levels of competence, the measure selected in our multivariate analysis (the inability to speak the minority language passably well) tends to underestimate the extent of anglicisation in both the Spanish and Residual language groups, particularly in the latter. Since even those children who reportedly speak the minority language 'pretty well' or 'very well' tend not to use it very often outside the home context, the definition tends to overestimate actual levels of use. And since the Residual language children use the minority language less frequently than the Spanish children at any given declared level of competence, this observation applies with particular force to the children of the Residual language group.

The multivariate analysis of the inability to speak the minority language revealed once again that parental nativity and language characteristics are the most important variables in predicting the retention or loss of minority language skills. Socioeconomic status does not appear to play a major role in the process of anglicisation, although there is a marked effect of the American environment *per se*. That is to say, children are everywhere more anglicized than their parents, although the extent of this anglicisation is partially structured by the factors retained in the baseline equation. One of the more interesting factors which structures the retention of minority language skills is the number of years of minority language education obtained by the child. It would appear that education in the minority language is associated with the retention of minority language skills. Restricting our analysis to the native born children who may be assumed to have received this education through some form of bilingual education programs, the results continue to confirm this hypothesis. However, we also found that the greater the anglicisation of the group, the greater the impact of bilingual education in preserving minimal competence in the minority language. The impact of bilingual education on the verbal skills of native born children of Spanish mother tongue was virtually nil.

While generally the membership group variables did not seem to play a very important role in determining the relative inability to speak the minority language, the data analysis did reveal some differences in the net rates of anglicisation of various groups. For the children of English mother tongue, the Filipino, Italian, Polish, and All Other groups tended to have the highest rates of anglicisation, while the French children were somewhat less anglicized than expected. In the Spanish group the Puerto Rican and Cuban children were more anglicized than those in other Hispanic groups. Intergroup differences seem less important among the children of minority mother tongues. The children of Filipino origin are more anglicized than most other groups; those of Greek and Portuguese origin are less anglicized than other groups of Residual children. In the Spanish language group the Puerto Rican and 'Other/

U.S. only' children are more anglicized than those in other groups. The differences are not, however, large.

By way of conclusion to this chapter, we should emphasize once again that the definition of anglicisation as used in the multivariate analysis differs from that used in the earlier part of this chapter (and more generally throughout the book). Anglicisation is properly defined by the use of English as the principal language spoken by a person of minority mother tongue. Having observed that this practice was nearly universal among these children, we were obliged to use an alternative definition. We defined anglicisation for our multivariate analysis as the relative inability to speak the minority language passably well. This definition should minimize the reported extent of anglicisation, because it is clearly possible to speak more than one language passably well. In fact, Tienda (1982) has criticized those who use the principal language of use as the salient definition of anglicisation on the grounds that such a choice maximizes the obtained rate of anglicisation. However, when using the minimalist definition which she requires, we find that anglicisation rates are relatively high in both minority language groups, particularly of course among those of English mother tongue. Furthermore, we have already presented a number of arguments, including that of the frequency of reported use in a variety of contexts, which suggest that the minimalist approach causes severe underestimates of the actual extent of language shift. The HSB is sufficiently rich in data to show that whatever the reported levels of competence in the minority language, children of high school age do not use them very frequently. Evidently this is most true for children of English mother tongue; it is also, however, true of children of minority mother tongue once they leave the home environment. The HSB data lead us to suggest that the actual extent of language shift will in fact be much greater than that currently observed, i.e., once these children establish their own households.

Chapter 6

Reflections on the Process of Anglicisation

The data presented in the three preceding chapters illustrate the power of the English language in the United States to subordinate and eradicate the languages of immigrants to that country. It is obviously not the language itself which carries such power but rather the power, the wealth, and the status, and the overwhelming numbers of those who speak that language, dominating as they do virtually every facet of the American economic and political scene.

This shift to the English language, in particular that form of it which we have called anglicisation, is evident in every table which we have presented. No ethnic group, however recently its members have arrived in the United States, has been immune to this process. Over thirty percent of those who claimed Hispanic ancestry in 1976 said that they had no knowledge or no background in the Spanish language. In the more heavily anglicized groups, this anglicisation of the ancestors of adults examined in the 1976 survey leads to the evolution of age pyramids having the shape of an inverted triangle, there being very few children and large numbers of older adults. This is the case, for example, for the French, German, Italian and Polish language groups which were in the not too distant past among the largest in the United States. The SIE data reveal that the numbers of persons who usually spoke these languages in 1976 was extremely limited, as were the numbers who retained their use as frequently spoken second languages.

When we examine the language shift patterns of adults of minority mother tongue, the data reveal that there are some differences in the rates at which people not born in the United States undergo language shift. These differences are partly related to time-of-arrival of specific language groups. The longer one lives in the United States, the more extensive the language shift to English. However, some differences between groups remain, the Chinese, Greek, Portuguese, and Spanish language groups tending to have somewhat lower rates of language shift to English. Nonetheless, on the whole the data reveal extensive and rapid adoption of the English language as the language usually spoken by the foreign born. Even the most recent immigrants in the most retentive language groups undergo such anglicisation. One in every eight immigrants of Spanish mother tongue who arrived in the United States between

January, 1970 and the spring of 1976 already spoke English more frequently than he or she spoke Spanish.

That which most characterizes the linguistic adaptation of the foreign born is the extent to which they retain the use of their mother tongue. Frequently it is only retained as a second language used rather often; in some cases, particularly among the most recent arrivals, the majority continue to retain the use of their mother tongue as their principal language. Generally speaking, however, the percentages of persons who abandon the use of their mother tongue as a daily language remain relatively low. Once again, the percentages increase as a function of length of residence in the United States.

If the anglicisation of the foreign born can be characterized as extensive and rapid, the process can only be classfied as 'epidemic' among the native born. The differences in rates of anglicisation between language groups which were observed among the foreign born virtually disappear. The anglicisation rates tend to oscillate around the ninety percent mark, and the English monolingual form of anglicisation tends to predominate over the English bilingual form. In short, the native born generation to all intents and purposes abandons the minority language. This holds true for the majority of persons in all language groups in all regions of the country. The two exceptions to this rule are the Spanish language group in certain specific regions and the Navajo language group.

In addition, the analysis indicates that the rates of anglicisation have been increasing over the past several decades. Each younger cohort is more anglicized than its predecessor. This is equally true of the French, Spanish, and Navajo language groups. It has also been found to be true of French language minorities in Canada, suggesting that North American society as a whole has been changing in ways that increasingly disfavor the retention of minority languages. For example, the lower rates of anglicisation of the native born in the Spanish and French groups may be largely explained by the agricultural character of their principal areas of settlement. However, the centralization and bureaucratization of the North American economy has severely undermined the viability of the family farm, which in most cases barely provided for a subsistence standard of living. Members of minority language groups are increasingly obliged to find employment opportunities in sectors of the economy where the language of work is English. Even when such opportunities do not entail out-migration, the risks of anglicisation are much greater than they were in the agricultural sector of the economy. Consequently, both those who migrate to urban areas and those who remain in the traditional areas of settlement are increasingly anglicized. The increasing penetration of national institutions, the mass media, fast-foods outlets, compulsory education, etc., also operate in the same direction, disrupting the traditional social patterns of minority language groups.

Thus, the analysis of the data indicates support for a two generation model of anglicisation for all groups with the exception of the Spanish and the Navajo. The first generation of immigrants undertake the process of learning the English language and making it their own. Those who make English their own language give it to their children as mother tongue. These latter may or may not be bilingual in the language which was their parents' mother tongue (and usual language). The children of those who retain their mother tongue as usual language may be expected to have the minority language as mother tongue. The data indicate that nearly all will adopt English as their language of use, most of them abandoning the use of their mother tongue as a second language. In any case, the data indicate that there will not be another generation of the native born having the language of their grandparents as their mother tongue.

This two-generational model of language shift is supported and expanded upon in our analysis of intergenerational language shift. The language behavior of children is explained by the interaction of three factors, parental language use, parental nativity, and the force of the American language environment itself. Observed differences in the retention rates of native born children are largely spurious, caused by differences in parental characteristics. With the single exception that Spanish children are more likely to have adopted English bilingualism as their form of anglicisation, the data reveal that children react in very similar ways to the language characteristics of their parents. They are everywhere much more anglicized than their parents, permitting us to discard the assumed link between parental and child language use.

Thus, while we can conceptualize a situation in which a minority language could be indefinitely transmitted as a second language, the same conditions which lead to its subordination as a second language also appear to lead to its abandonment. Approximately one-half of the children of English bilinguals in the Spanish language group have become English monolinguals before the age of seventeen, the data indicating that this process accelerates as children get older. Children of parents who usually speak a minority language have themselves most frequently adopted the English bilingual pattern of language use. There is a parallelism evident in the language use matrices which suggests that English bilingualism cannot be successfully maintained in the United States.

This analysis of data derived from the SIE is supported by the data reported by high school students in the HSB study. We find not only that children are less likely to actually use the minority language than are their parents; we also find that the parents themselves use English to a large extent in their relationships with their children. That is to say, there is a decline in both the use of the minority language by the parents themselves and a further decline in its use by their children. The children of English mother tongue rarely use the minority language, indicating the instability of English bilingualism, while those of minority mother tongue do not use it outside of the home. Thus, use of the minority language is largely confined to the home, language behavior outside the home occurring predominantly if not exclusively in English. Once again, while the rate of anglicisation in the Spanish language group is very high, children declare both greater competence and greater use of the minority language than do children in other groups.

These findings suggest that bilingualism is largely transitional in nature (Grosjean, 1982). That is to say, it appears to meet the linguistic and psychological needs of persons who are undergoing the anglicisation process, particularly among the foreign born. In general, English bilingualism should not be seen as a stable phenomenon which permits the transmission of the language to the next generation, but as an example of what Fishman (1966) has called 'unstable bilingualism'. It is a *modus vivendi*, a way by which persons of minority mother tongue come to terms with the American environment, a way in which they are not compelled to completely deny their linguistic heritage. This is particularly important for recent immigrants; it should not be expected to have the same importance for the native born. They are not called upon to deny the existence of a long personal history (childhood, adolescence, early adulthood) in which the minority language structured daily consciousness and self-identity, at least not to the same extent.

Nonetheless, the fact that parents in the Spanish language group have less anglicized language patterns than do those in the non-Spanish groups and that children are less frequently monolingual in English has been used to argue that the Spanish language group is generally more retentive than have been previous waves of immigrants (Lopez, 1981). While we concur that the Spanish language group was in 1976 more retentive than most other groups, we think it unlikely that their rates of language shift are lower than were those of other groups in the past.

First of all, there is no adequate data base which could sustain such an argument. Even the longitudinal inferences derived from the SIE do not permit us to make any serious assessments of the rates of anglicisation which might have prevailed before the Second World War. Thus, any such assertions of differential rates of language shift are inherently risky. Secondly, there is every reason to assume that anglicisation rates were generally lower in the past than they are now, due to the evolution of the American economy to which we have previously alluded. Thirdly, several of the minority language groups which came to the United States during the nineteenth century were characterized by large numbers, geographic concentration, and a minimal array of churches and other social institutions. This was probably particularly true of groups which settled in specific rural regions of the United States, the Germans and Scandinavians in the Midwest, the French Canadians in northern New England and the Cajuns in Louisiana. We suspect that these groups were characterized at some earlier date by substantially lower rates of anglicisation than those observed in 1976. Had the Acadian population of Louisiana been characterized either by their 1976 rate of anglicisation or by that of the Spanish language group, their final anglicisation would have not have required approximately two centuries to complete.

These considerations lead us to suggest that the greater retentiveness of Spanish language adults in 1976 is largely explained by demographic factors. The data clearly reveal that larger proportions of older people in the Spanish language group did not speak English well when compared to those in other minority language groups. In addition, larger proportions of persons of Spanish mother tongue had not adopted English as the language usually spoken, particularly in the states of Texas, Arizona, and New Mexico. While these facts are probably explained in turn by the structure of regional and local economies, the presence of such persons provides a basic pool of persons who normally converse in Spanish. Those who do not speak English well are likely to require dialogue in the minority language.

The existence of this basic pool of people usually speaking the minority language may have a braking effect on the anglicisation of immigrants. The new arrivals are received into relatively well-established communities of Spanish speaking people, whereas immigrants in other language groups must create small groups of compatriots or face the English language environment alone. The integration of new arrivals into the established Spanish communities may serve as a further brake on the anglicisation of both the native born and subsequent arrivals. This effect may take different forms for each group, the foreign born reacting by having lower rates of both anglicisation and English monolingualism, the native born by having lower rates of English monolingualism and higher rates of English bilingualism. And since English bilingualism appears to be inherently unstable, we cannot be certain that observed differences in rates of English monolingualism (measured either in the SIE or HSB) will remain as large as they currently are.

These same demographic factors can be invoked to explain intergroup and interregional variations in language shift. While geographic isolation may be related to the lower rates of anglicisation of the Navajo language group, it is likely to play an increasingly less important role in the anglicisation of the Spanish language groups. Where these latter do not already live in large cities (as in California), they are being brought into increasing contact with situations where the English language is normative. Nonetheless, where a native born group serves to integrate new arrivals, and where the minority language group is characterized by the continuous arrival of new immigrants, relatively large numbers, and a minimal set of minority language institutions, the anglicisation process, particularly of the foreign born, may be slowed to a certain extent. On the other hand, our analysis of the intergenerational transmission of minority languages suggests that whatever the sources of differentiation in the anglicisation of the foreign born, there appear to be relatively few sizeable differences in the anglicisation of the next generation. The language behavior of children is essentially determined by parental characterisitics in interaction with the American language environment.

There can be no doubt that the direction and extent of language shift in the United States is one aspect of what Gordon has defined as Anglo-conformity (1964). The existence of widespread and rapid anglicisation cannot be questioned; the process may vary somewhat by language group and region. However, if we exclude the Navajo language group as a special case (i.e., because Navajo is not an immigrant language), the data indicate that even for the Spanish language group in Texas, the anglicisation rate is so high that native born women cannot be expected to cover the losses by maintaining high birth rates. They would have to average more than five children each. In short, even in the most retentive region for the most retentive immigrant language, the anglicisation process is so extensive that the language group will not survive in the long run in the absence of continued immigration.

If these observations apply to the Spanish language group in Texas, they apply with still greater force to both the Spanish language group in other regions and to all other minority language groups. For example, the anglicisation rate of native born persons in the Spanish language group in California is equivalent to that of most other minority language groups elsewhere in the United States. Consequently, although the growth of the Spanish language group in absolute numbers over the past two decades has given most Americans the impression that Hispanics are resisting anglicisation, the analysis of the language shift process reveals that the language group has undergone (and is undergoing) such serious erosion that *only continued immigration can maintain a Spanish speaking population in the long run.* There is no language group in any region which possesses the retentive characteristics which would remotely sustain the theory that continued immigration is laying the groundwork for linguistic nationalism. In fact, the only minority language group with some survival potential is the Navajo language group, a group which must in any case rely on its own resources.

Although the data require us to conclude that continued immigration is the sole salvation of American minority language groups, such a conclusion does not necessarily imply that the structural integrity of the group is likewise threatened. For example, while many Americans fear that bilingual education programs are laying the basis for linguistic nationalism, the stated objective of such programs is the facilitation of the entry of minority language children into the English educational system. As we have seen, such programs may increase the probability that children will retain some minimal skills in the minority language, but the proportions of children who have nonetheless made English their preferred usual language remain exceptionally high. Thus, bilingual education programs do not retard in any specific way the general dominance of the English language. It would appear, then, that the pursuit of bilingual education objectives by Hispanic organizations is guided primarily by educational goals rather than by those pertaining to the linguistic integrity of the Spanish group. In addition, their support of bilingual educational initiatives are not in the slightest weakened by the fact that this is one area of the Federal bureaucracy where Hispanics have succeeded in establishing a foothold.

This line of analysis suggests that Hispanics are increasingly engaged in the classic American pattern of ethnic, not linguistic politics. Since bilingual educational objectives appear to rally both English and Spanish speaking Hispanics, as well as Hispanics of different national origins, they provide a focus around which all Hispanics can mobilize. This is true in spite of the fact that a common linguisitic tie in the full sense of the word no longer serves as a principal organizing factor. The salient criterion of social organization comes to be transformed over time, the sense of peoplehood deriving from a more broadly defined common heritage rather than a common language (Spanish). This sense of ethnic belongingness characterizes those who still speak Spanish, those in the process of anglicisation, and those who no longer speak the Spanish language (if they ever did). This sense of ethnic identity is frequently reinforced in the larger society, members of other groups reminding the teenager of

Puerto Rican ancestry that in their eyes he is still a Puerto Rican, even if he has been an English monolingual since birth.

Thus, the development of an ethnic identity is based upon the linguistic integration of persons of minority language groups into the English language group. When people do not speak the same language, the boundaries which distinguish them are clear to all. Language defines group membership. In fact, conceptions of membership may be relatively latent when most members of a group speak a minority language — the boundaries of the groups are so 'real'. When, however, a group undergoes anglicisation, a redefintion of the boundaries becomes imperative. In this sense ethnic consciousness is an emergent phenomenon, arising to replace 'real' boundaries which no longer serve to define group membership.

As a minority language group becomes progressively anglicized, we may presume that other aspects of American culture are also assimilated (as suggested by the model of Anglo-conformity). One important aspect of American political culture is the fact that structurally differentiated groups, particularly ethnic groups, may use group membership as the grounds for claiming an equitable share of community resources. We should expect that the most linguistically assimilated (most anglicized) members of minority language groups are those most likely to have adopted this view of American politics. As a result, the affirmation of ethnic claims by Hispanic groups, far from being the threat to the linguistic integrity of the nation as perceived by Anglo-chauvinists, may testify to the effectiveness of the cultural integration of Hispanics into American society.

Part Two:

The Role of Language Characteristics in the Attainment Process

While the comparative analysis of anglicisation in the United States permitted us to examine a certain number of prevalent myths, there is more to the study of linguistic assimilation than an analysis of the pace, the structure, and the extent of language shift. Implicit in the study of language shift is a theory (or theories) of the mechanisms which motivate (or determine) this process. Both demographic and economic models of language shift have been developed, the former emphasizing the demographic pressures which the English language group brings to bear on members of minority language groups. The need to communicate with other (English speaking) members of the society is evidently somewhat mitigated by the size, concentration, and linguistic composition of the minority language group. Where the group is large, highly concentrated, and contains a high percentage of the foreign born, the need to adopt the English language is not as urgent as when the opposing conditions are present.

On the other hand, the economic model of language shift tends to emphasize the importance of economic rewards in securing language shift to English in the United States. That is to say, those members of minority language groups who become English speaking are accorded preferential treatment in the attainment process, while those who retain their mother tongue as usual language are handicapped in the attainment race. The structure of attainment is consequently seen as more important than the demographic composition of the group in determining the extent and rapidity of language shift.

The data contained in the SIE and HSB are not really suited to permit us to distinguish the relative contribution of each theory to the explanation of observed language shift. We have seen in our analyses of intergenerational language shift that the language characteristics of children tend to be relatively well explained by demographic variables, the impact of socioeconomic status being relatively weak. Nonetheless, we cannot extricate or estimate the effects of attitudinal variables which may underlie (and explain) the observed move-. ment. Children may be more anglicized than their parents because they are responding to a set of anticipated rewards, believing, for example, that those who make English their usual language will do better in school and have higher socioeconomic attainments at some point in the not too distant future. The effects of such attitudinal variables can not be measured directly. They may, however, be hidden in the intercept term and in the values of the regression coefficients attached to the parental language indices. These estimates indicate that children are everywhere more anglicized than their parents.

The question which immediately arises, however, is whether such attitudes may exist only in the minds of members of minority language groups or whether such a set of rewards can be detected in the attainment process. Consequently, we shall attempt to measure the impact of language characteristics on the educational attainments and achievements of minority language children and on the occupational and earnings attainments of minority language adults. These analyses are multivariate (multiple regression) analyses which derive only the net effects of language characteristics, other differences which may have affected the attainment process having been already eliminated. In Chapter 7 we analyze the impact of language characteristics of persons of minority mother tongues on their occupational and income attainments. In Chapter 8 we present the analysis of the relationship between language characteristics and placement in grade level of minority language children, while a similar analysis of the educational achievements of children enrolled in secondary schools is presented in Chapter 9.

The fact that language characteristics may have a net impact on the socioeconomic attainments (achievements) of persons in minority language groups does not, however, indicate that the observed patterns of language shift were 'caused' by the observed structure of rewards (and punishments). Nonetheless, to the extent that language shift is rewarded in the attainment process, such findings provide presumptive evidence that the economic effects were anticipated and may have motivated children to alter their language behavior. The determination of the extent to which language shift is associated with higher attainments forms the subject of the second major section of this book.

Chapter Seven

The Impact of Language Characteristics on Occupational and Income Attainments of American Adults

Introduction. The principal objective of this chapter is to examine the role of language characteristics in the attainment process of persons of minority mother tongue. While we are not the only investigators interested in this topic, the previous research has been characterized by a lack of attention to the quality of the language variables used in the analysis. Mother tongue is sometimes included, sometimes not (Tienda et al., 1981). Complex indicators of language shift are developed with little attention to logic or theory (Tienda, 1981b). Since we have presented the grounds on which adequate indicators of language shift can be theoretically anchored, we can procede to a more rigorous definition of a set of language variables to be used in the analysis. While the models developed in this chapter are less complex than those developed by Tienda and her colleagues (1981) or in our earlier publication (1981b), they do permit us to make a relatively straight-forward evaluation of the role of language characteristics in the attainment process.

The analysis which we shall undertake in this chapter differs substantially from previous approaches to this problem in three important ways. First of all, unlike others who have also analyzed the SIE data (Garcia, 1979; Grenier, 1981; Tienda et al., 1981), we have chosen to exclude Hispanics of English mother tongue from our analysis. We have previously shown (Veltman, 1980b) that there appear to be no important attainment differences based on the mother tongue of English monolinguals or English bilinguals in the Spanish language group. Nonetheless, including persons of both Spanish and English mother tongue in the same analysis is similar to mixing apples and oranges. We should not take for granted that the work force experiences of these two groups are sufficiently similar that they can be easily mixed into a single group. On the one hand, the group of persons of English mother tongue is not very large (14.5% of the male sample and 13.2% of the female sample, Veltman, 1980b: Tables 2 and 15), so that their achievement pattern is submerged in the combined sample. On the other hand, if their attainment process is sufficiently different from that of persons of Spanish mother tongue, their presence could distort the analysis of the attainment process of the latter group. Since we are principally concerned with the impact of language shift on the attainment process, the persons of English mother tongue have been excluded from the minority language samples.

Secondly, we have placed the excluded persons of English mother tongue in the English language group. In our view, this is where they belong. This procedure permits us to ascertain whether there appear to be important differences in the attainment processes of specific ethnic groups in the English language population. To determine whether or not Hispanics suffer disadvantages in the workplace, they should be compared to persons of other ethnic origins in the English language group, rather than have their characteristics submerged in the Spanish language group.

Thirdly, while the previous research is concerned only with the analysis of the attainments of men and women of Hispanic origin, we shall also analyze in this chapter the attainment process of persons in other minority language groups. The non-Spanish (or Residual) language groups have been combined into a single minority language group in order to facilitate a comparative analysis. Such a procedure, while not eminently desirable, is made necessary because the percentages of persons in most minority language groups who were not anglicized were so low. That is to say, nearly everyone spoke English as his or her usual language. As may have been expected from our analysis in chapter three, the percentage of persons reporting low competence in spoken English is extremely low. In order to compare the impact of low proficiency in English in the Spanish language group to that in some other group, we must produce a sample which is sufficiently large to sustain such a procedure. The direct comparison of the Spanish and non-Spanish attainment processes has not been previously undertaken. This comparison is important because it may permit us to distinguish which aspects of the attainment process are common to all persons of minority mother tongue and which are specific (if any) to the Spanish language group.

The plan of analysis, then, consists first of all in presenting the occupational and income attainments of persons of Spanish mother tongue. This will be followed by the analysis of the attainments of those in the non-Spanish sample, i.e., those of mother tongues other than English or Spanish. After we have compared the results of these two analyses, we shall compare the attainments of both minority language samples to those of the White English monolingual population. Finally, we shall briefly examine the attainments of Hispanics (and other ethnic groups) in the English monolingual population. In addition, the presentation of the data is divided into two major sections, the first analyzing the occupational and income attainments of men, the second those of women. This division is not capricious. A variety of studies have shown that women earn considerably less income for equivalent educational and occupational attainments. These findings are presumably explained in part by an intermittent or inconsistent work force history for many women. As a result, any comparison of male and female attainments which does not include a history of work force participation is of relatively dubious validity. When using Census-type, cross-sectional data to do analyses of male income, the researcher assumes that all men have worked equivalent amounts of time during each year since they have left school. The relatively low percentages of 25-64 year old men who were employed full time in 1975 makes even this assumption highly questionable, but most researchers assume that this assumption is more likely to be true for men than it is for women. Since this factor is one of the more important determinants of income, separate analyses of the attainment processes of men and women are indicated.

In addition, there is no reason to suppose that language factors play the same role in the female attainment process that they do in the male attainment process. A number of studies have confirmed the existence of linguistic stratification in the Montreal labor market, but the data suggest asymetric stratification by sex. Boulet (1979), Vaillancourt (1979a, 1979b), and Veltman and Boulet (1980) found that at the beginning of the 1970's men of English mother tongue were located at the top of the economic hierarchy and benefitted from income premiums beyond the income predicted from their background characteristics.

However, with respect to the effects of language characteristics on the income of Motreal women the picture is somewhat less clear. Lussier (1978) found much less income stratification by language group, there being no net income differences between English monolinguals, English bilinguals, and French monolinguals. French bilingual women had somewhat higher net incomes (that is, after background characteristics have been controlled). However, Lacroix and Vaillancourt (1980) found that English monolingual women had the lowest net incomes while French monolingual women had the highest net incomes among women who possessed a university degree. These two studies make it clear, however, that language factors may not act in the same way in a labor market which is both sexually and linguistically stratified.

An age parameter has also been imposed on the analysis, only persons 25-64 years of age having been retained for examination. The upper limit was imposed to exclude retired or semi-retired persons. The lower limit was imposed for two reasons. First of all, we wished to exclude part time workers who were still enrolled in educational programs. Secondly, the language characteristics of young persons undergo a rapid evolution between the ages of 14 and 24. While there is some continued language shift after the age of twenty-five, a good deal of the most rapid movement has already been completed. Since an attempt to assess the role of language characteristics in the attainment process is predicted upon some reasonable stability of the phenomenon, an age limit lower than age twenty-five does not seem desirable.

The attainment process of Spanish language men. Applying these sample selection criteria to the Spanish language group results in an estimated population of 1,802,758 men. Their employment status and mean socioeconomic attainments are presented in Table 7.1.

Table 7.1 *Mean socioeconomic attainments of men aged 25-64, Spanish language group, United States, 1976*

Mean socioeconomic Attainments	Total	Employed	Employed Full time
Education	10.27	10.45	10.86
Occupation	26.01	29.36	31.21
Income ($)	8,504	9,483	10,818
Population estimate	1,802,758	1,596,838	1,248,114
Percent of total	(100.0)	(88.6)	(69.2)

Source: 1976 Survey of Income and Education

Beginning with the analysis of employment status, 69.2 percent of the male Spanish language sample was employed full time in 1975. Another 19.4 percent were employed for less than 1,750 hours, the figure selected to represent full time employment, while 11.4 percent of the weighted sample were not employed in 1975. As we have noted elsewhere, the employment status of Spanish language Americans is neither as favorable as that prevailing among the 'White' English monolingual population nor as unfavorable as that found for Black Americans (Veltman, 1980b). We shall return to this subject as additional data are presented.

Examining the socioeconomic attainments of Spanish language men, Table 7.1 shows that mean educational attainment is relatively low, 10.27 years of education. That increased educational attainment is related to more frequent and stable employment is evident from the mean attainment levels for each labor force status. Mean educational attainment for employed men is 10.45 years while it is 10.86 years for men employed full time.

Given the relatively low educational attainments of Spanish language men, the relatively low occupational and income attainments reported in Table 7.1 are not surprising. Full time employed men earned on the average only $10,818 in 1975 and had occupational attainments of only 31.21 Duncan points. Obviously, men who were not employed full time had still lower status and income, accounting for the lower means reported for all employed men. Men who did not work in 1975 were assigned a Duncan index of zero and a zero dollar income.

That which is most interesting for the analysis is not, however, the generally low levels of socioeconomic attainments of Spanish language men. These are largely explained by the relatively low levels of educational attainments in the Latin American countries in general and in Mexico in particular. Consequently, immigrants from these regions tend to have lower levels of educational attainments, which in the context of the American class system will lead to lower educational attainments in the succeeding, native born generation. What is most interesting for our purposes is to see whether within the Spanish language group itself there is evidence of linguistic stratification, and to see whether the most anglicized members of the group appear to enjoy significant socioeconomic benefits.

Our approach to this problem is two-fold. First of all, we examine the employment status of persons in the Spanish language group according to their language characteristics. The relevant data are presented in Table 7.2. Examining first of all the distribution of the language characteristics of the Spanish language men, 54.4 percent of the sampled men reported that they usually spoke the Spanish language. Of this group, the majority reported that they spoke English 'well' or 'very well.' Nonetheless, a sizeable percentage reported that their ability to speak English was relatively weak. Of those men who reported that they now usually speak the English language, the vast majority claimed that they continue to speak the Spanish language with some frequency. Only 9.0 percent of the sampled men said that they no longer spoke Spanish 'often.' This distribution conforms to the expectations derived from the analysis of language shift.

Table 7.2 suggests that there is indeed a relationship between the language characteristics of Spanish language men and their employment status. Approximately seventy-five percent of the men of English usual language were employed full time in 1975 and less than ten percent of such men were unemployed in 1975. The data show in fact that English bilingual men were

Table 7.2 *Employment status by language characteristics, men aged 25-64, Spanish language group, United States, 1976*

Language characteristics	Employment status			Weighted sample	
	Employed full time	Employed part time	Unemployed		
English usual language:					
English monolingual	74.7%	15.4%	9.9%	161,451	(9.0%)
English bilingual	76.7	13.6	9.7	660,393	(36.6%)
Spanish usual language:					
High English competence	66.8	21.8	11.4	542,433	(30.1%)
Low English competence	58.8	26.4	14.8	438,481	(24.3%)
Total	69.2	19.4	11.4	1,802,758	(100.0%)

Source: 1976 Survey of Income and Education

slightly more likely to have obtained full time employment and slightly less likely to have been unemployed than English monolingual men. Nonetheless, these two groups of English usual language men had markedly more favorable employment status characteristics than did the men of Spanish usual language.

For the men of Spanish usual language the type of employment obtained is also related to the degree of competence in English. Those who spoke English well had both higher rates of full time employment and lower rates of unemployment than did the men who did not speak English well. Only 58.8 percent of these latter had obtained full time employment in 1975, while the rate of unemployment (not in the labor force or unemployed) stood at 14.8 percent. These data suggest certain difficulties in obtaining employment (and in particular full time employement) which are associated with an inability to speak English well. Nonetheless, even those men who spoke English well but continued to speak Spanish as their primary language had less favorable employment patterns than did the men of English usual language.

It is not simply, however, the language characteristics of these men which are related to their employment status. Low competence in English is also associated with lower educational attainments. Consequently, the apparent link between language characteristics (competence levels in English and anglicisation patterns) and the employment status of such groups may simply reflect differences in the educational attainments of the respective groups. To test for this possibility we estimated an equation which included both educational attainment and the language characteristics of the male respondents. The dependent variable was a dummy variable representing full time employment. This equation was characterized by a very low coefficient of determination (r-squared = .043), indicating that neither education nor language characteristics explain much of the variation in full time employment. In addition, only the coefficient for the educational attainment variable attained statistical significance. Each additional year of education was associated with an additional 1.6 percent of the men having full time jobs. More importantly, none of the language characteristic coefficients attained the .05 level of statistical significance, indicating that for a sample of 2,465 cases the differences in the coefficients from the mean attainments of English monolingual men are not significant. Interestingly, the coefficients vary in the expected direction, some 2.9 percent more of the English bilingual men having obtained full time employment when compared to English monolingual men. On the other hand, 3.5 percent fewer of the men of high competence in English and 6.7 percent fewer of the men of low competence in English had obtained full time employment when compared to comparably qualified English monolingual men. Even were we to accept these non-significant findings as meaningful, they indicate nonetheless that the most important differences in full time employment revealed in Table 7.2 are due to educational differences between the language characteristics' groups. Thus, of the 15.9 percent difference in full time employment between English monolingual men and men of Spanish usual language with low competence in English (74.7 - 58.8 = 15.9), only 6.7 percent could be attributable to the differences in language characteristics of the two groups (that is, if we treat the lack of statistical significance as a function only of the sample sizes of the respective groups). At best the data suggest that there might be some small relationship between language characteristics and the ability to secure full time employment. The direction of this small relationship is clear. Men who continue to speak Spanish as their preferred, usual language have greater difficulty in obtaining full time employment, particularly those who do not speak English well.

Since this first attempt to examine the effects of language characteristics in the labor market has not been wholly successful, a somewhat different line of reasoning may be pursued. Examining only those men who are already employed full time, we may ask whether their language characteristics affect their levels of occupational and income attainments. Once again certain important background characteristics must be held constant to determine the net effects of language skills.

We begin this type of analysis by examining the gross differences in mean socioeconomic attainments of men who were employed full time in 1975. These data are presented in Table 7.3. As expected, the relative importance of men who usually speak Spanish has diminished. More than one-half of the men (40.6 + 9.7 = 50.3) usually speak English.

Table 7.3 *Mean socioeconomic attainments by language characteristics, full time employed men aged 25-64, Spanish language group, United States, 1976*

Language characteristics	Mean socioeconomic attainments			Weighted sample
	Education	Occupation	Income	
English usual language:				
English monolingual	12.87	37.63	$14,149	9.7%
English bilingual	12.54	37.75	12,398	40.6
Spanish usual language:				
High English competence	10.40	29.20	10,094	29.0
Low English competence	7.26	17.34	7,170	20.7
Total	10.86	31.21	$10,818	100.0%

Source: 1976 Survey of Income and Education

The examination of gross differences in the mean attainment levels of the various language characteristic groups reveals a clear pattern. The most anglicized men have the highest attainment levels, the least anglicized the lowest. The men of the two English usual language groups have on the average succeeded in obtaining a high school diploma (12.0 years). The mean attainment level of men who usually speak Spanish but who speak English well in only 10.40 years of education, while that of men who do not speak English well is only 7.26 years. These differences in educational attainment obviously affect the expected levels of occupational and income attainments.

If there are only small differences in the educational attainments of English bilingual and English monolingual men, the English bilingual men actually enjoy slightly higher occupational status. However, the English monolingual men have considerably higher earnings than the English bilingual men ($14,149 vs. $12,398). Still, both groups of men of English usual language have higher occupational status and higher incomes than do the men of Spanish usual language. These latter are in turn divided into two groups, the men of high competence in English having markedly higher attainments. Since, however, much of the differences in occupational and income attainments may be explained as functions of eductional attainments (and other background factors), an examination of the net impact of language characteristics is imperative.

Before turning to such an analysis we should like to address one further topic. Many observers of the American scene insist that ethnic differences in the Spanish language population must be examined in the attainment process. Once again we have divided the Spanish language group into four ethnic components, the Chicano or Mexican group, Puerto Rican, Cuban, and a residual group which is principally composed of Central American, South American, or Other Hispanic persons. The mean occupational and income attainments of these four groups are presented in Table 7.4.

Table 7.4 *Mean occupational and income attainments of 25-64 year old men employed full time, Spanish ethnic groups, United States, 1976*

Ethnic group	Occupation	Income	Percent of sample
Chicano/Mexican	28.11	$10,168	58.0%
Puerto Rican	31.61	10,631	12.9
Cuban	40.61	12,819	8.3
Other hispanic	35.86	11,952	20.8
Total	31.21	$10,818	100.0%

Source: 1976 Survey of Income and Education

Considering first of all the ethnic composition of the Spanish language group, the Chicano ethnic group contributes 58.0 percent to the sample. Puerto Ricans account for 12.9 percent and Cubans, 8.3 percent. The Other Hispanic group accounts for 20.8 percent of the Spanish language sample. With respect to mean socioeconomic attainments, Cuban men have the highest attainments. The Other Hispanic group has somewhat higher than average attainments, while the Puerto Rican group has mean attainment levels which correspond very closely to the mean of the entire Spanish language group. The Chicano men have lower than average attainment levels. Again, whether these oberved differences remain important once the background factors of the sampled men are taken into account merits an examination.

Before we examine the net contributions of language and ethnic factors to the explanation of the attainment process, we may well ask whether the mean occupational attainments of the language characteristic groups and of the ethnic groups differ significantly from one another. The relevant statistics are presented in Table 7.5. When we regress occupational attainment on the language characteristics of Spanish language men, we find that language characteristics explain 12.5 percent of the variance in occupational attainment (r-squared = .125). The regression coefficients indicate the difference between the mean of the specific language characteristic group and that of the reference group, the men of English monolingual language use. Thus, the regression coefficient of .12 for English bilingual men represents the difference between their mean of 37.75 (from Table 7.3) and the mean of the English monolingual men (37.63 from Table 7.3). This difference is not statistically significant according to Table 7.5. The difference in mean attainments of the two groups of Spanish usual language men and those of the two groups of men of English usual language are statistically significant (the data in Table 7.5 indicate statistically significant differentiation from the attainments of the English monolingual men; a t-test established the statistically significant differences between these men and the English bilingual men).

If the ability of the language characteristics to explain variation in occupational attainment is relatively limited, the r-squared produced for the equation which regresses occupational attainment on ethnic origin is still less impressive. Ethnic origin differences only explain 3.5 percent of the observed variation in occupational attainment. All of the regression coefficients differ significantly from those of the reference group. While a t-test shows that the differences between Puerto Rican men and Chicano men are not significant at these sample sizes, Cuban men have significantly higher occupational attainments than do the Puerto Rican and Chicano men. On the whole, however, the low r-squared suggests that ethnic origin is not a very important factor in the explanation of occupational attainment among Spanish language men.

To permit the assessment of the net impact of language and/or ethnic variables, a baseline equation must be estimated which takes into account the most important factors known to affect the occupational attainment process. We have retained four such factors, educational attainment, geographic residence, experience, and core-peripheral sector of employment.

Educational attainment is defined as the highest year of education completed by the respondent. It is entered as a metric variable in the analysis with a range of zero to nineteen, persons with post-graduate degrees being assigned the value nineteen irrespective of their actual attainments. Also entered in metric form is an experience surrogate which is conceptualized as represent-

Table 7.5 *Regression of occupational attainment on language characteristics and ethnic origin of full time employed men aged 25-64, Spanish language group, United States, 1976*

Regressors	Mean or percent	Regression coefficient
Language characteristics:		
English bilingual	40.62%	.12 (1.81)[1]
Spanish usual language:		
High English competence	29.66	−7.82 (1.87)*
Low English competence	20.66	−20.29 (1.97)*
Intercept (English monolingual)	(9.67)	37.63
R-squared		.125
Ethnic origin:		
Chicano/Mexican	58.04%	−7.75 (1.36)*
Puerto Rican	12.93	−4.25 (1.88)*
Cuban	8.34	4.75 (2.17)*
Intercept (other Hispanic)	(20.69)	35.86
R-squared		.035

[1] Standard errors in parentheses throughout Part II
*   p < .05
Source: 1976 Survey of Income and Education

ing the number of years of work force activity. It is actually defined as the number of years which have elapsed since the respondent completed his last year of formal education. Since the relationship between experience and attainment variables may be curvilinear in form, the square of the experience variable has also been entered into the equation.

Entered as a series of binary or dummy variables are the two sets of geographic variables. The nine regions developed by the U.S. Bureau of the Census have been restructured for this analysis, the New England and Middle Atlantic regions having been combined to produce the Northeast region, while the East North Central and West North Central regions have been collapsed into the Midwest region. The South Atlantic and East South Central regions have been combined into the South region, while we have renamed the West South Central region by calling it the Texas-Louisiana region. The list of states included in the original nine Census regions is reproduced in Appendix A.

This restructuring of the nine census regions is designed to facilitate an analysis of the Spanish language group. Since we have already demonstrated interregional variations in the rates of anglicisation, it is particularly important that regional differences not be submerged by creating a single southwestern region. On the other hand, an undue proliferation of regions would tend to produce categories which have very low percentages of persons. Under such circumstances the regression coefficients so estimated would likely be insignificant anyway (Veltman, 1980b: 23).

A second set of dummy variables defines the size of the place of residence. Persons may reside in the central city or suburban areas of the SMSA's defined in the SIE. They may also reside outside SMSA areas. These variables have been retained principally to distinguish between the types of occupational and income opportunities presented in these circumstances.

Finally, we have developed a dummy variable to distinguish between the core and the peripheral sectors of the economy (Beck, Horan, and Tolbert, 1978). Persons employed in the core sector presumably have greater opportunities for career advancement and receive rewards more likely to be commensurate with their human capital characteristics, while workers in the peripheral sector are treated more uniformly irrespective of their human capital characteristics. The data were classified using Tolbert's (1978) empirical classification of work force sector.

The baseline equation regressing occupational attainment of Spanish language men on these background variables is presented in Table 7.6. Examining first of all the column labelled 'percent or mean', we have already observed that the mean educational attainment of the sampled men is 10.86 years. Table 7.6 also shows that the average man of Spanish mother tongue finished his last year of schooling 24.13 years prior to the time of the survey. Nearly one-half of the men are employed in the core sector of the economy.

Examining the geographic variables, nearly three-quarters of the men sampled live in just three geographic regions, the Northeast, Texas-Louisiana, and the Pacific region. These regions correspond (roughly) to the New York metropolitan area, southern Texas, and southern California. The remaining men are relatively evenly divided among the three remaining regions, the Rocky Mountain region containing the three remaining southwestern states in the region originally settled by people of Mexican origin (Arizona, New Mexico, and Colorado). The data also show that most men live in central city or non-SMSA regions, the incidence of suburban residence being somewhat lower.

Examining the regression coefficients estimated in this equation, each additional year of education is associated with a 3.14 point increase in the Duncan index. Neither experience nor employment in the core sector is associated with statistically significant advantages (or disadvantages). While residence in

Table 7.6 *Regression of occupational attainment on selected background variables, full time employed men aged 25-64, Spanish language group, United States, 1976*

Regressors	Mean or percent	Regression coefficient
Education	10.86	3.14 (.12)*
Experience	24.13	.16 (.16)
Experience^2	720.29	.00 (.00)
Northeast	20.89%	2.19 (1.28)
Midwest	7.80	5.97 (1.77)*
South	8.12	6.82 (1.77)*
Texas-Louisiana	23.79	7.96 (1.25)*
Rocky Moutains	9.56	2.38 (1.68)
Pacific	29.84	(a)
Central city	38.74%	.11 (1.13)
Suburban	23.82	3.17 (1.24)*
Non-SMSA	37.44	(a)
Core sector	47.93%	1.11 (.89)
Intercept		-11.82
R-squared		.354

Notes:
(a) reference characteristic
* $p < .05$
Source: 1976 Survey of Income and Education

any region other than the Pacific region appears to be associated with positive occupational attainments, only three of the regression coefficients differ significantly from the attainment level of men in the Pacific region. Men in the Midwest, the South, and in Texas-Louisiana have higher net attainments than men in the Pacific region. The single remaining factor which attains statistical significance concerns size of place of residence. Men living in suburban regions have higher net attainments than men living in either of the two remaining areas.

To this baseline equation of occupational attainment we now add the language and ethnic variables. The relevant data are presented in Table 7.7. Considering the equation presented in column one which adds the language variables to the baseline equation, we observe first of all that the proportion of the variance explained is but slightly improved. The r-squared rises from .354 in

Table 7.7 *Regression of occupational attainment on selected background variables, full time employed men aged 25–64, Spanish language group, United States, 1976*

Regressors	Regression coefficient	Regression coefficient
Education	2.84 (.14)*	2.75 (.14)*
Experience	.20 (.16)	.19 (.16)
Experience^2	-.00 (.00)	-.00 (.00)
Northeast	2.39 (1.28)	-.95 (1.71)
Midwest	6.22 (1.76)*	5.52 (1.78)*
South	8.32 (1.74)*	4.41 (2.28)*
Texas-Louisiana	8.40 (1.26)*	8.75 (1.27)*
Rocky Mountains	1.85 (1.68)	1.35 (1.69)
Pacific Coast	(a)	(a)
Central City	.60 (1.13)	.36 (1.13)
Suburban	3.60 (1.23)*	3.17 (1.24)*
Non-SMSA	(a)	(a)
Core sector	.54 (.89)	.58 (.89)
English bilingual	1.60 (1.57)	1.60 (1.57)
Spanish usual language:		
High English competence	-2.56 (1.67)	-2.77 (1.68)
Low English competence	-5.29 (1.86)*	-5.42 (1.88)*
English monolingual	(a)	(a)
Chicano/Mexican		-3.76 (1.40)*
Puerto Rican		.58 (1.66)
Cuban		2.21 (2.09)
Other Hispanic		(a)
Intercept	-7.95	-3.44
R-squared	.365	.369

(a) reference characteristic
* p < .05
Source: 1976 Survey of Income and Education

the baseline equation to .365 when the language factors are added. This is a relatively small addition when we remember that the gross effects of language explained .125 of the variance in occupational attainment (Table 7.5). Thus, most of the gross differences in occupational attainment between men in the different language characteristic groups are explained by differences in educational attainment, experience, region of residence, or employment in the core sector. Very little is attributable to the effects of language characteristics *per se*.

Examining the regression coefficients for the language variables, Table 7.7 shows that men who usually speak Spanish and who have low competence in spoken English have net occupational attainments 5.29 points below those of the men who have become English monolinguals. This difference is statistically significant. A t-test confirms that English bilingual men also have significantly higher occupational status than these men of low English competence. These findings lead us to conclude that low English language competence is indeed penalized in the race for occupational attainment.

The pattern of the regression coefficients for the language variables has other interesting features. First of all, the data do not unambiguously indicate that the most anglicized men have the highest net occupational standing. The English bilingual men (of English usual language) have net occupational attainments 1.60 points higher than those of the English monolingual men. This difference is not, however, statistically significant. Secondly, while the men of Spanish usual language and high English competence have estimated net attainments 2.56 points below those of the English monolingual men, this difference is not significant. Thus, the data tend to indicate that good competence in spoken English is adequate to secure occupational attainments, commensurate with one's background characteristics. Thirdly, the English bilingual men have significantly higher net attainments than the men of Spanish usual language who have higher competence levels in English. This may suggest the existence of an occupational premium associated with continued bilingualism, once these men have made it clear that they are integrating into the English language community via anglicisation.

On the whole, then, the regression coefficients for the language characteristic variables present a relatively mixed picture. It appears that integration into the English language group by making English one's usual language is associated with positive occupational status gains. Not all differences between the men of English usual language and the men of Spanish usual language are, however, statistically significant. What appears most clearly are the occupational advantages of the men of English usual language when compared to the men who do not speak English well. The position of the men of high English competence is more ambiguous, statistically distinguishable only from the attainments of the English bilingual men.

As expected, the addition of the ethnic origin variables causes only slight changes in the proportion of the variance explained, the r-squared increasing by only .004. Briefly, the data indicate that there are no significant differences in the net occupational attainments of Cuban, Puerto Rican, and Other Hispanic men. All three groups have significantly higher net occupational attainments than have the men of Chicano origin. The addition of the ethnic variables, as in the case of the language characteristic variables, causes no appreciable changes in the regression coefficients of the background variables included in the respective equations.

Using similar procedures we can examine the importance of language and ethnic characteristics in the process of income attainment among men of Spanish language origin. The equations regressing employment income on the language and ethnic characteristics of Spanish language men are presented in Table 7.8. Once again the regression coefficients reflect the difference between the mean income of the group being considered and the mean income of the reference group (English monolinguals in the language characteristics equation; Other Hispanic in the ethnic origin equation).

Once again the proportion of the variance explained (r-squared) is rather

Table 7.8 *Regression of employment earnings on language characteristics and ethnic origin of full time employed men aged 25-64, Spanish language group, United States, 1976*

Regressors	Mean or percent	Regression coefficient
Language characteristics:		
English bilingual	40.62%	-1.751 (.577)*
Spanish usual language:		
High English competence	29.05	-4.055 (.594)*
Low English competence	20.66	-6.980 (.629)*
Intercept (English monolingual)	(9.67)	14.149
R-squared		.101
Ethnic origin:		
Chicano/Mexican	58.04%	-1.784 (.432)*
Puerto Rican	12.93	-1.321 (.598)*
Cuban	8.34	.867 (.692)
Intercept (other Hispanic)	(20.69)	11.952
R-squared		.017

* $p < .05$
Source: 1976 Survey of Income and Education

low, higher in the equation for language characteristics and approaching zero in the equation for ethnic origin. The first equation shows that English monolingual men have significantly higher gross earnings than men in the remaining three groups. English bilingual men have higher earnings than the men of Spanish usual language. Since the men of Spanish usual language who speak English well have significantly higher earnings than those who do not, the hierarchy of incomes is complete. Each additional increment of anglicisation is associated with significantly higher incomes. With respect to ethnic origin, the data indicate that Cuban and Other Hispanic men have significantly higher mean earnings than do the men of Chicano and Puerto Rican origins. In the case of both language and ethnic characteristics these are, of course, mean differences. Whether or not these differences remain after appropriate background factors have been controlled remains to be seen.

The baseline equation regressing employment earnings on the appropriate background factors is presented in Table 7.9. Having already examined the distribution of these factors, we may procede directly to the examination of the equation itself. Since the dependent variable is expressed in terms of thousands of dollars, the interpretation of the coefficients is relatively simple. Each additional year of education is associated with a $455 increase in employment income. Both of the experience variables attain statistical significance in this equation, indicating that each additional year of experience is associated with an income increment of $232 subject to a decline of $3 per year of experience squared. Roughly, these two coefficients indicate rapidly rising income following entry into the labor market. The percentage growth in income tends to decline over time, there being only small income increments after approximately twenty-five years of experience. The equation estimates that earnings begin to fall after forty years of work force experience. This conforms to the pattern expected according to human capital theory (Mincer, 1958).

Regional variables appear to play a lesser role in income attainment than in occupational attainment. From the data presented in Table 7.9 and from additional t-tests we find that men in the Texas-Louisiana region have lower net earnings than those men living in any region outside of the South. Only one other pair of coefficients present significant differences, men living in the Midwest having higher net earnings than men living in the South. In addition, men living in suburban regions have higher net earnings than men living in either the central cities or outside SMSA areas.

Table 7.9 also shows that employment in the core sector is associated with higher net income of $1,877 when compared to similarly qualified men

Table 7.9 *Regression of employment earnings on selected background variables, full time employed men aged 25-64, Spanish language group, United States, 1976*

Regressors	Mean or percent	Regression coefficient
Education	10.86	.455 (.048)*
Experience	24.13	.232 (.053)*
Experience^2	720.29	-.003 (.001)*
Northeast	20.89%	-.409 (.430)
Midwest	7.80	.356 (.595)
South	8.12	-1.042 (.599)
Texas-Louisiana	23.79	-1.557 (.424)*
Rocky Mountains	9.56	-.302 (.565)
Pacific Coast	29.84	(a)
Central City	38.74%	-.190 (.380)
Suburban	23.82	1.004 (.416)*
Non-SMSA	37.44	(a)
Core sector	47.93%	1.877 (.297)*
Duncan index	31.21	.093 (.008)*
Intercept		-1.274
R-squared		.271

(a) reference characteristic
* $p < .05$

employed in the peripheral sector. Thus, while employment in the core sector did not appear to confer significant occupational status advantages, the income associated with such employment is markedly higher. Finally, each additional point of Duncan-indexed status (occupational attainment) is associated with a $93 increase in net earnings.

Having examined the baseline regression of employment income on earnings, we present in Table 7.10 the two equations which add the language and ethnic variables. The introduction of the language variables improves the proportion of the variance explained by .001 (.282 - .271 = .001). While this improvement is well short of dramatic, the introduction of the language variables does cause some changes in the coefficients of the baseline variables. The estimated value of each additional year of experience rises by $16. The estimated value of living in a specific region or in a place of a given size changes but little, al-

Table 7.10 *Regression of employment earnings on selected background variables, full time employed men aged 25-64, Spanish language group, United States, 1976*

Regressors	Regression coefficient	Regression coefficient
Education	.372 (.051)*	.367 (.052)*
Experience	.248 (.053)*	.245 (.053)*
Experience^2	-.003 (.001)*	-.003 (.001)*
Northeast	-.335 (.429)	.176 (.574)
Midwest	.445 (.592)	.599 (.600)
South	-.550 (.605)	-.545 (.769)
Texas-Louisiana	-1.351 (.429)*	-1.407 (.432)*
Rocky Mountains	-.432 (.563)	-.436 (.567)
Pacific Coast	(a)	(a)
Central City	.017 (.380)	.069 (.381)
Suburban	1.062 (.415)*	1.037 (.419)
Non-SMSA	(a)	(a)
Core sector	1.652 (.299)*	1.658 (.299)*
Duncan index	.089 (.008)*	.089 (.008)*
English bilingual	-.989 (.526)	-1.044 (.527)*
Spanish usual language:		
High English competence	-1.897 (.562)	-1.930 (.567)*
Low English competence	-2.839 (.626)*	-3.001 (.634)*
English monolingual	(a)	(a)
Chicano/Mexican		.239 (.473)
Puerto Rican		-.834 (.559)
Cuban		.321 (.703)
Other Hispanic		(a)
Intercept	1.093	1.069
R-squared	.282	.284

(a) reference characteristic
* p < .05
Source: 1976 Survey of Income and Education

though residence in the South is no longer associated with significantly lower income when compared with residence in the Midwest. The value of employment in the core sector also declines somewhat.

Most importantly, while the equations for occupational attainment did not reveal definitive benefits accruing to the most anglicized, the regression of employment earnings certainly does. Net of baseline characteristics, English monolingual men earn an estimated $989 more than English bilingual men. While this coefficient fails to satisfy the criterion of being twice the size of its standard error, it very nearly satisfies the criterion of the .05 level of statistical significance.

In addition, both groups of men of English usual language have significantly higher net earnings than do the men of Spanish usual language. Since the men who speak English well among the latter group do not enjoy significantly higher earnings than do those who do not speak English well, the data reveal a clear division of Spanish language men into two groups, those who usually speak English and those who usually speak Spanish. The former enjoy net benefits of income above and beyond that which can be expected from their background (baseline) characteristics. It is quite evident, then, that employment income is tied not simply to competence in spoken English, but to integration into the English language group via anglicisation. At the very least, the men of English usual language have indicated a willingness to conform to the American credo of English as the language of the nation.

When the ethnic variables are added to the equation, only small changes are noted in the regression coefficients of the variables previously examined. The net negative income attainments ascribed to Puerto Rican origin permit the Northeast region of the United States to appear as a relatively privileged region. The superior estimated attainments of English monolingual men in in comparison to English bilingual men also attains statistical significance in this equation. However, none of the ethnic coefficients differ either from the intercept term which represents Other Hispanic origin or from one another. We are obliged to conclude that ethnic origin appears to play little role in the income attainment process of Spanish language men.

Summarizing briefly the findings for men of Spanish language, the data tend to indicate that men who usually speak Spanish experience some difficulty in obtaining full time employment. This is true even when the educational attainments of Spanish language men are held constant, although the sample size does not permit us to affirm that this finding holds true in the population at large. Men who do not speak English well have greater difficulty securing full time positions than those who do speak English well, but both groups of men who usually speak Spanish have greater difficulty than do those who usually speak English.

Among men employed full time the data tend to indicate that men of English usual language have higher net occupational attainments than do men of Spanish usual language. The pattern observed, however, does not completely satisfy the criteria of statistical significance. This is not the case in the analysis of income, where men of English usual language have statistically higher net earnings than do men of Spanish usual language. The data also tend to show that English monolingual men enjoy significant income premiums with respect to English bilingual men, lending credence to the theory that the American economy rewards not only integration into the English language group, but that it specifically rewards the most complete type of integration possible, the effective abandonment of the Spanish language as a daily language.

The attainment process of other minority language men. These findings immediately invite us to examine the extent to which they may be generalized. Can the same patterns of access to employment and rewards be found for men of minority language backgrounds other than Spanish? To ascertain the answer to this question we shall follow the same logic used to unravel the net impact of language characteristics on the attainments of Spanish language men. We begin by presenting the mean socioeconomic attainments and employment status characteristics of the non-Spanish men in Table 7.11.

Table 7.11 · *Mean socioeconomic attainments of men aged 25-64, non-Spanish minority language groups, United States, 1976*

Mean socioeconomic attainments	Total	Employed	Employed full time
Education	12.45	12.64	12.81
Occupation	35.55	40.10	41.77
Income ($)	11,620	13,023	14,367
Population estimate	3,862,717	3,424,865	2,841,821
Percent of total	(100.0)	(88.7)	(73.6)

Source: 1976 Survey of Income and Education

A comparison of this table with Table 7.1 reveals that the men of the non-Spanish minority language groups had mean educational attainment which was 2.18 years higher than that of the men of the Spanish language group (12.45 - 10.27 = 2.18). Consequently, their occupational and income attainments are markedly superior to those of the Spanish language men. When unemployed men are assigned zero values of occupational status and income, the non-Spanish men enjoy an additional 9.54 points of Duncan-indexed occupational status (35.55 - 26.01 = 9.54) and $3,116 of additional revenue ($11,620 - $8,504 = $3,116). The advantages are still greater when the figures for employed men and for men employed full time are compared, the non-Spanish men enjoying advantages of more than ten Duncan points and more than $3,500. These additional advantages are attributable to the larger percentage of non-Spanish men who had succeeded in obtaining full time employment in 1976. An additional 4.4 percent of the non-Spanish language men had obtained full time employment (73.6 - 69.2 = 4.4).

Although the non-Spanish men were more successful in having obtained full time employment, Table 7.11 reveals that approximately the same proportions of men in both groups succeeded in obtaining at least part time employment during the year 1975. The same pattern observed in Table 7.1 is again observed, the better educated men having easier access to the paid labor force in general and to full time employment in particular.

Beginning our analysis of the role of linguistic stratification in the non-Spanish minority language sample, we present in Table 7.12 the employment status of men by the language characteristics' category to which they belong. Examining first of all the distribution of the language characteristics of the non-Spanish men, over eighty-five percent of the men declared that they

Table 7.12 *Employment status by language characteristics, men aged 25-64, non-Spanish minority language groups, United States, 1976*

Language characteristics	Employment status			Weighted sample
	Employed full time	Employed part time	Unemployed	
English usual language:				
English monolingual	75.1%	13.4%	11.5%	2,153,535 (55.8%)
English bilingual	75.5	13.7	10.8	1,156,425 (29.9%)
Minority usual language:				
High English competence	66.4	23.6	10.0	390,111 (10.1%)
Low English competence	57.5	26.2	16.3	162,646 (4.2%)
Total	73.6	15.1	11.3	3,862,717 (100.0%)

Source: 1976 Survey of Income and Education

usually spoke the English language. Some 55.8 percent of the men of minority mother tongue declared that they now no longer spoke their mother tongue 'often.' An additional 29.9 percent of the sample declared English bilingual language use, having subordinated their mother tongue to the status of a second, frequently-spoken language. These data contrast markedly with the data presented in Table 7.2 for the Spanish language men. The comparable figures were 9.0 percent who declared English monolingual language use and 36.6 percent who reported English bilingual language usage. Obviously, the percentage of non-Spanish men who declared that they usually spoke the minority language is very much inferior to the percentage of men who usually spoke Spanish. Only 4.2 percent of the non-Spanish men reported that their competence in spoken English was relatively low as opposed to 24.3 percent of the Spanish language men. Similarly, only 10.1 percent of the non-Spanish men reported that they usually spoke a minority language but that their competence in English was relatively high, a figure which contrasts with the 30.1 percent of the Spanish language men who reported a similar pattern of language use.

These differences in the linguistic composition of the Spanish and non-Spanish samples have been amply explored in the first part of this book. What interests us here is how this distribution of language characteristics interacts with the employment status of the non-Spanish men to produce the mean employment status characteristics reported in the row labelled 'Total.' When compared to the Spanish language men, equal percentages of each group were not employed in 1975 but Spanish language men were more frequently found in part time employment. These findings are caused not by the ease or difficulty which men of the different language characteristic groups obtain employment; rather, they are caused by the distribution of the language characteristics in the two groups.

This point can be illustrated by examining and comparing the percentages of men in each language characteristic group who have obtained each employment status. Examining the English monolingual and English bilingual men, approximately seventy-five percent of the men in both the Spanish and non-Spanish groups obtained full time employment. However, slightly more of the non-Spanish men were unable to obtain any employment at all. We are obliged to conclude that for men who usually spoke the English language, the Spanish language men appear to enjoy slight advantages in terms of access to employment.

Among the men who usually spoke a language other than English, the Spanish language men who had low competence in English had more favorable employment status characteristics than did the non-Spanish men. An additional 1.3 percent of the Spanish men had obtained full time employment (58.8 - 57.5 = 1.3) while an additional 1.5 percent of the non-Spanish men were unemployed in 1975 (16.3 - 14.8 = 1.5). However, the non-Spanish men who spoke English well had somewhat lower rates of unemployment than did their Spanish language counterparts, although most of their advantages were secured via part time employment. Summarizing, the data show that men in the Spanish language group appear to enjoy slight advantages in access to the labor force once we control for the language characteristics of the men being compared. Since, however, the incidence of the various language characteristics varies between the two groups, the row totals appear to indicate that the men of the non-Spanish group enjoy access advantages to the labor force. These advantages are secured by means of the language shift patterns of the non-Spanish group, not because men of a given language characteristic group are favored with respect to Spanish language men.

As with the Spanish language men we have reason to suspect that the men of more retentive language characteristics also have lower educational attainments. Consequently, not all of the employment difficulties of the men who usually speak a (non-Spanish) minority language can be attributed to their language characteristics. If we estimate an equation where full time employment is the dependent variable and where the independent variables are educational attainment and the language characteristics of the non-Spanish men, we find that each additional year of educational attainment is associated with a net increase of 1.7 percent in number of men obtaining full time employment. This figure compares favorably with the regression coefficient obtained in the equation estimated for the Spanish language men (1.6 percent). As in the case of these latter men, the estimated equation for the non-Spanish men only explains a small proportion of the variability observed (r-squared = .030). Thus, the association between the educational and language characteristics of men and their access to full time employment is not very strong.

Nonetheless, an examination of the regression coefficients for the language characteristic groups reveals an interesting pattern. While English bilingual men have a net rate of full time employment which is less than one percent below that of the English monolingual men, this difference is not significant. However, both groups of men who usually speak English have significantly higher rates of access to full time employment than have the men who usually speak a minority language and who do not speak English well. The English monolingual men have a rate of full time employment which is 10.3 percent higher; the English bilingual men a rate which is 9.3 percent higher. In addition, the men who usually speak a minority language and who speak English well have a significantly higher rate of full time employment than do the men who do not speak English well. The estimated difference is 8.4 percent. Thus, net of educational differences this equation shows that the men who do not speak English well have significantly lower rates of access to full time employment. An inability to speak English well is a liability in terms of access to full time employment, a finding which was presaged in our analysis of the Spanish language men.

The position of the men who usually speak a minority language but who also speak English well is also quite interesting. Although only 1.9 percent fewer of these men had obtained full time employment in 1975 when compared to the English monolingual men, this difference is statistically significant. Nonetheless, the vast majority of their access difficulties are explained by their lower mean educational attainment. Table 7.12 showed that 8.7 percent fewer of these men had obtained full time positions when compared to the English monolingual men (75.1 - 66.4 = 8.7). Nearly all of this difference is explained by educational attainment differences. Since the differences between the coefficients estimated for the English bilingual men and these men of minority usual language are not significant, the 9.1 percent difference in rates of full time employment which separate these groups may be attributed to educational differences as well (75.5 - 66.4 = 9.1). These findings oblige us to conclude that in general the language characteristics of men who at a minimum speak English well seem relatively unimportant in the struggle to obtain full time employment. Educational factors are by far more important. However, men who do not speak English well suffer additional handicaps beyond those already imposed by their generally lower levels of educational attainment. These findings conform in their essentials to those already obtained for the Spanish language men and may consequently be generalized to the minority language population as a whole.

Turning to the analysis of the role of language characteristics once men have succeeded in obtaining full time employment, we present in Table 7.13 the mean socioeconomic attainments of the non-Spanish minority language men. This table reveals first of all the expected change in the distribution of men in the language characteristic categories. The percentage of men who usually speak a minority language is lower among full time workers than it is in the population as a whole. Secondly, Table 7.13 reveals that the English bilingual men have somewhat higher mean educational and occupational attainments than do the English monolingual men. The mean incomes of the two groups are, however, nearly equivalent, a finding which leads us to expect

Table 7.13 *Mean socioeconomic attainments by language characteristics, full time employed men aged 25-64, non-Spanish minority language groups, United States, 1976*

Language characteristics	Mean socioeconomic attainments			Weighted sample
	Education	Occupation	Income	
English usual language:				
English monolingual	12.80	41.47	$14,775	56.9%
English bilingual	13.52	45.44	14,801	30.7
Minority usual language:				
High English competence	12.09	37.71	12,125	9.1
Low English competence	8.23	24.14	9,476	3.3
Total	12.81	41.77	14,367	100.0%

Source: 1976 Survey of Income and Education

that the English monolingual men may enjoy an income premium. As expected, the men of minority language have lower than average socioeconomic attainments, those men who do not speak English well having substantially lower educational, occupational and income attainments.

When compared to comparable Spanish language men (Table 7.3), the men of minority usual language (both groups) and the English bilingual men in the non-Spanish group had completed approximately one additional year of education than had their Spanish language counterparts. Their occupational standing was approximately seven points higher and their incomes more than $2,000 higher than those of the comparable group of Spanish language men. Given the differences in educational attainment levels, these differences may be expected. However, the occupational differential (37.63 - 41.47 = -3.84) and the income differential ($14,149 - $14,775 = -$626) which separates the English monolingual men of the Spanish language group from those of the non-Spanish minority language groups cannot be explained by educational differences between the two groups. Although disadvantaged in terms of occupational and income attainments, the men of the Spanish language group have a slightly higher level of educational attainment than do the men of the non-Spanish group.

The importance of this finding should not be minimized. When we compare the mean attainments of the Spanish language group as a whole to those of the non-Spanish men or to those of the White English monolingual men, we may find that the actual attainments of the Spanish language men closely parallel their predicted attainments. However, since so few men in the Spanish language group have become English monolinguals, their importance in such an analysis is minimized. Thus, the importance of such an attainment gap which appears to exist only for the English monolingual men is also minimized. Nonetheless, we may expect that English monolingualism in the Spanish language group will increase (sharply) in the future. If this should occur and the attainment gap continue into the future, we may expect that the actual attainments of the Spanish language men will increasingly diverge from that predicted.

As may have been anticipated there is considerable variation in the mean occupational and income attainments of the men in specific minority language groups. The relevant data are presented in Table 7.14. There are several groups of men whose mean attainment levels differ from the mean attainment level of the entire sample to an important extent. Most notably, the men of Yiddish minority language have occupational attainments fifteen points above the mean attainment level of the entire sample and income which is more than

Table 7.14 *Mean occupational and income attainment of 25-64 year old men employed full time, non-Spanish minority language groups, United States, 1976*

Language group	Occupation	Income	Percent of sample
Chinese	51.17	$13,645	3.1%
Filipino	43.83	13,556	2.4
French	37.86	14,156	9.6
German	41.05	14,814	14.3
Greek	40.30	13,050	3.3
Italian	40.46	14,410	19.7
Japanese	41.55	17,180	2.6
Polish	37.08	13,370	10.7
Portuguese	29.30	11,721	3.1
Scandinavian	42.68	15,376	3.0
Native American	31.30	9,977	1.0
Yiddish	57.17	17,684	3.8
All others	45.28	14,470	23.5
Total	41.77	$14,367	100.0%

Source: 1976 Survey of Income and Education

$3,000 higher than the sample mean (57.17 - 41.77 = 15.40 and $17,684 - $14,367 = $3,317). Men of the Portuguese and Native American language groups (largely Navajo) have mean attainment levels markedly below the mean levels of the entire sample. Certain other groups have more ambiguous patterns, Chinese language men having high occupational attainments but income below that of the sample mean, while Japanese language men have mean occupational attainment equivalent to that of the entire sample but earnings which are markedly higher. The remaining groups have attainment levels roughly comparable to those of the means of the minority language sample.

To begin our analysis of occupational attainment of the non-Spanish men, we may ask whether the mean attainment levels of the language characteristic groupings differ significantly from one another. Similarly, we should like to know whether the mean attainment levels of the specific minority language groups differ significantly from one another. The relevant data to address both of these issues is presented in Table 7.15.

Beginning with the impact of the language characteristic groups on occupational attainment, we observe first of all that the proportion of the variance explained is extremely low (r-squared = .027). That is to say, the language characteristic categories are only slightly related to occupational achievement. Nonetheless, each of the regression coefficients differs significantly both from the intercept representing English monolingualism and from each of the remaining coefficients. Thus, the observed means reported in Table 7.13 differ significantly from one another.

Turning to the examination of the equation regressing occupational attainment on membership in specific minority language groups, the proportion of the variance explained remains low. It is, however, somewhat higher than that observed for the language characteristic variables. The coefficients estimated for each of the specific minority language groups represent deviations from the reference category. This category is defined as the men not belonging to the specific language groupings already defined. They constitute 23.47 percent of the entire sample and had a mean occupational attainment of 45.28 Duncan points, a figure 3.51 points higher than that of the sample as a whole (45.28 - 41.77 = 3.51). Since this group is relatively privileged with respect to the sample as a whole, its mean attainment level is significantly higher than that of many of the remaining groups. Only the Yiddish and Chinese groups have significantly higher mean occupational attainments.

When t-tests are applied to examine the extent to which the regression coefficients differ from one another, the Yiddish group is found to have sig-

Table 7.15 *Regression of occupational attainment on language characteristics and language group of full time employed men aged 25-64, non-Spanish minority language groups, United States, 1976*

Regressors	Mean or percent	Regression coefficient
Language characteristics:		
English bilingual	30.71%	3.97 (.69)*
Minority usual language:		
High English competence	9.11	−3.76 (1.09)*
Low English competence	3.29	−17.32 (1.74)*
Intercept (English monolingual)	(56.89)	41.47
R-squared		.027
Language group:		
Chinese	3.07%	5.89 (1.83)*
Filipino	2.37	−1.45 (2.05)
French	9.60	−7.42 (1.15)*
German	14.25	−4.23 (1.01)*
Greek	3.31	−4.98 (1.77)*
Italian	19.74	−4.82 (.92)*
Japanese	2.57	−3.73 (1.98)
Polish	10.75	−8.20 (1.11)*
Portuguese	3.09	−15.98 (1.82)*
Scandinavian	2.96	−2.60 (1.86)
Native American	.97	−13.92 (3.11)*
Yiddish	3.85	11.89 (1.65)*
Intercept (all others)	(23.47)	45.28
R-squared		.042

* p < .05
Source: 1976 Survey of Income and Education

nificantly higher attainments than all other groups, while the Chinese group has higher attainment levels than the remaining non-Yiddish groups. There are no significant differences in the mean attainment levels of the Scandinavian, Japanese, Italian, Greek, German, and Filipino language men, while the men of the French and Polish language groups have significantly lower attainment levels than have the men of these six minority language groups. Finally, the men of the Portuguese and Native American language groups have significantly lower occupational attainment levels than have the men in all the other minority language groups.

This brief portrait of linguistic stratification based on language characteristics or on membership in specific language groups is, however, based only on gross differences in mean attainment. A more refined analysis requires us to take into account differences in the educational attainments and other background characteristics of the minority language men. We begin by presenting the relevant baseline equation for the occupational attainment of the non-Spanish men. These data are presented in Table 7.16.

Table 7.16 *Regression of occupational attainment on selected background variables, full time employed men aged 25-64, non-Spanish minority language groups, United States, 1976*

Variable	Mean or percent	Regression coefficient
Education	12.81	4.18 (.08)*
Experience	29.08	-.27 (.09)*
Experience^2	990.93	.01 (.00)*
Northeast	43.89%	4.28 (.72)*
Midwest	25.03	1.87 (.78)*
South	6.50	6.99 (1.13)*
Texas-Louisiana	5.78	5.76 (1.20)*
Rocky Mountains	2.87	2.56 (1.56)
Pacific Coast	15.93	(a)
Central City	26.53%	2.74 (.62)*
Suburban	35.21	2.62 (.58)*
Non-SMSA	38.26	(a)
Core sector	58.80	5.30 (.49)*
Intercept		-17.66
R-squared		.387

Notes:
(a) reference characteristic
* $p < .05$
Source: 1976 Survey of Income and Education

Examining first of all the characteristics of the non-Spanish sample, we observe that the non-Spanish men have nearly five additional years of work force experience than had the Spanish language men (29.08 - 24.13 = 4.95).

Logically, this indicates that the non-Spanish men are on the whole at a somewhat different position in their work force careers than are the Spanish men. This is not, moreover, the only difference worthy of note. The non-Spanish men are much more heavily concentrated in the Northeast and Midwest regions of the United States, and they are much more likely to reside in the suburban areas of SMSA regions. In addition, a much higher proportion of the non-Spanish men have obtained positions in the core sector of the economy. Since core sector employment has already been shown to confer significant income advantages, the sources of the Spanish/non-Spanish differential warrant some exploration.

Logically, we expect that educational attainment is related to the ability to obtain core sector employment. When we regress core sector employment on educational attainment for a combined sample of Spanish and non-Spanish men, higher educational attainment is indeed related to core sector employment. However, once the language characteristic variables are added to the equation, this relationship disappears. Although the proportion of the variance explained is very low (.029), access to core employment is positively related to anglicisation. The more anglicized the language characteristic group, the higher the percentage of men obtaining core sector employment.

When we add to this equation a regressor for membership in the Spanish language group, the findings indicate that net of educational and language characteristics an additional 2.8 percent of the non-Spanish men obtained core sector employment. Thus, the 10.9 percent gap between the two groups in core sector employment can be partitioned as follows: 1.6 percent is explained by the lower mean educational attainments of the Spanish men, 2.8 percent by differential treatment, and 6.5 percent by the less anglicized language patterns of the Spanish men.

Examining the regression of occupational attainment on these selected background factors, we observe that each additional year of educational attainment is associated with a net increase of 4.18 Duncan points. The experience coefficients, both of which are statistically significant, indicate the presence of a curvilinear relationship between experience and occupational attainment. Men who have been in the labor market for twenty or more years have net occupational attainments which are positively associated with age. The longer the men have been in the labor market the higher their occupational status. Men who completed their educations ten to fifteen years have occupational attainments nearly two points lower than predicted. The more recent entries into the labor market also appear to have lower than expected net occupational attainment, but the gap between expectation and attainment tends to close for the most recent entrants.

The regression equation also reveals that men living in regions other than the Pacific Coast appear to enjoy higher occupational attainments, men living in the two southern regions (South and Texas-Louisiana) having the highest attainment levels. Men living in both the central city and suburban parts of the identified SMSAs have higher net attainments than do rural men. The equation also shows that core employment is associated with significant gains in occupational status, employment in the core sector being associated with a net advantage of 5.30 points. Finally, we should note that the proportion of the variance explained (.387) is quite satisfactory for this type of analysis.

Comparing briefly the results of the baseline equation estimated in Table 7.16 for the non-Spanish men with those presented in Table 7.6 for the Spanish language men, we note first of all that the proportion of the variance explained in both equations is very similar. Also similar are the findings that men in the Pacific Coast region tend to have lower net occupational attainments. However, in other respects the findings diverge. Each additional year of education was associated with only 3.14 points of Duncan status among Spanish language men, while it is associated with 4.18 points among the non-Spanish minority language men. The experience variables were not associated with net differences in attainment among the Spanish language men, while among the non-Spanish men a curvilinear relationship was observed. And while Spanish language men living in central cities had occupational attainments equivalent to those of rural men, the non-Spanish men living in central cities had occupational attainments equivalent to those of suburban men. Finally, employment in the core sector was not related to occupational attainment among Spanish language men.

These findings suggest that there is greater uniformity in the labor force treatment of Spanish language men than there is in the treatment of non-Spanish minority language men. That is to say, additional years of education are associated with much less stratification in terms of occupational attainment among Spanish language men. This may suggest in turn that the value of the educational attainment of Spanish language men is discounted by the employer. Alternatively, the perceived differences between a seventh and eighth grade education may be substantially less than those perceived to obtain between a twelfth grade education and the completion of the first year of university. In other words, the Spanish language men tend to to be concentrated at the lower end of the educational attainment scale. The association between educational attainment and occupational attainment being not completely linear in nature, the observed results of differential educational atttainment are less. On the other hand, we also observe that employment in the core sector does not bring additional occupational status rewards to Spanish language men. This tends to suggest that employers do tend to apply criteria which devalue the objective attainments of the Spanish language men. Consequently, it appears that both the nonlinear relationship between education and the Duncan index and the devaluation of the objective attainments of the Spanish language men contribute to an explanation of the differences observed in the two equations.

We shall now procede to the estimation of equations which add the language characteristic variables and the membership group variables to this baseline equation. The relevant data are presented in Table 7.17. Examining first of all the equation which includes the language characteristic variables, we observe that the proportion of the variance explained is virtually unchanged. Thus, the addition of the language characteristic variables improves but very little the explanation of occupational attainment. Secondly, the regression coefficients for the variables used in the baseline equation are therefore unchanged or changed very little. Thirdly, the gross advantages observed in Table 7.15 are almost completely eliminated once the appropriate baseline variables have been controlled. For example, the observed advantage of 3.97 Duncan points which the English bilingual men enjoyed in comparison to the English monolingual men is reduced to 1.14 points, a difference which while still statistically significant is indeed quite small. The remaining differences reported in Table 7.15 have been completely eliminated. To underline that fact we note that the group of men who usually spoke a minority language and who did not speak English well had an occupational attainment mean 17.32 points below those of the English monolingual men; not only is this difference eradicated but the equation estimates that these men had net occupational attainments 1.50 points higher than the English monolingual men, once their background characteristics were taken into account. We are obliged to conclude that there is little relationship between the language characteristics of the non-Spanish men and their net occupational attainments. Their occupational attainments are adequately explained by the variables contained in the baseline equation.

When we add the specific language groups to the equation, we observe that the proportion of the variance explained rises from .387 to .397. Once again, this is not a dramatic improvement. In addition, the regression coefficients estimated for most groups do not depart in any important way from the attainment of the reference group. Very briefly, men in the Yiddish

Table 7.17 *Regression of occupational attainment on selected background variables, full time employed men aged 24-64, non-Spanish minority language groups, United States, 1976*

Regressor variables	Regression coefficient	Regression coefficient
Education	4.20 (.09)*	4.11 (.09)*
Experience	-.25 (.09)*	-.28 (.09)*
Experience^2	.01 (.00)*	.01 (.00)*
Northeast	4.32 (.71)*	3.58 (.79)*
Midwest	1.98 (.78)*	1.99 (.85)*
South	7.02 (1.13)*	6.12 (1.17)*
Texas-Louisiana	5.77 (1.20)*	5.46 (1.29)*
Rocky Mountains	2.62 (1.56)	2.06 (1.65)
Pacific Coast	(a)	(a)
Central City	2.57 (.63)*	1.89 (.64)*
Suburban	2.57 (.58)*	2.23 (.59)*
Non-SMSA	(a)	(a)
Core sector	5.33 (.50)*	5.96 (.50)*
English bilingual	1.14 (.55)	1.36 (.56)*
MUL: High competence (1)	.30 (.90)	.32 (.93)
MUL: Low competence	1.50 (1.44)	1.72 (1.48)
English monolingual	(a)	(a)
Chinese		3.99 (1.50)*
Filipino		-2.68 (1.70)
French		.28 (.99)
German		.70 (.82)
Greek		1.07 (1.43)
Italian		1.51 (.77)
Japanese		-.24 (1.68)
Polish		-2.42 (.90)*
Portuguese		-2.77 (1.50)
Scandinavian		.59 (1.49)
Native American		.52 (2.63)
Yiddish		10.83 (1.35)*
All others		(a)

Continued on next page

Table 7.17 Continued

Regressor variables	Regression coefficient	Regression coefficient
Intercept	−18.66	−17.31
R-squared	.387	.397

(a) reference characteristic
(1) minority usual language
* $p < .05$
Source: 1976 Survey of Income and Education

language group enjoy important advantages in occupational attainment, advantages which differ significantly from the attainments of all other minority language groups. The Chinese language men enjoy modest but statistically significant advantages when compared to the men of the reference group and when compared to the men of most other groups. Only the Filipino, Polish, and Portuguese men have attainment levels which are marginally lower than those predicted by their baseline characteristics and by their language characteristics. Nonetheless, in most instances their attainment levels are not significantly lower than those of most other groups. We are obliged to conclude that the gross differences reported in Table 7.15 are largely explained by the remaining factors explained in this equation. Membership in one minority language group or in another does not appear to have a great deal of significance. Only the men of the Yiddish language group are clearly distinguished from men of the other language groups examined.

Although language factors do not appear to play an important role in the occupational attainment process of the non-Spanish language men, they may play a more important role in the income attainment process. We begin our examination of this problem by presenting the regression of employment income on the language characteristics and on the language membership groups of the non-Spanish men. The relevant data are presented in Table 7.18. The means for each of the specific minority language groups on which this equation is based are those presented in Table 7.14.

Beginning with the regression of employment earnings on the language characteristic variables, we observe that the differences between the earnings of the English monolingual men and those of the English bilingual men are not significant. The earnings of both of these groups of men who usually speak English are significantly higher than those of the men of minority usual

Table 7.18 *Regression of employment earnings on language characteristics and language group of full time employed men aged 25-64, non-Spanish minority language groups, United States, 1976*

Regressors	Mean or percent	Regression coefficient
Language characteristics:		
English bilingual	30.71%	.027 (.224)
Minority usual language:		
High English competence	9.11	-2.649 (.358)*
Low English competence	3.29	-5.298 (.568)*
Intercept (English monolingual)	(56.89)	14.775
R-squared		.022
Language group:		
Chinese	3.07%	-.825 (.609)
Filipino	2.37	-.914 (.684)
French	9.60	-.314 (.384)
German	14.25	.344 (.337)
Greek	3.31	-1.420 (.589)*
Italian	19.74	-.060 (.307)
Japanese	2.57	2.710 (.659)*
Polish	10.75	-1.000 (.370)*
Portuguese	3.09	-2.749 (.607)*
Scandinavian	2.96	.906 (.619)
Native American	.97	-4.493 (1.038)*
Yiddish	3.85	3.214 (.552)*
Intercept (all others)	(23.47)	14.470
R-squared		.020

* $p < .05$
Source: 1976 Survey of Income and Education

language who speak English well. The earnings of these latter are significantly higher than those of the men who do not speak English well. The proportion of the variance explained by these language characteristic variables is once again very low.

The regression of earnings on membership in specific minority language groups is also associated with a very low proportion of the variance explained (r-squared = .020). The findings show that Yiddish and Japanese language men have mean earnings which are significantly higher than those of the men in the remaining groups. Similar t-test results show that the men in the Native

American and Portuguese language groups have earnings which are significantly lower than those of the men in the remaining groups. The data also reveal that the differences between the earnings of men in the remaining groups are not statisitically significant, although the data presented show that the Greek and Polish language men have mean incomes significantly lower than those of the men in the reference group. If we look only at the four major minority language groups, the income of German men is significantly higher than that of the Polish men. The income of Italian men is also significantly higher than that of the Polish men, but all remaining paired income comparisons do not differ significantly.

Once again these are gross comparisons based only on the differerences between the means of the observed group. To observe net differences a certain number of background characteristics must be controlled in a baseline equation. This equation is presented in Table 7.19. The regression coefficients obtained in this equation show that each additional year of education is associated with a net increase of $536 in income. Each additional year of experience is associated with a $430 increase in earnings, subject to a decline of $7 for each additional squared year of experience. This indicates a curvilinear relationship between earnings and experience. There is a rapid increase in earnings after initial entry into the labor force but the rate of increase is constantly decelerating. Earnings peak after approximately thirty years of labor force experience and then begin a slow decline.

Table 7.19 also shows that residence in the Pacific Coast region is associated with significantly higher earnings when compared to residence in the Northeast, the Midwest, or the South. This contrasts with the findings for occupational attainment where Pacific residence was the least favorable. And while the occupational attainment equation showed that central city residence was associated with positive attainments, only residence in a suburban area is associated with significantly higher income attainments. The income attainment equation also finds that employment in the core sector is associated with positive earnings, and each additional point of Duncan status is associated with an additional $96 of earnings. The proportion of the variance explained is .248.

When we compare the equation estimated in Table 7.19 to that estimated for the Spanish language men in Table 7.9, there are a number of evident similarities. First of all, returns from additional points of Duncan-indexed occupational attainments are vey similar. The returns associated with urban, suburban, and rural residence are also quite similar, as is the return to employment in the core as opposed to the peripheral sector. There are also, however, a number of differences in the earnings attainment process in the two language

Table 7.19 *Regression of employment earnings on selected background variables, full time employed men aged 25-64, non-Spanish minority language groups, United States, 1976*

Regressors	Mean or percent	Regression coefficient
Education	12.81	.536 (.036)*
Experience	29.08	.430 (.039)*
Experience^2	990.93	-.007 (.001)*
Northeast	43.89%	-1.022 (.261)*
Midwest	25.03	-.984 (.285)*
South	6.50	-1.528 (.412)*
Texas-Louisiana	5.78	.287 (.438)
Rocky Mountains	2.87	-.606 (.569)
Pacific Coast	15.93	(a)
Central City	26.53%	.018 (.228)
Suburban	35.21	1.124 (.213)*
Non-SMSA	38.26	(a)
Core sector	58.80%	1.426 (.182)*
Duncan index	41.77	.096 (.005)*
Intercept		-2.956
R-squared		.248

(a) reference characteristic
* $p < .05$
Source: 1976 Survey of Income and Education

groups. Men in the entire region east of the Mississippi River in the non-Spanish group appear to have lower net earnings, while in the Spanish language group it is men living in the South or in the Texas-Louisiana region who have the lower earnings. More importantly, the returns to education are somewhat lower in the Spanish language group, each additional year of educational attainment being associated with $81 less than that observed for non-Spanish men ($536 - $455 = $81). In itself this would not seem extremely important since the difference in mean attainment levels between the two groups are only two years. However, this $81 gap again points to a discounting of the value of the objective attainments of the Spanish language men.

This discounted value is most evidenced in the returns to work force experience. The earnings associated with additional work force experience are substantially higher in the non-Spanish group. After ten years of experience the income of the non-Spanish men is $3,600 higher than that of comparably qualified recruits, while that of the comparable Spanish language men is only $2,020 higher. After twenty years of experience that income of the non-Spanish men is $5,600 higher than that of the recent entry; that of the Spanish men, $3,400. Thus, the first twenty years of productive work force activity are characterized by widening gaps in the net earnings of the Spanish and non-Spanish minority language men. While these findings may be at least in part attributable to a curvilinear relationship between educational attainment and the experience variable, the data do seem to indicate some further discounting of objective background factors of men in the Spanish language group.

To test the effects of adding the language characteristic and language group variables to the baseline equation, we present the appropriate regression equations in Table 7.20. The pattern of the regression coefficients remain essentially unchanged for the baseline variables. The addition of the language characteristic variables causes very little change in the proportion of the variance explained. In addition, the pattern of the regression coefficients is somewhat unexpected. The men of minority usual language who speak English well have lower net income attainments than do those who reported that they did not speak English well. Earnings differences between the English monolingual men, the English bilingual men, and the minority usual language men who do not speak English well are not significant. The differences are either not large enough, the sample sizes too small, or the variability within a given group too large to attain statistical significance. We are obliged to conclude that there is a relative absence of stratification based on language characteristics when the variable being examined is employment earnings.

The addition of the minority language membership group variables confirms this interpretation. None of the language characteristic groups enjoys significant net income advantages. However, it does appear that certain minority language groups enjoy comparative advantages in the earnings process. Net of other characteristics the men of the Yiddish and Japanese language groups enjoy the highest earnings, earnings significantly higher than the men in all other groups with the exception of the French language men. Three groups seem to have particular difficulties in obtaining earnings commensurate with their baseline characteristics, the Chinese, Filipino, and Native American men. The estimated earnings (net) of these three groups of men do not differ significantly from the estimated earnings of the men in most of the remaining groups. Such findings are at the least indicative of a problem which may have racial overtones. The earnings of the groups generally perceived to be 'White'

Table 7.20 *Regression of employment earnings on selected background variables, full time employed men aged 25-64, non-Spanish minority language groups, United States, 1976*

Regressors	Regression coefficient	Regression coefficient
Education	.512 (.037)*	.532 (.038)*
Experience	.419 (.034)*	.396 (.034)*
Experience^2	-.006 (.001)*	-.006 (.001)*
Northeast	-1.057 (.261)*	-1.089 (.292)*
Midwest	-1.048 (.285)*	-.951 (.313)*
South	-1.530 (.413)*	-1.459 (.430)*
Texas-Louisiana	.297 (.438)	.113 (.475)
Rocky Mountains	-.618 (.569)	-.336 (.605)
Pacific Coast	(a)	(a)
Central City	.114 (.231)	.102 (.235)
Suburban	1.136 (.214)*	1.121 (.215)*
Non-SMSA	(a)	(a)
Core Sector	1.367 (.183)	1.490 (.185)*
Duncan index	.096 (.005)*	.094 (.005)*
English bilingual	-.268 (.202)	-.107 (.205)
MUL: High competence (1)	-.980 (.328)*	-.503 (.341)
MUL: Low competence	-.759 (.525)	-.160 (.542)
English monolingual	(a)	(a)
Chinese		-1.250 (.552)*
Filipino		-.693 (.624)
French		1.131 (.364)*
German		.956 (.301)*
Greek		.308 (.525)
Italian		.890 (.281)*
Japanese		1.985 (.614)*
Polish		.141 (.331)
Portuguese		.223 (.549)
Scandinavian		.901 (.547)
Native American		-1.456 (.966)
Yiddish		2.083 (.496)*
All others		(a)

Continued on next page

Table 7.20 continued

Regressors	Regression coefficient	Regression coefficient
Intercept	−2.172	−2.747
R-squared	.249	.256

(a) reference characteristic
(1) MUL = minority usual language
* $p < .05$
Source: 1976 Survey of Income and Education

are quite positive by comparison, at least after their background characteristics have been controlled. It should also be observed that the French, German, and Italian groups benefit from comparably high levels of net earnings, while the earnings of the Polish language men are significantly lower than those of the men in these three largest minority language groups. Once again we should observe that the proportion of the variance explained is but slightly augmented by the addition of the language group variables.

Summarizing our findings for the non-Spanish men, we have found that the men who usually speak a minority language have greater difficulties obtaining full time employment. These difficulties are partly explained by their lower educational attainments and partly by the impact of their language characteristics. In the case of the men who usually speak a minority language and who also speak English well, it is principally their lower educational attainments which account for their employment difficulties. However, in the case of the men who do not speak English well both language and educational factors contribute equally to the explanation of their lower rates of full time employment. Thus, an inability to speak English well is associated with liabilities in access to full time employment.

Turning to a consideration of the impact of language characteristics on the attainments of the non-Spanish men employed full time in 1975, the SIE data reveal a clear hierarchy of socioeconomic attainments. The two groups of men who usually speak English have higher mean occupational and income attainments than have the men who speak English well but who usually speak a minority language. These latter men have higher mean attainments than have the men who do not speak English well. However, once the relevant background characteristics of the four language characteristic groups have been taken into account, each language characteristic group has occupational and income attainment commensurate with their background characteristics. Thus, after language characteristics have played their role in the process of securing full time employment, we are obliged to conclude that there is little evidence of further differentiation in the labor market.

A similar type of analysis reveals that some groups have socioeconomic attainments which are quite distinctive. Men of the Yiddish language group have markedly higher mean occupational and income attainments, while men in the Filipino and Native American language groups had socioeconomic attainments considerably lower than those of the men in the remaining minority language groups. However, once the background characteristics of the non-Spanish men are taken into consideration, most differences in mean attainment levels are found to be insignificant, rather small, or both. The attainments of the Yiddish language men remain markedly higher, however, than those of the men in most other minority language groups. Nonetheless, on the whole we should conclude that membership in one or another of the specific minority language groups which are present in the non-Spanish sample does not appear to be an extremely important determinant of socioeconomic attainments. Differences in the mean attainments of the various minority language groups are largely explained by differences in the background characteristics of the men in each specific group.

Summarizing our comparative findings for the Spanish and non-Spanish minority language group men, we begin by noting that there are important differences in the characteristics of the two groups. The non-Spanish men are better educated, they are more anglicized, they are older, and they tend to be concentrated in the Midwest and in the Northeast rather than in the Southwest. One important similarity which characterizes the two groups of men should be underlined: anglicisation is related to the mean level of educational attainment. In both groups the men who had made English their usual language had higher mean levels of educational attainment when compared to the men who usually spoke Spanish or some other minority language. Within the group of men which usually spoke a language other than English the men who spoke English well had higher educational attainments than did those men who did not speak English well.

When we considered the relationship between language characteristics and access to full time employment, we noted on the one hand that the effects of educational attainment needed to be segregated from those of language characteristics. We found that an important proportion of the differences between the language characteristic groups in obtaining access to full time employment was explained by differences in educational attainment. However, the inability to speak English well is clearly associated with difficulties in obtaining full time employment. On the other hand, we observed that the Spanish language men appear to be more successful in obtaining full time jobs than were men of the non-Spanish group when we compared men of equivalent language characteristics. This proposition can be easily tested by regressing full time employment on the language characteristics, educational attainment, and language group membership (Spanish vs. non-Spanish) of the sampled men. When such an equation is estimated, we find that net of language characteristics and educational attainment, an additional 2.7 percent of the Spanish language men succeeded in obtaining full time employment. The proportion of the variance explained remains very low (r-squared = .036), but the findings do not suggest that the Spanish language men have special difficulties in obtaining full time jobs. Obviously, their difficulties derive from their lower educational attainments and from their more retentive pattern of language shift. While the effects of this latter variable negatively affect the access of Spanish language men to full time employment, the American interpretation of civil rights does not consider such differentiation to be discriminatory. Nonetheless, the SIE data do suggest that the language characteristics of both Spanish and non-Spanish men are related to employment access opportunities.

The second major aspect of our analysis consisted of an examination of the impact of language characteristics on the attainment process of men who had succeeded in obtaining full time employment. Essentially, the data analysis reveals the presence of linguistic stratification in the Spanish language group but not in the non-Spanish minority language sample. In both groups we found that the men who usually speak English (both the English monolinguals and the English bilinguals) have higher mean attainment levels than the remaining men. Among the men who usually speak a language other than English those who speak English well have higher attainments than those who do not. Nonetheless, in the non-Spanish sample these differences in mean attainment levels are rather adequately explained by differences in the background characteristics of the men in each language characteristic group.

This is not, however, the case in the Spanish language group. The data reveal that men who usually speak the English language enjoy net advantages of occupational and income attainments, that is, over and above those generated by their favorable background characteristics. The pattern of generated occupational benefits is somewhat more ambiguous than that observed for income attainments. With respect to occupational attainment it is only the men of Spanish usual language who do not speak English well who are clearly disadvantaged. The net occupational advantages of the men of English usual language over those men who usually speak Spanish but who speak English well are not significant. However, with respect to earned income, the English monolinugal men enjoy significantly higher income than the English bilingual men, while both groups of English usual language men enjoy significant income advantages when compared to the men who usually speak Spanish. This analysis suggests that there are labor market rewards for abandoning Spanish as one's usual langauge and making English the language which one principally speaks. In addition to undergoing such anglicisation, however, the data also suggest that the simple abandonment of Spanish as a frequently spoken language is also associated with positive income returns. Why this pattern is only observable for the Spanish language is a matter for speculation to which we shall return somewhat later.

The examination of the baseline equations for the Spanish and non-Spanish attainment processes suggests that the objective background variables of the Spanish language men are discounted in the national labor market. In the occupational attainment process each additional year of education brings lower net benefits to the Spanish language men, while employment in the core sector of the economy confers no occupational status advantages at all. This contrasts markedly with the situation observable for the non-Spanish men, who succeeded both in placing a higher percentage of men in the core sector and in obtaining a significant premium associated with employment in the core sector (5.30 points).

While these findings indicate that there is a more uniform treatment of the Spanish language men irrespective of their objective characteristics in the occupational attainment process, the estimated returns to work force experience suggest a similar finding for the income attainment process. While Spanish language men have the expected curvilinear relationship between experience and income, the curvilinear relationship is, however, flatter. Employment earnings do not rise as rapidly nor as high with additional experience as they do in the non-Spanish group. Finally, one further finding is particularly troubling. While the English monolingual men in both groups enjoy equivalent educational attainments, the Spanish language men have occupational and income attainments which are considerably lower than those of the non-Spanish men.

The comparative attainments of White English language men. Although the comparison of the Spanish and non-Spanish men provides interesting insights into the relationship between language characteristics and the attainment process, one further comparison is also warranted. We shall proceed to a comparison of the attainment processes of minority language men to that of White English monolingual, American men. The sampled men come from entirely English language backgrounds. They had English as mother tongue, they currently speak English, and they do not often speak a second language (again, probably not at all). The sample used in the analysis is a stratified subsample of the appropriate cases contained in the SIE. All of the cases where a Chinese, Filipino, French, German, Greek, Italian, Japanese, Polish, Portuguese, Native American, or Scandinavian ethnic identity was selected have been included in this sample. A ten percent random sample of the remaining cases was drawn. The population weights of the cases contained in the 100 percent sample were divided by ten to permit the construction of an appropriately weighted national sample.

The mean socioeconomic attainments of this sample of White English monolingual men are presented in Table 7.21. An examination of the mean attainments reported in this table reveals that the White English monolingual men had mean educational attainments that were 1.12 years higher than those of the non-Spanish men and 3.30 years higher than those of the Spanish language men (from Tables 7.1 and 7.11). It is not, therefore, surprising to observe that the mean occupational attainments of the White English sample are approximately five points higher than those of the non-Spanish men and fifteen points higher than those of the Spanish language men. Nonetheless, the mean incomes of the White English and the non-Spanish men are approximately the same, that of the latter group being only marginally lower. The mean income of these two groups is in turn approximately $4,000 higher than that of the Spanish language men.

Table 7.21 *Mean socioeconomic attainments of white English monolingual men aged 25-64, United States, 1976*

Mean socioeconomic attainments	Total	Employed	Employed full time
Education	13.57	13.77	13.87
Occupation	40.15	44.32	46.22
Income ($)	12,406	13,496	14,771
Population estimate	3,566,458	3,230,869	2,706,553
Percent of total	(100.0)	(90.6)	(75.9)

Source: 1976 Survey of Income and Education

When we examine the proportion of the men who succeeded in obtaining employment in 1975, we find that the White English monolingual men enjoy employment advantages. Some 90.6 percent of these men obtained some employment in 1975 as opposed to 88.7 percent of the non-Spanish men and 88.6 percent of the Spanish language men. A similar situation obtains with respect to having secured full time employment, 75.9 percent of the White English men, 73.6 percent of the non-Spanish men, and 69.2 percent of the Spanish language men having secured full time employment. When, however, the White English men are compared only to the men who usually speak English in the two other groups, the observed differences in employment status disappear. Thus, the overall differences between the percentages of men who obtained either employment in general or full time employment in particular are attributable to the presence of men who continue to use their minority language as the principal language of use. We have already explored the sources of their difficulties. Suffice it to say that among men who usually speak English, the language group of origin, English, Spanish, or non-Spanish, is not related to the ability to secure employment (at least not among men who declare a non-Black ethnic origin, Veltman, 1980b).

Turning to the examination of the determinants of the occupational attainment of the White English monolingual men, their baseline equation is presented in Table 7.22. An examination of the characteristics of this sample shows that these men have on the average less work force experience than the men of the Spanish and non-Spanish groups. However, since the White English men have an educational superiority of three years when compared to the Spanish language men, and since they lack only a single year of work force experience when compared to the Spanish men, it follows that the Spanish language men are approximately two (chronological) years younger. Both the Spanish language group and the White English group are much younger than the men of the non-Spanish group.

The data presented in Table 7.22 also reveal differences in the residence patterns of the White English men. They are less frequently found in the Northeastern region of the United States than the non-Spanish minority language men, and less frequently found in the American Southwest (included in the Texas-Louisiana, Rocky Mountain, and Pacific Coast regions) than the Spanish language men. In addition, the White English men are much less likely to reside in central city areas of the identified SMSA's and much more likely to reside in the non-SMSA regions of the United States.

When we examine the baseline equation itself, a number of findings are quite striking. First of all, each additional year of education is associated with

Table 7.22 *Regression of occupational attainment on selected background variables, full time employed white English monolingual men aged 25-64, United States, 1976*

Variable	Mean or percent	Regression coefficient
Education	13.87	5.19 (.09)*
Experience	22.76	.38 (.08)*
Experience^2	662.98	-.00 (.00)
Northeast	21.07%	.27 (.84)
Midwest	30.35	-1.74 (.80)*
South	21.41	2.65 (.85)*
Texas-Louisiana	9.33	.08 (1.02)
Rocky Mountains	5.37	-1.28 (1.22)
Pacific Coast	12.47	(a)
Central City	13.81%	2.26 (.72)*
Suburban	32.37	3.59 (.54)*
Non-SMSA	53.82	(a)
Core sector	62.27%	3.43 (.49)*
Intercept		-36.18
R-squared		.384

(a) reference characteristic
* $p < .05$
Source: 1976 Survey of Income and Education

a net occupational gain of 5.19 points. This compares with an estimated gain of 4.18 points for non-Spanish men and 3.14 points for the Spanish language men. Secondly, the net impact of experience is positive, rather large (.38), and statistically significant. These two findings suggest that the employers of White English monolingual men appear to differentiate more thoroughly between men of different educational and work experience characteristics. In short, it appears that the objective characteristics of both groups of minority language men are discounted. As we have previously observed, those of the Spanish language men are discounted still more than those of the non-Spanish men.

There are certain other findings which merit discussion as well. The regression equation again shows that men in the South tend to enjoy small net advantages when compared to men in other regions. However, men living in the

Pacific region do not appear to be as disfavored as the men of the minority language groups. Thus, residence in the Pacific Coast region is not unambiguously negative for English language men, whereas it was found to be so in the equations for the Spanish and non-Spanish language men.

In two other respects the equation for the occupational attainment of the White English language men resembles that of the non-Spanish men. Residence in both central city and suburban regions of SMSA regions is associated with positive occupational attainment, and employment in the core sector of the economy is associated with net occupational gains. The net gain associated with core employment is 3.43 points for the English language men, which is intermediate to that obtained for the non-Spanish men (5.30 points) and for the Spanish language men (1.11 points).

The regression equation estimated in Table 7.22 permits us to make one further comparison. If we consider this equation as giving the normative values for each of the background characteristics under examination, we may substitute the observed population characteristics of the minority language samples for those of the White English monolingual men. That is to say, we shall use the regression coefficients estimated for the White English language men estimated in Table 7.22 and the sample characteristics reported in Tables 7.6 and 7.16. This permits us to answer in an approximate way the following question: 'What if the minority language groups were rewarded according to the pattern observed for the White English language men?'

Using the coefficients estimated in Table 7.22, the expected (or predicted) level of occupational attainment for the Spanish language men is 32.75 Duncan points. Their actual attainment was 31.21 points, 95.3 percent of that predicted. There is, therefore, some evidence of a small attainment gap between the Spanish language men and the White English monolingual men which is not attributable to the factors included in the baseline equation. Thus, although the mean occupational attainments of the Spanish language men were 15.01 points lower than those of the White English language men, the largest share of this difference is attributable to their background characteristics.

Moreover, the small gap of 4.7 percent which remains unexplained using the baseline equation is principally attributable to the patterns of geographic residence which differentiate the White English language men and the Spanish language men. If the Spanish language men were rewarded according to an equation based only on education and experience variables, their predicted attainment level is 30.72 Duncan points. This figure is lower than their actual attainment level. Further analysis confirms that the lower percentage of

Spanish language men in the core sector is not an important factor in the explanation of the gap, leaving the residence patterns as the major determinant. Consequently, we are obliged to conclude that this type of comparison does not provide evidence of discrimination against Spanish language men.

Applying a similar procedure to the characteristics of the non-Spanish minority language men, their estimated attainments are 45.05 Duncan points. Actual attainment is 41.77 points, only 92.7 percent of that expected. This comparison suggests that the non-Spanish men have greater difficulty in realizing occupational attainments which correspond to their backgrounds than do the Spanish language men. Once again it is the differential residence patterns which explain this finding. Based only on returns to education and experience, the estimated mean occupational attainment of the non-Spanish men is 42.09 Duncan points. Actual attainment in these circumstances attains 99.2 percent of that anticipated.

A similar type of analysis of the income attainments of White English monolingual men begins with the presentation of the appropriate baseline equation in Table 7.23. An examination of the regional coefficients tends to confirm previous findings that men living in the Pacific Coast region tend to enjoy income premiums when compared to men living in other regions. The data also show that White English monolingual men living in central city regions enjoy income premiums when compared to non-SMSA men. Thus, both groups of men living in SMSA areas have higher earnings than men living outside such areas. Central city men in the Spanish and non-Spanish groups did not enjoy net income advantages when compared to their non-SMSA counterparts.

With respect to the non-geographic variables the findings indicate once again a greater differentiation in earnings associated with changes in background characterisitics. Thus, each additional year of education is associated with a net increase in earnings of $685. Comparable figures for the non-Spanish and Spanish language men were $536 and $455 respectively. Similarly, the experience coefficients indicate a sharper curvilinear relationship between earnings and experience than previously observed. Thus, earnings rise more sharply with additional experience in the English language group. We have previously observed a similar pattern when comparing the Spanish and non-Spanish groups, the Spanish men having lower rates of increase with additional experience. While the return to points of Duncan status is similar irrespective of the sampled group, the returns to core employment in the English language group are higher than those obtained for the minority language men. Core employment is associated with $2,243 of additional income in the White English

Table 7.23 *Regression of employment earnings on selected background variables, full time employed white English monolingual men aged 25-64, United States, 1976*

Regressors	Mean or percent	Regression coefficient
Education	13.87	.685 (.041)*
Experience	22.76	.566 (.032)*
Experience^2	662.98	-.009 (.001)*
Northeast	21.07%	.104 (.313)
Midwest	30.35	-.365 (.296)
South	21.41	-.867 (.318)*
Texas-Louisiana	9.33	-.993 (.382)*
Rocky Mountains	5.37	-.503 (.456)
Pacific Coast	12.47	(a)
Central City	13.81%	.649 (.269)*
Suburban	32.37	1.820 (.203)*
Non-SMSA	53.82	(a)
Core sector	62.27%	2.243 (.182)*
Duncan index	46.22	.098 (.005)*
Intercept		-7.783
R-squared		.281

(a) reference characteristic
* $p < .05$
Source: 1976 Survey of Income and Education

language group, whereas it was associated with $1,426 in the non-Spanish group and $1,877 in the Spanish language group. These education, experience, and core sector coefficients indicate that the minority language men are treated in a similar way, their objective characteristics playing lesser roles in the earnings' determination process.

If we reward the characteristics of the Spanish language men according to the returns estimated in Table 7.23, predicted mean earnings are $11,289. Actual earnings were $10,818 or 95.8 percent of the predicted amount. Regional variables do not explain the 4.2 percent gap which remains. In fact, when an equation which regresses income on education and experience is used for the comparison, predicted earnings are slightly higher, $11,320. Thus, this comparison finds that Spanish language men do not obtain employment earnings commensurate with their educational and experience characteristics, and that their regional distribution, patterns of core employment, or Duncan-indexed attainments change but little the magnitude of the gap. In fairness, however, it should be observed that this gap is markedly less than that which we observed between Black and White men in a previous study (Veltman, 1980b).

A similar comparison predicts mean earnings of $14,584 for the non-Spanish men. Actual earnings were $14,367 or 98.5 percent of that expected. The equation based on education and experience predicted mean income of $14,194, a figure lower than that observed. Thus, the data do not show a residual income gap between the non-Spanish men and the White English monolingual men. Such differences in mean earnings as were observed are adequately explained by differences in background characteristics.

The process of rewarding the minority language men according to the attainment equations of the White English language men does not reveal important differences between the expected and observed attainments of the minority language men. Where such differences were observed, they were largely explained by differences in the residential patterns of the various groups. Only one comparison revealed unexplained residual differences, Spanish language men attaining only 95.6 to 95.8 percent of their predicted earnings. This gap may be attributable to a variety of factors: the negative impact of the large percentages of men who could not speak English well, the negative impact of the retention of Spanish as a usual language, the high proportion of recent immigrants, or a curvilinear relationship (even a very modest one) between education and earnings.

Nonetheless, there is some evidence that the objective characteristics of both the Spanish and the non-Spanish minority language men are ignored to a greater extent than seems to be the case in the White English group. Still, the relative level of occupational attainment and earnings' attainments is sufficiently high such that no major attainment gaps were found in the comparative analysis. This is not to say, however, that this discounting of the value of the objective characteristics of the minority language men is without importance. While the men with poorer labor force characteristics in these groups may not be treated as poorly as may have been anticipated, there is no guarantee that the better prepared men will attain rewards equivalent to those obtained in the White English language group at some future point in time. This point is particularly important with respect to the Spanish language men. The data already suggest that the better prepared, English language men are not receiving labor force rewards which correspond to their educational attainments. Consequently, as higher proportions of men in the Spanish language group come to have higher attainments in the future, continued discounting of their objective characteristics will tend to widen the earnings' gap which already separates English language men and the men of the Spanish language group. In addition, a similar occupational attainment gap may appear even though the 1976 SIE data do not now show that such a gap exists.

A second way of attacking this problem is to examine ethnic differentials in attainment among English language men. This analysis is not entirely satisfactory due to the problem of appropriately weighting the data. If the groups for which one hundred percent samples were drawn are not reduced in relative importance (dividing the population weights by ten), then the resulting sampling means and estimated coefficients do not resemble those of the entire American population. If these groups are reduced in importance, then the standard errors of the estimates are much larger in the resulting equation than they would be had we not adopted this procedure. Briefly, we have estimated the regression coefficients by reducing the importance of the groups which were sampled at one hundred percent, while we estimated the standard errors of the estimate from an equation where these groups were not reduced in importance.

To determine the impact of ethnic origin, we added a set of ethnic variables to the baseline equations reported in Tables 7.23 and 7.24. The ethnic groups so examined were British, Chinese, Filipino, French, German, Greek, Irish, Italian, Japanese, Native American, Polish, Portuguese, Scandinavian, Spanish, and Other Ethnic groups. When the dependent variable was occupational attainment, the men of Spanish ethnic origin had net negative attainment levels 4.40 Duncan points below those of the reference category (Other Ethnic). In addition, this coefficient was significantly lower than those estimated for most of the remaining groups. Similarly, in the income attainment analysis the men of Spanish ethnic origin had net earnings $1,447 below those of the men of the reference group. Again, this figure is significantly different from the coefficients estimated for most of the remaining ethnic groups under examination. These findings which are based on the analysis of the attainments of the White English monolingual men confirm those which we derived from our analysis of the Spanish language men. Together they suggest a pattern of emerging problems for the men of Spanish origin.

This fact needs to be well understood. It is not the differences in the mean occupational and income attainments between the English language men and the men of the Spanish language group which provides evidence for discrimination (or differential treatment). While there is evidence which confirms the existence of the linguistic structuring of labor market achievements within the Spanish group itself, the direct comparison of the men of the Spanish language group to the White English language men is relatively favorable. This is due to the fact that the men who do not speak English well (or more generally, all those men who usually speak Spanish) have attainment profiles which correspond relatively well to their objective educational and experience characteristics. Consequently, the direct comparison of the two groups reveals little or no problem.

However, when we isolate the men who are monolingual in English, the data show that their occupational and income attainments do not compare so favorably with those of their similarly qualified non-Spanish counterparts. When we also examine the experience of the White English monolingual men of Hispanic ethnic origin(s), we find a similar pattern of lower attainments for equivalent characteristics. Thus, it is the most advantaged Spanish-American men, those who have the higher mean educational attainments, those who are the most anglicized, who are experiencing difficulties in obtaining occupational attainments and earnings which correspond to their objective preparation. Since the proportions of Spanish-American men who are English monolinguals may be expected to increase, and since the anglicisation rates of persons of Spanish mother tongue are also increasing over time, this problem should become increasingly important over time. Analytically, it should produce widening gaps between expected and observed attainments of those Spanish-Americans who have most fully embraced two important American values, the English language and a good education.

The attainment process of Spanish language women. The discussion of this topic will be somewhat abbreviated in comparison to our discussion of the attainment process of Spanish language men. Our fundamental interest in this section is the determination of the extent to which the process of linguistic stratification is symmetric or asymetric by sex. Since the background characteristics of men and women in the Spanish language group are very similar, a detailed discussion is not necessary. And since the labor force history of women in the Spanish language group cannot be adequately inferred, the estimated impact of language and other factors is less reliable than that estimated for men. Nonetheless, the data should prove sufficiently reliable to permit us to determine the apparent nature of linguistic stratification in the female work force.

The mean socioeconomic attainments and employment characteristics of

Spanish language women are presented in Table 7.24. Examining first of all the employment characteristics of these women, we observe that only 26.2 percent of the estimated 2,014,645 women represented in the sample worked full time in 1975. Another 23.9 percent obtained part time employment, bringing to 50.1 percent the number of employed women in the Spanish language group. Thus, approximately one-half of the women were not employed outside the home in 1975.

Table 7.24 *Mean socioeconomic attainments of women aged 25-64, Spanish language group, United States, 1976*

Mean socioeconomic attainments	Total	Employed	Employed full time
Education	9.73	10.59	11.12
Occupation	15.30	30.54	33.16
Income ($)	2,382	4,754	6,770
Population estimate	2,014,645	1,009,427	528,197
Percent of total	(100.0)	(50.1)	(26.2)

Source: 1976 Survey of Income and Education

Table 7.24 also shows that the mean educational attainment of Spanish language women was 9.73 years, an attainment level which was .54 of a year lower than that found for Spanish language men (10.27 - 9.73 = .54). However, the employed women had slightly higher educational attainments than did the employed men. These higher educational attainments are associated with slightly higher occupational attainments as measured by the Duncan index. For example, the Spanish language women employed full time had a mean Duncan index of 33.16 while that of their male counterparts was 31.21. As has been frequently found, however, the higher Duncan indices of women are not matched by higher salaries. The average earnings of the full time employed Spanish language woman was $4,048 lower than that of the Spanish language man employed full time ($10,818 - $6,770 = $4,048).

To begin our analysis of the role of language factors in the attainment process, we present in Table 7.25 the employment status of Spanish language women according to their language characteristics. Table 7.25 reveals that the Spanish language women have less anglicized language characteristics than have the Spanish language men. While 45.6 percent of the men reported that they usually spoke English, 'only' 40.9 percent of the women of Spanish

Table 7.25 *Employment status by language characteristics, women aged 25-64, Spanish language group, United States, 1976*

Language characteristics	Employed full time	Employment status Employed part time	Unemployed	Weighted sample	
English usual language:					
English monolingual	34.6%	24.8%	40.6%	151,290	(7.5%)
English bilingual	34.1	26.7	39.2	672,590	(33.4%)
Spanish usual language:					
High English competence	26.9	22.6	50.5	529,220	(26.3%)
Low English competence	15.7	21.9	62.4	661,545	(32.8%)
Total	26.2	23.9	49.9	2,014,645	(100.0%)

Source: 1976 Survey of Income and Education

mother tongue reported that they did so. And while only 24.3 percent of the men reported low competence in English, the figure was 32.8 percent for the women.

Examining the employment patterns of the various language characteristic groups, the two groups of women who usually speak English had similar employment status characteristics. Approximately forty percent of the women in both groups did not work in 1975, while thirty-four percent held full time positions in that year. For the women who usually spoke Spanish the picture was different. Only 26.9 percent of those who reported high competence in English held full time positions, while only 15.7 percent of the women who reported low competence in English succeeded in obtaining full time work. On the other hand, 50.5 percent of those with high competence in English and 62.4 percent of those with low competence in English did not work outside the home in 1975.

This pattern conforms to the pattern previously observed for Spanish language men in Table 7.2. The anglicized women are those most likely to secure employment in general and full time employment in particular. Those who retain Spanish as their principal language experience greater difficulty in securing both types of employment, the women who reportedly did not speak English well having the greatest difficulty.

Since anglicisation is positively related to educational attainment, we have once again estimated an equation to determine the net impact of language characteristics on employment status. When the dependent variable is employment as a whole, both full and part time, the proportion of the variance explained is .052, somewhat higher than that obtained in similar equations for minority language men. Each additional year of education is associated with a net 1.6 percent increase in the number of employed women. Net of educational differences, 1.1 percent more of the English bilingual women were employed in 1975 when compared to English monolingual women. This difference is not, however, statistically significant.

Both groups of women who usually speak English enjoy significant employment advantages when compared to the two groups of women who usually speak Spanish. Net of educational attainments, seven to eight percent fewer of the women who usually spoke Spanish but who had good English skills obtained employment in 1975. The figure attains fourteen to fifteen percent when the women with low competence in English are compared to the women who usually speak English. These differences are statistically significant for all paired comparisons at the .10 level of statistical significance, and for three of the four comparison pairs at the .05 level of significance.

Similar results are obtained when the dependent variable is defined as having been employed full time in 1975. With an r-square of .047 the equation suggests that the impact of language factors on the prospect of obtaining full time employment is somewhat less than that observed previously. Thus, language characteristics appear to play a greater role in gaining access to the labor market as a whole than they do in determining which women obtain full time employment. The differences between the two equations are, nonetheless, relatively minor.

When the equation estimated for the percentage of women employed full time is compared to the similar equation estimated for men, the data suggest that language factors play a more important role in determining the access of women to full time employment than they do for men. For example, when compared to comparably educated English monolinguals, some 3.5 percent less of the men but 5.6 percent less of the women who usually spoke Spanish but who also spoke English well had obtained full time employment in 1975. Comparable figures for those who did not speak English well are 6.7 percent for men and 12.3 percent for women. Presumably, employers are more likely to discriminate on the basis of language criteria when the position being filled is a white collar position, less likely to do so when the job is a blue collar position. The sexual stratification of the labor market works to the disadvantage of Spanish language women who continue to speak Spanish as their principal language. In addition, these women are disadvantaged when compared to Spanish language men, there being higher concentrations of Spanish language women in the more retentive categories.

Turning now to the role of language characteristics among women employed full time, we present the mean socioeconomic attainments of such women in Table 7.26. Briefly, this table shows that the English bilingual women clearly enjoy the highest attainments. They have an educational attainment mean which is more than one year higher than that of the English monolingual women. These latter women have a mean level of educational attainment which is only marginally higher than that of the women who usually speak Spanish but who have high reported competence in English. The women with low reported competence in English have socioeconomic attainments far below those of the remaining groups of women.

When we examine the ethnic composition of the sample of full time employed Spanish language women, we find that it differs in certain respects from the male sample. The relevant data are presented in Table 7.27. The percentage of persons of Cuban ancestry is 6.5 percent higher in the women's sample (14.8 − 8.3 = 6.5), while that of Other Hispanic origins is 6.1 percent

Table 7.26 *Mean socioeconomic attainments by language characteristics, full time employed women aged 25-64, Spanish language group, United States, 1976*

Language characteristics	Mean socioeconomic attainments			Weighted sample
	Education	Occupation	Income	
English usual language:				
English monolingual	11.54	32.09	$7,164	7.5%
English bilingual	12.59	39.87	7,632	33.4
Spanish usual language:				
High English competence	11.04	32.75	6,570	26.3
Low English competence	7.78	19.48	4,947	32.8
Total	11.12	33.16	$6,770	100.0

Source: 1976 Survey of Income and Education

higher (26.9 - 20.8 = 6.1). (The relevant data for men are obtained from Table 7.4). On the other hand, the percentage of Chicanos falls from 58.0 percent in the male sample to 46.9 percent in the female sample. The percentage of Puerto Ricans in the female sample is also lower than that found in the male sample.

The sources of these compositional differences are not hard to find. When a series of ethnic variables are added to the regression of full time employment on educational and language characteristics, both Puerto Rican and Chicano women are found to have significantly lower rates of full time em-

Table 7.27 *Mean occupational and income attainments of 25-64 year old women employed full time, Spanish ethnic groups, United States, 1976*

Ethnic group	Occupation	Income	Percent of sample
Chicano/Mexican	31.10	$6,075	46.9%
Puerto Rican	31.04	7,318	11.4
Cuban	38.92	6,960	14.8
Other Hispanic	34.48	7,317	26.9
Total	33.16	$6,770	100.0%

Source: 1976 Survey of Income and Education

ployment than the women in the remaining two ethnic groups. Cuban women are more likely to have been employed full time than were the Other Hispanic women. Thus, it is not the language or educational characteristics of the various Spanish ethnic groups which account for differences in the rates of full time employment. It is either a systematic pattern of discrimination which benefits Cuban women and disadvantages Chicano and Puerto Rican women, or it is a differential pattern of preferences for employment in the home rather than in the labor market. Some combination of the two explanations is probably likely. These observed ethnic differences in full time employment among Spanish language women were generally absent among the men of the Spanish language group. In fact, the data indicate that Chicano men were slightly more likely to have been employed full time than expected, Puerto Rican men slightly less likely. The intergroup differences, however, are generally small among the men.

Table 7.27 also reveals that Cuban and Other Hispanic women have the highest occupational attainments. The observed patterns by ethnic group parallel rather closely those obtained for Spanish language men. The occupational status of Chicano women is, nonetheless, three points higher than that of their male counterparts. With respect to earnings, however, the Puerto Rican, Cuban, and Other Hispanic women have similar mean incomes. While mean earnings of the Chicano women are markedly lower than those of the women in the three other groups, the clear hierarchy of occupational and income attainments by ethnic origin which was visible among men in the Spanish language group is nearly absent among women. Ethnic differentiation appears largely restricted to the male work force, where, as we have seen, the observed differences in mean earnings are adequately explained by (non-ethnic) background characteristics.

To ascertain the extent to which observed mean differences in occupational attainment are explained by language or ethnic characteristics, we present in Table 7.28 the results of the appropriate regression equations. Examining the equation regressing the Duncan index on language characteristics, Table 7.28 shows that the proportion of the variance explained is .132, a figure smaller in size to that observed in the equation estimated for Spanish language men (Table 7.5). The English bilingual women have significantly higher occupational attainments than the English monolingual women, while the women of low English competence have significantly lower attainments than all other groups of women. As expected, the difference in attainment between the English monolingual women and the women who usually speak Spanish but who also reported high competence in spoken English is not significant. The

Table 7.28 *Regression of occupational attainment on language characteristics and ethnic origin of full time employed women aged 25-64, Spanish language group, United States, 1976*

Regressors	Mean or percent	Regression coefficient
Language characteristics:		
English bilingual	43.39%	7.78 (2.51)*
Spanish usual language:		
High English competency	26.99	.65 (2.65)
Low English competency	19.71	-12.62 (2.77)*
Intercept (English monolingual)	(9.91)	32.09
R-squared		.132
Ethnic origin:		
Chicano/Mexican	46.92%	-3.38 (1.83)
Puerto Rican	11.38	-3.44 (2.68)
Cuban	14.81	4.44 (2.45)
Intercept (other Hispanic)	(26.89)	34.48
R-squared		.018

* p < .05
Source: 1976 Survey of Income and Education

equation regressing occupational attainment on ethnicity is characterized by a very low proportion of the variance explained (r-squared = .018). In addition, most of the between-group differences are not statistically significant, although Cuban women have significantly higher occupational attainments than do Puerto Rican or Chicano women.

However, even such language characteristic and ethnic differences as have been observed may be adequately explained by uncontrolled background differences. In Table 7.29 we present the regression of occupational attainment on the baseline factors retained in previous analyses. We note first of all that there are some differences in the distribution of background characteristics when we compare the male and female Spanish language samples. Full time employed women are more likely to be found in the Northeast and Southern regions of the United States, and in the suburban areas of SMSA's. In addition, the percentage of women who obtained such employment in the core sector of the economy is substantially lower (47.93 - 35.58 = 12.35%).

The estimated net effects of the specific background variables show a

Table 7.29 *Regression of occupational attainment on selected background variables, full time employed women aged 25-64, Spanish language group, United States, 1976*

Regressors	Mean or percent	Regression coefficient
Education	11.12	2.95 (.19)*
Experience	23.08	-1.36 (.21)*
Experience^2	667.19	.03 (.00)*
Northeast	23.46%	.04 (1.74)
Midwest	6.29	-.70 (2.62)
South	15.02	3.26 (2.03)
Texas-Louisiana	20.66	5.35 (1.85)*
Rocky Mountains	7.76	6.79 (2.53)*
Pacific	26.81	(a)
Central City	39.95%	.55 (1.70)
Suburban	28.44	4.03 (1.77)*
Non-SMSA	31.61	(a)
Core sector	35.58%	3.96 (1.26)*
Intercept		10.54
R-squared		.416

(a) reference characteristic
* $p < .05$
Source: 1976 Survey of Income and Education

marked similarity in many respects to the equation estimated for Spanish language men in Table 7.6. Each additional year of education is assoicated with a net increase of approximately three Duncan points. While regional variation appears to be somewhat less important, residence in suburban areas confers statistically significant occupational advantages. In two respects, however, the findings by sex differ. First of all, employment in the core sector is associated with the anticipated advantages for the Spanish language women, whereas it was not for the men. Secondly, the experience variables are statistically significant in the equation for the Spanish language women. Interestingly, the findings indicate that younger women enjoy significant occupational attainment advantages when compared to older women (net of other characteristics). Furthermore, the pattern is curvilinear in form, women who terminated their formal education twenty or more years ago (prior to the Survey) having net occupational attainments approximately fifteen points lower than those of the most recent entrants to the labor force. In fact, the data indicate consistent improvements in the status of Spanish language women over the past ten to fifteen years. Despite the dubious value of the experience variable when used in the analysis of female attainment, such a finding suggests that affirmative action programs may have had some effect in this particular area.

In Table 7.30 we present the results of the regression equations which add the language and ethnic variables to this baseline set of background variables. Examining the equation which adds the language variables to the baseline equation, we observe that the English bilingual women enjoy significantly higher occupational attainments than do the women in the English monolingual group. T-tests show that their attainments are significantly higher than those of the women of Spanish usual language who do not speak English well. No other differences satisfy the criteria of statistical significance. The women who do not speak English well have attainment levels which compare favorably to those of the Spanish (usual) language women who speak English well and to those of the English monolingual women. Thus, the lower attainments of the women who do not speak English well are adequately explained by their background characteristics, most notably their lower mean educational attainment. The addition of the ethnic variables to the equation causes no change in these observations, nor does it reveal any unexplained differences between ethnic groups in occupational attainment.

This examination of the data does not indicate the presence of extensive linguistic stratification among women of the Spanish language group once their background characteristics have been taken into account. Thus, once access to full time employment has been achieved, it appears that the retention of the Spanish language as a second language is accorded a premium in occupational status. Such a premium appears to be accorded only after Spanish language women have been anglicized. For those women who continue to speak Spanish as their principal language, no such premium is evident. On the whole, however, the data indicate a relative absence of extensive linguistic stratification.

The equations regressing employment income on the language and ethnic characteristics of Spanish language women are presented in Table 7.31. Once again, the proportion of the variance explained is not very high in either equation, although the effects of language characteristics on earnings are more pronounced than are the effects of ethnic origin. When compared to English monolinguals, only the women of Spanish usual language who did not speak English well had significantly lower incomes. T-tests reveal, nonetheless,

Table 7.30 *Regression of occupational attainment on selected background variables, full time employed women aged 25-64, Spanish language group, United States, 1976*

Regressors	Regression coefficient		Regression coefficient	
Education	2.63	(.21)*	2.66	(.22)*
Experience	-1.32	(.21)*	-1.32	(.21)*
Experience^2	.02	(.00)*	.02	(.00)*
Northeast	1.31	(1.74)	.78	(2.27)
Midwest	.41	(2.62)	.31	(2.64)
South	5.15	(2.13)*	5.47	(2.59)*
Texas-Louisiana	5.57	(1.85)*	5.66	(1.89)*
Rocky Mountains	6.78	(2.51)*	6.72	(2.52)*
Pacific Coast	(a)		(a)	
Central City	.83	(1.70)	.72	(1.72)
Suburban	4.01	(1.77)*	4.10	(1.78)*
Non-SMSA	(a)		(a)	
Core sector	3.58	(1.26)*	3.58	(1.27)*
English bilingual	4.44	(2.09)*	4.56	(2.11)*
Spanish usual language:				
High English competence	1.58	(2.23)	1.73	(2.28)
Low English competence	-1.70	(2.46)	-1.36	(2.52)
English monolingual	(a)		(a)	
Chicano/Mexican			-.38	(1.77)
Puerto Rican			.92	(2.39)
Cuban			-1.08	(2.30)
Other Hispanic			(a)	
Intercept	10.68		10.45	
R-squared	.426		.426	

(a) reference characteristic
* $p < .05$
Source: 1976 Survey of Income and Education

that the women of high English competence and the English bilingual women also had significantly higher incomes than women who did not speak English well. The English bilingual women also had mean earnings significantly higher than the Spanish language women who spoke English well. These findings tend to indicate the presence of relatively weak linguistic stratification, the

Table 7.31 *Regression of employment earnings on language characteristics and ethnic origin of full time employed women aged 25-64, Spanish language group, United States, 1976*

Regressors	Mean or percent	Regression coefficient
Language characteristics:		
English bilingual	43.39%	.468 (.414)
Spanish usual language:		
High English competence	26.99	−.594 (.437)
Low English competence	19.71	−2.217 (.458)*
Intercept (English monolingual)	(9.91)	7.164
R-squared		.090
Ethnic origin:		
Chicano/Mexican	46.92%	−1.242 (.291)*
Puerto Rican	11.38	.775 (.426)
Cuban	14.81	−.357 (.390)
Intercept (other Hispanic)	(26.89)	7.317
R-squared		.046

* $p < .05$
Source: 1976 Survey of Income and Education

women of English usual language tending to enjoy marginally higher earnings than the women who usually spoke Spanish. Once again, among these latter the women who did not speak English well had markedly lower earnings.

Examining the equation which regresses employment income on ethnic origin, Chicano women are found to have lower mean earnings than women in any other group. The only other statistically significant difference indicates that Puerto Rican women had higher incomes than did Cuban women. As we suggested earlier, ethnic differentiation in earnings does not appear to be an important factor in the determination of female earnings in the Spanish language group.

The regression results obtained by estimating the appropriate baseline equation are reported in Table 7.32. A number of findings which characterize the earnings' process of women as a whole are immediately evident. The net return to both educational and occupational attainment is approximately one-half that observed for men of similar backgrounds. The same is true for returns from core sector employment. Frequently, the returns to experience

Table 7.32 *Regression of employment earnings on selected background variables, full time employed women aged 25-64, Spanish language group, United States, 1976*

Regressors	Mean or percent	Regression coefficient
Education	11.12	.237 (.038)*
Experience	23.08	.025 (.037)
Experience²	667.19	-.000 (.001)
Northeast	23.46%	1.267 (.302)*
Midwest	6.29	.552 (.454)
South	15.02	-.310 (.352)
Texas-Louisiana	20.66	-.602 (.324)
Rocky Mountains	7.76	-.043 (.441)
Pacific Coast	26.81	(a)
Central City	39.95%	.906 (.294)*
Suburban	28.44	.527 (.309)
Non-SMSA	31.61	(a)
Core sector	35.58%	.556 (.220)*
Duncan index	33.16	.048 (.006)*
Intercept		1.230
R-squared		.326

(a) reference characteristic
* $p < .05$
Source: 1976 Survey of Income and Education

are not significant or do not show the familiar curvilinear pattern. These differences in the income attainment process are clearly evident in the Spanish language group.

In addition, the returns to region and place of residence differ in the equation estimated for Spanish women. Residence in the Northeast and/or in central cities is associated with net earnings' advantages. Midwestern and/or suburban residence also appears to be relatively advantageous, although not always statistically significant.

The results of the regression equations which add language and ethnic characteristics to the baseline equation are presented in Table 7.33. Adding the language characteristics causes some changes in the coefficients estimated for certain of the baseline variables. Once the language characteristics of

Table 7.33 *Regression of employment earnings on selected background variables, full time employed women aged 25-64, Spanish language group, United States, 1976*

Regressors	Regression coefficient		Regression coefficient	
Education	.168	(.040)*	.190	(.041)*
Experience	.026	(.037)	.028	(.037)
Experience^2	-.000	(.001)	-.000	(.001)
Northeast	1.648	(.307)*	1.914	(.388)*
Midwest	.687	(.450)	.717	(.452)
South	.247	(.366)	.858	(.444)
Texas-Louisiana	-.482	(.320)	-.565	(.325)
Rocky Mountains	-.000	(.434)	.018	(.434)
Pacific Coast	(a)		(a)	
Central City	1.089	(.292)*	1.100	(.293)*
Suburban	.605	(.304)	.703	(.306)*
Non-SMSA	(a)		(a)	
Core sector	.425	(.218)	.430	(.217)
Duncan index	.044	(.006)*	.044	(.006)*
English bilingual	-.064	(.360)	-.017	(.363)
Spanish usual language:				
High English competence	-.858	(.383)*	-.757	(.384)
Low English competence	-1.700	(.422)*	-1.540	(.430)*
English monolingual	(a)		(a)	
Chicano/Mexican			.417	(.304)
Puerto Rican			.116	(.409)
Cuban			-.702	(.374)
Other Hispanic			(a)	
Intercept	2.462		1.797	
R-squared	.351		.357	

(a) reference characteristic
* $p < .05$
Source: 1976 Survey of Income and Education

Spanish language women have been controlled, residence in the South is associated with relatively positive income returns, while residence in the Northeast and in the Midwest is still more advantageous than previously estimated. However, due to the impact of language characteristics on placement in the core sector, employment in the core sector is no longer associated with statistically higher earnings.

The examination of the net impact of language characteristics on the earnings of Spanish language women reveals a clear pattern of linguistic differentiation. The women of English usual language, both bilingual and monolingual, have net earnings significantly higher than those of the women of Spanish usual language. Among these latter the women who speak English well have significantly higher earnings than those who do not speak English well.

When the ethnic variables are added to the analysis, the proportion of the variance explained is increased but slightly. T-tests reveal that at these sample sizes only one pair of coefficients differ significantly. Chicano women, net of all other included factors, have higher net earnings than Cuban women. Thus, it is the remaining factors which explain the lower mean earnings of Chicano women. The addition of the ethnic variables causes one other minor change in the language coefficients. The women of English usual language no longer enjoy statistically significant income advantages when compared to the women who usually speak English well. However, the differences in the estimated regression coefficients still satisfy the .10 criterion of statistical significance, a finding which may reassure us with respect to the general direction of the results obtained.

Summarizing our principal findings for the role of language characteristics in the attainment process of Spanish language women, we found first of all that women who usually spoke English were more likely to be found in the labor force in 1975. The observed advantages of these women persisted even after the educational attainments of Spanish language women were held constant. This pattern of advantages is similar to that observed for Spanish language men except that the impact of language characteristics on both full time employment in particular and employment of any type in general appears to be stronger among women. Since larger percentages of the women were found in the more retentive categories of language use, they are doubly disadvantaged in the attempt to secure access to employment. Once again, the women who did not speak English well suffered the greatest access problems.

Once having obtained full time employment, the language characteristics of Spanish language women appeared to play a relatively minor role in the occupational attainment process. English bilingual women appear to have secured an occupational premium associated with their bilingualism. However, linguistic stratification appears to play a more important role in the earnings' process. The women of English usual language enjoy earnings' premia, while the women of Spanish usual language who did not speak English well were found to be under-rewarded with respect to their other background characteristics. The pattern of earnings' stratification is similar to that observed for men save that English monolingualism confers no additional benefits on Spanish language women.

These findings suggest a symmetric pattern of linguistic stratification in the marketplace for both the men and women of the Spanish language group. The process of access to employment opportunities and to subsequent occupational status and earnings operates in essentially the same manner. Unearned premia are associated with anglicisation, unearned penalties with the retention of Spanish as one's usual language. Additional penalties accrue to persons who do not speak English well. The extent of the rewards and penalties varies somewhat by sex, but the model is the same. Anglicisation pays off in the labor market for persons of Spanish mother tongue.

The attainment process of other minority language women. The objective pursued in this section of the chapter is the determination of the extent to which the model developed to explain the role of language among Spanish language women also explains the role of language among non-Spanish minority language women. Alternatively, the attainment process of these latter women may resemble that of their male minority language counterparts.

The mean socioeconomic attainments and employment characteristics of the non-Spanish women are presented in Table 7.34. This table shows first of all that 29.1 percent of the estimated 4,148,300 women of the non-Spanish minority language groups were employed full time in 1975. Another 25.9 percent were employed part time during the same year, bringing to 55.0 per-

Table 7.34 *Mean socioeconomic attainments of women aged 25-64, non-Spanish minority language groups, United States, 1976*

Mean socioeconomic attainments	Total	Employed	Employed full time
Education	11.93	12.46	12.70
Occupation	20.58	37.43	41.05
Income ($)	3,212	5,840	8,119
Population estimate	4,148,300	2,281,454	1,208,109
Percent of total	(100.0)	(55.0)	(29.1)

Source: 1976 Survey of Income and Education

cent the number of employed women in this group. Thus, a larger percentage of the non-Spanish women were employed in 1975 than was observed for the Spanish language women.

Table 7.34 also shows that the better educated women were more likely to be employed. However, the mean educational attainments of the non-Spanish women in each category of employment status are lower than those observed for men in the same group (Table 7.11). This finding contrasts with the relationship observed in the Spanish language group, where the employed Spanish women had higher mean educational attainments than did the men. The marginally lower educational attainments of the non-Spanish women are associated with occupational attainments which are also somewhat lower than those observed for non-Spanish men. As expected, their income attainments are markedly lower than those observed for their male counterparts. The average earnings of the full time employed women were $6,248 lower than that observed in Table 7.11 for full time employed non-Spanish men ($14,367 − $8,119 = $6,248).

Beginning our analysis of the role of language characteristics in the attainment process of non-Spanish women, we present in Table 7.35 the employment status of these women according to their language characteristics. As we found for the Spanish language group, the women of the non-Spanish group have more retentive language characteristics than the men. While 55.8 percent of the non-Spanish men were English monolinguals, 51.4 percent of the women had such a language use pattern. On the other hand, 6.6 percent of the women reported that they did not speak English well while only 4.2 percent of the men claimed such low competence in English. Needless to say, the non-Spanish women remain markedly more anglicized than their Spanish language counterparts.

Examining the distribution of employment status by language characteristics, the data conform to previous findings. The more anglicized women are more likely to have obtained full time employment, those women who retain the use of the minority language as usual language, less likely. However, when we compare Table 7.35 to the comparable table for Spanish language women (Table 7.25), certain differences merit comment. First of all, among women who usually speak English, the proportion of Spanish language women in both the paid labor force in general and in full time employment in particular is approximately four percent higher. For example, while 34.6 percent of the English monolingual women in the Spanish group had obtained full time employment, the figure is only 29.7 percent for the non-Spanish women. Secondly, among the women of minority usual language who had high

Table 7.35 *Employment status by language characteristics, women aged 25–64, non-Spanish minority language groups, United States, 1976*

Language characteristics	Employed full time	Employment status Employed part time	Unemployed	Weighted sample	
English usual language:					
English monolingual	29.7%	25.9%	44.4%	2,132,048	(51.4%)
English bilingual	30.6	26.1	43.3	1,331,283	(32.1%)
Minority usual language:					
High English competence	27.7	26.6	45.7	410,415	(9.9%)
Low English competence	19.8	23.6	56.6	274,552	(6.6%)
Total	29.1	25.9	45.0	4,148,298	(100.0%)

Source: 1976 Survey of Income and Education

competence levels in English, a greater percentage of the non-Spanish women worked part time in 1975, causing a lower percentage of the non-Spanish women to remain outside the paid labor force in 1975. Thirdly, among women who did not speak English well, the percentage of non-Spanish women who obtained both part time and full time employment was higher. Consequently, while 62.4 percent of the Spanish language women remained unemployed in 1975, the figure was 5.8 percent. lower in the non-Spanish group (62.4 - 56.6 = 5.8).

These findings lead us to suggest that language characteristics play a much weaker role in determining access to the labor force in the non-Spanish group. In fact, once we take into account the educational attainments of women in the various language characteristic groupings, the language variables are unrelated either to employment in general or to full time employment in particular. The differences in percentages of women employed full time and women unemployed (not in the paid labor force) are explained by differences in the mean educational attainments of women in each language characteristic group. This finding contrasts with that previously observed not only for the Spanish language women, but also with that observed for the Spanish and non-Spanish minority language men.

Turning to the analysis of the role of language characteristics once the non-Spanish women have obtained full time employment, we present in Table 7.36 the mean socioeconomic attainments of these women. This table reveals

Table 7.36 *Mean socioeconomic attainments by language characteristics, full time employed women aged 25-64, non-Spanish minority language groups, United States, 1976*

Language characteristics	Mean socioeconomic attainments			Weighted sample
	Education	Occupation	Income	
English usual language:				
English monolingual	12.72	41.69	$8,049	52.4%
English bilingual	13.32	44.19	8,717	33.7
Minority usual language:				
High English competence	13.00	36.42	7,487	9.4
Low English competence	7.23	19.83	5,770	4.5
Total	12.70	41.05	8,119	100.0

Source: 1976 Survey of Income and Education

that English bilingual women have the highest mean educational, occupational, and income attainments. The second highest educational attainments belong to the women of high competence in spoken English but who usually speak a minority language. However, their occupational and income attainments are lower than those of the English monolingual women, a finding which suggests a pattern of additional rewards for anglicized women. The women who do not speak English well have by far the lowest mean socioeconomic attainments.

Differences in the mean occupational and income attainments of women in specific minority language groups are presented in Table 7.37.

Table 7.37 *Mean occupational and income attainments of 25-64 year old women employed full time, non-Spanish minority language groups, United States, 1976*

Language group	Occupation	Income	Percent of sample
Chinese	40.68	$8,926	3.6%
Filipino	45.75	9,778	5.8
French	40.91	7,482	10.7
German	40.86	7,603	16.8
Greek	42.76	7,567	2.3
Italian	41.40	8,264	16.5
Japanese	35.12	7,003	4.3
Polish	34.90	7,861	9.4
Portuguese	28.29	5,949	2.8
Scandinavian	45.18	8,002	3.0
Native American	39.10	6,603	1.1
Yiddish	55.89	8,930	2.1
All others	43.21	8,821	21.6
Total	41.05	$8,119	100.0%

Source: 1976 Survey of Income and Education

With respect to occupational attainment only two groups depart markedly from the mean. Portuguese language women have attainments substantially lower than those of women in most other groups, Yiddish language women higher than those of women in most other groups. Similar findings were obtained for men.

With respect to income attainments the women of the Japanese, Native American, and Portuguese language groups have mean earnings which are more than $1,000 below the sample mean. While the men in the two latter minority language groups also had lower mean earnings than those in most other groups, the men of the Japanese language group enjoyed mean earnings well above the male sample mean. While Filipino men had mean earnings relatively close to that of the sample mean, Filipino women are the only group of women having mean earnings more than $1,000 higher than the female sample mean. These findings suggest that there may be an element of asymmetric stratification for specific minority language groups. On the whole, however, it appears that both the men and women of certain language groups tend to enjoy higher mean earnings, while those in other groups have similarly lower mean earnings.

We shall now examine whether the observed differences in mean occupational attainments of specific minority language groups and specific language characteristic groups meet the established tests of statistical significance. The results of the appropriate equations are presented in Table 7.38. Examining first of all the regression of occupational attainment on the language characteristics of non-Spanish women, we find that English bilingual women have attainments which are significantly higher than those of English monolingual women. Both groups of women of English usual language have significantly higher attainments than do the women of minority usual language who speak English well. All three of these groups of non-Spanish women have superior attainments when compared to the women who did not speak English well. The proportion of the variance in occupational attainment explained by the language characteristics of the non-Spanish women remains quite low (r-squared = .053).

The effects of membership in specific language groups appears even weaker (r-squared = .035). While most minority language groups have mean occupational attainments similar to those of the reference group (Other minority languages), four groups of women have mean attainment levels which differ significantly from that of the reference group (and from that of most other groups). Japanese and Polish language women have mean attainments approximately eight points lower than the attainment of women in the reference group. However, the attainment level of Portuguese language women is nearly fifteen points below that of the reference group, while that of the Yiddish women is more than twelve points higher.

Since these observed effects are based simply on differences in the mean occupational attainments of the specific language characteristic and minority language groups, a more refined analysis which controls for the background characteristics of the non-Spanish women is imperative. The appropriate base-

Table 7.38 *Regression of occupational attainment on language characteristics and language group of full time employed women aged 25-64, non-Spanish minority language groups, United States, 1976*

Regressors	Mean or percent	Regression coefficient
Language characteristics:		
English bilingual	33.69%	2.50 (.92)*
Minority usual language:		
High English competence	9.42	−5.27 (1.47)*
Low English competence	4.51	−21.86 (2.04)*
Intercept (English monolingual)	(52.38)	41.69
R-squared		.053
Language group:		
Chinese	3.62%	−2.53 (2.38)
Filipino	5.85	2.54 (1.95)
French	10.73	−2.30 (1.57)
German	16.75	−2.35 (1.36)
Greek	2.27	−.45 (2.93)
Italian	16.51	−1.81 (1.37)
Japanese	4.25	−8.09 (2.23)*
Polish	9.45	−8.31 (1.63)*
Portuguese	2.77	−14.92 (2.67)*
Scandinavian	3.02	1.97 (2.58)
Native American	1.10	−4.11 (4.10)
Yiddish	2.05	12.68 (3.06)*
Intercept (all others)	(21.63)	43.21
R-squared		.035

* $p < .05$
Source: 1976 Survey of Income and Education

line regression results are reported in Table 7.39. The background characteristics of the non-Spanish women parallel in almost every respect those of the non-Spanish men. Two exceptions seem worth noting. Central city women appear more likely to have obtained full time employment than suburban women. While only 26.53 percent of the non-Spanish men employed full time lived in the central city, the equivalent percentage is 30.68 percent for women. Suburban women are less likely to be employed full time. In addition, the percentage of men employed in the core sector is again markedly superior to

Table 7.39 *Regression of occupational attainment on selected background variables, full time employed women aged 25-64, non-Spanish minority language groups, United States, 1976*

Regressors	Mean or percent	Regression coefficient
Education	12.70	3.60 (.13)*
Experience	29.03	-.19 (.12)
Experience^2	995.90	.00 (.00)
Northeast	41.48%	1.31 (1.00)
Midwest	24.67	-1.26 (1.09)
South	7.60	.99 (1.52)
Texas-Louisiana	5.41	3.55 (1.72)*
Rocky Mountains	3.10	3.61 (2.15)
Pacific Coast	17.74	(a)
Central City	30.68%	3.11 (.87)*
Suburban	31.66	3.77 (.86)*
Non-SMSA	37.66	(a)
Core sector	41.37	5.14 (.71)*
Intercept		-7.02
R-squared		.341

(a) reference characteristic
* $p < .05$
Source: 1976 Survey of Income and Education

that found for the women, an additional 17.43 percent of the non-Spanish men being employed in the core sector (58.80 - 41.37 = 17.43).

An examination of the regression coefficients also shows a strong relationship between the occupational attainment process of the non-Spanish men and women. While the net returns of educational attainment to the non-Spanish women is .58 Duncan points lower than that estimated for the men (4.18 - 3.60 = .58), the pattern of net returns to experience, size of place of residence, and core sector are similar. Only with respect to the impact of regional variables does the equation for the non-Spanish women resemble that estimated for the Spanish language women (Table 7.29). In general, then, the occupational attainment process of non-Spanish women strongly resembles that observed for the non-Spanish men. While returns to education are higher than those estimated for the Spanish language women, there is no evidence that recent entrants to the labor market enjoy improved occupational status. The occupational attainment process apparently differs very little for older as opposed to younger women, a finding which contrasts with that observed for Spanish language women.

We shall now procede to the estimation of equations which add the language characteristic and language group membership variables to this baseline equation. The relevant data are presented in Table 7.40. The introduction of the language variables causes little change in the estimated impact of the baseline variables. However, a very slight pattern of increased net occupational attainment for the most recent entrants to the labor market is apparent. The impact of the language characteristics themselves on the occupational attainment process is minimal. The perceived advantages of English bilingual women are adequately explained by their background characteristics, as are the perceived disadvantages of women with low competence in spoken English. However, the women who usually speak a minority language but who report high verbal competency in English suffer distinct disadvantages when compared to the other three groups of women. The exact nature of the problem can only be imagined. Perhaps employers do not expect that women with seventh grade educations who do not speak English well should make English their principal language of use. They accord employment opportunities which correspond to seventh grade educations (more or less). On the other hand, there is perhaps a tendancy to penalize women who speak English sufficiently well to make it their personal (preferred) language but who do not do so. They may be expected to anglicize but have not done so. However, why such a phenomenon should exist among non-Spanish women but not among Spanish language women nor among non-Spanish men is unexplainable.

The pattern of the language coefficients is unchanged by the introduction of the membership group variables. Membership in a number of minority language groups is associated with higher than expected attainments. Yiddish language women have net occupational attainments significantly higher than women in all other groups. Women in the Greek, Scandinavian, and Italian language groups have lower but still positive advantages, whereas membership in the Filipino and Japanese language groups is associated with net disadvantages. These findings suggest that language group membership may be a more important variable in the labor force stratification of women than it is for non-Spanish men, a finding reinforced by the fact that the proportion of the variance explained rises by .020 when the minority language group variables are added to the equation. The improvement in the male equation was only .010.

Table 7.40 *Regression of occupational attainment on selected background variables, full time employed women aged 25-64, non-Spanish minority language groups, United States, 1976*

Regressor variables	Regression coefficient	Regression coefficient
Education	3.45 (.14)*	3.52 (.14)*
Experience	-.28 (.12)*	-.45 (.13)*
Experience^2	.00 (.00)	.01 (.00)*
Northeast	1.10 (1.00)	-1.60 (1.11)
Midwest	-1.61 (1.10)	-3.18 (1.20)*
South	.70 (1.51)	-1.28 (1.55)
Texas-Louisiana	3.13 (1.71)	1.97 (1.78)
Rocky Mountains	4.05 (2.15)	2.13 (2.28)
Pacific Coast	(a)	(a)
Central City	3.97 (.88)*	3.49 (.88)*
Suburban	3.97 (.85)*	3.35 (.85)*
Non-SMSA	(a)	(a)
Core sector	4.92 (.71)*	4.65 (.71)*
English bilingual	-.48 (.78)	-.29 (.78)
MUL: High competence (1)	-7.79 (1.29)*	-6.71 (1.34)*
MUL: Low competence	-2.60 (1.87)	-2.57 (1.94)
English monolingual	(a)	(a)
Chinese		-.07 (2.08)
Filipino		-7.36 (1.70)*
French		.36 (1.32)
German		-.42 (1.15)
Greek		6.82 (2.39)*
Italian		3.62 (1.16)*
Japanese		-6.44 (1.95)*
Polish		-1.17 (1.37)
Portuguese		3.88 (2.28)
Scandinavian		4.50 (2.18)*
Native American		.38 (3.61)
Yiddish		11.49 (2.52)*
All others		(a)
Intercept	-2.18	1.04
R-squared	.350	.370

(a) reference characteristic
(1) minority usual language
* p < .05
Source: 1976 Survey of Income and Education

One other finding seems worthy of note. The addition of the language group variables has revealed a curvilinear relationship between experience and occupational attainment. The pattern is stronger than that observed for the non-Spanish men but not as strong as that observed for the Spanish language women. Nonetheless, the data now indicate that, net of language characteristic and other background variables, more recent entrants into the labor market enjoy significantly higher occupational status than similar qualified older women. If these findings may be in part attributable to the existence of affirmative action programs, then the Spanish language women appear to have experienced somewhat more rapid progress than the non-Spanish women. Progress is evident, however, for both groups.

The equations regressing employment income on the language characteristics and the minority language group of non-Spanish women are presented in Table 7.41. Once again, the proportion of the variance in earnings explained by either set of variables is very low. Examining the impact of language chararcteristics on earnings, the English bilingual women have significantly higher mean earnings than do the women in the remaining three groups. The women of minority and usual language who do not speak English well have earnings which are significantly lower than those of the remaining groups of women. As in the case of occupational attainment, it is likely that these differences are due to differences in background characteristics.

Table 7.41 also shows that eight different groups of minority language women have mean earnings significantly lower than those of women in the residual (All others) reference group. There are, nonetheless, few significant differences in earnings between the women of these groups nor between these groups and those women in most other groups. Suffice it to say that women in the Filipino language group enjoy mean earnings which are substantially higher than those of women in most of the remaining minority language groups. On the other hand, women in the Portuguese and Native American groups have earnings which appear to be substantially lower than those of women in the remaining groups, most of the differences not attaining, however, statistical significance.

To determine the extent to which the observed gross differences in earnings between language characteristic groups and between specific minority language groups remain after background characteristics are controlled, we present the appropriate baseline equation in Table 7.42. In general, the earnings' process of the non-Spanish women tends to resemble rather closely that already observed for the Spanish language women. The estimated net value of each year of educational attainment is approximately the same. In neither group is

Table 7.41 *Regression of employment earnings on language characteristics and language group of full time employed women aged 25-64, non-Spanish minority language groups, United States, 1976*

Regressors	Mean or percent	Regression coefficient
Language characteristics:		
English bilingual	33.69%	.668 (.209)*
Minority usual language:		
High English competence	9.42	-.563 (.335)
Low English competence	4.51	-2.280 (.464)*
Intercept (English monolingual)	(52.38)	8.049
R-squared		.017
Language group:		
Chinese	3.62%	.105 (.536)
Filipino	5.85	.957 (.440)*
French	10.73	-1.339 (.352)*
German	16.75	-1.218 (.307)*
Greek	2.27	-1.254 (.658)
Italian	16.51	-.557 (.308)
Japanese	4.25	-1.818 (.501)*
Polish	9.45	-.960 (.368)*
Portuguese	2.77	-2.872 (.602)*
Scandinavian	3.02	-.819 (.580)
Native American	1.10	-2.218 (.922)*
Yiddish	2.05	.109 (.689)
Intercept (all others)	(21.63)	8.821
R-squared		.025

* $p < .05$
Source: 1976 Survey of Income and Education

experience significantly related to earnings, a finding which is probably a function of the poor quality of the experience variable when applied to women. In addition, while the magnitude of the net values of region of residence vary for the two groups of women, residence in the Northeast is associated with higher earnings while residence in the South, Texas-Louisiana, or Rocky Mountain regions is associated with lower earnings. And while residence in an SMSA is generally associated with higher earnings, non-Spanish women enjoy a higher premium.

Table 7.42 *Regression of employment earnings on selected background variables, full time employed women aged 25-64, non-Spanish minority language groups, United States, 1976*

Regressors	Mean or percent	Regression coefficient
Education	12.70	.248 (.035)*
Experience	29.03	.007 (.030)
Experience^2	995.90	.000 (.001)
Northeast	41.48%	.508 (.242)*
Midwest	24.67	.098 (.264)
South	7.60	-.329 (.366)
Texas-Louisiana	5.41	-1.792 (.414)*
Rocky Mountains	3.10	-.517 (.520)
Pacific Coast	17.74	(a)
Central City	30.68%	1.350 (.211)*
Suburban	31.66	.940 (.207)*
Non-SMSA	37.66	(a)
Core sector	41.37	.757 (.173)*
Duncan index	41.05	.069 (.005)*
Intercept		1.104
R-squared		.235

(a) reference characteristic
* $p < .05$
Source: 1976 Survey of Income and Education

This is not, however, the only area in which the non-Spanish women seem to obtain higher net rewards for their background characteristics. Employment in the core sector is associated with a net income gain of $757, a gain which is $201 higher than that estimated for Spanish language women. Each additional point of Duncan-indexed occupational attainment is associated with a net gain of $69, a figure $21 higher than that estimated for Spanish language women. Since the mean occupational attainment of Spanish language women is nearly eight points lower, the lost income is approximately $170. These findings indicate once again that the objective background characteristics of men and women in the Spanish language group are subject to discounting in the employment marketplace.

While these findings suggest that the non-Spanish women are more closely rewarded in accordance with their background characteristics than are the Spanish women, the data indicate that the value of the background characteristics of the non-Spanish women appears severely discounted when compared to the non-Spanish men. The net value of educational attainment, employment in the core sector, and occupational attainment are higher for the non-Spanish men. And since the percentage of non-Spanish women employed in the core sector is markedly inferior to the percentage of the non-Spanish men (58.80 − 41.37 = 17.43), even the rewards secured by employment in the core sector are not as widely shared.

To test the effects of adding the language characteristic and specific language group variables to the baseline equation, we present the appropriate regression results in Table 7.43. The observed pattern of the regression coefficients remains essentially unchanged by the introduction of the language variables. An examination of the language characteristic coefficients reveals that none of the remaining groups enjoy earnings which differ significantly from those of the English monolinguals. However, the women who usually speak a minority language but who also speak English well are found to have net earnings which are significantly lower than those of both the English bilingual women and the women of minority usual language who do not speak English well. This finding parallels that obtained for occupational attainment, indicating cumulative comparative losses for the women in this group. They not only do not obtain occupational status commensurate with their background characteristics; given this lower occupational status, they do not attain income commensurate with their background characteristics.

This situation is essentially unchanged when the minority language group variables are added to the equation. The data indicate that four groups have earnings significantly lower than those of the residual reference group. However, since nearly all of the regression coefficients are negative and since the standard error of most of the regression coefficients is so large, there are few significant differences in earnings. The magnitude of the negative coefficient of the Yiddish language women warrants comment. This is caused by the extraordinarily high occupational status of the women of this group. Table 7.40 revealed that Yiddish women had occupational attainments 11.49 points higher than that predicted by their assorted background characteristics. Since each point of Duncan status is associated with net earnings of $70 (Table 7.43), the equation forces us to expect that the Yiddish language women will have earnings which are approximately $805 higher than their non-occupational background characteristics alone would lead us to predict. If this amount were to be subtracted, Yiddish women might be expected to have net earnings

Table 7.43 *Regression of employment earnings on selected background variables, full time employed women aged 25-64, non-Spanish minority language groups, United States, 1976*

Regressors	Regression coefficient	Regression coefficient
Education	.253 (.037)*	.233 (.038)*
Experience	-.009 (.030)	.024 (.031)
Experience^2	.000 (.001)	-.000 (.001)
Northeast	.521 (.243)*	.651 (.271)*
Midwest	-.074 (.266)	.042 (.294)
South	-.342 (.366)	-.227 (.379)
Texas-Louisiana	-1.788 (.416)*	-1.596 (.436)*
Rocky Mountains	-.433 (.521)	-.254 (.559)
Pacific Coast	(a)	(a)
Central City	1.385 (.215)*	1.333 (.217)*
Suburban	.926 (.207)*	.876 (.209)*
Non-SMSA	(a)	(a)
Core sector	.759 (.174)*	.765 (.175)*
Duncan index	.068 (.005)*	.070 (.005)*
English bilingual	.265 (.189)	.296 (.191)
MUL: High competence (1)	-.541 (.316)	-.738 (.330)*
MUL: Low competence	.314 (.454)	.082 (.476)
English monolingual	(a)	(a)
Chinese		.603 (.509)
Filipino		.430 (.419)
French		-.728 (.324)*
German		-.745 (.281)*
Greek		-1.009 (.588)
Italian		-.381 (.285)
Japanese		-.619 (.480)
Polish		-.180 (.335)
Portuguese		-.929 (.560)
Scandinavian		-.737 (.520)
Native American		-.327 (.887)
Yiddish		-1.517 (.622)*
All others		(a)

Continued on next page

Table 7.43 continued

Regressors	Regression coefficient	Regression coefficient
Intercept	1.074	1.103
R-squared	.237	.244

(a) reference characteristic
(1) MUL = minority usual language
* p < .05
Source: 1976 Survey of Income and Education

which are only $712 lower than those of the reference group women ($1,517 - $805 = $712). The situation of the Yiddish women is unique. They have succeeded in obtaining positions which confer much higher occupational status than their backgrounds would lead us to expect; however, these same positions are rather low-paying given their high status. On the whole, the Yiddish language women have employment earnings which are more or less consonant with their non-occupational background characteristics and which differ little from most of the remaining language groups.

Summarizing our principal findings for the attainment process of non-Spanish women, we have found that differences in the rates of access to employment for women of different language characteristics are adequately explained by their educational backgrounds. There is no evidence of linguistic stratification at this point in the employment process. Little evidence was found for the existence of stratification by language characteristics among women who obtained full time employment in 1975. Only the women who retained the principal use of a minority language but who also spoke English well appear to experience particular difficulties. Why this should be the case cannot be explained by prevalent theory. Nonetheless, the examination of the data lead us to conclude that there is little, if any, linguistic stratification or discrimination evident in the attainment process of non-Spanish minority language women. Since this finding so closely parallels that obtained for the non-Spanish minority language men, we may have greater confidence in its validity.

The relative absence of linguistic stratification in the non-Spanish group contrasts with the findings obtained for Spanish language women. Language factors played a role both in access to the labor market and in the attainment process for these latter women. When comparing the employment process of

Spanish and non-Spanish minority language women, however, one further question needs to be addressed. What are the causes of the lower percentage of Spanish language women who obtained part time or full time positions in 1975? Do the data indicate discrimination against Spanish language women in terms of access to employment opportunities? To respond to this question we have once again combined the two minority language samples and estimated an equation which regresses full time employment on educational attainment, language characteristics, and a dummy variable representing membership in the Spanish language group. The results of this equation suggest that the lower rates of full time employment of Spanish language women are explained by their educational attainments and by their language characteristics. Net of these two factors the rate of full time employment of Spanish language women was nearly three percent higher than that of non-Spanish women.

Since the role of language characteristics in the employment process differs in the two minority language samples, combining the two samples may not provide an optimal solution to the problem. A second way to approach this problem is to reward Spanish women according to the pattern observed for the non-Spanish women. We insert the mean educational attainments of the Spanish women into the equation regressing full time employment on the educational attainments of non-Spanish women. This procedure leads us to predict a rate of full time employment of Spanish language women. The predicted rate is 24.9 percent; the observed rate, 26.2 percent. Thus, the educational characteristics of the Spanish language women are themselves adequate to explain their lower rates of full time employment. In fact, the data continue to suggest that Spanish language women actually enjoy slight access advantages to full time employment.

When a similar procedure is applied to examine access rates to employment in general, we predict that 49.5 percent of the Spanish language women should have been employed in 1975. The actual figure was 50.1 percent, indicating once again that net of educational attainments Spanish language women do not appear disadvantaged in terms of access to employment opportunities. One may be permitted to observe that given the lower mean salaries of Spanish language men, Spanish language women are frequently obliged to seek employment to increase family income. While this is likely to be the case, the point is nonetheless the same. When Spanish language women seek employment, they appear to be at least as likely to find it as are the non-Spanish women given their educational attainments.

The comparative attainments of White English language women. To ascertain the relative success of both the Spanish and non-Spanish minority language women in the marketplace, we shall again compare their experience to those of White English monolingual women whose mean socioeconomic attainments are presented in Table 7.44. These women are better educated and have higher rates of both employment in general and full time employment in particular. These latter advantages derive directly from the former. The higher mean educational attainments of the White English language women are reflected in higher occupational attainments, attainments which are slightly superior to those of the White English language men. However, when we compare the mean earnings of the White English language women to those of the non-Spanish minority language women, it appears that the White English language women have not been able to translate their superior backgrounds into additional earnings.

Table 7.44 *Mean socioeconomic attainments of white English monolingual women aged 25-64, United States, 1976*

Mean socioeconomic attainments	Total	Employed	Employed full time
Education	13.21	13.63	13.63
Occupation	26.87	44.31	47.21
Income ($)	3,504	5,794	8,239
Population estimate	3,809,370	2,302,633	1,184,849
Percent of total	(100.0)	(60.4)	(31.1)

Source: 1976 Survey of Income and Education

That which interests us the most is, of course, the attainment process of the White English women. The appropriate baseline equation regressing occupational attainment on the background characteristics of White English language women is reported in Table 7.45. Apart from the fact that the net value of educational attainment is associated with higher occupational attainment in the White English language sample, the pattern of regression coefficients presented in Table 7.45 strongly resembles that obtained for the non-Spanish minority language women (Table 7.39). The net value of experience, size of place of residence, and placement in the core sector is approximately the same for both sets of women. There are, however, also some differences in the impact of region of residence, location in the Pacific Coast states being

Table 7.45 *Regression of occupational attainment on selected background variables, full time employed white English monolingual women aged 25-64, United States, 1976*

Variable	Mean or percent	Regression coefficient
Education	13.63	4.25 (.15)*
Experience	23.40	-.20 (.12)
Experience^2	698.10	.00 (.00)
Northeast	23.41%	-2.19 (1.16)
Midwest	27.19	-3.93 (1.14)*
South	23.43	-1.71 (1.18)
Texas-Louisiana	8.51	.38 (1.49)
Rocky Mountains	4.66	1.00 (1.18)
Pacific Coast	12.80	(a)
Central City	17.07%	2.51 (.95)*
Suburban	29.70	3.46 (.79)*
Non-SMSA	54.23	(a)
Core sector	45.24%	5.74 (.68)*
Intercept		-10.85
R-squared		.309

(a) reference characteristic
* p < .05
Source: 1976 Survey of Income and Education

associated with more positive returns in the equation for the White English language women. On the whole, however, the process of attainment for the White English language women and the non-Spanish minority language women is quite similar, there being perhaps some slight discounting of the value of educational attainment and core placement for the non-Spanish women.

Taking once again the equation for the White English language women as giving the normative net values for each of the background characteristics under examination, we may calculate the expected values of occupational attainment for each group of minority language women by substituting their sample characteristics for those of the White English language women. The predicted level of occupational attainment for the Spanish language women is 34.96 Duncan points. Their actual attainment was 33.16 points, 94.9 percent of that predicted. There is some evidence of a small attainment gap which is not explained by differences in background characteristics. The gap is similar in size to that observed previously for the attainments of Spanish language men and to that estimated elsewhere for all women of Hispanic ethnic origin (Veltman, 1980b). Nonetheless, all but 1.80 Duncan points of the 14.05 point gap in the mean attainments of White English language women and Spanish language women is explained by differences in the background characteristics of the two groups of women, notably differences in educational attainments.

When we apply this procedure to the characteristics of the non-Spanish minority language women, predicted attainment is 39.60 points. Since actual attainment was 41.05 points, the data indicate that the non-Spanish women had occupational attainments 3.7 percent higher than that predicted. There is, consequently, no evidence of possible discrimination based on ethnic criteria against women of the non-Spanish minority language group.

Turning to the analysis of the income attainment process of White English language women, the appropriate baseline equation is presented in Table 7.46. The findings once again confirm the desirability of residence in the Pacific Coast region, a finding which contrasts with those obtained for the minority language women. Residence in the Northeast region appears clearly preferable for women of the Spanish and non-Spanish minority language groups.

With respect to personal background characteristics the findings suggest a pattern of stronger net rewards for experience, education, and employment in the core sector than was found for Spanish or non-Spanish women. The return to points of Duncan-indexed occupational status is somewhat lower than that obtained in the previous analyses. On the whole, however, these findings suggest greater differentiation between English language women of varying backgrounds than is found in the two groups of minority language women. In other words, the value of the personal characteristics of the minority language women is discounted in the marketplace.

Nonetheless, when we assign the return rates of the characteristics of the White English language women to the sample characteristics of the minority language women, the minority language women enjoy actual earnings which exceed their predicted earnings. Predicted earnings for the Spanish language women were $6,152, while actual earnings were $6,770. Expected earnings for the non-Spanish women were $7,788, while actual earnings were $8,119. We conclude that the data do not support a theory which finds that White English language women enjoy income premia when compared to women from minority language backgrounds. In fact, the women from minority language backgrounds have earnings which exceed those predicted from their baseline background characteristics.

Table 7.46 *Regression of employment earnings on selected background variables, full time employed white English monolingual women aged 25-64, United States, 1976*

Regressors	Mean or percent	Regression coefficient
Education	13.63	.593 (.039)*
Experience	23.40	.086 (.027)*
Experience^2	698.10	-.001 (.001)
Northeast	23.41%	-.198 (.258)
Midwest	27.19	-.464 (.253)
South	23.43	-.717 (.261)*
Texas-Louisiana	8.51	-1.121 (.329)*
Rocky Mountains	4.66	-.737 (.402)
Pacific Coast	12.80	(a)
Central City	17.07%	.871 (.210)*
Suburban	28.70	1.111 (.176)*
Non-SMSA	54.23	(a)
Core sector	45.24%	1.454 (.153)*
Duncan index	47.21	.043 (.004)*
Intercept		-3.895
R-squared		.260

(a) reference characteristic
* $p < .05$
Source: 1976 Survey of Income and Education

When a series of ethnic variables are added to the baseline occupational and income determination equations of the White English language women, the data do not suggest that women of Hispanic ancestry have particular difficulties in the marketplace. In terms of occupational attainment the net value of membership in the Hispanic ancestry group is slightly positive when compared to membership in most other groups. With respect to income attainments the women of Hispanic origin have net earnings which are slightly lower than those of women of most other origins. The differences are not sufficiently large to attain statistical significance. In fact, the single group of White English monolingual women which has both occupational and income attainments signficantly lower than those of comparably qualified women from other groups is the group of Filipino ethnic origin. Otherwise, ethnic differentiation in the White English monolingual sample of women appears to be relatively unimportant.

Conclusion. The impact of language characteristics on the attainment process of minority language men and women can be rather readily summarized. The data generally support the proposition that the more anglicized men and women are generally more likely to have obtained access to full time positions. These differences tend to persist even after educational attainment has been controlled, although the relationship between language characteristics and employment access is relatively weak.

However, once access to full time employment has been accomplished, the data indicate the presence of a pattern of linguistic rewards and liabilities with respect to men and women of the Spanish language group, a pattern which is not to be found in the non-Spanish minority language group. More anglicized men and women in the Spanish language group have mean attainment levels which are somewhat higher than those of similarly qualified, more retentive men and women. Consequently, the findings suggest the presence of discrimination based on linguistic grounds against men and women in the Spanish language group who have more retentive patterns of language use. This linguistic discrimination is not found in the attainment analyses of non-Spanish minority language men and women.

The particularistic nature of this discrimination suggests that it is in fact ethnic rather than linguistic in nature. More properly, we might label it ethnolinguistic discrimination. Moreover, the data analysis indicates that the disadvantages of Hispanic-Americans, particularly males, are evolutionary in nature. Although the data tend to support the proposition that the form of discrimination against men and women of Spanish mother tongue is linguistic in nature, the data do not support a theory of widespread ethnic discrimination against such persons. Ethnic discrimination is an emergent phenomenon. As members of the Spanish language group undergo the anglicisation process, linguistic stratification necessarily diminishes. As linguistic stratification declines, discrimination based on ethnic origin criteria arises to take its place. One of the consequences of the emergence of ethnic discrimination may be the finding that men and women of English mother tongue in the Hispanic origin groups do not appear to enjoy occupational and income attainments which differ significantly from those of their peers of Spanish mother tongue (Veltman, 1980b; Grenier, 1981). Their achievement levels are suppressed below those predicted by their background characteristics.

The nature, extent, and future of this emergent pattern of discrimination based on ethnic criteria is difficult to assess. Whether the discrimination is intended and perceived as racial in character is impossible to ascertain from Census-type data. It is also rather difficult to determine whether the eventual earnings' gap between White English monolingual men and an anglicized male population of Hispanic origin will come to approximate the Black-White earnings' differential. This problem can again be partitioned into two parts, access to full time employment and treatment once employed full time.

When we isolated the English monolingual men of Hispanic ancestry and compared them to the English monolingual men of non-Hispanic ancestries, an estimated 3.9 percent less of the Hispanic men had obtained full time employment when education was held constant. This difference was statistically significant when the appropriate estimates of standard errors were calculated. However, when we assign Blacks to full time employment at the rates observed for White English monolingual men, we expect to find that 71.9 percent of the Black men were employed full time in 1975. The observed percentage was 61.8 percent. Consequently, we conclude that the Hispanic men of English monolingual language characteristics have markedly more favorable rates of full time employment than do Black men. As a result, the mean earnings of such Hispanic men should remain somewhat higher in the future than those of Black men.

On the other hand, once access to full time employment has been secured, the estimated earnings' gap which separates White English monolingual men of Hispanic and non-Hispanic ancestry resembles very strongly the Black-White income gap. Once we control for the education and experience characteristics of the White English monolingual men, the income of the Hispanic origin men is $1,725 lower than that of their non-Hispanic peers. This figure is comparable in magnitude to the $1,800 differential which we have previously obtained for Black men (Veltman, 1980b: 51). These findings suggest that the earnings' differential separating English monolingual men of Hispanic ancestry from those of non-Hispanic origins may come to approximate that which separates Black and White men, at least among those who have succeeded in obtaining full time employment.

Thus, as the Spanish language population undergoes anglicisation, individuals obtain educational attainments similar to those of other members of the American population and are increasingly forced to compete for employment opportunities which correspond to their educational attainments. Once this competition is engaged, the English monolinguals of Hispanic origin experience some difficulty in obtaining full time employment but not nearly as much difficulty as do Black Americans. However, once employed full time, ethnic factors appear to play as large a role in the income determination process as they do in Black-White comparisons.

Once again, while our prinicipal concern is not with male-female differentiation in the work force, sex differentiation in earnings is much more powerful than is ethnic or linguistic differentiation. For example, English monolingual women of Hispanic ancestry are somewhat more likely to have obtained full time employment than similarly qualified women of non-Hispanic origins. Black women are also more likely to have obtained full time employment when the effects of education are controlled. On the other hand, there are no significant differences in the earnings of similarly qualified non-Hispanic women and Hispanic women in the White English monolingual language group. These findings tend to confirm the general pattern of the lack of importance of ethnic criteria previously observed for White non-Spanish, Black, and Hispanic origin women (Veltman, 1980b).

Briefly, then, we have found that discrimination against Hispanic origin Americans is ethno-linguistic in nature. The pattern of linguistic stratification which accords premia to persons who usually speak English tends to be particularistic, a reward applied only to persons of Spanish mother tongue. The type of discrimination found appears to evolve with the anglicisation of the Spanish language population, becoming more serious as English monolinguals of Hispanic origin compete with English monolinguals from non-Hispanic groups. Such discrimination based on ethno-linguistic criteria appears to be most specifically a problem for men in the American labor force, more serious for Black than for Hispanic origin men. Should sexual stratification of the labor force diminish over the coming decades, we might expect that ethno-linguistic factors may become increasingly important in the analysis of the attainments of American women as well.

Chapter Eight

The Impact of Language Characteristics on the Educational Attainments of American Children

Introduction. Given the importance of the educational attainments of adults in minority language groups in the socioeconomic attainment process, we shall turn in this chpater to an analysis of the determinants of educational attainment itself. In the previous chapter we treated educational attainment as a given, a fact which potential employees and persons already employed present to those in a position to accord both employment and promotions. We then ascertained whether the language characteristics of these adults had any additional impact on the socioeconomic attainments of minority language men and women.

However, as Garcia (1979) has pointed out, it may well be that the language characteristics of adults determined (or caused), at least in part, their level of educational attainments. That is to say, the more anglicized members of the group have higher educational attainments partly because they have a better grasp of the English language. Nonetheless, when considering the case of minority language adults, the contrasting point of view can also be argued. The better educated adults are more anglicized because they are better educated. They are more likely to have had greater exposure to formal training in English. It is difficult to tell which factors are causal when the two are so intimately associated. Consequently, some other procedure must be developed to examine the role of language characteristics in the process of securing formal education.

A somewhat better approximation of the impact of language characteristics may be obtained by examining the relative attainments of children currently enrolled in school (or who have recently left school). The SIE permits us to ascertain the highest grade of education attained by children aged 4 to 17 in 1976. This measure of educational attainment is relatively crude, permitting us to examine current placement in grade level as a function of the age of the child. We have no information on the actual performance level of children still enrolled in school and we have no information on the age at which school-leaving is either anticipated or already accomplished. Nonetheless, measures of relative educational attainment have come to be used with increasing frequency by educational analysts in U.S. government agencies. Consequently, we shall examine in this chapter the relative educational attainments of minority language children. In the next we shall examine more closely the correlates of educational performance.

Two factors in particular have retained the attention of previous analysts of the SIE data, the role of language characteristics and the role of social class origins. Silverman (1978), McArthur (1979), and Brown et al. (1980) have shown from cross-tabular analyses that children who live in households where a minority language is frequently spoken (or who themselves speak a minority language) are more likely than other children to be found in lower than expected grade levels. McArthur (1979) and Brown et al. (1980) have also demonstrated the presence of the expected social class effects, children from higher income households or having better educated parents being less likely to be enrolled below anticipated grade level. Both language and social class effects are similarly related to decisions to terminate formal schooling (Silverman, 1978; McArthur, 1979; Brown et al. 1980). However, in none of these studies have the authors attempted to distinguish the relative contribution of each of these factors. It is, for example, quite likely that social class factors account for a large proportion of the lowered educational attainment of children living in minority language homes.

Methodology. Following the approach of the previously published reports, we have selected as a sampling parameter the presence of a minority language as the usual household language or that of a second household language spoken with some frequency. Our sample of Spanish language children consists of all children living in homes where the Spanish language is frequently spoken. The application of the sample parameters leads to a sample which closely resembles that presented in our chapter on intergenerational language shift, except that children under six years of age were excluded since they had not yet begun their formal, state-sponsored education. Also excluded were children for whom the educational attainment data were missing. Once again, we have grouped into a single sample all children from non-Spanish minority language homes.

The measure of educational attainment which serves as the dependent variable in this chapter differs somewhat from that used by the previous investigators and is more fully described in our earlier study of educational attainment (Veltman, 1980a). Both types of measures are, nonetheless, based on an expected relationship between the age of the child and the grade in which the child is enrolled. Empirically, for example, McArthur (1979) observed that older seven year olds will be found in the second grade in the spring of a given year while the younger ones will be enrolled in first grade. She considers these two years to be modal grades for seven year old children. On the other hand, Silverman (1978) and Brown et al. (1980) fix first grade as the norm for seven year old children, children eight or more years of age in the first grade being considered to be below expected grade level. In practice, all three investigators consider the same children to be enrolled below grade level, since it is only with this end of the attainment spectrum with which they are concerned.

Nonetheless, educational attainment is normally a variable which is measured in metric (continuous) form. While some children may be expected to be enrolled below grade level, others may be enrolled in a grade considered advanced for their age. In addition, some children will be found to be further below or further above grade level than others, a fact which is unmeasured by previous investigators. Consequently, we have developed a metric measure of educational attainment which permits a more global assessment of the total range of educational advantages and disadvantages which may be observed in any given group.

This measure of educational attainment is based on the norm defined by Silverman (1978) and Brown et al. (1980). Seven year old children in the first grade were assigned a score of zero (0), indicating no deviation from expectation. An eight year old child in the first grade was assigned a score of minus one (-1), since this child is considered to be one grade lower than expected. Similarly, a nine year old child in first grade is assigned a value of minus two (-2), while a six year old in first grade received a score of plus one (+1). This method was applied to each combination of grade level and age.

The choice of a metric measure of educational attainment facilitates the integration of children no longer enrolled in school into the attainment analysis. They were assigned the highest grade of schooling already completed on the assumption that re-enrollment would likely require the completion of the entire year of schooling for those who had left during an academic year. In any case, a separate analysis for those who had already left school is no longer necessary.

The selection of the metric measure of educational attainment as opposed to the one-tailed measure used by Federal investigators is not without consequence. We have previously shown (1980a: Appendix B) that only children from the Spanish language group have lower than expected educational attainments when the metric measure is adopted. When using the one-tailed measure proposed by previous analysts, both Black children and English monolingual children of anglicized Hispanics also have lower than expected educational attainments. Moreover, social class factors play a more powerful role in predicting which children are enrolled below grade level (one-tailed) than they do in predicting the specific grade in which children are enrolled (metric). Regardless of the measure selected, however, the proportion of the variance explained is quite low, a finding which suggests that placement in grade level is largely indeterminate. At the very least, it is not determined to an important extent by the variables retained as explanatory.

Since we are principally interested in the effects of the language characteristics of children on their educational attainments, we have developed a series of language indices. Children were defined as being English monolinguals or English bilinguals according to the usual criteria. Children who usually spoke a minority language were divided into two groups, those who reported that they also spoke English frequently (from the second language question) and those who reported that they did not. The former are defined as Spanish bilinguals; the latter as monolingual in a minority language. Since the principal home language is likely related to the child's language characteristics, and since the child's own characteristics are those presented to the teacher in the school setting, the language of the home has not been retained as an explanatory variable.

The language characteristic variables have been combined with a variable representing the nativity of the child to produce a series of interactive variables. That is to say, each language characteristic group is divided into two parts, those children born outside the United States being separated from native born children. The decision to create an interactive set of variables was reached after tests indicated that the interactive variables produced much more satisfactory equations. The proportion of the variance explained was much higher than that produced when the two variable sets were separated.

The remaining independent variables used in the analysis are the age of the child, the geographic region of the United States, parental education, and membership group. The age of the child was included because we expected that increased age would be associated with lower educational attainments. First of all, the opportunity to fall behind in grade level should increase as the child progresses through school. Secondly, the introduction of the age variable may permit us to make longitudinal-type interpretations of the findings. The maximum period of time in which important changes may have altered the structure of educational attainment for 6 to 13 year old children is eight years (the period of time which elapsed since the thirteen year olds began school). Since it is unlikely that such major changes have occurred during such a short period, differences in the net educational attainments of the older children in the age group may capture the rate at which children are falling behind in school. Two forms of the age variable were tested, a linear form in which increased age may have a constant effect on attainment, and a non-linear form in which the rate of change may vary.

Also retained for analysis is a set of regional variables similar to those used in the previous chapter. The United States is divided into six regions, the Northeast, the Midwest, the South, Texas-Louisiana, the Rocky Mountains, and the Pacific Coast. In addition, each region is divided into an urban (central city and suburb) and rural region, an interactive set of variables proving much more satisfactory in this case as well. This produces a set of twelve regional variables. As we found in our chapter on intergenerational language shift, the parental education variable is the best single predictor of the socioeconomic status variables. Consequently, the occupational status of the head of the household and household income were dropped as predictor variables (see Veltman, 1980a for a detailed discussion).

The final set of variables to be used in the analysis consists of the membership group variables to which specific groups of children belong. We have again divided the Spanish language group into its Cuban, Chicano, Puerto Rican, and Other origins components, while the Residual group is divided into Chinese, Filipino, French, German, Greek, Italian, Japanese, Navajo, Polish, Portuguese, Scandinavian, Yiddish, and Other groups. These membership group variables are introduced both to see whether specific groups have specific difficulties or advantages and to statistically reduce the heterogeneity of the sample.

The plan of analysis is relatively simple. We shall first of all examine the attainment process of 6 to 13 year old children. The planners of the SIE made no provision to identify drop-outs in this age group, so that the analysis is restricted to children enrolled in school. We shall subsequently examine the attainments of the 14 to 17 year old children, a group which contains both drop-outs and those still enrolled in educational institutions. We begin our presentation of the data by reporting the mean attainments of children in specific groups. This is followed by the estimation of a baseline equation regressing educational attainment on geographic region and educational attainment. We then add in a stepwise fashion the nativity/language, membership group, and age variables. The chapter concludes with a comparative analysis of the educational attainments of minority language children and White English language children.

The educational attainments of Spanish language children. The principal data pertaining to the educational attainments of Spanish language children are presented in Table 8.1.

Table 8.1 *Mean educational attainment by nativity and language characteristics, by ethnic origin and by age, Spanish language children aged 6-17, United States, 1976*

Characteristics	Children aged 6-13		Children aged 14-17	
	Percent	Mean educational attainment	Percent	Mean educational attainment
Nativity and language:				
Native born:				
English monolingual	24.58	.433	27.36	.147
English bilingual	41.75	.431	41.29	.127
Spanish bilingual	15.00	.276	9.47	-.529
Spanish monolingual	0.61	.221	0.40	-.391
Foreign born:				
English monolingual	0.79	.176	0.67	.101
English bilingual	9.16	.316	9.70	.112
Spanish bilingual	6.86	.090	8.02	-.258
Spanish monolingual	1.25	.033	3.09	-2.196
Ethnic origin:				
Chicano/Mexican	58.48	.299	61.12	-.080
Puerto Rican	15.75	.428	13.74	-.048
Cuban	5.27	.327	5.56	-.027
Other ethnic groups	20.50	.480	19.58	.080
Total	100.00	.357	100.00	-.036
N (unweighted)	2,723		1,387	
N (weighted, 000's)	1,830		890	

Source: 1976 Survey of Income and Education

Table 8.1 reveals first of all that as expected, there is an important difference in the mean attainments of the younger and older children. Younger children had a mean attainment level of .356, while older children had a mean of -.036. The score for the younger children indicates that on the the average, 35.6 percent of the Spanish language children were found in the upper half of the modal year established for their age by McArthur (1979); the score for the older children indicating that nearly all children were found in the lower grade appropriate for children their age, while 3.6 percent were enrolled in the grade just below their appropriate grade level.

Turning our attention to the educational attainments of the 6 to 13 year old children, Table 8.1 reveals that the sample includes 2,723 children which when weighted appropriately gives a national estimate of 1,830,000 children. As expected from our chapter on intergenerational anglicisation, there is an important group of English monolingual children, nearly all of whom are native born. The percentage of children who usually speak Spanish is quite low (15.00 + 0.61 + 6.86 + 1.25 = 23.72%). The percentages who do not speak English often are still lower, 1.86 percent (0.61 + 1.25 = 1.86%).

When educational attainment is related to the set of language and nativity variables, two preliminary conclusions are obtained. First of all, native born children have somewhat higher mean educational attainments. Secondly, within nativity categories the children who usually speak English have higher educational attainments. The data also indicate that Cuban and Chicano children have somewhat lower mean educational attainments than do children in the two remaining Spanish groups.

Turning to the examination of the older children, the data reveal that the native born children are more anglicized and the foreign born children are less anglicized than are the younger children in the Spanish language group. The mean attainment scores suggest that while language characteristics appear to have become more important, the effects of nativity seem markedly attenuated among the older children. For example, the native born Spanish bilinguals have an attainment level still lower than their foreign born counterparts. The most striking finding in the table, however, concerns the mean attainment level of foreign born Spanish monolinguals. The data indicate that the average child in this group is more than two years behind expected grade level. Even though the percentage of children in this category is relatively small, it is apparent that they suffer from severe educational difficulties. Young persons in the remaining groups of children who usually speak Spanish also have attainment levels lower than those of the children who usually speak English but the magnitude of the problem is not as great.

To examine the extent to which these mean differences in language and nativity characteristics are associated with differences in educational attainment, we present in Table 8.2 the results of the regression of educational attainment on these two factors for the younger Spanish children. Also included are the results of a similar equation regressing educational attainment on the ethnic origin characteristics of these children.

The results reported in Table 8.2 indicate that the children who are both

Table 8.2 *Regression of educational attainment on selected background characteristics of Spanish language children aged 6-13, United States, 1976*

Characteristics	Percent	Regression coefficient
Nativity and language characteristics:		
Native born:		
English bilingual	41.75%	-.002 (.004)
Spanish bilingual	15.00	-.157 (.046)*
Spanish monolingual	0.61	-.212 (.180)
Foreign born:		
English monolingual	0.79	-.257 (.159)
English bilingual	9.16	-.117 (.054)*
Spanish bilingual	6.86	-.343 (.060)*
Spanish monolingual	1.25	-.400 (.128)*
Intercept (Native born, English monolingual)	24.58	.433
R-squared		.022
Ethnic origin:		
Chicano/Mexican	58.48%	-.181 (.036)*
Puerto Rican	15.75	-.052 (.047)
Cuban	5.27	-.153 (.068)*
Intercept (Other ethnic origins)	20.50	.480
R-squared		.011

* $p < .05$
Source: 1976 Survey of Income and Education

native born and who usually speak English enjoy significant attainment advantages with respect to other groups of children. When the differences do not attain statistical significance (as measured by t-tests), it appears to be due simply to the small number of children in the category to which they are being compared. The native born Spanish bilinguals also enjoy significantly higher attainments when compared to similar children of foreign birth. Thus, it would appear that both native birth and the usual use of English are related to educational attainment. Nonetheless, the proportion of the variance explained as measured by r-squared is very low, indicating only a weak general relationship between these characteristics and educational attainment.

The contribution of ethnic origin to the explanation of educational attainment is still lower (r-squared = .011). The data presented in Table 8.2 indicate that both Puerto Rican and Other Hispanic children enjoy statistically significant educational advantages in comparison to Cuban and Chicano children.

These observed differences are, of course, gross differences based on the mean educational attainments of the various groups examined. To permit the isolation of language and nativity factors we procede to the estimation of multiple regression equations. The percentages of children for each of the dummy (binarized) variables and the mean value of metric variables are presented in column one of Table 8.3.

The first column reveals that large percentages of the sampled children live in the SMSA areas of the Northeastern United States, the rural areas of the Texas-Louisiana region, and in both subregions of the Pacific Coast states. There are also relatively large concentrations in the urban areas of the Texas-Louisiana region and in the non-metropolitan areas of the Rocky Mountain states. The first column also shows that the mean educational attainment of the best educated parent was only 10.53 years.

The results of the baseline equation are presented in column two of Table 8.3. The data reveal a small but statistically significant effect of parental education on the attainment of children. Each additional year of parental education is associated with a .024 increase in the grade level of the children. In addition, the data indicate that residence in the rural areas of the Northeast or in either of the subregions of the Texas-Louisiana region is associated with educational attainments significantly lower than those prevailing in most other regions. Residence in the metropolitan areas of the American Midwest is associated with positive levels of educational attainment when compared to most other regions. However, if we restrict our attention only to those areas containing the largest proportion of Spanish children, it is only those children living in the Texas-Louisiana region who have markedly lower attainments than similar children living elsewhere.

In column three of Table 8.3 we present the results of a regression equation which adds the nativity and language variables to the baseline variables. The addition of these variables causes little change in the observed coefficients of the baseline regressors. The impact of parental education is somewhat less than that observed in column two, a finding explained by the interaction between parental education and the language characteristics of the children. Better educated parents have children in the most favored language and nativity characteristics categories.

The pattern of the regression coefficients for the nativity and language variables is particularly interesting. All four groups of foreign born children

Table 8.3 Regression of educational attainment on selected background characteristics, Spanish language children aged 6-13, United States, 1976

Regressors	Mean or percent	Regression coefficient	Regression coefficient	Regression coefficient	Regression coefficient
Northeast SMSA	19.46	.008 (.050)	.059 (.052)	.026 (.069)	.021 (.068)
Northeast non-SMSA	2.28	-.326 (.099)*	-.288 (.097)*	-.311 (.109)*	-.330 (.107)*
Midwest SMSA	4.59	.168 (.075)*	.169 (.074)*	.157 (.078)*	.147 (.077)
Midwest non-SMSA	2.06	-.164 (.102)	-.129 (.102)	-.159 (.103)	-.190 (.102)
South SMSA	4.84	-.106 (.074)	-.001 (.076)	-.011 (.087)	-.021 (.086)
South non-SMSA	1.51	.013 (.117)	.102 (.117)	.073 (.122)	.049 (.120)
Texas-Louisiana SMSA	9.23	-.261 (.060)*	-.253 (.060)*	-.252 (.060)*	-.278 (.059)*
Texas-Louisiana non-SMSA	18.11	-.201 (.051)*	-.205 (.052)*	-.206 (.052)*	-.278 (.059)*
Rocky Mountains SMSA	2.56	-.059 (.093)	-.063 (.093)	-.063 (.093)	-.054 (.091)
Rocky Mountains non-SMSA	7.79	-.086 (.063)	-.085 (.062)	-.106 (.063)	-.107 (.062)
Pacific Coast SMSA	16.22	-.087 (.052)	-.043 (.052)	-.050 (.053)	-.081 (.052)
Pacific Coast non-SMSA	11.35	(a)	(a)	(a)	(a)
Parental education	10.53	.024 (.003)*	.021 (.004)*	.019 (.004)*	.016 (.004)*
Native born:					
English bilingual	41.75		.051 (.035)	.057 (.035)	.045 (.035)
Spanish bilingual	15.00		-.009 (.049)	-.007 (.049)	-.054 (.049)
Spanish monolingual	0.61		-.020 (.176)	-.011 (.176)	-.124 (.174)
English monolingual	24.58		(a)	(a)	(a)
Foreign born:					
English monolingual	0.79		-.338 (.154)*	-.371 (.154)*	-.324 (.152)*
English bilingual	9.16		-.142 (.054)*	-.140 (.055)*	-.114 (.055)*
Spanish bilingual	6.86		-.269 (.062)*	-.265 (.063)*	-.270 (.062)*
Spanish monolingual	1.25		-.311 (.126)*	-.314 (.126)*	-.388 (.124)*

Continued on next page

Table 8.3 continued

Regressors	Mean or percent	Regression coefficient	Regression coefficient	Regression coefficient	Regression coefficient
Chicano/Mexican	58.48			-.087 (.044)	-.083 (.043)
Puerto Rican	15.75			-.065 (.054)	-.050 (.053)
Cuban	5.27			-.110 (.073)	-.077 (.072)
Other ethnic origins	20.50			(a)	(a)
Age of child	9.59				-.051 (.006)*
Intercept		.189	.223	.316	.843
R-squared		.048	.065	.067	.092

(a) reference characteristic
* p < .05

have mean attainment levels which are significantly lower than those of the native born, English monolingual children (the reference group). Furthermore, the attainments of these latter children do not differ significantly from those of other native born children. While not all pairs of coefficients differ significantly from one another, these findings suggest that foreign born children, irrespective of their language characteristics tend to have lower than expected educational attainments for their age. On the other hand, the findings do not sustain the previous observation that there is linguistic stratification in the educational attainment process of these children. No significant differences within nativity categories were found for children having different language characteristics. Nonetheless, the improvement in the proportion of the variance explained when the nativity and language variables are included in the equation indicates the importance of the nativity variables for these younger children.

As can be seen from column four, the ethnic origin of Spanish language children has little impact on their educational attainments. The proportion of the variance explained in the equation is only slightly higher, and none of the coefficients differs significantly from another. Consequently, the data suggest that the ethnic origin of the Spanish language child plays little role in the educational attainments of 6 to 13 year old children. The differences observed in Table 8.1 are adequately explained by other background factors.

Including the age variable (column five) improves the proportion of the variance explained by 2.5 percent (.092 - .067 = .025), a rather sizeable increase considering the low percentage of the variance which we have succeeded in explaining. And while the addition of the age variable does not produce major changes in the estimated impact of the variables previously entered, language characteristics of foreign born children are revealed to play a stronger role than previously estimated. Considering only the three largest groups, the English bilingual children have significantly higher net attainments than do the two groups of children who usually speak Spanish. The data do not, however, indicate significant differences between the Spanish monolingual children and those who have been classified as Spanish bilingual. Thus, the data presented in the last column indicate some support for the proposition that language factors do play a role in the educational attainment process. The support is, nonetheless, relatively weak.

The effect of age itself on the educational attainments of children has the expected direction. Each additional year of age, net of other factors, is associated with a decline of .051 years of educational attainment. This suggests that the educational attainment of thirteen year olds has dropped by more than four-tenths of one year since they began school (.051 × 8 = .408). Alternatively, an additional 40.8 percent of the Spanish language had fallen one year below their expected grade level. Furthermore, although a linear relationship between age and educational attainment best fits the data, a curvilinear relationship fits the data nearly as well, indicating that falling behind expected grade level tends to accelerate as children get older.

Turning to the analysis of the educational attainments of the older Spanish language children, we present in Table 8.4 the regression of educational attainment on the nativity and language characteristics and on the ethnic origin characteristics of the sampled individuals. Examining the proportions of the variance explained, it is evident that ethnic origin remains a relatively un-

Table 8.4 *Regression of educational attainment on selected background characteristics of Spanish language children aged 14-17, United States, 1976*

Regressors	Percent	Regression coefficient
Nativity and language characteristics:		
Native born:		
English bilingual	41.29%	-.020 (.065)
Spanish bilingual	9.47	-.676 (.100)*
Spanish monolingual	0.40	-.538 (.425)
Foreign born:		
English monolingual	0.67	-.046 (.328)
English bilingual	9.70	-.035 (.099)
Spanish bilingual	8.02	-.405 (.107)*
Spanish monolingual	3.09	-2.343 (.159)*
Intercept (Native born, English monolingual)	27.36	.147
R-squared		.166
Ethnic origin:		
Chicano/Mexican	61.12%	-.160 (.075)*
Puerto Rican	13.74	-.128 (.101)
Cuban	5.56	-.107 (.139)
Intercept (Other ethnic origins)	19.58	.080
R-squared		.004

* $p < .05$
Source: 1976 Survey of Income and Education

important factor in the educational attainment process while nativity and language factors play a much more important role than that observed for younger children. In fact, this set of variables alone explains a higher proportion of the variance than did the complete set of variables for the younger children.

As we have previously observed the effect of nativity appears to have been markedly reduced for the older children. Emerging instead is the linguistic stratification of the older children. The educational attainments of all groups of children who usually speak English are statistically equivalent. They are also statistically superior to the attainments of children who usually speak Spanish, at least when the percentage of children contained in the language categories surpasses one percent. One further observation should be made: all groups of children have educational attainment levels which are markedly superior to those of the children who are both foreign born and monolingual in Spanish.

The regression of educational attainment on the baseline and other background characteristics of the older Spanish language children are presented in Table 8.5. The baseline equation reveals a somewhat different pattern of regional advantages and disadvantages than that found for the younger children. First of all, most of the regression coefficients in this equation are positive, whereas most of the coefficients were negative in Table 8.3. This indicates that younger children in the non-metropolitan Pacific Coast regions had somewhat higher net attainments than children in most other regions, whereas the reverse is the case for the older children. Nonetheless, residence in the metropolitan areas of the Texas-Louisiana region continues to be associated with net negative attainments when compared to most other regions. On the other hand, residence in the urban areas of the Pacific Coast region is associated with high net attainments when compared to children in a number of other regions.

Also worthy of note is the net impact of educational attainment of the parents. The coefficient obtained in this equation is nearly double that found for the younger children, indicating the greater importance of social class factors as children decide to leave school during the teenage years. The impact of this factor is, however, markedly reduced when the nativity and language characteristics of the 14-17 year olds are introduced, indicating that the children in the less favored language and nativity categories are those who also have the least educated parents.

While the estimated liabilities of children who usually speak Spanish are not as great as those estimated in Table 8.4, the essential pattern has not changed. Children who usually speak English have higher net attainments

Table 8.5 Regression of educational attainment on selected background characteristics, Spanish language children aged 14-17, United States, 1976

Regressors	Mean or percent	Regression coefficient	Regression coefficient	Regression coefficient	Regression coefficient
Northeast SMSA	14.22	.028 (.108)	.053 (.104)	.207 (.141)	.186 (.139)
Northeast non-SMSA	1.74	-.023 (.226)	-.058 (.217)	.083 (.234)	.038 (.230)
Midwest	6.15	.203 (.138)	.186 (.130)	.254 (.137)	.237 (.134)
Midwest non-SMSA	1.57	.175 (.143)	.208 (.221)	.247 (.224)	.300 (.220)
South SMSA	5.62	.157 (.143)	.217 (.141)	.374 (.174)*	.372 (.171)*
South non-SMSA	1.37	-.038 (.252)	-.031 (.239)	.070 (.247)	.075 (.243)
Texas-Louisiana SMSA	7.83	-.243 (.127)	-.280 (.120)*	-.275 (.120)*	-.268 (.118)*
Texas-Louisiana non-SMSA	18.95	-.039 (.102)	-.080 (.098)	-.070 (.099)	-.066 (.098)
Rocky Mountains SMSA	2.73	.263 (.187)	.196 (.174)	.205 (.174)	.215 (.171)
Rocky Mountains non-SMSA	9.33	.211 (.121)	.178 (.113)	.216 (.118)	.210 (.116)
Pacific Coast SMSA	17.96	.304 (.103)*	.392 (.097)*	.405 (.098)*	.392 (.096)*
Pacific Coast non-SMSA	14.10	(a)	(a)	(a)	(a)
Parental education	9.85	.054 (.077)*	.028 (.007)*	.030 (.007)*	.030 (.007)*
Native born:					
English monolingual	27.36		(a)	(a)	(a)
English bilingual	41.29		.108 (.067)	.112 (.068)	.141 (.067)*
Spanish bilingual	9.47		-.373 (.109)*	-.371 (.109)*	-.342 (.107)*
Spanish monolingual	0.40		-.143 (.421)	-.112 (.422)	.026 (.415)
Foreign born:					
English monolingual	0.67		-.029 (.334)	-.001 (.334)	-.007 (.329)
English bilingual	9.70		.004 (.103)	.020 (.107)	.027 (.105)
Spanish bilingual	8.02		-.315 (.113)*	-.314 (.115)*	-.291 (.113)*
Spanish monolingual	3.09		-2.189 (.164)*	-2.193 (.165)*	-2.166 (.162)*

Continued on next page

Table 8.5 continued

Regressors	Mean or percent	Regression coefficient	Regression coefficient	Regression coefficient	Regression coefficient
Chicano/Mexican	61.12			.099 (.082)	.084 (.081)
Puerto Rican	13.74			-.084 (.115)	-.081 (.113)
Cuban	5.56			-.121 (.155)	-.135 (.152)
Other ethnic origins	19.56			(a)	(a)
Age of child	15.46				-2.253 (.797)*
Age of child squared	240.41				.068 (.026)*
Intercept		-.646	-.316	-.428	18.073
R-squared		.080	.211	.213	.240

(a) reference characteristic
* p < .05
Source: 1976 Survey of Income and Education

than those who usually speak Spanish. These differences are statistically significant in all instances where the percentage of the children in the category being compared exceeds one percent. Nonetheless, the exceptional position of the 3.09 percent of the children who are both foreign born and Spanish monolingual must be underscored. Net of parental education and regional distribution, these children average 2.189 years below expected grade level, significantly below the attainments of all other groups of children.

The entry of the ethnic origin variables causes little change in the proportion of the variance explained. While none of the estimated coefficients for ethnic origin differ from one another, the negative sign for Cuban and Puerto Rican ethnic origin children may surprise some observers. However, these children tend to reside in geographic areas which are associated with net higher attainments. The net impact of residence in the metropolitan areas of the Northeast and of the South is considerably more positive than that estimated in the baseline equation. The negative impact of Chicano origin estimated in Table 8.4 is probably largely subsumed under residence in the urban areas of the Texas-Louisiana region. These interactive effects of ethnicity and region of residence make it difficult to isolate the sole effect of ethnic origin. Nonetheless, it would appear that residence in the Texas-Louisiana region is more likely to 'cause' low educational attainments of Chicano children than is the presence of such children to cause low educational attainments in the region. The presence of large numbers of Chicano children in the Pacific Coast region is not associated with negative attainment levels, and their presence in general is associated with a relatively positive attainment level (regression coefficient = .099).

The final equation reported in Table 8.5 adds two age variables to the equation, the age of the child and its square. Since both variables are statistically significant, a curvilinear relationship between age and educational attainment is indicated. In previously published research we included only a linear estimate of the effect of age, an estimate which found Spanish language children falling behind expected grade level at the rate of .149 years of educational attainment for each additional (net) year of age (Veltman, 1980a: Table 3). This figure is three times higher than that found for the younger children. Given the four years of age represented in this sample, this figure would indicate a net decline of more than two-thirds of a grade level over this period. Obviously, such a decline is caused both by dropping-out of school and by the necessity to repeat grades.

The use of two age variables reveals a curvilinear relationship between age of the child and educational attainment and permits us to specify the nature of the relationship. Briefly, the two regression coefficients indicate that the most rapid decline in educational attainment occurs during the early teenage years. Part of this rapid decline may be attributable to children who actually dropped-out before the age of fourteen but whose educational attainments are captured for the first time at age fourteen. However, it is also quite plausible that large numbers of Spanish language children decide to leave school during the early teenage years. For those who decide to remain at school the rate of decline in educational attainment is much less rapid.

The introduction of the age variables causes one change in the nativity and language variables worthy of some comment. The observed educational attainments of native born, English bilingual children are now seen to be significantly higher than those of native born, English monolingual children. Since these two groups are so large, the significance of this finding should not be underestimated. This finding suggests that the maintenance of the Spanish language as a second language is related to positive educational attainment, once an appropriate set of background variables has been controlled. The general pattern of the language variables remains intact, however, children of English usual language enjoying educational advantages when compared to children who usually speak Spanish.

Summarizing the findings for the younger and older children living in homes where the Spanish language is frequently spoken, we have found small but positive relationships between higher parental educational attainments and the educational attainments of children. The effect is more pronounced for the older children. We have also found age effects which indicate that the older the child, the farther behind he or she has fallen behind expected grade level. The rate of falling behind in school is also more pronounced for the older than for the younger children and is particularly high during the early teenage years.

The situation with respect to the nativity and language characteristics of the children is more complex. The most pronounced effect found for the younger children is a nativity effect, most groups of foreign born children having lower net educational attainments than most groups of native born children. Some evidence was found which indicates the development of linguistic stratification among the younger children. Increased movement toward the English language as the principal language of use tended to be associated with higher educational attainments. The relationship is, however, weak.

If the older children can be presumed to have followed a similar educational career, then the latent linguistic stratification observed for the younger children explodes into a clear pattern of manifest stratification during the teenage years. Nativity distinctions lose much of their importance. Children who usually speak English enjoy statistically significant educational advantages over children who usually speak Spanish. Ironically, in spite of the evidence which suggests that making English one's usual language is associated with positive levels of educational attainment, the abandonment of Spanish is not associated with the highest levels of educational attainment. English bilingualism among the native born confers greater educational benefits, a finding which suggests that too rapid a movement to conform to normative American monolingualism has negative consequences for the child.

The educational attainments of other (non-Spanish) minority language children. Our objective in this section is to ascertain the extent to which nativity and language factors have the same effect for the Residual language children as has been observed for the Spanish language children. More generally, we should like to know whether the process of educational attainment is the same for children living in non-Spanish minority language homes as it is for children living in Spanish language households. The mean educational attainments of the Residual language children are presented in Table 8.6. The raw sample sizes are quite similar to those observed for the Spanish language children even though the population estimates are lower. This is due to the fact that the Residual language children are more frequently found in areas of the United States which were oversampled by the Bureau of the Census.

When we examine the educational attainments of the 6-13 year old children by their nativity and language characteristics, the data generally show that children who usually speak English have somewhat higher educational attainments than the bilingual children who usually speak a minority language. There do not appear to be important nativity effects, nor does it appear that the inability to speak English is associated with negative educational attainment. However, the children in the two NEL monolingual categories represent such a small proportion of the population that they are perhaps better ignored.

With respect to the older children, the native born children who usually speak English have markedly higher educational attainments than their foreign born counterparts. They also have higher attainments than the two small groups of native born children who usually speak a minority language. However, the relatively important group of NEL bilinguals who were not born in the United States enjoy relatively high levels of educational attainment as well, a finding which would appear to disrupt a clear pattern of linguistic

Table 8.6 *Mean educational attainments by nativity and language characteristics and by age, residual language children aged 6-17, United States, 1976*

Characteristics	Children aged 6-13		Children aged 14-17	
	Percent	Mean educational attainment	Percent	Mean educational attainment
Nativity and language:				
Native born:				
English monolingual	45.09	.438	55.52	.369
English bilingual	26.62	.552	19.11	.572
NEL bilingual (1)	6.20	.304	2.82	-.857
NEL monolingual	0.24	.783	1.58	-.513
Foreign born:				
English monolingual	3.58	.652	2.88	.042
English bilingual	12.14	.403	11.57	.345
NEL bilingual	5.67	.235	5.71	.432
NEL monolingual	0.46	.487	0.81	.086
Total	100.00	.454	100.00	.349
N (unweighted)	2,673		1,515	
N (weighted, 000's)	1,132		598	

(1) NEL = usual language a language other than English
Source: 1976 Survey of Income and Education

and nativity stratification. Moreover, both groups of foreign born children who usually speak a minority language have higher educational attainments than do the native born children with similar language characteristics.

When we compare Table 8.6 with the comparable table for Spanish language children (Table 8.1), we find that the Residual language children aged 6-13 had somewhat higher educational attainments (.454 vs. .357). However, that which is most striking to the observer is the small decline in educational attainment when the younger and older children in the Residual language group are compared. Mean educational attainment of the older children is only .105 grade level lower than that of the younger children (.454 - .349 = .105). The decline observed in the Spanish language groups was .393 (.357 - (-.036) = .393), a much sharper decline associated with increased age.

Since we shall control for membership in specific minority language groups during the regression analysis (in an attempt to reduce some of the heterogeneity of the Residual language group sample), we present the mean educational attainments of younger and older children in Table 8.7. An examination of Table 8.7 shows that Yiddish, Greek, and Chinese language group children, both younger and older, have attainment means which are markedly superior to those of the sample mean. Only the attainment mean of the Navajo children is markedly lower than the attainment levels of other groups of 6-13 year old children. However, that of their 14-17 year old counterparts is more than one year lower than that of any other group of minority language children. While the figures are not nearly so negative, it may also be observed that 14-17 year old French and Portuguese language children also have educational attainment means quite a bit lower than those of children in the remaining groups.

To examine the extent to which the nativity and language characteristics and to which minority language group membership explain variability in

Table 8.7 *Mean educational attainments by language group and by age, residual language children aged 6-17, United States, 1976*

Characteristics	Children aged 6-13		Children aged 14-17	
	Percent	Mean educational attainments	Percent	Mean educational attainments
Language group:				
Chinese	4.77	.721	3.02	.657
Filipino	6.39	.502	3.13	.474
French	13.13	.437	19.13	.180
German	13.97	.401	13.88	.393
Greek	4.61	.763	3.72	.559
Italian	14.87	.374	16.16	.486
Japanese	1.82	.437	1.76	.438
Navajo	2.71	-.205	3.04	-.958
Polish	4.04	.522	4.54	.461
Portuguese	3.46	.348	3.96	.120
Scandinavian	0.93	.499	1.77	.376
Yiddish	2.47	.954	3.05	.972
Other groups	26.83	.438	22.84	.374
Total	100.00	.454	100.00	.349
N (unweighted)	2,673		1,515	
N (weighted, 000's)	1,132		598	

Source: 1976 Survey of Income and Education

educational attainment, we present the results of two equations which regress educational attainment on these characteristics in Table 8.8. Examining the proportion of the variance explained, we note once again that the r-squared is

Table 8.8 *Regression of educational attainment on selected background characteristics of residual language children aged 6-13, United States 1976*

Characteristics	Percent	Regression coefficient
Nativity and language characteristics:		
Native born:		
English bilingual	26.62%	.114 (.034)*
NEL bilingual (1)	6.20	-.134 (.060)*
NEL monolingual	0.24	.345 (.290)
Foreign born:		
English monolingual	3.58	.214 (.077)*
English bilingual	12.14	-.035 (.045)
NEL bilingual	5.67	-.202 (.063)*
NEL monolingual	0.46	.049 (.207)
Intercept (Native born, English monolingual)	45.09	.438
R-squared		.016
Language group:		
Chinese	4.77%	.283 (.069)*
Filipino	6.39	.064 (.061)
French	13.13	-.001 (.046)
German	13.97	-.037 (.046)
Greek	4.61	.325 (.070)*
Italian	14.87	-.064 (.045)
Japanese	1.82	-.001 (.106)
Navajo	2.71	-.643 (.088)*
Polish	4.04	.114 (.074)
Portuguese	3.46	-.090 (.079)
Scandinavian	0.93	.061 (.146)
Yiddish	2.47	.515 (.092)*
Intercept (Other)	26.83	.438
R-squared		.053

* $p < .05$
(1) Usual language is the non-English language
Source: 1976 Survey of Income and Education

very low in both equations. Nativity and language characteristics only explain 1.6 percent of the variance in educational attainment, while language group membership explains 5.3 percent.

Given the extremely small percentages of NEL monolingual children, it is not surprising that their mean attainment levels do not differ significantly from those of children in other nativity and language categories. Nonetheless, their positive educational attainments seem somewhat surprising in view of their limited or non-existent English-speaking ability. When we compare the six larger nativity and language categories, one finding clearly emerges. The children who usually speak English have higher net educational attainments than the NEL bilinguals. All pairs of regression coefficients differ significantly except when foreign born, English bilingual children are compared to the native born children who usually speak a minority language (NEL bilingual). Table 8.8 reveals two other interesting findings. First of all, the native born, English bilingual children have higher educational attainments than do their native born, English monolingual counterparts, a finding which conforms to that obtained for Spanish language children. Secondly, foreign born, English monolingual children also have higher net attainments than have their native born counterparts. Before attempting to explain such a finding, we shall see whether the pattern remains after other background variables are controlled.

Turning to the examination of the effect of language group membership, the equation supports our previous observations. Yiddish language children have mean educational attainments which are significantly higher than those of children in any other language group. The attainments of Chinese and Greek language children are also significantly higher than those of children in any of the remaining groups. Those of the Navajo language children are significantly lower than those of children in any other group. Once again, we need to examine the extent to which such findings are maintained after other important factors are controlled.

The appropriate baseline equation to which these factors will be subsequently added is presented in Table 8.9. Examining the column which presents the distribution of the Residual language children throughout the United States, we observe once again that these children tend to be concentrated in three regions of the country, the Northeast, the Midwest, and the Pacific Coast regions. In addition to different patterns of residence, the level of parental educational attainment also distinguishes the Residual language children from the Spanish language children. The parents of the Residual language 6-13 year old children have mean educational attainments more than two years

Table 8.9 Regression of educational attainment on selected background characteristics, residual language children aged 6-13, United States, 1976

Regressors	Mean or percent	Regression coefficient	Regression coefficient	Regression coefficient	Regression coefficient
Northeast SMSA	26.18	.044 (.057)	.043 (.057)	.032 (.060)	.008 (.059)
Northeast non-SMSA	10.92	-.009 (.066)	-.004 (.066)	.001 (.068)	-.017 (.067)
Midwest SMSA	11.80	-.186 (.064)*	-.188 (.064)*	-.183 (.066)*	-.201 (.066)*
Midwest non-SMSA	6.88	-.087 (.073)	-.104 (.075)	-.083 (.077)	-.092 (.076)
South SMSA	5.08	-.146 (.080)	-.144 (.080)	-.087 (.080)	-.105 (.080)
South non-SMSA	3.13	.112 (.093)	.045 (.093)	.099 (.094)	.007 (.094)
Texas-Louisiana SMSA	1.58	-.430 (.122)*	-.389 (.121)*	-.358 (.121)*	-.364 (.121)*
Texas-Louisiana non-SMSA	7.62	-.111 (.071)	-.108 (.071)	-.109 (.079)	-.114 (.079)
Rocky Mountains SMSA	0.75	-.320 (.168)	-.321 (.168)	-.297 (.166)	-.306 (.165)
Rocky Mountains non-SMSA	5.50	-.362 (.079)*	-.395 (.081)*	-.105 (.095)	-.116 (.095)
Pacific Coast SMSA	12.84	-.028 (.063)	-.018 (.064)	-.003 (.063)	-.013 (.062)
Pacific Coast non-SMSA	7.72	(a)	(a)	(a)	(a)
Parental education	12.83	.017 (.003)*	.015 (.004)*	.010 (.004)*	.008 (.004)*
Native born:	45.09				
English monolingual	26.62		(a)	(a)	(a)
English bilingual	6.20		.119 (.035)*	.112 (.035)*	.104 (.035)*
NEL bilingual (1)	0.24		.044 (.067)	.110 (.070)	.082 (.070)
NEL monolingual			.498 (.298)	.530 (.285)	.461 (.283)
Foreign born	3.58				
English monolingual	12.14		.209 (.077)*	.218 (.077)*	.233 (.077)*
English bilingual	5.67		-.031 (.046)	-.080 (.047)	-.065 (.047)
NEL bilingual	0.46		-.181 (.064)*	-.205 (.065)*	-.189 (.065)*
NEL monolingual			-.011 (.205)	-.033 (.203)	-.023 (.202)

Continued on next page

Table 8.9 continued

Regressors	Mean or percent	Regression coefficient	Regression coefficient	Regression coefficient	Regression coefficient
Chinese	4.77			.274 (.070)*	.272 (.069)*
Filipino	6.39			.028 (.064)	.013 (.064)
French	13.13			.031 (.053)	.049 (.053)
German	13.97			-.058 (.046)	-.045 (.046)
Greek	4.61			.328 (.070)*	.342 (.070)*
Italian	14.87			-.091 (.048)	-.086 (.048)
Japanese	1.82			-.026 (.107)	-.032 (.106)
Navajo	2.71			-.622 (.122)*	-.594 (.122)*
Polish	4.04			.128 (.075)	.155 (.075)*
Portuguese	3.46			-.060 (.082)	-.070 (.081)
Scandinavian	0.93			.055 (.145)	.066 (.145)
Yiddish	2.47			.421 (.093)*	.424 (.092)*
Other groups	26.83			(a)	(a)
Age of child	9.56		.300		-.034 (.006)*
Intercept		.305		.338	.688
R-squared		.035	.048	.084	.095

Notes:
(1) Usual language = Non-English language
(a) reference characteristic
Source: 1976 Survey of Income and Education

higher than those of the parents of the Spanish language children (12.83 − 10.53 = 2.30 years).

Examining the baseline regression equation itself, we observe that the proportion of the variance explained is again rather low (r-squared = .035). The baseline variables explain rather poorly differences in expected educational attainment. Nonetheless, the impact of social class factors on the educational attainment of the Residual language children appears to be somewhat less than that observed for the Spanish language children. Each additional year of parental education was associated with a net increase of .017 years of educational attainment for the Residual language children as opposed to .024 in the case of the Spanish language children.

Regional factors do not appear to play a major role in the attainment process of 6-13 year old Residual children. While residence in the non-metropolitan areas of the Pacific Coast region appears to be associated with relatively positive attainment levels, it does not differ significantly from residence in most other areas. Only residence in the urban Midwest, the urban areas of the Texas-Louisiana region, or the rural regions of the Rocky Mountain states is associated with significantly lower levels of educational attainment when compared to residence in most other regions.

When the nativity and language factors are added to the baseline factors, the effect of parental education on educational attainment is somewhat minimized, indicating that the children in the less favored nativity and language categories are those who have the less educated parents. There is, however, only one group of children which has significantly lower educational attainments when compared to most other groups of children, the foreign born bilingual children who usually speak a minority language. Their net educational attainments are significantly lower than those of their native born counterparts and lower than those of all groups of children who usually speak English. Given the small sizes of the two groups of children who are minority language monolinguals, the estimated coefficients for these groups do not differ significantly from any others. Nonetheless, it is clear that these children are enrolled in grade levels appropriate for their age.

In addition, two groups of children have higher net attainments than the native born, English monolingual children. As in the case of the Spanish language children, the native born, English bilinguals tend to have higher net educational attainments. However, the findings indicate that foreign born, English monolinguals also have higher net attainments than do their native born counterparts. Why this should be the case is not self-evident. Perhaps school administrators and teachers perceive that children educated outside the United States have received education which is superior in quality to that received by children of the same age in American institutions. When such children are enrolled in American institutions, they may be placed in a grade level higher than that expected for their age.

If such a positive evaluation of the previous educational experiences may explain the superior attainments of the foreign born, English monolingual children in the Residual language group, it appears that the same type of positive evaluation is not applied to children who come from Latin American countries. The principal finding derived in our analysis of the young children in the Spanish language group was that foreign birth was associated with significantly lower educational attainments in most cases. That which is most striking in the analysis of the Residual language children is the absence of this pattern and the presence of a pattern of linguistic stratification. Foreign birth in itself is not perceived to be an educational liability. If, however, the child continues to speak a minority language as his principal language, this may be perceived as an educational liability. Nonetheless, if the child does not speak English with frequency (NEL monolingual), it appears that he or she is simply integrated into the grade which is appropriate for children of that age. Since their numbers are so small, they may not be perceived as posing a threat to the linguistic integrity of the classroom, at least not at this age level.

When the language group membership variables are added to the equation, the proportion of the variance explained is markedly improved (.084 as compared to .048 in the previous equation). Only two important changes in the coefficients of the variables previously analyzed are observed. First of all, residence in the rural regions of the Rocky Mountain states is no longer associated with statistically significant lower mean attainments, a portion of this lower attainment being explained by the concentration of the Navajo language children in this region. Secondly, the net impact of class effects is substantially reduced, children in the most favored language groups having the better educated parents, in the less favored groups having the more poorly educated parents. It is important to note, however, that the addition of the membership group variables causes only minor changes in the estimated impact of the language and nativity characteristic variables. Thus, while the heterogeneity of the Residual language sample is statistically minimized, the net impact of the language and nativity variables remains unchanged.

The coefficients obtained in this equation for language group membership continue to correspond to those presented in Table 8.8. Children of the Yiddish language group have higher net attainments than children in any other group, while Navajo language children have lower net attainments than

Educational Attainments of American Children

children in any other group. Children in the Greek and Chinese language groups enjoy higher net attainments than those of children in all other groups with the exception of Yiddish children. Since part of these differences may be explained by intra-regional state differences in permissable dates for enrolling children in the first grade, these findings should be taken as indicative rather than definitive and interpreted with some prudence.

The introduction of the age variable, while increasing the proportion of the variance explained, modifies but slightly the estimated net impact of the remaining variables. As the negative coefficient of the age variable shows, each additional year of age is associated with a net decline of .034 years of educational attainment. This figure indicates that the thirteen year old children have a net educational attainment level which is .272 lower than that of six year olds (.034 $\times$ 8 = .272). This decline, while significant, is lower than that observed for the 6-13 year old Spanish language children (.408).

Beginning our analysis of the educational attainment process of the older Residual language children, we present in Table 8.10 the results of the regression of educational attainment on the nativity and language characteristics and on the language membership group characteristics of these children. The proportion of the variance explained by each of these equations is markedly higher than that observed for the 6-13 year old Residual language children.

The examination of the gross impact of the nativity and language characteristics on the educational attainment process of 14-17 year old Residual language children reveals that all four groups of children who usually speak English have higher net attainments than the two groups of native born children who usually speak a minority language. However, the bilingual foreign born children who usually speak a minority language have educational attainments which, while inferior to those of the native born, English bilingual children and similar to those of the native born, English monolingual children, are also significantly superior to those of the native born children who usually speak a minority language. The sample sizes are too small to permit the coefficient attached to the children who were both foreign born and monolingual in a minority language to differ significantly from those of the other groups of children, although the expected negative impact is apparent.

The gross impact of language group membership corresponds in many respects to that observed for younger Residual language children. Membership in the Yiddish language group is associated with the highest educational attainments; in the Navajo language group with the lowest. Chinese language children have relatively high attainment levels, while Table 8.10 reveals that the

Table 8.10 *Regression of educational attainment on selected background characteristics of residual language children aged 14-17, United States 1976*

Characteristics	Percent	Regression coefficient
Nativity and language characteristics:		
Native born:		
English bilingual	19.11%	.203 (.059)*
NEL bilingual (1)	2.82	-1.226 (.136)*
NEL monolingual	1.58	-.882 (.180)*
Foreign born:		
English monolingual	2.88	-.337 (.135)*
English bilingual	11.57	-.024 (.720)
NEL bilingual	5.71	.063 (.098)
NEL monolingual	0.81	-.283 (.250)
Intercept (Native born, English monolingual)	55.52	.369
R-squared		.081
Language group:		
Chinese	3.02%	.283 (.135)*
Filipino	3.13	.100 (.133)
French	19.13	-.194 (.068)*
German	13.88	.019 (.075)
Greek	3.72	.185 (.124)
Italian	16.16	.112 (.072)
Japanese	1.76	.064 (.173)
Navajo	3.04	-1.332 (.135)*
Polish	4.54	.087 (.114)
Portuguese	3.96	-.254 (.120)*
Scandinavian	1.77	.002 (.173)
Yiddish	3.05	.598 (.135)*
Intercept (Other)	22.84	.374
R-squared		.099

(1) Usual language is the non-English language
* p < .05
Source: 1976 Survey of Income and Education

French and Portuguese language children have attainment levels which are significantly lower than those of children in most other groups.

To examine the extent to which the observed gross language and nativity effects and the gross effects of language group membership remain after other factors are controlled, we present the appropriate baseline equation in Table 8.11. We observe first of all that the estimated net impact of parental education is .046, a figure only slightly lower than that observed in the baseline equation for the 14-17 year old Spanish language children. Thus, the impact of social class factors appears roughly equivalent for both groups of minority language children.

Table 8.11 also reveals that residence in the urban areas of the Northeast and the Pacific Coast regions is associated with significantly higher educational attainments for these children than is residence in most other regions. Residence in the urban areas of the Pacific Coast region was also associated with higher net educational attainment for the 14-17 year old Spanish language children. Table 8.11 fails to reveal a statistically significant educational penalty attached to residence in the urban areas of the Texas-Louisiana region, indicating that it is only the Spanish language children who experience particular difficulties in this region.

That which differs most in the educational attainment processes of Spanish and Residual language 14-17 year olds is the estimated value of the intercept term. While social class and regional factors do not exhibit a great deal of variation from one group to another, the mean educational attainment of Residual language children living in the rural regions of the Pacific Coast states and who have parents with zero (0) years of education is -.242. When the level of parental education is twelve years, the educational attainment of the children is estimated to be .310 (-.242 + (12 $\times$ .046) = .310). The comparable figure for Spanish language children having parents with zero (0) years of education is -.646, for those having parents with twelve years of education, .002 (-.646 + (12 $\times$ .054) = .002). Thus, Table 8.11 shows that the basic difference in the attainment process of the Spanish language children when compared to 14-17 year olds in the Residual language group is simply that the attainment level of the Spanish language children is generally lower. The impact of social class is approximately the same. There are some greater differences in the impact of regional variables.

The addition of the nativity and language variables improves the proportion of the variance explained by 3.3 percent. This is, nonetheless, substantially less than the 13.1 percent improvement observed for the 14-17 year old Spanish

Table 8.11 Regression of educational attainment on selected background characteristics, residual language children aged 14-17, United States, 1976

Regressors	Mean or percent	Regression coefficient	Regression coefficient	Regression coefficient
Northeast	23.46	.293 (.092)*	.282 (.091)*	.246 (.108)*
Northeast non-SMSA	11.85	-.035 (.102)	-.045 (.101)	.013 (.115)
Midwest SMSA	14.55	-.044 (.099)	-.072 (.097)	-.079 (.112)
Midwest non-SMSA	5.43	-.182 (.123)	-.079 (.123)	-.092 (.132)
South SMSA	3.83	.076 (.138)	.128 (.136)	.143 (.145)
South non-SMSA	3.77	.261 (.138)	.272 (.136)*	.305 (.146)*
Texas-Louisiana SMSA	1.42	.072 (.199)	.039 (.197)	.102 (.203)
Texas-Louisiana non-SMSA	12.53	-.150 (.101)	-.191 (.101)	-.055 (.120)
Rocky Mountains SMSA	0.71	-.440 (.271)	-.438 (.267)	-.449 (.271)
Rocky Mountains non-SMSA	6.47	-.606 (.118)*	-.400 (.124)*	-.152 (.146)
Pacific Coast SMSA	8.63	.282 (.110)*	.258 (.110)*	.261 (.119)*
Pacific Coast non-SMSA	7.35	(a)	(a)	(a)
Parental education	12.42	.046 (.006)*	.038 (.006)*	.034 (.006)*
Native born:				
English monolingual	55.52		(a)	(a)
English bilingual	19.11		.156 (.058)*	.167 (.059)*
NEL bilingual (1)	2.82		-.718 (.148)*	-.601 (.155)*
NEL monolingual	1.58		-.616 (.179)*	-.461 (.182)*
Foreign born:				
English monolingual	2.88		-.444 (.131)*	-.423 (.131)*
English bilingual	11.57		-.035 (.070)	-.023 (.072)
NEL bilingual	5.71		.016 (.099)	.039 (.102)
NEL monolingual	0.81		-.477 (.242)*	-.441 (.241)

Continued on next page

Table 8.11 continued

Regressors	Mean or percent	Regression coefficent	Regression coefficient	Regression coefficient
Chinese	3.02			.030 (.136)
Filipino	3.13			.125 (.139)
French	19.13			-.142 (.077)
German	13.88			.028 (.075)
Greek	3.72			.219 (.122)
Italian	16.16			.079 (.077)
Japanese	1.76			.072 (.180)
Navajo	3.04			-.612 (.176)*
Polish	4.54			.089 (.115)
Portuguese	3.96			-.151 (.122)
Scandinavian	1.77			-.017 (.169)
Yiddish	3.05			.428 (.136)*
Other groups	22.84			(a)
Intercept		-.242	-.137	-.131
R-squared		.130	.163	.184

Notes:
(1) Usual language = Non-English language
(a) reference characteristic
* p < .05

language children, indicating the greater importance of these characteristics for the educational attainment process of the Spanish language children.

The pattern of the regression coefficients does not differ from that observed in Table 8.10 save that the educational attainments of the foreign born children who are monolingual in a minority language are significantly lower than those of children in a number of other groups. Still, these findings differ in important respects from those obtained for the younger children in the Residual language group. The most notable point of correspondance continues to be that of the superior educational attainments of the native born, English bilingual children when compared to their English monolingual counterparts. Both groups of children who usually speak English have significantly higher attainment levels than the native born children who usually speak a minority language.

The pattern of the regression coefficients obtained for the foreign born children is curious. The educational attainments of both the English bilinguals and the NEL bilinguals are significantly higher than those of the English monolinguals and the children who are monolingual in a minority language. That the children who are NEL monolinguals should tend to have lower educational attainments is perhaps not surprising; that the English monolinguals should have lower attainments is surprising, particularly in view of the positive educational attainments observed for their younger counterparts.

In the light of such conflicting findings any attempt to offer an explanation is indeed tentative. As in the case of the older Spanish language children, the pattern of linguistic structuring of educational attainment is clearly visible. Children who usually speak English generally have higher educational attainments, the native born English bilinguals having higher attainments than their monolingual peers. However, in the case of the Residual language children, the poor performance of the English monolingual children of foreign birth demands some kind of explication.

Let us propose an interpretation of this coefficient based on both age and community norms. First of all, in the case of both the Spanish language children and the Residual language children aged 6-13, the data tended to indicate relatively undifferentiated educational attainments in early childhood. The r-squareds, for example, were considerably lower than those obtained in the analysis of the 14-17 year old children. The impact of social class and language factors were markedly lower for the younger children, although as previously noted nativity factors play a stronger role for Spanish language children. In the case of the Residual language children, there may be a positive evaluation of the value of education received abroad, children being placed in age-appropriate grades.

However, when the teenage years are reached, the incipient pattern of educational stratification observed in early childhood emerges with greater force. Social class factors become more important. Language factors not only become more important; they may be the object of an evaluation which itself changes. We suggest that there may be social penalties attached to what is perceived as aberrant social behavior, penalties applied either by educational authorities, peer and community authorities, or both. In the case of native born children it may be considered aberrant to continue to speak a minority language as one's principal language during the teenage years, whereas such a pattern may more or less be accepted for younger children. In the case of foreign born children the adoption of English monolingualism may be negatively viewed by family, peers, and community authorities — at least in some minority language groups. Such a negative evaluation might undermine the motivation of such students to perform well in school and may indicate the presence of cultural norms which value non-material goals (for example, community integrity) at the expense of educational attainment. This problem is restricted in effect to the Residual language group since few foreign born children in the Spanish language group opt for a pattern of English monolingual language use. Once again, we reiterate the tentativeness of this explanation, an explanation which would require field investigation. In any event, since the category of foreign born, English monolingual children in the Residual language group only contains 2.88 percent of the children, the aberrant nature of their academic performance is relatively marginal and does not generally infirm the finding that children who usually speak English have higher educational attainments.

The addition of the language membership group variables tends to cause changes in the net impact of three variables previously analyzed. Less negative in impact are residence in the rural regions of the Rocky Mountain states, the presence of the NEL bilingual pattern among native born children, and the presence of the NEL monolingual pattern among native born children. As expected, the negative coefficient associated with membership in the Navajo language group explains to a certain extent the negative sign attached to these categories in the previous equation. Navajo language children have significantly lower attainments than children in all other minority language groups. At the other extreme, Yiddish language children enjoy superior educational attainments when compared to other groups of children. Only one other group seems relatively distinctive, French language children tending to have lower educational attainments than children in a number of other groups, most notably those of the German and Italian language groups.

In contrast to the findings obtained for the Spanish language children aged 14-17, no age effects attained statistical significance for the Residual language children. Consequently, the relevant regression results are not presented in Table 8.11.

The educational attainments of White English language children. To permit an assessment of the extent to which the educational attainments of the minority language children resemble those of English-speaking American children, we have assembled a ten percent sample of the White children who have not been previously defined into the minority language groups. The procedures are defined more fully in Veltman, 1980a (Appendix A). Also excluded from most of the analysis presented in this section are children living in English monolingual homes where one or both of the parents came from a minority language background (normally defined by their mother tongue). These children were defined in our previous analysis as Anglo-Spanish or as Anglo-Residual. The exclusion of these children leaves us with a sample which consists of children having parents who themselves came from English monolingual backgrounds. The mean educational attainments of the 6-13 year olds was .415 while that of the 14-17 year olds was .315.

The results of the baseline equation regressing educational attainment on parental education and geographic factors are presented in Table 8.12. Examining first of all the characteristics of the White English children, we find the highest concentrations of such children in the Northeast and in the Midwest. The South, particularly the non-urban areas, also contains a high percentage of these children. In most respects the geographic concentration of the White English language children resembles more closely the distribution of the Residual language children than it does that of the Spanish language children. However, both groups of minority language children tend to be more concentrated in urban areas than are the White English language children.

The net impact of the residence variables tends to conform to previous findings. Residence in the urban areas of the Texas-Louisiana region is again associated with negative net attainments. However, White English children residing in the urban areas of the Northeast, the South, and the Pacific Coast regions have higher net attainments than children living in other regions, a

Table 8.12 *Regression of educational attainment on selected background characteristics of white English children aged 6-13, United States, 1976*

Characteristics	Percent or mean	Regression coefficient
Northeast SMSA	11.35	.114 (.050)*
Northeast non-SMSA	10.29	.032 (.050)
Midwest SMSA	13.03	.039 (.049)
Midwest non-SMSA	18.41	-.058 (.047)
South SMSA	5.52	.152 (.057)*
South non-SMSA	17.08	.078 (.047)
Texas-Louisiana SMSA	4.07	-.175 (.061)*
Texas-Louisiana non-SMSA	4.17	.023 (.061)
Rocky Mountains SMSA	1.47	-.032 (.086)
Rocky Mountains non-SMSA	3.73	-.060 (.063)
Pacific Coast SMSA	6.12	.137 (.056)*
Pacific Coast non-SMSA	4.76	(a)
Parental education	13.94	.023 (.003)*
Intercept		.069
R-squared		.026

Notes:
(a) reference characteristic
* $p < .05$
Source: 1976 Survey of Income and Education

finding which tends to indicate that urban children enjoy educational advantages when compared to rural children (Veltman, 1980a: Table 12). This difference does not appear to obtain for either of the two groups of younger minority language children.

The parents of the White English language children had an educational attainment mean of 13.94 years, more than one full year higher than that of the parents of the Residual language children (13.94 - 12.83 = 1.11) and more than three years higher than that of the parents of the Spanish language children (13.94 - 10.53 = 3.41). The net impact of parental education on the attainment of the children is approximately the same as that observed in the Spanish language group, each additional year of parental education associated with a net increase of .023 years of educational attainment. This figure is somewhat higher than that observed for the Residual language group. In any event, both social class and residence effects are extremely weak, explaining only 2.6 percent of the variability in educational attainment.

Taking the baseline equation estimated in Table 8.12 as indicating the normative process of educational attainment for White English language children in the United States, we may compare the actual attainments of minority language to an attainment level predicted by inserting their characteristics into the regression equation estimated in Table 8.12. Predicted educational attainment for the younger Spanish children given their geographic distribution and the educational attainments of their parents is .348; their actual attainment, .357. Predicted attainment for the younger Residual language children is .421; actual attainment, .454. In both instances, then, once parental education and geographic distribution have been taken into account, the children of minority language background have obtained educational attainments commensurate with expectation. Whatever the effects of nativity and language characteristics which we have previously documented, the relative level of the educational attainments of minority language children is adequately explained by geographic and social class factors.

To determine whether there is evidence of ethnic effects for English monolingual children defined as Anglo-Spanish or Anglo-Residual, we added these children to the White English language sample and created a binary (dummy) variable to test the effects of membership in each group. When these ethnic variables were added to the baseline equation and standard errors were re-estimated in accordance with the procedure previously outlined, the data indicate that both Anglo-Spanish and Anglo-Residual children enjoyed significantly higher educational attainments than predicted by the baseline equation. These findings suggest that the children of anglicized persons have significantly higher educational attainments than children of English monolinguals, at least for 6-13 year old children and as measured in this study. This result is not altogether unexpected, since we reported similar results using a different methodology in an earlier study (Veltman, 1980a). The net educational attainments of the Anglo-Spanish children are superior to those of the White English language children by .046 years of educational attainment; those of the Anglo-Residual children by .038 years. These findings also conform to the paradigm provided by Featherman (1971) which indicates that the children of immigrants tend to have higher socioeconomic attainments than do the children of the native born.

To determine the extent to which a similar set of findings prevail among the older children, we begin by presenting the baseline equation for 14-17 year old White English language children. The relevant data are presented in

Table 8.13. Since the characteristics of the 14-17 year old children so strongly resemble those of their younger counterparts, we shall immediately procede to an examination of the equation. Once again we note that the proportion of the variance explained is higher in the equation for older than for the younger children. Nonetheless, regional and parental education variables appear to play a less important role in the educational attainment process of the White English language children than they do in the educational attainment process of the minority language children, the r-squareds reported in Table 8.5 and 8.11 being somewhat higher than that obtained in this equation.

Table 8.13 *Regression of educational attainment on selected background characteristics of white English children aged 14-17, United States, 1976*

Characteristics	Percent or mean	Regression coefficient
Northeast SMSA	10.57	-.087 (.090)
Northeast non-SMSA	9.99	.047 (.091)
Midwest SMSA	14.42	.122 (.086)
Midwest non-SMSA	17.52	.042 (.084)
South SMSA	6.09	.151 (.102)
South non-SMSA	14.84	-.005 (.086)
Texas-Louisiana SMSA	4.02	.060 (.114)
Texas-Louisiana non-SMSA	5.23	.012 (.106)
Rocky Mountains SMSA	1.36	.114 (.115)
Rocky Mountains non-SMSA	3.90	.011 (.106)
Pacific Coast SMSA	5.86	.143 (.103)
Pacific Coast non-SMSA	6.20	(a)
Parental education	13.61	.058 (.006)*
Intercept		-.514
R-squared		.041

Notes:
(a) reference characteristic
* $p < .05$
Source: 1976 Survey of Income and Education

Table 8.13 also shows that regional factors do not appear to be particularly important in differentiating the educational attainments of the White English language teenagers. None of the coefficients differs significantly from the mean attainment level of the reference group (children living in the non-urban areas of the Pacific Coast states). Furthermore, most of the coefficients do not differ significantly from one another. However, residence in the urban areas of the Midwest, the South, and the Pacific Coast states is relatively advantageous compared to residence in most other regions. While residence in the Northeastern urban areas was found to be relatively advantageous for the younger White English language children, it has ceased to be so for the older children of this group.

Further examination of Table 8.13 shows that the impact of parental educational attainment on the educational attainment of White English language children is similar in magnitude to that observed in the equations for the Spanish and Residual language children. Each additional year of parental education is associated with a net increase of .058 years of educational attainment for the children. In addition, the impact of parental education is stronger for the older children than was found to be the case for the younger children, supporting once again the proposition that social class factors become more important as children get older.

Using the equation estimated for the White English language children in Table 8.13 as the standard according to which other groups may be expected to obtain educational attainment, we begin by rewarding the Spanish language children according to their geographic distribution and the educational attainments of their parents. Their predicted educational attainment is .093 units of expected grade level. That is to say, based only on parental education and geographic residence, the educational attainment of Spanish language children may be expected to be .222 of a grade level lower than that of the White English language children (.315 - .093 = .222). This expected attainment level is also lower than that observed for Black children and is principally explained by social class factors (Veltman, 1980a). Nonetheless, the actual attainment level of the Spanish langauge 14-17 year olds is still .129 years below that predicted (.093 - (-.036) = .129), indicating that about one-third of the gap which separates the educational attainments of White English language teenagers from those of the Spanish language teenagers is attributable to membership in the Spanish language group. Two-thirds is explained by class and regional factors. When, however, the foreign born Spanish monolinguals are excluded from the comparison, the educational attainment gap is reduced from .129 to .073, indicating that the particular problem of this group of children accounts for some of the lower observed attainment attributable to language factors. Nonetheless, it does appear that children from Spanish language homes *per se* do have somewhat lower than expected attainments during the teenage years. Part of this problem may be attributed to difficulties with the English language (unmeasured in this study), part perhaps to educational discrimination (also unmeasured).

When the predicted attainment level of the 14-17 year old Residual language children is calculated, actual attainment (.349) exceeds expected attainment (.233) by .116. It is evident, then, that in general the educational attainment problem afflicts teenagers of the Spanish language group in particular. While there may be some specific minority language groups in the Residual language group which have specific problems (notably the Navajo language children), the data do not show that the children of the Residual language group as a whole have difficulties obtaining educational placement commensurate with their age, at least not after class and geographic factors have been controlled. The particular treatment of the Spanish language group is once again revealed.

When the Anglo-Spanish and Anglo-Residual ethnic groups are added to the White English language group, the data indicate that the Anglo-Residual children have an estimated attainment level .096 years higher than that of the White English language children and .087 years higher than that of the Anglo-Spanish children. Both differences are statistically significant, indicating that both the younger and older Anglo-Residual children enjoy significant educational advantages when compared to the White English monolingual children. The educational attainments of the Anglo-Spanish children aged 14-17 do not, of course, differ significantly from those of the White English language children, indicating that they have lost the modest educational advantages which they (presumably) had when they were younger.

In addition, further analysis of the educational attainment process of the Anglo-Spanish teenagers tends to show a negative relationship between placement in grade level and age, indicating that net of other factors, the older the child, the further behind grade level he or she is found to be. No such findings were obtained for the Anglo-Residual or White English language children (Veltman, 1980a: Tables 9 to 13). Thus, while in general the data analysis provides no evidence for the presence of ethnic discrimination against Anglo-Spanish or Anglo-Residual children (and in fact tends to show the contrary), the data may indicate an emergent problem of educational attainment among the 14-17 year old Anglo-Spanish teenagers. Such a problem is likely to be associated with decisions to terminate formal schooling, the resultant divergence in educational attainments of Anglo-Spanish and other White English monolingual teenagers accelerating over time.

Summary and conclusion. When we examine the educational attainments of 6–13 year old children, the data indicate that the selected background variables explain rather poorly the variability in observed educational attainment. The proportion of the variance explained is relatively low in all the equations examined for 6–13 year old children, indicating that most of the variance in age-appropriate placement in grade is randomly produced (or partly explained by other unmeasured factors). Nonetheless, the data analysis revealed the presence of relatively weak stratification based on social class origins and on nativity and/or language characteristics.

When we examine the educational attainment process of the older children, we find that the retained explanatory variables more completely determine the observed educational attainments of the sampled children. The r-squareds are notably higher in the equations estimated for the older children. Language characteristics and social class origins play a greater role among the older children, while nativity factors seem to become relatively unimportant. Generally speaking, children who usually speak English have significantly higher educational attainments than children who usually speak a minority language. Among native born children who usually speak English, English bilingual children generally have higher educational attainments than their English monolingual peers.

Moving away from the examination of the internal structuring of educational attainment in the Spanish and in the Residual language groups, we then attempted to compare the general attainment levels of each group with that of a sample of White English language children. After controlling for the social class origins and the regional distribution of the minority language children, we found that the younger children generally enjoyed equivalent or superior educational attainments when compared to the White English language children. Similar findings were obtained when comparing the older Residual language children to the older White English language children. However, the older Spanish language children had educational attainments .129 years below expectation, only part of which was attributable to the disastrous educational position of the foreign born, Spanish monolingual children. The older Spanish language children appear to experience particular difficulties in the American educational system, the analysis of the attainment process indicating a severe drop-out problem in the early teenage years.

When we compared Anglo-Spanish and Anglo-Residual children to White English monolingual children, we found little or no evidence of ethnic discrimination. In fact, Anglo-Spanish and Anglo-Residual children aged 6–13 had significantly higher educational attainments than did the White English language children. The older Anglo-Residual children also enjoyed attainment levels superior to those of their White English language peers, while the attainment level of the Anglo-Spanish children compared favorably with that of the White English language sample. However, the fact that their initial advantage has disappeared may be a harbinger of projected declining rates of educational attainment, an hypothesis also presaged by the negative relationship between age and educational attainment in this group. Since this extrapolation rests on such a small sample size (N = 365), such an interpretation (while plausible) must be offered and accepted with extreme caution. It is tempting, nonetheless, to see this as a second example of the particularistic treatment of Hispanic origin adolescents in the American educational system.

Finally, we need to ask ourselves whether the results would have been different had we adopted the prevalent Federal definition of educational attainment, the percentage of children enrolled *below* expected grade level. As we have previously indicated (Veltman, 1980a: Appendix B), the answer to this question is relatively complex. Two points seem particularly important, however. First of all, when using the one-tailed measure used by Federal investigators, the position of the White English language children is stronger than when using the metric measure reported in this chapter. Consequently, when controlling for social class origin and regional distribution, the proportion of Spanish language children aged 6-13 enrolled below expected grade level is greater than that predicted using the metric measure of attainment. Similarly, the proportion of younger Residual language children enrolled below grade level is larger than predicted. Thus, the measure used by the Federal investigators tends to find higher percentages of educationally disadvantaged children than does the metric measure used in this study. Both measures show, however, that the only group of severely disadvantaged children is the group of Spanish language children aged 14-17.

Secondly, the general relationships discovered in the analysis of the educational attainment process of the Spanish and Residual language groups are not modified in any unimportant manner when the one-tailed measure is used. While social class factors are more strongly related to the proportion of children enrolled below grade level than to our metric measure of educational attainment, the data continue to show that class factors play a stronger role in the educational attainment process of teenagers than they do among younger children. Likewise, the same pattern of language and nativity effects is obtained using the one-tailed measure of educational attainment. Thus, the essential effect of using the one-tailed measure is restricted to changing the estimated relationship between the educational attainments of the White

English language children and that of any other group of children to whom they are being compared. The use of the one-tailed measure does not alter in any important way the findings obtained when analyzing any single group of children.

Chapter 9

The Impact of Language Characteristics on the Educational Achievements of American Children

Introduction. In the previous chapter we suggested that the measure of educational attainment used by analysts of the SIE data presents certain drawbacks, notably that it was applied only to children still enrolled in school. On the other hand, the measure which we proposed has certain advantages, particularly since we were able to analyze at the same time persons who were still enrolled in school and those who had already dropped out. Thus, we were able to propose a single measure of educational attainment for all the children of a given age group rather than a measure limited to those children who were still enrolled in school.

This is not, however, the case in this chapter. Since the data are derived from *High School and Beyond*, the sample is restricted to those students of minority language background who were still enrolled in school in the Spring of 1980. Consequently, the impact of language (and other) variables on the decision to terminate schooling is excluded from the analysis. Nonetheless, the HSB data contribute enormously to the analysis of the impact of language variables because the data collection process included the administration of a number of so-called achievement tests. Thus, the analysis presented in this chapter is oriented toward the impact of language characteristics on classroom performance, at least insofar as this latter is captured by the achievment testing process.

The sample of children analyzed in this chapter resembles very strongly, of course, that used in our analysis of the language shift process of the HSB students (Chapter 5). However, not all students who completed the language questionnaire also completed the battery of tests devised by NCES researchers to measure achievement. Consequently, the sample sizes retained for the analysis of educational achievement are somewhat smaller than those previously reported. The fact that not all of the sampled children completed the tests introduces as well some changes into the characteristics of the achievement sample. The percentages of children declaring high, medium, and low ability to speak the minority language are reported by mother tongue in Table 9.1.

While Table 9.1 reveals (as expected) a high degree of similarity between

Table 9.1 *Characteristics of the language and achievement samples by language group, United States, 1980*

Mother tongue/minority language competence	Language group							
	Spanish			Residual				
	Language	Achievement	Change		Language	Achievement	Change	
English Mother tongue:								
High	6.48%	6.55%	+0.07%		4.69%	4.47%	−0.22%	
Medium	19.98	21.30	+1.32		18.60	19.53	+0.93	
Low	27.06	28.31	+1.25		49.15	50.55	+1.40	
Subtotal	53.52	56.16	+2.64		72.44	74.55	+2.11	
Minority mother tongue:								
High	19.91	18.60	−1.31		10.54	9.57	−0.97	
Medium	20.86	19.80	−1.06		9.60	8.91	−0.69	
Low	5.71	5.44	−0.27		7.42	6.97	−0.45	
Subtotal	46.48	43.84	−2.64		27.56	25.45	−2.11	
Estimated sample	5,353	4,350			3,757	3,325		

Source: High School and Beyond

the language shift and educational achievement samples, it seems that children who completed the achievement tests were more likely to have English for their mother tongue. The proportion of children of minority mother tongue falls by 2.64 percent (46.48 - 43.84 = 2.64%) in the Spanish language sample and by 2.11 percent (27.56 - 25.45 = 2.11%) in the Residual language group. Consequently, the children of minority mother tongue are under-represented in the achievement sample.

Furthermore, an examination of the columns labelled 'change' indicates that the children having the highest declared ability to speak the minority language are those most likely to be absent from the achievement samples. The proportion of such children declines for children of both English and minority mother tongue in the Residual language group. In the Spanish language group, this group also undergoes the greatest decline among children of Spanish mother tongue and experiences the least increase among those of English mother tongue. Thus, children who best speak the minority language are those least likely to have completed the achievement questionnaire. This finding leads us to suggest that the children of English mother tongue and little ability to speak the minority language were somewhat more comfortable when faced with the battery of achievement questions, presumably because their English language skills were better. This suggests that the samples retained for analysis over-estimate the mean achievements of children in both minority language groups, particularly those children of minority mother tongue. A certain percentage of the lowest achievers failed to complete the questionnaire.

That which seems most striking, however, in Table 9.1 is the difference in sample sizes between the achievement and language shift samples. It would appear that only 81.3 percent (4,350 / 5,353 = .813) of the children who completed the language questionnaire also completed the educational achievement tests in the Spanish language group. Similarly, only 88.5 percent (3,325 / 3,757 = .885) of the Residual language children completed both sets of questions. Why so many children, particularly Spanish language children, failed to finish the achievement tests is nowhere explained in the NCES literature on High School and Beyond. Presumably, however, the same factors which explain differences in educational achievement may also explain differences in completion rates of the educational achievement questionnaire. For example, if a high level of ability to speak the minority language is associated with lower achievement levels in reading or vocabulary scores, it is quite likely that the same factor may act on the completion rates. Furthermore, since so many more Spanish language children retain relatively high skill levels in the minority language, this factor would also explain differences in the completion rates by

Spanish and Residual children. In any case, we should remember the fact that the minority language samples retained for the achievement analysis are likely to overstate achievement of these students, a relatively large proportion of the presumably weaker students having failed to respond to the questionnaire.

Procedures. As we have indicated in our earlier chapter on the HSB children, mother tongue is a variable which appears to be extremely important in terms of its behavioral consequences. While we could treat children of both Spanish and English mother tongues in the same multiple regression analysis, such a comparison would tend to minimize these differences. This is still more true in the case of the Residual children where the size of the population of English mother tongue would lead to the masking of any independant effects which may be found for the children of minority mother tongues. We have, therefore, elected to divide both language groups into two components, those of English mother tongue and those of minority mother tongues.

As in the previous chapter we should like to ascertain the effects of a number of relatively important variables on the process of educational achievement. Educational achievement is defined in the HSB study as performance on a series of achievement tests which were given to both seniors (last year of secondary school) and to sophomores (third to last year). In its processing of the data NCES developed measures of achievement which were common to both groups of students by selecting a certain number of items which were included in both sets of questionnaires. Each such measure was normalized to yield a national mean of fifty (50) with a standard deviation of ten (10) points. We have retained for analysis in this chapter the mean scores achieved for the vocabulary, reading, and mathematics tests.

Since in the previous chapter the data indicated that English bilingual children tended to have higher educational attainments than English monolingual children of similar backgrounds, we have created an independent variable which measures retention of the minority language. Children of both English and minority mother tongues were classified by their declared ability to speak the minority language. Those who said that they spoke it very well were placed in the category defining high competence, those who declared a 'pretty good' knowledge in that defining medium competence, while those who declared either no competence or poor competence were placed in the category defining low competence in the ability to speak the minority language.

We also retained for analysis a number of other independent variables. We have previously described in chapter five the nature of variables representing minority language education (MLE), parental education, socioeconomic status (SES), ethnic origin or language group membership, and region of residence. We also conducted extensive tests regarding the impact of place of birth on the educational achievement process, since native born children may be thought to have significant advantages in terms, for example, of vocabulary achievements. Such advantages may extend to the greater ability to read achievement tests and consequently confer significant advantages on native born children. The appropriate multiple regression analyses did not show the hypothesized effects. Since place of birth has little or no impact on the achievement process, it has been excluded from the analyses which follow.

The educational achievements of children of minority mother tongue. Since we normally think of children of minority mother tongue when we speak of the potential educational problems of minority language children, we shall begin our analysis by presenting the characteristics of the children of Spanish and other minority mother tongues. The relevant data are presented in Table 9.2. Since this table is so similar to that presented in our analysis of the language shift characteristics of these children (Table 5.18), we shall not present an in-depth analysis. Briefly, the parents of the children of Spanish mother tongue have on the whole markedly lower socioeconomic status than do the parents of the Residual language children. Table 9.2 also reveals that the Residual language children are more anglicized. Only 37.61 percent of the children of Residual mother tongues declared that they spoke the minority language 'very well', while 27.36 percent said they either did not speak it at all or did not speak it very well. The comparable figures in the Spanish language group are 42.42 percent and 12.44 percent respectively. The children in both groups completed nearly three years of education in their respective minority languages.

1. The educational achievements of children of Spanish mother tongue. The relevant data for the mean educational achievements of children of Spanish mother tongue are presented in Table 9.3. Looking first of all at the mean scores, it is evident that there is a strong relationship between the achievement means. The range of the achievement means is only 0.51 points (45.83 - 45.32 = 0.51), indicating that children of Spanish mother tongue scored equally well on all three aspects of measured achievement. This may surprise some observers since one would expect that mathematics is relatively more symbolic and less embedded in English language culture than are English reading and vocabularly.

Table 9.2 *Characteristics of children of minority mother tongue by language group, achievement sample, United States, 1980*

Characteristics	Language group	
	Spanish	Residual
Socioeconomic status	35.52	47.65
Minority language competence:		
High	42.42	37.61
Medium	45.14	35.03
Low	12.44	27.36
Region:		
Northeast	22.22	35.60
South Atlantic	10.28	8.31
South	26.05	5.20
Midwest	7.13	18.91
Rocky Mountains	9.50	5.93
Pacific Coast	24.82	26.05
Minority language education	2.90	2.78
Ethnic group:		
Chicano	49.39	
Cuban	9.97	
Puerto Rican	16.76	
Other Latino	11.92	
Other	11.96	
Language group:		
Italian		8.48
Chinese		9.50
French		9.34
German		14.17
Greek		6.27
Portuguese		3.81
Filipino		6.85
Polish		3.34
All other		38.26
Sample size (raw)	1,907	846
Sample size (weighted)	123,574	103,669

Source: High School and Beyond

Table 9.3 *Mean educational achievements of children of Spanish mother tongue, United States, 1980*

Characteristics	Mean educational achievements		
	Reading	Vocabulary	Mathematics
Ethnic origin:			
Chicano/Mexican	44.66	44.51	45.21
Cuban	50.51	51.20	50.81
Puerto Rican	44.17	44.63	43.15
Other Latino	46.23	49.16	45.69
Other	44.89	45.18	43.87
Minority language competence:			
High	45.55	46.47	45.51
Medium	45.10	45.22	45.00
Low	45.75	45.90	45.82
Total	45.37	45.83	45.32

Source: High School and Beyond

When we examine the effects of ethnic origin on the achievement means, the data reveal that Cuban children, although of Spanish mother tongue, have mean scores which exceed the national average. This holds true for all three aspects of educational achievement. The performance of children in the remaining Hispanic groups is distinctly poorer, tending to hover around 45 points in nearly all cases. In only one other instance does a mean score tend to approach the national average, the children of Other Latino origins having a vocabulary score which approximates the national mean. On the whole, however, Chicano, Puerto Rican, Other Latino, and Other (U.S. only) children tend to have scores well below the national averages on all three tests.

When we examine the mean achievements of children who report various degrees of ability to speak the Spanish language, the data do not seem to indicate that the retention of Spanish is associated with either higher or lower educational achievement. The differences in the scores of the children having high, medium, or low competence are always inferior to one point, irrespective of the area of educational achievement being examined.

The presentation of the regression analyses will be less rich than that presented in the preceding chapters. Were we to present the results of the regression of each dependent variable on each (set) of the independent variables, the presentation of data would become quite cumbersome. In order not to impede the ready understanding of the regression equations we have accordingly decided to present only two equations for each group being analyzed. We present first of all in Table 9.4 the regression of each type of educational achievement on the variables representing socioeconomic status, region, ability to speak Spanish, and bilingual education.

Table 9.4 *Regression of selected factors on the educational achievement of children of Spanish mother tongue, United States, 1980*

Background characteristics	Regression coefficients (standard errors)		
	Reading	Vocabulary	Mathematics
Socioeconomic status	.11 (.01)*	.14 (.01)*	.12 (.01)*
Region:			
Northeast	.29 (.58)	-.30 (.57)	-1.67 (.57)*
South Atlantic	1.84 (.74)*	1.97 (.74)*	1.93 (.74)*
South	-1.05 (.56)	-2.76 (.55)*	-1.24 (.55)*
Midwest	2.25 (.84)*	.90 (.83)	.65 (.83)
Rocky Mountains	-.06 (.75)	-.33 (.74)	-.81 (.75)
Minority language competence:			
High	.37 (.64)	1.01 (.64)	.46 (.64)
Medium	-.15 (.63)	.01 (.63)	-.34 (.63)
Minority language education	-.49 (.06)*	-.34 (.06)*	-.52 (.06)*
Constant	43.07	42.53	43.41
R-squared	.110	.141	.131

* $p < .05$
Source: High School and Beyond

Examining first of all the general characteristics of the three equations, Table 9.4 reveals that the proportion of the variance explained by the equations is relatively low. Only eleven (.110) to fourteen (.141) percent of the differences in educational achievement is explained by the four factors combined. The equations resemble one another in other respects as well. Socioeconomic status has a positive effect on educational achievement, each additional point being associated with a net increase in achievement scores of slightly more than one-tenth of one point. The magnitude of the effects is approximately the same for each subject area.

Table 9.4 also confirms the impressions gathered from Table 9.3 with respect to the impact of minority language retention. There are no significant differences in educational achievement between children declaring high, medium, or low ability to speak Spanish. If anything, the children declaring high levels of competence seem to do slightly better than do children having medium or low competence.

The examination of the coefficients for the regional variables reveals that there are regional differences in the process of educational achievement. There are, however, somewhat different regional effects according to the subject area being examined, rendering rather difficult the interpretation of the results. Generally, it appears that children in the South Atlantic and Midwest regions have somewhat higher achievements than do children in the other regions. Since, however, we are principally concerned with eliminating as much heterogeneity in the sample as possible, the precise nature of regional differences is not extremely interesting. Rather, we wish to avoid attributing to other variables qualities which are best explained by regional differences.

Finally, Table 9.4 reveals that minority language education has a negative impact on all three types of achievement. MLE has the least negative effects on vocabulary achievement, somewhat greater negative effects on reading scores, and the most negative effects on mathematics achievement. These figures are, of course, net of other factors and capture the independent contribution of MLE alone. The detractors of MLE programs will be certain to note this negative effect; those who support them may be surprised by this finding, since MLE programs are supposed to facilitate the educational achievement of minority language children.

In Table 9.5 we have estimated a similar set of equations, having added the ethnic origin variables for the Hispanic ancestry group. The addition of ethnic variables to the equations increases by approximately 1.5 to 1.9 percent the proportion of the variance explained, indicating that ethnicity does play an independent role in the achievement process. While no major changes in the coefficients of the baseline variables can be observed, there are several minor changes. First of all, it would appear that the independent impact of socioeconomic status is marginally lower than that estimated in Table 9.4. The regional and minority language education effects are also somewhat smaller than previously estimated, while the effects of the ability to speak Spanish are somewhat more negative than estimated (although not statistically significant).

The pattern revealed by the estimated coefficients for ethnic origin itself is relatively clear. The Cuban children have educational achievements which average approximately four points higher than their other background characteristics would lead us to expect, i.e., when compared to the reference group

Table 9.5 *Regression of selected background variables and ethnic origin on the educational achievement of children of Spanish mother tongue, United States, 1980*

	Regression coefficients (standard errors)		
Background characteristics	Reading	Vocabulary	Mathematics
Socioeconomic status	.10 (.01)*	.12 (.01)*	.12 (.01)*
Region:			
Northeast	1.10 (.77)	−.36 (.76)	−.25 (.76)
South Atlantic	.50 (.94)	.08 (.93)	1.11 (.93)
South	−1.11 (.55)*	−2.72 (.55)*	−1.36 (.55)*
Midwest	2.53 (.85)*	.98 (.84)	1.11 (.84)
Rocky Mountains	−.09 (.75)	−.44 (.74)	−.82 (.74)
Minority language competence:			
High	−.48 (.63)	.45 (.64)	.07 (.64)
Medium	−.06 (.65)	−.33 (.63)	−.77 (.63)
Minority language education	−.45 (.06)*	−.31 (.06)*	−.47 (.06)*
Ethnic origin:			
Chicano	.76 (.67)	.52 (.66)	2.31 (.66)*
Cuban	3.75 (.98)*	3.95 (.97)*	4.46 (.97)*
Puerto Rican	−1.14 (.85)	−.38 (.84)	−.42 (.84)
Other Latino	.58 (.83)	3.18 (.82)*	1.11 (.82)
Constant	42.81	42.44	41.82
R-squared	.125	.160	.150

* $p < 0.5$

Source: High School and Beyond

of children of 'Other U.S. only' ethnic origin. Their reading and mathematics scores are significantly higher than those of children in any other group, while their vocabulary scores are significantly higher than those of all other groups except that of the Other Latinos. The net achievement scores of most other groups of children do not differ from one another. While the Other Latinos have mean vocabulary scores which are significantly higher than those of children in the two remaining (non-Cuban) groups, it is the performance of the Cuban children which is the most strikingly consistent from one equation to another.

2. The educational achievements of children of non-Spanish (Residual) mother tongue. Having examined the achievement process of the children of Spanish mother tongue, we turn our attention now to the achievements of the children of Residual mother tongue. The achievement means for each group of children are reported in Table 9.6.

Table 9.6   *Mean educational achievements of children of residual mother tongues, United States, 1980*

Characteristics	Mean educational achievements		
	Reading	Vocabulary	Mathematics
Language group:			
Italian	47.78	49.16	48.69
Chinese	52.42	48.66	56.43
French	51.56	50.46	52.26
German	52.74	52.79	52.97
Greek	50.74	51.20	52.25
Portuguese	48.63	45.22	50.28
Filipino	49.16	47.26	50.61
Polish	52.99	55.56	55.43
Other	49.64	48.86	52.97
Minority language competence:			
High	49.82	47.90	52.64
Medium	50.16	49.88	52.80
Low	51.79	51.93	52.44
Total	50.47	49.69	52.64

Source: High School and Beyond

Examining first of all the achievement means for the language group as a whole, we note that the mean scores are markedly higher than those observed for the children of Spanish mother tongue. In fact, only the mean vocabulary achievement, 46.69 falls just below the national average. Nonetheless, it is nearly four points higher (46.69 - 45.83 = 3.86) than that observed for the children of Spanish mother tongue. This is a quite interesting finding when the mean vocabulary scores are compared to self-reports of the ability to speak English. One would assiume that there is a relatively close correspondence between the two. However, in Table 5.9 we showed that the self-reported scores for the two groups of children were relatively close. The children of Residual mother tongue had an index score of 2.62 points, those of Spanish mother tongue 2.57 points of the three point scale. There would appear, then, to be some inconsistency between self-perceived ability to speak English and the measured ability of vocabulary achievement for the children of Spanish mother tongue. Their perceived ability is higher than their measured ability, at least when compared to the children of Residual mother tongue.

The reading and mathematics achievements of children of Residual mother tongue are also higher than those of the Spanish language children. Their reading achievement is just slightly superior to the national norm, while their mathematics achievement is 2.64 points higher than the national average. Thus, the expectation that mathematics achievement should be higher for children of non-English language backgrounds is found to hold true for the Residual language children, a finding which contrasts with that observed for the children of Spanish mother tongue. Unlike the children of Spanish mother tongue, however, the data show evidence of linguistic stratification in the achievement process. The greater the ability to speak the minority language, the lower the reading and vocabulary scores of the children, particularly the latter. There does not appear to be a relationship between minority language competence and mathematics achievement.

When we examine the mean achievement scores of children of specific mother tongues, the Filipino, Italian, and Portuguese children appear to have generally lower achievements than those in other groups. These findings seem, however, to vary by subject area, the Italian children having vocabulary scores relatively close to the national norm, mathematics scores over one point lower, and reading scores more than two points lower than the national average. Similarly, the Filipino and Portuguese children are weakest in vocabulary, have scores which approach the national average in reading, and have mathematics achievements superior to the national norm. This pattern of increased achievements as one moves from vocabulary to reading to mathematics scores is not only observable among these groups. The same pattern characterizes the Chinese, French, and the "other" minority language groups. The French, German, and Greek language children have attainments which are close to but always exceed the national norm, while the Polish children seem to have generally superior attainments. The Chinese children have reading scores which are among the highest and their mathematics achievements exceed those of all other groups of children. On the whole, however, we must conclude that the children of minority mother tongues other than Spanish appear to do quite well in the American classroom. In only one instance, that of the reading scores of Portuguese children, is a mean score inferior to 47 points. These children seem generally to perform at or near the national average, somewhat more poorly in the case of vocabulary scores, somewhat superior in terms of mathematics scores.

To examine the effects of the independent background variables on educational achievement, we present in Table 9.7 the results of our baseline equations.

Table 9.7 *Regression of selected variables on the educational achievements of children of residual mother tongues, United States, 1980*

Background characteristics	Regression coefficients (standard errors)		
	Reading	Vocabulary	Mathematics
Socioeconomic status	.11 (.02)*	.17 (.02)*	.18 (.02)*
Region:			
Northeast	-.01 (.85)	.77 (.87)	-.53 (.83)
South Atlantic	-1.82 (1.29)	-1.17 (1.33)	-.78 (1.26)
South	-1.40 (1.56)	-.37 (1.61)	-.39 (1.53)
Midwest	-.67 (.98)	.57 (1.01)	-2.44 (.96)*
Rocky Mountains	-2.75 (1.48)	-1.45 (1.53)	-5.90 (1.45)*
Minority language competence:			
High	.65 (.86)	-1.48 (.88)	1.41 (.84)
Medium	-.37 (.84)	-.71 (.86)	1.20 (.82)
Minority language education	-.89 (.10)*	-.83 (.10)*	-.30 (.10)*
Constant	48.23	44.66	45.26
R-squared	.159	.205	.169

* $p < 0.5$
Source: High School and Beyond

We observe first of all that the proportion of the variance explained is marginally higher than that obtained for the children of Spanish mother tongue. As in the equations for the children of Spanish mother tongue, socioeconomic status is positively associated with educational achievement, while the number of years of minority language education is negatively associated with achievement of all types.

Nonetheless, when we examine the equations in greater detail, we observe both less uniformity between the equations in the Residual language group and some interesting differences from those estimated for the children of Spanish mother tongue. For example, we find that MLE has a much stronger negative effect on the reading and vocabulary achievements of the Residual children than on their mathematics achievements. The effect on reading and vocabulary is approximately double that found for the Spanish language children. Each additional year of MLE is associated with nearly one point less of achievement scores. The effect of minority language education on mathematics achievement is somewhat stronger in the Spanish language group than that found among Residual children. And while children in the South Atlantic region were found to have higher achievements in the Spanish group, the principal regional finding for the Residual children is the negative impact of residence in the Rocky Mountain states.

As we found for the Spanish language children, the impact of the ability to speak the minority language fails to attain statistical significance in the equations examined. The data suggest, however, that the retention of the minority language is associated with positive mathematics achievements and negative vocabulary scores. Were the sample sizes larger these effects would undoubtedly attain statistical significance. Nonetheless, the effects are relatively weak, the retentive children having higher or lower achievement scores of approximately one point.

To examine the effect of belonging to a specific language group, we added the language group variables to the baseline equation. The results are presented in Table 9.8. As we found for the Spanish language group, the addition of the membership group variables improves the proportion of the variance explained. The increase is somewhat larger than that observed when adding the ethnic variables to the Spanish equations, a fact no doubt related to the greater heterogeneity of language as opposed to ethnic groups. Once again, there is little change in any of the regression coefficients previously estimated. While the impact of minority language education remains unchanged, regional effects appear to be somewhat weaker than previously thought. There are also some changes in the significance of retaining a minority language. Children of high competence are found to have significantly lower vocabulary scores, while those of medium competence have a disadvantage of just over one point, a finding which does not attain statistical significance. However, the relative advantages of retentive children in the area of mathematics achievement have been markedly reduced, no longer approaching the criterion of statistical significance.

With respect to membership in a specific minority language group, many of the estimated coefficients not only do not differ from that of children in the reference group (All others) having equivalent characteristics; they also do not differ from one another. There are, however, several exceptions worth noting. Children of Italian mother tongue have reading scores significantly

Table 9.8 *Regression of selected variables and language group on the educational achievements of children of residual mother tongues, United States, 1980*

Background characteristics	Regression coefficients (standard errors)		
	Reading	Vocabulary	Mathematics
Socioeconomic status	.10 (.02)*	.17 (.02)*	.18 (.02)*
Region:			
Northeast	.90 (.94)	.45 (.97)	.90 (.91)
South Atlantic	-1.63 (1.32)	-2.02 (1.36)	-.35 (1.27)
South	-1.44 (1.60)	-1.36 (1.65)	.32 (1.55)
Midwest	-.14 (1.04)	-.31 (1.07)	-1.49 (1.00)
Rocky Mountains	-2.54 (1.53)	-2.17 (1.58)	-5.71 (1.48)*
Minority language competence:			
High	.66 (.88)	-1.99 (.90)*	.92 (.85)
Medium	-.55 (.84)	-1.08 (.87)	.77 (.81)
Language group:			
Italian	-3.77 (1.30)*	-.77 (1.35)	-4.77 (1.26)*
Chinese	2.68 (1.22)*	-.05 (1.26)	3.53 (1.18)*
French	-.47 (1.25)	-.88 (1.29)	-2.76 (1.21)*
German	.96 (1.04)	1.18 (1.07)	-1.90 (1.00)
Greek	-.25 (1.44)	2.30 (1.49)	-.70 (1.39)
Portuguese	-.88 (1.81)	-2.10 (1.87)	-1.68 (1.75)
Filipino	-1.97 (1.38)	-3.89 (1.42)*	-4.02 (1.33)*
Polish	.07 (1.90)	3.92 (1.96)*	.83 (1.84)
Constant	48.18	45.35	45.60
R-squared	.180	.224	.211

* p < .05
Source: High School and Beyond

lower than those of children in most other groups, while Chinese children have significantly higher scores. A more or less similar pattern is found for mathematics achievement, the children of Italian mother tongue and Filipino mother tongue having the lowest scores, the Chinese children the highest scores. The pattern differs for vocabulary achievement, Polish and Greek children having significantly higher scores than most other groups of children, Filipino children lower scores. These are the principal exceptions to the general rule which finds that language of origin does not appear to play a very important role in the process of educational achievement. Differences in the mean scores reported in Table 9.6 seem relatively well explained by the other variables in the equation. The only such differences as seem to remain suggest that Italian and Filipino children experience greater difficulties in the achievement process, while children of Chinese mother tongue seem to have higher achievements than their other characteristics would lead us to expect.

The educational achievement of children of English mother tongue. Having obtained a certain number of interesting findings from our analysis of the achievements of children of minority mother tongues, we shall now ascertain whether the process of educational achievement is similar for children of English mother tongue. We present the characteristics of the two samples of children in Table 9.9.

There is no doubt but that the sample characteristics of the children of English mother tongue differ markedly from those of the children previously analyzed. The socioeconomic status of the parents is higher, particularly that of the children in the Spanish group, while the ability to speak the minority language is markedly lower. We have previously observed that children of English mother tongue are more likely to have declared a non-Hispanic or U.S. only ethnic origin in the Spanish group. In the Residual group, they are more likely to belong to the older, larger immigrant groups (Italian, French, and German) than to the smaller groups more recently arrived. In both groups children of English mother tongue have obtained more than one year of minority language education, a finding which is somewhat surprising since the avowed objective of U.S. language programs is the promotion of the integration of children of minority *mother tongue*. Nonetheless, the Residual children averaged 1.45 years of MLE, Spanish children, 2.05 years.

1. The educational achievements of children of English mother tongue in the Spanish language group. We begin our analysis of the educational achievements of English language children by presenting in Table 9.10 the mean achievement scores for children in the Spanish language group. The mean scores obtained by the children of English mother tongue correspond much more closely to the national average than those obtained by their peers of Spanish mother tongue. Nonetheless, all scores remain slightly below those obtained by American children as a whole. That data also reveal that the more anglicized children have higher mean achievement scores. Those children who said they spoke the minority language very well had mean achievement scores approximately two points lower than those of children declaring a medium level of

Table 9.9 *Characteristics of children of English mother tongue in the achievement samples, by language group, United States, 1980*

Characteristics:	Language group	
	Spanish	Residual
Socioeconomic status	47.36	53.56
Region:		
Northeast	13.57	32.56
South Atlantic	9.33	8.86
South	19.63	10.32
Midwest	16.87	28.29
Rocky Mountains	16.95	3.36
Pacific Coast	23.65	16.61
Minority language competence:		
High	11.66	6.00
Medium	37.93	26.20
Low	50.41	67.80
Minority language education	2.05	1.45
Ethnic group:		
Chicano	37.76	
Cuban	1.28	
Puerto Rican	4.61	
Other Latino	9.43	
Other/U.S. only	46.92	
Language group:		
Italian		15.86
Chinese		1.49
French		22.61
German		24.94
Greek		2.81
Portuguese		1.79
Filipino		2.10
Polish		6.31
All others		22.10
Sample size (raw)	2,442	2,479
Sample size (weighted)	158,242	303,777

Source: High School and Beyond

Table 9.10 *Mean educational achievements of children of English mother tongue, Spanish language group, United States, 1980*

Characteristics	Mean educational achievements		
	Reading	Vocabulary	Mathematics
Ethnic origin:			
Chicano/Mexican	47.03	47.14	46.68
Cuban	50.43	52.50	52.23
Puerto Rican	49.49	49.56	47.81
Other Latino	49.37	50.41	48.50
Other/U.S. only	51.15	51.69	51.18
Minority language competence:			
High	46.77	47.88	45.92
Medium	48.77	49.68	48.81
Low	50.36	50.25	50.03
Total	49.09	49.75	49.34

Source: High School and Beyond

competence. In fact, the observed difference is nearly three points for mathematics scores. Similarly, children of low ability to speak the minority language had still higher achievements than did those who claimed a medium of level of competence. This pattern is found for all three types of measured achievement. These differences suggest that the bilingual child of English mother tongue may incur educational penalties as a function of learning the Spanish language.

The examination of the mean achievements of children in specific Hispanic ancestry groups reveals that Cuban and Other and U.S. only children obtained achievement scores higher than the national mean. Children of Chicano origin were the only ones scoring consistently below the national mean, Puerto Rican and Other Latino children having scores very near the national average for vocabulary and reading, somewhat lower for mathematics. It appears, then, that differentiation within the Hispanic group takes a different form among children of English mother tongue than was found for children of Spanish mother tongue.

To examine the impact of the variables retained for analysis, we present in Table 9.11 the results of the appropriate regression equations. We observe first of all that the proportion of variance explained by these equations is from 3.7 to 4.7 percent higher than that obtained in the equations for the children of Spanish mother tongue. That is to say, the variables retained

Table 9.11 *Regression of selected variables on the educational achievements of children of Spanish mother tongue, United States, 1980*

Background characteristics	Regression coefficients (standard errors)		
	Reading	Vocabulary	Mathematics
Socioeconomic status	.13 (.01)*	.16 (.01)*	.16 (.01)*
Region:			
Northeast	2.33 (.60)*	.50 (.63)	1.22 (.62)
South Atlantic	-1.28 (.69)	-2.80 (.72)*	-.90 (.71)
South	.18 (.54)	-3.08 (.56)*	-.84 (.56)
Midwest	1.79 (.57)*	.29 (.59)	2.30 (.58)*
Rocky Mountains	-.03 (.56)	-2.51 (.59)*	-.17 (.58)
Minority language competence:			
High	-1.36 (.60)*	.01 (.62)	-1.69 (.61)*
Medium	-1.30 (.38)*	-.30 (.40)	-1.01 (.40)*
Minority language education	-.66 (.06)*	-.69 (.06)*	-.68 (.06)*
Constant	44.56	44.88	43.21
R-squared	.152	.177	.178

* p < .05
Source: High School and Beyond

in the equation have a stronger impact on the determination of educational achievement for the children of English mother tongue. This observation can also be supported by examining the regression coefficients estimated for the various factors. The impact of socioeconomic status on the achievement process is somewhat higher for the children of English mother tongue. Similarly, the number of years of minority language education is also more strongly related to achievement, each additional year of MLE being associated with still more negative achievement levels than those found for the children of Spanish mother tongue. On the other hand, the effects of region of residence do not appear to play as important a role among the children of English mother tongue.

However, the most significant difference in the educational achievement process of the children of English mother tongue concerns the impact of the ability to speak the minority language. While most of the differences in the mean attainment levels of the three competence groups (from Table 9.10) are explained by the other variables included in the equation, the data generally indicate that there are statistically significant disadvantages associated with the retention of the Spanish language. This is particularly true in the area of reading achievement but appears to hold true as well in the area of mathematics. The data do not reveal significant (net) differences in the area of measured vocabulary achievements.

The addition of the ethnic origin variables increases the proportion of the variance explained by 1.2 to 1.5 percent. The relevant data are presented in Table 9.12. Once again, the addition of the ethnic origin variables causes only small changes in the size of the coefficients estimated for the variables previ-

Table 9.12 *Regression of selected variables and ethnic origin on the educational achievements of children of English mother tongue, Spanish language group, United States, 1980*

Background characteristics	Regression coefficients (standard errors)		
	Reading	Vocabulary	Mathematics
Socioeconomic status	.11 (.01)*	.14 (.01)*	.14 (.01)*
Region:			
Northeast	1.10 (.67)	-.71 (.69)	.30 (.69)
South Atlantic	-2.35 (.71)*	-3.87 (.74)*	-1.90 (.73)*
South	.24 (.54)	-3.03 (.56)*	-.76 (.55)
Midwest	.96 (.58)	-.50 (.60)	1.51 (.60)*
Rocky Mountains	.16 (.56)	-2.38 (.58)*	.05 (.58)
Minority language competence:			
High	-1.34 (.60)*	-.04 (.62)	-1.62 (.61)*
Medium	-1.32 (.38)*	-.32 (.40)	-1.00 (.40)*
Minority language education	-.69 (.06)*	-.71 (.06)*	-.71 (.06)*
Ethnic origin:			
Chicano	-2.86 (.45)*	-2.73 (.47)*	-2.68 (.46)*
Cuban	-.13 (1.58)	1.28 (1.65)	1.77 (1.63)
Puerto Rican	-.42 (.92)	-.63 (.96)	-1.36 (.95)
Other Latino	-2.01 (.64)*	-1.18 (.66)	-2.56 (.66)*
Constant	47.15	47.32	45.70
R-squared	.167	.189	.192

* $p < .05$
Source: High School and Beyond

ously examined. Socioeconomic status has a slightly weaker effect while the number of years of MLE has a slightly stronger effect on educational achievement. There are no changes, however, in the estimated impact of the relative ability to speak the Spanish language. Both high and medium levels of competence are associated with significant educational disadvantages on the reading and mathematics tests. No such effect is found for vocabulary achievement.

With respect to the impact of ethnic origin itself, the findings are very clear. Membership in either the Chicano or Other Latino group is generally associated with educational achievement significantly lower than that of similar children in the Other/U.S. only group. The application of t-tests also shows that Cuban children enjoy generally higher educational attainments when compared to all groups of children except those of Other/U.S. only origins. In addition, the Puerto Rican children tend to have higher attainment levels when compared to those of Chicano origins. These findings tend to differ from those found for children of Spanish mother tongue, where only children of Cuban ancestry were differentiated from children in the other ethnic groups. There would appear to be greater differentiation among children of English mother tongue. There appears to be a relatively clear hierarchy of achievement by ethnic origin, even though not all of the paired comparisons differ significantly from one another. Cuban children have the highest educational achievements, followed closely by those of Other and U.S. only origins. Puerto Rican children have intermediate achievement levels, while Chicano and Other Latino children have the lowest net levels of achievement. Since similar findings are obtained when regional factors are omitted, these ethnic differences cannot be dismissed as being contaminated by the presence of the regional variables.

2. The educational achievements of children of English mother tongue in the non-Spanish (Residual) language group. Having completed our examination of the achievement process for Hispanic children of English mother tongue, we turn our attention to those of Residual origin. Their educational achievement means are presented in Table 9.13.

The examination of the educational achievements of children in the Residual group as a whole reveals that these children have mean scores approximately three points superior to the national mean. These scores are approximately four points higher than those found for the children of English mother tongue in the Spanish language group. Once again, the comparison of the vocabulary scores to the self-reported scores of the ability to speak the English language (Table 5.9) indicates that the children in the Spanish lan-

Table 9.13 *Mean educational achievements of children of English mother tongue, residual language group, United States, 1980*

Characteristics	Mean educational achievements		
	Reading	Vocabulary	Mathematics
Language group:			
Italian	51.58	52.01	52.75
Chinese	55.13	58.22	56.94
French	52.37	53.06	52.97
German	53.15	53.35	53.06
Greek	52.77	53.33	52.72
Portuguese	50.12	51.88	49.76
Filipino	49.83	51.75	51.27
Polish	54.26	53.34	53.09
All other	53.65	54.59	54.52
Minority language competence:			
High	48.53	50.52	50.51
Medium	53.21	54.53	53.24
Low	53.07	53.58	53.51
Total	52.80	53.42	53.26

Source: High School and Beyond

guage group appear to overestimate their verbal abilities. The two groups of children declared equivalent levels of the ability to speak the English language. However, the measured vocabulary scores reveal that the Residual language children enjoy distinct advantages in this respect.

Table 9.13 also reveals that the more anglicized children have higher educational achievements. Those who speak the minority language very well have mean achievement levels ranging from three to three and one-half points lower than do children having medium or low competence in the minortiy language. There do not appear to be important differences between the two latter groups of children, a finding which contrasts with that obtained for the Spanish children.

When we examine the mean achievement scores by language group of origin, the data reveal that nearly all groups have achievement scores which meet or exceed the national average. The lowest scores are obtained by Portuguese and Filipino children. In both instances the achievement scores exceed the national mean on two of three tests. On the third test their scores are marginally lower than the national average. The highest scores are obtained by the children of Chinese language origin, the scores of most other groups falling in the 52 to 54 points range.

To examine the educational achievement process of these children we estimated the baseline equations presented in Table 9.14.

Table 9.14 *Regression of selected variables on the educational achievements of children of English mother tongue, residual language group, United States, 1980*

Background characteristics	Regression coefficients (standard errors)		
	Reading	Vocabulary	Mathematics
Socioeconomic status	.12 (.01)*	.18 (.01)*	.14 (.01)*
Region:			
Northeast	1.51 (.55)*	1.58 (.53)*	1.56 (.55)*
South Atlantic	.39 (.76)	-1.39 (.73)	-1.66 (.75)*
South	-1.41 (.73)	-1.58 (.70)*	-1.01 (.72)
Midwest	1.24 (.57)*	-.39 (.55)	1.09 (.56)
Rocky Mountains	-1.53 (1.09)	-1.21 (1.06)	-2.68 (1.08)*
Minority language competence:			
High	-2.68 (.80)*	-1.47 (.77)	-1.52 (.78)
Medium	.30 (.43)	.09 (.41)	-.12 (.42)
Minority language education	-.68 (.07)*	-.56 (.07)*	-.48 (.07)*
Constant	46.68	44.58	46.12
R-squared	.118	.167	.114

* $p < .05$
Source: High School and Beyond

Examining first of all the proportion of the variance explained, Table 9.14 reveals that the equations for reading and mathematics achievement are more indeterminate than the equations previously estimated. That is to say, the retained variables are not as important in determining the educational achievements of these children as is the case for the three groups of children previously examined.

Nonetheless, the pattern of the regression coefficients resembles rather strongly that obtained for the children of English mother tongue in the Spanish language group. The impact of socioeconomic status is approximately the same, while that of minority language education is generally slightly weaker. The data also reveal significant regional variation in the achievement process of these children, children living in the South Atlantic, South, and Rocky Mountain regions tending to have more negative achievements, those in the Northeast and Pacific Coast regions more positive achievements. Once again, there are also variations according to the area of achievement examined. In addition, the data clearly sustain the proposition that a high degree of ability to speak a minority language is associated with negative academic performance, ranging from a low of 1.48 points on the vocabulary test to 2.68 points on the reading test. This finding clearly resembles that obtained for the children of English mother tongue in the Spanish language group.

The addition of the language membership group variables has a very small impact on the proportion of the variance explained. The relevant data are presented in Table 9.15. The addition of the language group variables does not change in any appreciable way the size of the coefficients for the remaining variables included in the equations. The direction of the coefficients attached to the language group variables indicates that the group of children in the 'All other' language group tend to have higher mean achievements, net of other factors, than do children in most other groups. Nonetheless, the data indicate that children in the Italian, Filipino, and Portuguese language groups tend to have educational achievement scores which are significantly lower than those of children in most other groups. On the other hand, children of Chinese origin tend to have somewhat higher achievement levels than do other children, particularly, in the area of vocabulary and mathematics achievement.

Conclusion. The examination of the regression equations for the two groups of Spanish and Residual children reveals few differences in the process of educational achievement. This process appears to be largely indeterminate, the proportion of the variance explained by the variables retained for analysis being generally rather low (.15 to .20). Nonetheless, a number of factors have been found to consistently affect the educational achievement process.

First of all, the analysis reveals the importance of socioeconomic status in the educational achievement process, a finding similar to that observed in the preceding chapter on educational attainment. Social class origins continue to play a role in the results achieved by children in the process of educational attainment. The intergenerational transmission of status and privilege through the educational system is particularly important for the Spanish language group, since so many immigrants enter the U.S. work force at the bottom of the socioeconomic ladder. Nonetheless, the net impact of socioeconomic

Table 9.15 *Regression of selected variables and language group on the educational achievements of children of English mother tongue, residual language group, United States, 1980*

Background characteristics	Regression coefficients (standard errors)		
	Reading	Vocabulary	Mathematics
Socioeconomic status	.12 (.01)*	.18 (.01)*	.13 (.01)*
Region:			
Northeast	1.84 (.58)*	2.18 (.56)*	2.02 (.58)*
South Atlantic	.51 (.77)	-1.05 (.75)	-1.40 (.76)
South	-1.55 (.75)*	-1.57 (.72)*	-.86 (.74)
Midwest	1.03 (.58)	-.27 (.56)	1.26 (.58)*
Rocky Mountains	-1.83 (1.09)	-1.31 (1.06)	-2.71 (1.08)*
Minority language competence:			
High	-2.73 (.80)*	-1.54 (.77)*	-1.50 (.79)
Medium	.24 (.44)	-.04 (.42)	-.16 (.43)
Minority language education	-.68 (.07)*	-.56 (.07)*	-.48 (.07)*
Language group:			
Italian	-2.35 (.62)*	-2.89 (.60)*	-2.01 (.61)*
Chinese	.60 (1.54)	2.31 (1.49)	1.46 (1.53)
French	-.82 (.57)	-.80 (.55)	-1.10 (.57)
German	-.20 (.54)	-.71 (.52)	-1.18 (.53)*
Greek	-.40 (1.16)	-.83 (1.12)	-1.32 (1.15)
Portuguese	-2.71 (1.42)	-2.00 (1.37)	-4.10 (1.41)*
Filipino	-4.02 (1.32)*	-2.98 (1.28)*	-3.23 (1.31)*
Polish	.24 (.84)	-1.15 (.81)	-1.82 (.83)*
Constant	47.53	45.52	47.21
R-squared	.128	.178	.123

* $p < .05$
Source: High School and Beyond

status on the achievements of children is relatively weak. According to the equations estimated it takes approximately six to ten points of additional SES to change the achievement scores of children by a single point. Thus, one group would have to enjoy exceptional SES advantages to greatly affect the educational performance of their children.

Secondly, the data do not show consistent relationships between retention of the minority language and academic performance. Nonetheless, certain trends seem relatively clear. First of all, among children of minority mother tongue, either Spanish or other, the data indicate that there is little or no relationship between the ability to speak the minority language and performance on these educational tests. That is to say, increased anglicisation, the progressive abandonment of the mother tongue, is not associated with positive educational gains. Secondly, the data clearly indicate that children of English mother tongue who have good verbal skills in the minority language do indeed have lower than expected educational achievement scores. This was found to be true for children who declared either medium or high competence in Spanish but only for those declaring high verbal competence in one of the Residual languages. This latter difference is not surprising, since we have previously discovered that Residual children declaring medium competence actually used the minority language somewhat less than did Spanish children declaring the same level of competence. Nonetheless, for those who would argue that bilingualism is associated with positive academic achievement, these findings must be relatively disheartening, particularly when the same data also find that minority language education programs are also associated with negative results.

Thirdly, we have clearly established the negative impact of minority language education on the educational achievements of children in all four subgroups and for each of the three subject areas tested. Furthermore, similar findings can be obtained for native born children in all four groups, permitting us to make some inferences about the utility of bilingual education programs. The data suggest that such programs have an effect which depresses the educational achievements of children of *both* English mother tongue and those of minority mother tongues. This is equally true for vocabulary, reading, and mathematics skills as measured in these tests. It is also true for children in both the Residual and Spanish language groups, although the negative effects of MLE programs appear to be somewhat stronger for the non-Spanish children.

This finding, of course, leads us to consider the real goals of parents who enroll their children in such programs. We have already established in chapter five that such programs are indeed associated with the retention of greater skills in the minority language. If this is the objective of parents enrolling their children in such programs, MLE programs appear to meet this expectation, at least within the terms defined and measured in this study. If, rather, MLE programs seek to render less traumatic the transition from a minority language background to the English language school setting, this kind of social objective may also be met. We may wish to see some psychological evidence demonstrating that this is the case. In addition, parents may wish to be consulted as to whether they prefer smoother social integration or higher educational achievements, since these two features of MLE programs appear to be inversely related. If, on the other hand, bilingual education programs exist to further the upward mobility of adults in minority ethnic groups, a relatively common feature of the Federal bureaucracy, then it would seem that parents may wish to know the educational costs of enrolling their children in such programs. If, finally, the goal of MLE programs is to equalize educational opportunity by permitting minority language children to begin their formal education in a more familiar language, the data indicate that the opposite is in fact the result.

Fourthly, the data indicate that some minority language or background groups have either higher or lower achievements than others. Among children of minority mother tongues, Cuban children in the Spanish language group and Chinese children in the Residual language group have higher than expected educational achievements. Children of Italian and Filipino mother tongues have lower than expected achievements in the Residual language group. There is also some tendancy for the children of Portuguese mother tongue to have lower than expected achievement scores. Relatively similar findings are obtained for the children of English mother tongue in the Residual language group. However, the situation is somewhat different in the Spanish language group. While Cuban children continue to have the highest net achievement scores, those of Other/U.S. only children are nearly as high (and do not differ significantly). On the other hand, Chicano and Other Latino children have net achievements which are significantly lower than those of the Cuban and Other/U.S. only children. These findings suggest greater ethnic stratification among Spanish children of English mother tongue than was found for their peers of Spanish mother tongue.

Finally, we should like to address two remaining questions. The presentation of the achievement means for the children in each of the four groups examined showed important differences in the general levels of their educational achievements. The children of Spanish mother tongue had mean scores of approximately 45 points, while those of English mother tongue in the Spanish language group had scores approximately four points higher. The children of Residual mother tongue enjoyed achievement levels slightly superior to the national average in the areas of reading and vocabulary, three points higher in the area of mathematics. Their peers of English mother tongue had mean achievement scores of approximately 53 points.

The first question we should like to ask is whether the lower educational achievements of children of minority mother tongue are due to their mother tongue or to their remaining characteristics. We may examine this problem by treating the educational achievement processes of the children of English mother tongue as normative. If we then reward the children of minority mother tongue according to the equations estimated for the children of English mother tongue, we can compare observed achievements to expected values. The relevant data for this comparison are presented in Table 9.16.

Table 9.16 *Expected educational achievements of children of minority mother tongue, United States, 1980*

Language group	Mean educational achievements		
	Reading	Vocabulary	Mathematics
Spanish:			
Expected	46.34	46.90	45.38
Observed	45.37	45.83	45.32
Observed − Expected	−0.97	−1.07	−0.06
Observed / Expected	0.98	0.98	1.00
Residual:			
Expected	50.31	51.30	51.24
Observed	50.47	49.69	52.65
Observed − Expected	0.16	−1.61	1.41
Observed / Expected	1.00	0.97	1.03

Source: Tables 2, 11 and 14

The examination of this table reveals that the lower educational achievements of the children of minority mother tongue correspond relatively well to their background characteristics, i.e., parental SES, region of residence, the number of years of MLE, and their ability to speak the minority language. The vocabulary scores of the children of Spanish mother tongue are 1.07 points lower than expected, while those of children of Residual mother tongue are 1.61 points lower than indicated. The reading score of children of Spanish mother tongue is also nearly a point lower than predicted. On the other hand, the mathematics scores of the Spanish children approximate very closely those expected, while those of Residual children exceed expectation. We should probably conclude that within language groups, the mother tongue of the child does not appear to be associated with large differences in the educational achievements of children, at least once their background characteristics have been taken into consideration.

We may then ask whether there are differences in the expected and observed levels of achievement between children in the Spanish language group and those in the Residual language group. To accomplish this comparison we have accepted as normative the achievement process of the Residual language children. Inserting the characteristics of the children of the Spanish into the equations estimated for the Residual children produces the results reported in Table 9.17.

Table 9.17 *Expected educational achievements of children in the Spanish language group, United States, 1980*

Mother tongue	Mean educational achievements		
	Reading	Vocabulary	Mathematics
English:			
Expected	50.75	50.91	51.12
Observed	40.09	49.75	49.34
Observed − Expected	−1.66	−1.16	−1.78
Observed / Expected	0.97	0.98	0.97
Spanish:			
Expected	48.39	46.60	50.18
Observed	45.37	45.83	45.32
Observed − Expected	−3.02	−0.77	−4.86
Observed / Expected	0.94	0.98	0.90

Source: Table 3, 7, 10, and 14

The examination of Table 9.17 reveals that the lower educational test scores of the children in the Spanish language group are not completely explained by their background characteristics. The achievements of the children of English mother tongue in the Spanish language group remain from 1.16 to 1.78 points lower than anticipated, i.e., after their background characteristics have been taken into account. Since the mean achievement scores separating the Residual and Spanish children differed by four points, approximately two-thirds is explained by differences in the characteristics of the children. The other one-half is not explained. Actual achievements are approximately 97 to 98 percent of those expected.

When we examine the children of minority mother tongues, we find that in general the achievement gap is somewhat wider. In the comparison of vocabulary achievement, the unexplained gap is less than one point; it is three points for reading achievement, nearly five for mathematics scores. Thus, the differences in vocabulary means are nearly entirely explained by differences in the background characteristics of the children of minority mother tongue. The vocabulary scores of the children of Spanish mother tongue are nearly as high as anticipated. However, their reading and mathematics achievement scores are definitely lower than expected, indicating particular educational difficulties in these areas. The unexplained differences remain relatively large. Whether these differences are due to discrimination is, of course, open to interpretation. Suffice it to say that the evidence indicates that the outcomes are unequal, Residual language children benefitting from educational advantages, those of Spanish mother tongue suffering from comparative disadvantages.

Finally, we should emphasize once again that the data presented in this chapter concern only those children enrolled in high school during the Spring of 1980. Still more accurately, the sample retained for analysis appears to exclude the weaker students who did not complete the achievement questionnaire, particularly those of Spanish mother tongue. It may well be that the analysis of the achievements of children still enrolled in school minimizes the impact of the independent variables on the total educational process. Some children have already dropped out. Were their achievement scores added to those included in the study, the impact of the baseline variables might have been still greater. Furthermore, the total impact of these variables may not be known until these children have completed their educational attainments, since the same factors which account for lower achievements at the moment of the study may also be associated with decisions to terminate one's formal education. In this sense, then, the data presented in this chapter are relatively minimal estimates of the impact of the independent variables retained for analysis.

Chapter Ten

Reflections on the Role of Language Characteristics
in the Attainment Process of Minority Language Groups

The data presented in the preceding three chapters tends to indicate that persons of Spanish language or background experience particular difficulties in obtaining expected levels of socioeconomic attainment. This conclusion is based on a number of analyses which produce convergent results. Before we attempt an interpretation which might explain this situation, we shall briefly review the evidence which supports this observation.

We began our analysis of the socioeconomic attainment process of minority language adults in chapter seven with the examination of mean levels of occupational and income attainments. We found that men and women in the Spanish language group, i.e., of Spanish mother tongue, had mean attainment levels which were markedly lower than those of the men and women in the non-Spanish (Residual) language group. Needless to say, they were also lower than those of White English monolinguals. However, most of these gross differences in mean attainment levels are adequately explained by the relatively unfavorable background characteristics of persons in the Spanish language group, especially their low levels of educational attainment. The mean educational attainment of persons employed full time who were 25 to 64 years old in 1976 varies significantly from one group to another. Men of Spanish mother tongue, for example, averaged 10.86 years of completed education, while those of Residual mother tongues had completed 12.81 years and White English monolingual men, 13.87 years.

In spite of the fact that most of the gross differences in mean attainment levels are explained by background factors, the comparative analysis of the attainment processes of persons in the Spanish and Residual language groups permitted us to specify with much greater precision the role of language characteristics in the American labor market. As expected, there are some important sex differences in the attainment process, differences which extend to the impact of language characteristics as well. First of all, there do not appear to be major differences in the ability of Spanish and non-Spanish women to obtain employment, once their educational characteristics have been taken into account. Secondly, the extent of retention or anglicisation of the minority language women does not appear to be related to the ability to obtain employment. These two findings contrast sharply with those obtained for minority language men. On the one hand, men in the Spanish language group seem more likely to have obtained full time employment, i.e., once their language and educational characteristics have been controlled. On the other hand, the more anglicized men in both the Spanish and Residual groups were more likely to have obtained full time employment, even after the effects of education have been eliminated. Thus, among men in the minority language sample, access to employment appears to be related to their language characteristics, the more anglicized enjoying small advantages, the less anglicized incurring small (net) disadvantages.

Once persons had obtained access to full time employment, the data do not indicate important sex differences with respect to the impact of language characteristics on occupational status and income. Rather, membership in either the Spanish or non-Spanish groups appears to play a determinative role. The examination of the attainment process of the non-Spanish men and women revealed that language characteristics played no significant role once other background characteristics had been taken into account. In the Spanish language group, however, the most anglicized persons tended to enjoy socioeconomic attainments, particularly earnings, which were significantly higher than those of persons who usually spoke Spanish. Since this linguistic structuring of occupational and income attainments is not observed in the Residual language group, it is not an inherent, universal characteristic of the American economy.

We also discovered two further types of particularistic treatment of the men of Hispanic origin. First of all, when compared to similar men in the non-Spanish language group, the English monolingual men of Spanish mother tongue were found to have occupational and income attainments considerably lower than expected. Secondly, when English monolinguals of Hispanic origin are compared to other groups of men of English mother tongue, they have more difficulty obtaining full time employment and their occupational and income attainments are significantly lower than expected for men having their background characteristics.

When we compared the net returns to certain key variables, notably educational attainment, the data analysis revealed that men and women in the Spanish language group did not obtain equivalent rewards for equivalent characteristics. Generally speaking, the men and women of the White English monolingual language group obtained the highest net returns, those of the non-Spanish language group intermediate returns, while those in the Spanish language group secured the lowest returns. These findings suggest that employers 'discount' the value of the objective characteristics of Spanish language men and women. This discounting may be expressed in the relationship between expected and observed attainments of persons in the Spanish language group. The men and women of the Spanish language group have occupational attainments which are approximately 95 percent of those expected on the basis of their background characteristics. While Spanish women have earnings which exceed expectation, the men of the Spanish language group have earnings which are approximately four percent lower than those predicted.

On the whole, then, the data analysis of the attainment process of adults in minority language groups suggests particularistic treatment of Spanish mother tongue. Furthermore, net of educational attainments, the data suggest an evolution of the criteria by which Hispanics, particularly the men, are assigned lower levels of occupational and income attainments. As persons of Spanish mother tongue respond to the rewards associated with integration into the English language group (easier access to employment and occupational and income premia), they are confronted with an evolving pattern of ethnic stratification. Linguistic-based stratification is replaced by ethnic-based stratification.

All of the preceding observations are, of course, derived after appropriate background characteristics have been controlled. However, since language characteristics have been shown to be related to two types of socioeconomic attainment (occupation and earnings), it is quite likely that they are also related to the educational attainment process as well. In other words, the lower educational attainments of persons of Spanish mother tongue are perhaps partly explained by their more retentive language characteristics. If, then, those who have more retentive language characteristics can be shown to have lower (net) levels of educational attainment, language characteristics must play a larger role in the attainment process than those estimated in the occupational and income analyses.

Since there is no way to unravel the relationship between educational attainment and the language characteristics of adults, we examined instead the relationship between language characteristics and the educational attainments of children. Our first analysis, based on the Survey of Income and Education, examined the relationship between placement in grade level and the age of the child. Since all children start school at approximately the same age, the net effect of language variables may be expected to become more important as children get older. This relationship is in fact observed, linguistic stratification playing a greater role in the attainment process of older children in both the Spanish and Residual language groups. Very little linguistic structuring of placement in grade level was observed for the younger children. It would appear, then, that the more retentive children fall behind in school more rapidly than do the anglicized children. These effects are, once again, net of the effects of other variables, including social class origins. Since the social class origins of parents in the Spanish language group are lower, and since children in the Spanish language group have more retentive language characteristics, the children of Spanish language origin are subjected simultaneously to a double system of penalties, the first deriving from the impact of the class structure, the second from the impact of language characteristics on the process of obtaining educational attainment.

While the problem of class and linguistic stratification affects children in both the Spanish and Residual language groups, the data also reveal a third problem for the Spanish children. When the 14-17 year olds are compared to either the Residual or White English language children, the data indicate that the Spanish children have lower than expected educational attainments, even after social class origins and regional factors have been controlled. While part of this attainment gap is explained by the extremely low attainments of foreign born, Spanish monolingual children, most of it can be attributed to the generally lower educational attainments of Spanish children as a whole.

Furthermore, the data indicate that the problems of the Spanish language children are far from finished. They are falling behind grade level at faster rates than are children in the two comparison groups. Moreover, the data also reveal that English monolingual children of Hispanic ancestry appear to share a similar fate (Veltman, 1980a). Since falling behind grade level is likely to be related to decisions to terminate one's formal education, these findings are harbingers of still greater educational attainment gaps between Hispanics and other groups at some later point in time. Presumably, the educational gap between retentive and anglicized children will also widen appreciably.

Having obtained these general conclusions from the analysis of the SIE data, we then proceded to analyze the relationship between educational achievement and language characteristics. While the High School and Beyond data do not permit us to make inferences about those students who have already dropped out, they do permit us to refine our analyses concerning those still enrolled. The HSB data make it clear that the social class effects observed for placement in grade level are also operative in the achievement process. Children from higher social class backgrounds have more positive achievement scores although the relationship is relatively weak.

The HSB data generally support the second observation derived from the SIE, namely that the more anglicized children have higher net levels of educational achievement. However, this finding applies only to the children of English mother tongue, for whom the presence of high or medium levels of ability to speak the minority language is associated with lower test scores. No such relationship is found for the children of either Spanish or Residual mother tongues. Nonetheless, since so many children in both language samples had English as first language, this relationship between retention of a minority language and lower educational achievement characterizes the larger samples of children as well (i.e., when mother tongue is ignored, as in the SIE samples).

The third general finding from the SIE is also supported by the HSB data. Children in the Spanish language group have somewhat lower educational achievements than do the Residual language children, even after their language characteristics, region of residence, social class origins, and minority language educational experiences have been standardized. While there remains only a relatively small educational disadvantage for the Hispanic children of English mother tongue, the gap is somewhat larger for those of Spanish mother tongue. These findings confirm the lower general levels of educational achievement of children in the Spanish language group.

Thus, data from two separate national studies produce convergent conclusions. Three inter-related processes seem to 'cause' the lower than expected educational achievements of children in the Spanish language group, the effects of the class structure, the linguistic bias of the system in favor of more anglicized children, and a residual difference which may be provisionally attributed to membership in the Spanish language group (or more generally, Hispanic ancestry group) itself. While the class and linguistic biases of the American educational system also affect the children of the Residual language group, the impact of these factors is less important, since these children are both highly anglicized and come from more favorable social class origins.

Since the data analysis itself suggests that the role of both ethnic and linguistic factors is likely to become still more important as children decide to terminate their formal educations, we can be relatively confident that the educational attainment variable used in our analyses of occupational and income attainments is partly determined by these factors. That is to say, educational attainment carries within it the effects of language characteristics. The regression coefficients estimated for educational attainment are consequently larger than they should be, while those attached to language characteristics are smaller than they should be. Educational attainment expresses to a certain extent the effects of language characteristics in the equations estimated in chapter seven, both in terms of access to employment opportunities and in terms of premia or penalties associated with language shift and retention. The exact extent of this difficulty cannot, however, be determined, since we have no way of making inferences as to the final impact of language characteristics on the educational attainment process. If the final impact is relatively strong, then it may be possible to observe net language effects in the occupational and income equations for men and women in the non-Spanish groups. In any case, the impact of language characteristics in the Spanish language group is certainly stronger than that estimated in our chapter on occupational and income attainments, although the extent to which this is true cannot be determined with any accuracy.

Having explored the extent to which Hispanic-Americans seem singled out for particularistic treatment in the process of socioeconomic attainment, we may well ask why this should be the case. It appears that there is initially only rather weak evidence for the existence of possible discrimination against persons of Spanish mother tongue. For example, when compared to the men of the Residual language group, the men of the Spanish language group are somewhat more likely to have obtained full time employment. This finding is probably due to the fact that Spanish-speaking immigrants arrive in the United States with low educational attainments. They obtain as a result low status, low paid jobs, jobs which are nonetheless relatively commensurate with their educational attainments. Access to different positions is stratified by linguistic criteria since some jobs require little or no knowledge of English, while others require a relatively high degree of fluency. Social contacts within the Spanish speaking community facilitate access to the former type of employment opportunities, whereas access to the latter presumably depends on contacts either with anglicized Hispanics or with members of the larger English speaking community.

As long as Spanish speaking Americans continue to speak Spanish as their usual language, they are relatively well insulated from direct job competition with members of the White English speaking group. Thus, their observed levels of achievement are relatively close to the predicted level of achievement, particularly were we to allow for non-linear relationships between, for example, education and income. However, since anglicisation is associated with both greater access to full time employment and with subsequent socioeconomic advantages, the desire to improve one's lot in life produces voluntary compliance with the American norm requiring that Americans speak English as their preferred (and preferably their only) usual language. As anglicisation produces increasingly large numbers of English speaking persons of Hispanic ancestry, members of this group are increasingly drawn into competition for jobs with members of the White English language group. It is at this point that the data suggest that Hispanic Americans are experiencing particular difficulties. Actual occupational and income attainments fail to attain the predicted levels for English monolingual men of either Spanish or English mother tongue.

Two explanations seem ready-made to explain why it is at this point that the brakes are applied to Hispanic mobility. The first suggests that White English language Americans employ racist criteria to protect their own access to employment opportunities. Since many Americans do not consider Hispanics to be fully 'White,' there is a certain plausibility to this explanation. However, dual labor market theory also offers an avenue of explanation. Since the workforce is in any case stratified by ethnic criteria, members of ethnic groups associated overwhelmingly with proletarian occupations tend to become victims of class prejudice. Members of the group are viewed as belonging in proletarian occupations irrespective of their objective characteristics. Their objective characteristics are de-valued or discounted, a theory which would explain quite well the findings presented in chapter seven.

The theory of dual labor markets does not, however, explain why Hispanic men and women are singled out for particular treatment. While White racism may be invoked to explain the residual attainment gaps observed for Spanish language children and adults, it does not seem sufficiently refined to explain variations within the Spanish and/or Residual language groups. For example, persons of Cuban origin tend to have somewhat higher attainments than do other Hispanics; yet it is unlikely that they are any more 'White' than are other Hispanics. Similarly, Chinese children do exceptionally well in school while Italian and Filipino children experience greater difficulties. A theory of White racism has some difficulty adjusting to such realities. Consequently, we are obliged to offer a somewhat more general theory which may subsume certain aspects of the racial explanation.

We propose that a theory of linguistic ethnocentricism best explains the relatively lower than expected attainment of the Spanish language group. In the area of language, for example, most Americans are fundamentally committed to the supremacy of the English language. Since this commitment sometimes takes the form of nativistic rejections of 'foreigners,' we shall pejoratively call this form of ethnocentricism 'anglo-chauvinsim'. When minority groups arrive in relatively small numbers, they are not seen by anglo-chauvinists as a threat to the supremacy of the English language. Consequently, members of such minority language groups enjoy a certain level of acceptance, employers, school officials, neighbors and peers believing that the newcomers will undoubtedly come to subscribe to the English language norm in a relatively short period of time. The data analysis presented in chapter three shows that these expectations are realized. Since no long term menace to the English language group is perceived, there is no need to mobilize resistence to the minority language groups in question. Hence little linguistic or ethnic differentiation is observed when comparing the Residual language group as a whole to the White English language group.

However, when a minority language group arrives in large numbers, as have the Spanish, they are perceived as threatening the supremacy of the English language. If the group is sufficiently large, this fear may be generalized still further: the minority language group threatens not only the divine place accorded the English language; it threatens the integrity of the nation. As a result, linguistic differentiation emerges both in the educational system and in the American labor market. Persons who continue to speak the specific minority language singled out for special treatment are assigned penalties in the attainment race beyond those normally associated with their other background characteristics. Further penalties may be accorded to simple membership in the group, driving home the point that ethnic groups perceived as resisting the American norm of English monolingualism may be expected to pay for their resistance.

While the theory of linguistic ethnocentricism may well explain the dynamics of the linguistic stratification observed among persons of Spanish mother tongue and the ascribed value of membership in the group, it would seem to explain less well why English monolinguals should have lower net levels of occupational and income attainments, particularly when their educational attainments are relatively high. It may be that a theory of White racism, suitably adjusted to the color realities of the Hispanic origin group, may account for the relatively favorable position of Hispanic origin men when compared to Black men in the United States.

An alternative explanation, of course, to theories having as their focus the nature of American society, is to attribute the lower attainments of Hispanics to their cultural characteristics. Otherwise known as 'blaming the victim,' this theory would argue that Hispanics embrace certain values (unspecified) which limit their progress in American society. The data do indeed suggest that some groups enjoy distinct advantages when compared to others. The Yiddish group, for example, enjoys singularly high attainment levels. The Cuban group has the highest net attainments in the Spanish group. Nonetheless, the data also show, for example, that given their background characteristics, the proportion of men of Spanish mother tongue at work full time in 1975 exceeds expectation. The proportion of women of Spanish mother tongue having a similar employment pattern conforms exactly to prediction. Thus, the data suggest that once the educational characteristics of the Spanish language group have been taken into account, they are more likely to be employed, to actively participate in the struggle for socioeconomic attainment. In fact, the percentages of employed persons may be as high as they are in the Spanish language group because people are willing to do jobs that persons of other language groups, including English, are unwilling to do. Consequently, the data do not suggest that the lower socioeconomic attainments of Hispanic Americans are due to a lack of initiative or effort stemming from their cultural origins. The data in fact suggest the opposite, lending greater credibility to the alternative explanations anchoring the experience of Spanish Americans in the nature of the host society.

Part Three:

Language Planning in the Context of Identified Needs

In this last chapter of the book we shall attempt to derive some public policy implications which logically flow from the research findings throughout this book. In the first part of the chapter we shall discuss the educational needs of minority language children, in the second the occupational and income problems of adults in minority language groups, and in the third the problem of the relationship between educational programming and the retention of minority languages in the United States. Our objective in this chapter is to provide rather general orientations for policy initiatives, leaving to those who implement public policy the task of translating these orientations into specific recommendations. Furthermore, since policy orientations are generally formulated to satisfy the needs of politicians and technocrats, we are not so naive as to believe that more specific recommendations would be any more helpful.

Language planning for educational progress. Although we are most concerned with language planning in this chapter, we would be remiss were we to ignore two related problems. First of all, the intergenerational transmission of social class privileges via the educational system is a problem which affects the children of every origin group. However, since the socioeconomic status of Hispanic American adults is markedly lower than those of other groups in the American population, this problem affects children of Hispanic origin with particular acuity. Thus, any broader attempt to control or mitigate the class bias of the American educational system should elicit the enthusiastic support of Hispanic Americans.

Secondly, the proportion of the variance explained in all of our equations relating to educational achievement or attainment suggests that the process is largely indeterminate, i.e., not highly determined by the factors retained as explanatory variables. Consequently, any type of intervention designed to promote the academic performance of children, particularly those of the Spanish language group, is likely to be relatively ineffective. The data analysis indicates that we simply do not adequately understand which factors promote better educational performances.

Nonetheless, the first finding of some public policy relevance is that which indicates that adolescents in the Spanish language group experience relatively unique diffiuclties in the American educational system. Both educational achievement (as measured by testing in High School and Beyond) and attainment (as measured by placement in grade level) are below expected levels, the expected levels being determined by their background characteristics. Since the Residual language children enjoy educational performances which equal or exceed the national averages in most instances, it is clear that special attention to the needs of Spanish language teenagers is warranted. We are not suggesting that the Federal government ignore the situation of non-Spanish minority language groups. For example, our analysis revealed that the Navajo, Italian, Filipino, and Portuguese children may also experience some difficulties in obtaining educational achievement commensurate with expectation. Rather, we suggest that the Government respond first of all to the area of greatest defined need. This need is not simply determined by the language characteristics of Spanish children; it is also a function of their membership in a specific group and thus ethnic in nature.

The second general policy orientation derived from our research suggests that the improvement of the academic performance of children who usually speak a minority language is extremely important. While the number of children in both the Spanish and Residual language groups who retain the minority language as usual language is rather small, those who do so appear to incur educational penalties. They have educational attainment levels which are lower than their background characteristics would lead us to expect. Even the presence of substantial bilingual skills among children of English mother tongue is associated with lower educational achievement. Consequently, there is pressure within the American educational system to secure monolingual English language behavior. That bilingualism should be associated with negative educational performance appears neither salutary nor just.

On the other hand, the data analysis makes it quite clear that children having been enrolled in minority language education programs do more poorly than others on achievement tests. Furthermore, we are led to suspect that these tests minimize the full impact of both language characteristics and minority language education, since the most retentive children are underrepresented in the achievement sample. Furthermore, these same children are likely to have had still greater exposure to MLE programs than have those who completed the questionnaire. Thus, the negative effects of MLE programs are probably underestimated. Nonetheless, the findings suggest that current MLE programming is not improving the educational achievement of minority language children. In addition, enrollment in such programs while it increases the percentage of children capable of speaking the minority language with minimal competence, is more detrimental to the academic performance of children of English mother tongue than it is to that of children of minority mother tongues. These findings suggest that bilingualism is, to use Lambert's terms (1980), 'subtractive' rather than 'additive.' Once we step outside the psychologist's laboratory, real world bilingualism in the United States is associated with lower levels of educational achievement.

It would appear, then, that some serious experimental studies need to be undertaken in the United States to attempt to improve the educational achievements and attainments of children in minority language groups. These studies may include, among other types of programming, much heavier content in the minority language. In other words, a little education in the minority language may be a bad thing, not using enough of the child's first language to build a solid intellectual base from which reading and writing skills in the English language could be generalized. Much heavier minority language content may provide such a transition. On the other hand, the available data from the HSB suggest that the most effective course of action is immediate insertion in the English language classroom, a possibility which no doubt delights the anglo-chauvinist. Clearly this is an issue where our study raises serious questions. Given the methodological difficulties inherent in our measure of MLE, we are inclined simply to suggest that much greater attention be directed to the issue.

The third general orientation derived from our educational research suggests that specific programming should be directed to minority language monolinguals not born in the United States, particularly once again in the Spanish language group. Since there are few such children in the Residual language group, it is difficult to know whether such a program should be generalized to similar children in this group. Nonetheless, the educational problems of 14 to 17 year old Spanish monolinguals are particularly serious. They were already more than two years further behind in grade level than their backgrounds would lead us to expect. Obviously, they will continue to fall further behind as children in other groups complete their formal educations. In addition, as these children enter the labor market, they will be subjected to the difficulties which we have already documented for adults who do not speak English well.

Since the majority of these children are relatively recent immigrants, the most desirable time to intervene in their educational attainment process is upon arrival in the United States. Services must evidently be provided initially in the Spanish language, since these children have little knowledge of English. However, the principal objective should be a rapid improvement in the English language skills of such teenagers. One may also consider adding a vocational component to such a program, since these children are likely to come from homes where the parents themselves have low educational attainments. Consequently, many of these children already are or soon will be early entrants to the labor force as they attempt to supplement low family income. Such an observation suggests that stipends be accorded to immigrant children for a certain period of time. While the idea that students should be paid to remain in school seems repugnant to many Americans, we observe simply that most other 14 to 17 year olds are normally provided with free educational services during their high school years and with state-subsidized services at the university level. Since it is highly unlikely that the target population will attend university, the payment of stipends for a short period of time is clearly less expensive to the State than the educations of those who will be subsidized with indirect higher education payments. In effect, the Government would be required to invest in relatively short-term training programs which should have an extremely positive cost-benefit ratio.

Language planning for the labor market equality. Once the educational attainment process has been completed, minority language men and women must compete in the labor market to obtain employment opportunities. The analysis of the data suggests that the problems of Hispanic men and women tend to differ depending on both sex and mother tongue. With respect to the problems of Hispanic women, it appears that they have relatively few difficulties obtaining employment commensurate with their educational attainments. Furthermore, while there is some evidence that the most anglicized women enjoy higher than expected earnings, Hispanic women as a whole tend to have earnings which compare favorably with those of other groups of women. Their principal problem would appear to be related to the fact that they are women, not that they are Hispanics. Consequently, their employment difficulties would appear to be adequately covered in existing equal opportunity and affirmative action guidelines.

On the other hand, the data reveal that men who usually speak a minority language have somewhat greater difficulties in obtaining full time employment than their educational attainments would lead us to expect. In addition, the less anglicized men of Spanish mother tongue incur additional losses in terms of occupational and income attainments. Consequently, the retention of a minority language does present certain problems in the American labor market, i.e., over and above those associated with lowered educational attainment.

Generally speaking, discrimination based on linguistic grounds is not forbidden in the United States. Technically, a complainant must show that alleged wrong-doing by an employer (or prospective employer) was motivated by the illegal application of national origin criteria. Should the employer respond that the person did not possess the degree of fluency in English required for the job, it becomes impossible to prove discrimination based on ethnic origin. Consequently, the vast majority of the Hispanic population, those of Spanish mother tongue (approximately 85 percent), is not effectively covered by the regulations governing fair play in the labor market. It would seem appropriate, then, to forbid discrimination based on specifically linguistic criteria. Obviously, some balance must be struck between the objective needs of employers and the level of fluency which they demand. Since such a balance appears to have been struck in the case of persons who usually speak some other minority language, it would appear that the use of language criteria by employers constitutes a hidden form of ethnic discrimination against persons of Spanish mother tongue. If persons were permitted to file anti-discrimination suits when language criteria have been applied in an abusive manner, persons who usually speak Spanish would be provided a recourse which members of other minority language groups appear to enjoy as a natural right.

Language planning to retain minority language bilingualism. There is much in the general policy orientations just outlined which runs against the grain of American prejudices, largely because they imply that one (or all) minority language groups will come to enjoy legal recognition and protection. The doctrine of the supremacy of the English language is deeply engrained in the American character, particularly among those whose own ancestors were recently subjected to the anglicisation process. For example, Unites States' Senator Hayakawa (Republican, California) believes that the Spanish language group has become so strong that he proposes to make English the official national language, other minority languages being subjected as a result to more or less official repression. At the very least, persons should not be encouraged to retain minority languages, particularly not the Spanish language population. Even were the majority of Federal politicians and policy-makers convinced of the wisdom of adopting a realistic language policy aimed at creating social justice, many would be hesitant to enact the necessary legislation on the grounds that it would appear to represent a concession to Hispanic Americans. Concessions in the world of Washington politics are extremely bad things, indicating that Federal policy can be effectively changed by small, well-organized pressure groups. Thus, any change in American language policy would likely encourage Hispanic organizations to push for still further concessions.

There is undoubtedly a great deal of truth in this view of the world. Nonetheless, once can expect nothing else. Hispanic organizations must be expected to defend the interests of Hispanic Americans, just as the NAACP defends the interests of Black Americans. Still, there is a fundamental misunderstanding of the nature of American reality that motivates the cynical view of the anglo-chauvinist. American reality is organized in ethnic, not linguistic terms. The support of Hispanic organizations for desegregation assistance centers and bilingual education programs serve above all the ethnic interests of Hispanic Americans. Desegration assistance centers, for example, threaten the fundamental integrity of the language group. Furthermore, the integrity of the language group is ravaged daily by the process of anglicisation, so that only an organization totally out of touch with the daily lives of Hispanics could seriously propose linguistically-grounded political activity. Rather, Hispanic organizations support programs which are supposed to promote the educational attainments of children who will live their entire adult lives in the United States. If a better way can be found to promote the educational attainments of Hispanic children (without at the same time seriously damaging the current interests of Hispanic adults in the Federal bureaucracy), it is logical to assume that Hispanic organizations will support it.

There are, however, several reasons both moral and political, which support programmatic efforts to minimize (or eliminate) the negative consequence of retaining a minority language as one's usual language. First of all, since discrimination against Hispanic Americans is already forbidden, the policy of ethnic justice requires that linguistic justice be done. It is only reasonable to extend to persons of Spanish mother tongue what other groups already obtain as a matter of right. Current interpretation of equal opportunity is too narrow to guarantee such equality. If inaction with respect to the labor market has relatively serious consequences for those who usually speak a minority language, inaction with respect to the educational situation of Hispanic children is unconsciounable. Children should not be expected to pay the price extracted by the social class position of their parents, the language characteristics of their parents (which play a large role in determining their own language skills), and membership in the Hispanic group.

A second reason which might warrant intervention to ensure linguistic justice stems from the new economic realities which have come to characterize the relationship between the United States and its Latin American neighbors. The United States has, for example, indicated its interest in securing stable, long-term oil supplies from the Mexican States. In this kind of economic situation the government of Mexico may decide to take official notice of the way its nationals are received in the United States. In short, a vigorous defense of the rights of Spanish speaking citizens (and others) may constitute a symbolic recognition of the importance of the Spanish speaking group in the United States. Such recognition may facilitate relationships with the Spanish speaking countries from which these immigrants have come.

A third reason to support a positive language planning policy is that some method to retard anglicisation is in itself a desirable national goal. Even though this is precisely that which the anglo-chauvininst most fears, universal monolingualism in English does not serve the long-term interests of American business and government. A Presidential Commission has already indicated the pressing need to find competent personnel who speak minority languages with great fluency. Given the extent of English monolingualism in the United States and the smug self-assurance that personal bilingualism is both impossible and unnecessary, it is extremely difficult to transform English monolinguals into competent speakers of other languages.

An alternative program to produce competent bilinguals in the United States, a program probably much cheaper than those currently being pursued, is to consider immigrants as furnishing a natural pool of persons who already speak minority languages with fluency. If immigrants themselves do not have sufficiently high levels of skills to meet manpower needs, their children certainly constitute a potential reservoir of persons who can respond to these new demands. However, the current rates of anglicisation are so high that comparatively few native born children will be competent bilinguals when they are adults. A program which facilitates the retention of minority languages offers a more realistic escape from the confines of English monolingualism than does massive instruction in foreign languages.

As we have suggested from the data analysis, the implementation of more extensive minority language education programs would not eliminate anglicisation as such. Anglicisation appears to be a very powerful process, increasingly so. Furthermore, even those children who report high levels of minority language skills do not speak minority languages either exclusively or in most settings. Institutional structures, employment, government services, the media, etc. simply do not permit the development of sufficiently large areas of social life to produce a marked decline in the rate of anglicisation. Even were minority language programs significantly expanded, they might slow the observed rates of anglicisation, but they could not eliminate it altogether. The English language, in addition to the rewards which it confers in the workplace, is still the language of the vast majority of the population.

More importantly, any program designed to retard anglicisation rates must also come to terms with the negative effects of MLE programs on educational achievement. Parents may be willing to accept the 'costs' of one or two points on achievement scores in order to maintain minimal skills in the minority language; they are unlikely to accept successive declines of as much as one point per year in the achievement scores of their children. It would not appear that the contradiction between the goals of greater retention and those of greater achievement has been adequately recognized. To overcome this difficulty, to create educational programming which realizes both goals at the same time, is the challenge set before those who wish to achieve linguistic justice or who desire to modify the omnipresent English monolingualism which characterizes American society.

Appendix A:

Source and Reliability of the SIE Estimates*

1. *Source of the Data*

The estimates for school enrollment from the Survey of Income and Education (SIE) are based on data collected during the spring months of 1976. This survey was conducted by the Bureau of the Census acting as collection agent for the Department of Health, Education, and Welfare.

Approximately 158,500 households, selected independently in the 50 Staes and the District of Columbia, were eligible for interview in SIE. Of this number, 7,300 interviews were not obtained because the occupants were temporarily absent, refused to be interviewed, or, after repeated callbacks, could not be found at home. In addition to the 158,500 households, there were about 33,000 sample units which were visited and found to be vacant, condemned, unfit, demolished, etc., and therefore were ineligible for interview. The distribution of the occupied households, noninterviews, and households ineligible for interview by State is shown in Table A1.

The sample design for the SIE sample was a stratified multi-stage cluster design. Each State was divided into areas made up of counties and independent cities referred to as primary sampling units (PSU'S). These PSU's were then grouped to form strata within each State according to the proportion of persons who were children 5 through 17 years old living in poverty families at the time of the 1970 census. Some strata consisted of only one PSU (generally the larger metropolitan areas and some larger nonmetropolitan PSU's) which came into sample with certainty and which were called self-representing. In nine States (Connecticut, Delaware, District of Columbia, Hawaii, Maryland, Massachusetts, New Hampshire, Rhode Island, and Vermont) every PSU was made self-representing. In the remaining States, two PSU's were selected without replacement from each of the strata which were not self-representing. These sample PSU's are called non-self-representing PSU's.

Within selected PSU's, a sample of housing units enumerated in the 1970 Census of Population and Housing was selected. In addition, a sample of new construction building permits was also selected to represent the units constructed in areas under the jurisdictions of building permit offices (permit-

---

* Partial reprint from McArthur (1979)

Table A1. SIE households and noninterview rates

States	Total households (1)	Number (2)	Eligible households			Ineligible households	
			Interviewed (3)	Noninterviewed			
				Number (4)	Rate (4÷2) (5)	Number (6)	Rate (6÷1)
United States	191,459	158,475	151,170	7,305	4.6	32,984	17.2
New England	26,970	21,604	20,754	850	3.9	5,366	19.9
Maine	3,123	2,240	2,189	51	2.3	883	28.3
New Hampshire	5,834	4,434	4,261	173	3.9	1,450	24.6
Vermont	3,752	2,796	2,723	73	2.6	956	25.5
Massachusetts	4,614	3,879	3,664	215	5.5	735	15.9
Rhode Island	4,193	3,509	3,386	123	3.5	684	16.3
Connecticut	5,404	4,746	4,531	215	4.5	658	12.2
Middle Atlantic	16,506	14,323	13,459	864	6.0	2,183	13.2
New York	5,276	4,521	4,211	310	6.9	755	14.3
New Jersey	5,684	5,007	4,694	313	6.3	677	11.9
Pennsylvania	5,546	4,795	4,554	241	5.0	751	13.5
East North Central	25,797	21,905	20,933	972	4.4	3,892	15.1
Ohio	5,508	4,766	4,501	265	5.6	742	13.5
Indiana	4,820	4,083	3,965	118	2.9	737	15.3
Illinois	5,480	4,776	4,499	277	5.8	704	12.8
Michigan	5,744	4,669	4,450	219	4.7	1,075	18.6
Wisconsin	4,245	3,611	3,518	93	2.6	634	14.9

(continued on next page)

Table A1 continued

States	Total households (1)	Eligible households		Noninterviewed		Ineligible households	
		Number (2)	Interviewed (3)	Number (4)	Rate (4 ÷ 2) (5)	Number (6)	Rate (6 ÷ 1)
West North Central	25,592	21,230	20,448	782	3.7	4,362	17.0
Minnesota	4,238	3,579	3,458	94	2.6	659	15.5
Iowa	4,694	4,000	3,879	121	3.0	694	14.8
Missouri	3,088	2,463	2,343	120	4.9	625	20.2
North Dakota	3,644	3,007	2,922	85	2.8	637	17.5
South Dakota	2,365	1,846	1,765	81	4.4	519	21.9
Nebraska	3,624	3,075	2,932	143	4.7	549	15.1
Kansas	3,939	3,260	3,122	138	4.2	679	17.2
South Atlantic	22,052	18,031	17,098	933	5.2	4,021	18.2
Delaware	3,001	2,455	2,310	145	5.9	546	18.2
Maryland	3,262	2,869	2,714	155	5.4	393	12.0
District of Columbia	2,172	1,824	1,578	246	13.5	348	16.0
Virginia	2,478	2,122	2,036	86	4.1	356	14.4
West Virginia	2,073	1,709	1,671	38	2.2	364	17.6
North Carolina	1,997	1,613	1,555	58	3.6	384	19.2
South Carolina	1,895	1,441	1,380	61	4.2	454	24.0
Georgia	1,937	1,582	1,534	48	3.0	355	18.3
Florida	3,237	2,416	2,320	96	4.0	821	25.4
East South Central	8,057	6,552	6,361	191	2.9	1,505	18.7
Kentucky	1,970	1,587	1,517	70	4.4	383	19.4
Tennessee	2,185	1,791	1,736	55	3.1	394	13.0
Alabama	2,055	1,686	1,653	33	2.0	369	18.0
Mississippi	1,847	1,488	1,455	33	2.2	359	19.4

(continued on next page)

Table A1 continued

States	Total households (1)	Eligible households		Noninterviewed		Ineligible households	
		Number (2)	Interviewed (3)	Number (4)	Rate (4÷2) (5)	Number (6)	Rate (6÷1)
West South Central	11,531	9,511	9,158	353	3.7	2,020	17.5
Arkansas	1,925	1,531	1,505	26	1.7	394	20.5
Louisiana	2,065	1,735	1,659	76	4.4	330	16.0
Oklahoma	2,429	1,989	1,896	93	4.7	440	18.1
Texas	5,112	4,256	4,098	158	3.7	856	16.7
Mountain	33,755	27.773	26,383	1,390	5.0	5,982	17.7
Montana	3,963	3,190	3,034	156	4.9	773	19.5
Idaho	5,879	4,773	4,568	205	4.3	1,106	18.8
Wyoming	4,536	3,741	3,569	172	4.6	795	17.5
Colorado	3,782	3,174	3,014	160	5.0	608	16.1
New Mexico	2,589	2,164	2,077	87	4.0	425	16.4
Arizona	2,705	2,160	2,042	118	5.5	545	20.1
Utah	5,110	4,309	4,136	173	4.0	801	15.7
Nevada	5,191	4,262	3,943	319	7.5	929	17.9
Pacific	21,199	17,546	16,576	970	5.5	3,653	17.2
Washington	4,406	3,743	3,567	176	4.7	663	15.0
Oregon	4,841	4,141	3,944	197	4.8	700	14.5
California	5,067	4,432	4,202	230	5.2	635	12.5
Alaska	3,677	2,568	2,360	208	8.1	1,109	30.2
Hawaii	3,208	2,662	2,503	159	6.0	546	17.0

issuing areas) since the 1970 census. Further, a sample of units constructed since the 1970 census in areas not under the jurisdiction of building permit offices (nonpermit-issuing areas) and units from mobile home parks established since the 1970 census was selected.

Estimation procedure for SIE. The first step in the estimation procedure involved the inflation of the sample data by the reciprocal of the probability of its selection. Next, adjustments were made to account for occupied households in which interviews were not obtained because the occupants were temporarily absent, refused to be interviewed, or, after repeated callbacks, could not be found at home. This adjustment was made separately to households in different race of head residence (1970 Census) poverty level categories. Table A1 shows the overall noninterview rates for the United States, Divisions, and States.

In order to obtain more reliable estimates, various stages of ratio estimation were employed which made extensive use of available auxiliary data on characteristics of the survey population. The source of most of this auxiliary data was geographic information about the sample units, 1970 census data and current independent population counts.

The first stage of ratio estimation was employed for sample households from non-self-representing (NSR) PSU's only. This procedure adjusted for the differences that existed at the time of the 1970 census in the distribution of persons by race and residence as estimated from the sample NSR PSU's and from the NSR population in each State. This ratio estimation was designed to reduce the variance attributable to the sampling of PSU's.

Additional stages of ratio estimation were employed to adjust for coverage problems and to bring the distribution of the sample population into agreement with the distribution of the population from which the sample was selected. The second stage of ratio estimation was only employed for new construction sample units (i.e., sample units built April 1, 1970 or later) in permit-issuing areas. The sample estimate of new construction in these areas was ratio-adjusted to agree with an independently derived estimate from the Survey of Construction (SOC), a survey of building permits conducted monthly by the Bureau of the Census.

In the third stage the national sample estimates of civilian persons were controlled to independently derived national estimates for various age, race, and sex categories. To these totals were added the population estimates of those in the armed forces living off post or with their families on post. The fourth stage adjustment was made so that the husband and wife of a family received the same weight. Finally, the last stage adjusted the State sample estimates of civilian persons to agree with independently derived estimates of State population for three age categories in each State.

The last three stages in the estimation procedure were iterated in order to bring the SIE estimates into close agreement with both the national and State independent estimates. The effect of these final stages of ratio estimation, as well as the overall estimation procedure, was to reduce the error for most statistics below what would have been obtained by simply weighting the results of the SIE sample by the inverse of the probability of selection.

The estimates pertaining to the 1970 population (i.e., the population that existed at the time of the 1970 census) are based on either the 20-percent, 15-percent, or 5-percent sample data collected in April 1970 for the Decennial Census of Population and Housing. A detailed description of the sample design and estimation procedure can be obtained in the 1970 census reports PC(1), *Detailed Characteristics*.

2. Reliability of the Estimates

There are two types of possible errors associated with estimates based on data from sample surveys, sampling and nonsampling errors. The following is a description of the sampling and nonsampling errors associated with the SIE sample. A description of the sampling errors and nonerrors associated with the sample estimates from the 1970 census appears in the 1970 census reports, PC(1), *Detailed Characteristics*. The sampling errors for 1970 census data are much smaller than those for SIE data and therefore, when making comparisons between the two data sources, it can be safely assumed that the census data are subject to negligible sampling errors.

2.1 *Nonsampling variability*. In general, nonsampling errors can be attributed to many sources: inability to obtain information about all cases, definitional difficulties, differences in the interpretation of question, inability or unwillingness to provide correct information on the part of respondents, mistakes in recording or coding the data, and other errors of collection, response, processing, coverage, and estimation for missing data. As can be seen from the above list, nonsampling errors are not unique to sample surveys since they can, and do occur in complete censuses as well.

Source and Reliability of the SIE Estimates

It should be pointed out that steps used in the estimation procedure to reduce errors due to nonresponse and coverage deficiencies introduce nonsampling errors of their own. However, the errors introduced are believed to be smaller than the errors due to nonresponse and coverage deficiences.

2.2 *Coverage errors*. It was mentioned previously that the SIE sample was selected from four frames: (1) the 1970 census, (2) new construction in permit-issuing areas, (3) new construction from non-permit-issuing areas, and (4) mobile home parks established since the 1970 census. These four frames do not completely cover the total housing unit inventory, and hence there are some coverage deficiencies in the SIE sample.

It has been estimated that the 1970 census missed about 2½ percent (i.e., about 1.7 million units) of the total 1970 housing inventory. These units have also been missed by SIE.

During the sampling of building permits, only those permits issued between January 1, 1970 and November 1975 inclusive, were eligible to be sampled to represent new construction in permit-issuing areas. It had been assumed that units with permits issued prior to 1970 would have been completed by the time of the 1970 census (i.e., April 1970) and, therefore, would have been represented in the sample selected from the 1970 census units. Due to time constraints, it was not possible for units whose permits were issued after November 1975 to be selected in time to be interviewed during the SIE interview period. It has been estimated that the new construction misses were about 8 percent (i.e., about 900,000 units) of all new construction units.

In addition to the above missed units, mobile homes that were not in parks and that were either placed in their current site after the 1970 census or were vacant at the time of the census, housing units that were converted from nonresidential to residential use since the census, and housing units that have been moved since the census had no chance of being selected for the SIE sample. No estimate currently exists of the total number of missed units in these categories.

The ratio estimation procedure discussed above has partially corrected the survey data for these coverage deficiencies. That is, the ratio estimation has tended to bring the survey estimates to the appropriate level though there still may remain small errors in the distribution.

2.3 *Evaluation studies*. Although it would be exceptionally difficult to assess fully each source of error, an attempt was made to measure the possible effects of some of these sources as they might affect estimates from the Survey of Income and Education. Acting to comply with the congressional legislation, particular effort was concentrated in evaluating the accuracy of the measurement of poverty according to the present definition. A principal component of this evaluation was a return visit, by different interviewers, to approximately 5 percent of the households in the SIE sample. For these selected households, which were concentrated in low to moderate income households, an independent interview was conducted, referring only to necessary identifying information from the first interview. The small size of the sample, approximately 9,000 designated households, permitted inclusion of features intended to produce a more accurate measurement. For example, persons age 16 and over were asked to respond for themselves, wherever possible, even when repeated callbacks to the households were required. A new questionnaire was designed to ask each respondent first about the sources of income the respondent had during 1975 and then to obtain the amount for each of these sources by detailed questions. A comparison of these interviews with the original interviews measured the potential biases that the choice of survey procedures may have had on the estimates of poverty.

At the national level, the reinterview results on the number of children age 5 to 17 in poverty families were within sampling error of the SIE result. However, the reinterview changed the poverty classification of a substantial number of families. The principal reason for reclassification for the majority of cases was a change in reported earnings income, and for this group there was a slight tendency (although not statistically significant) for the reinterview to increase the count of poverty. On the smaller number of cases reclassified because of changes in reported transfer payments, there was weak statistical evidence that the effect of interview was to move families out of poverty. In addition, the reinterview provided no firm statistical evidence that any particular region of the country was inequitably treated relative to the others by systematic error. The comparison has been carried down to the level of the nine census divisions, the lowest level at which the reinterview results can be reliably interpreted. The results of the evaluation have been recorded in the census report, 'Assessment of the Accuracy of the Survey of Income and Education: A Report to Congress as Mandated by the Educational Amendments of 1974'.

The second component was an evaluation of the coverage of the SIE sample frame. From 2,632 SIE sample units in primarily rural areas, four neighbor-

Source and Reliability of the SIE Estimates

ing units were identified and interviews were conducted at those neighboring units which had no chance of being included in the SIE sample (i.e., missed units). In addition, approximately 6,800 structures in both rural and nonrural areas that contained a unit from the SIE sample were matched to the 1970 census and interviews were conducted at missed households (households that had no chance of selection). The objective of this study was the measurement of coverage biases due to missed units in primarily rural areas and to missed households within structures. The results of this evaluation study were not available at the time of this report.

2.4 *Sampling error.* The particular sample used for this survey is one of a large number of possible samples of the same size that could have been selected using the same sample design. Even if the same schedules, instructions, and enumerators were used, estimates from each of the different samples would differ from each other. The variability between estimates from all possible samples is defined as the sampling error. One common measure of sampling error is standard error which measures the precision with which an estimate from a sample approximates the average result of all possible samples. In addition, the standard error, as calculated for this report, also partially reflects the variation in the estimates due to some nonsampling errors, but it does not measure, as such, any systematic biases in the data. Therefore, the accuracy of the estimates depends on both the sampling and nonsampling errors, measured by the standard error, and biases and some additional nonsampling errors not measured by the standard error.

The procedure, as illustrated below provides a method to construct interval estimates such that a known proportion of the intervals would contain the average of all possible samples. For example, if all possible samples were selected, each of these surveyed under identical conditions and an estimate and its estimated standard error were calculated from each sample, then:
1. Approximately 68 percent of the intervals from one standard error below the estimate to one standard error above the estimate would include the average results of all possible samples;
2. Approximately 90 percent of the intervals from 1.6 standard errors below the estimate to 1.6 standard errors above the estimate would include the average results of all possible samples;
3. Approximately 95 percent of the intervals from two standard errors below the estimate to two standard errors above the estimate would include the average result of all possible samples.

The average result of all possible samples either is or is not contained in any particular computed interval. However, for a particular sample one can say with specified confidence that the average result of all possible samples is included in the constructed interval.

The figures presented in the tables below are preliminary standard errors of various estimates based on data and assumptions used to design the survey. The tables of standard errors provide an indication of the order of magnitude of the standard errors rather than the precise standard error for any specified item.

The reliability of an estimated percentage, computed by using sample for both numerator and denominator, depends upon both the size of the percentage and the size of the total upon which the percentage is based. Estimated percentages are relatively more reliable than the corresponding absolute estimates of the numerators and denominators of the percentages, particularly if the percentages are 50 percent or more.

Table A2 presents a generalized table of standard errors for estimates of percentages. To find the standard error of a percentage for a specific State, region, division or for the entire country, the standard error obtained from Table A2 must be multiplied by an appropriate error factor for the region so selected. These error factors are reported in Table A3. Finally, the estimates of the standard errors associated with different characteristics examined also varies according to the type of characteristic examined. In most instances in our report we have dealt with characteristics which are individual in nature, for example, mother tongue. Characteristics referring to specific persons are considered to be more reliable than those pertaining to households as a whole. Consequently, the error factor obtained from Tables A2 and A3 should be multiplied by 0.6 as indicated in McArthur (1979: Table B-5).

2.5 *Standard error of a difference*. For a difference between two sample estimates (means), the standard error is approximately equal to the square root of the sum of the squared standard errors of the estimates. This will represent the actual standard error quite accurately for the difference between two estimates of the same characteristic in two different areas, or for the difference between separate and uncorrelated characteristics in the same area. If, however, there is a high positive correlation between the two characteristics, the formula will overestimate the true standard error; whereas, if there is a high negative correlation, the formula will underestimate the true standard error.

Source and Reliability of the SIE Estimates

Table A2. *Standard errors of estimated percentages*
(68 chances out of 100)

Base of percentage	Estimated percentage						
	1 or 99	2 or 98	5 or 95	10 or 90	15 or 85	25 or 75	50
500.0	21.4	30.1	46.9	64.6	76.8	93.2	107.6
750.0	17.5	24.6	38.3	52.7	62.7	76.1	87.9
1,000.0	15.1	21.3	33.2	45.7	54.3	65.9	76.1
1,500.0	12.4	17.4	27.1	37.3	44.4	53.8	62.1
2,500.0	9.6	13.5	21.0	28.9	34.4	41.7	48.1
5,000.0	6.6	9.5	14.0	20.4	24.3	29.3	34.0
7,500.0	5.5	7.8	12.1	16.7	19.8	24.1	27.8
10,000.0	4.8	6.7	10.5	14.4	17.2	20.8	24.1
15,000.0	3.9	5.5	8.6	11.8	14.0	17.0	19.6
25,000.0	3.0	4.3	6.6	9.1	10.9	13.2	15.2
50,000.0	2.1	3.0	4.7	6.5	7.7	9.3	10.8
75,000.0	1.7	2.5	3.8	5.3	6.3	7.6	8.8
100,000.0	1.5	2.1	3.3	4.6	5.4	6.6	7.6
150,000.0	1.2	1.7	2.7	3.7	4.4	5.4	6.2
250,000.0	1.0	1.3	2.1	2.9	3.4	4.2	4.8
500,000.0	0.7	1.0	1.5	2.0	2.4	2.9	3.4
750,000.0	0.6	0.8	1.2	1.7	2.0	2.4	2.8
1,000,000.0	0.5	0.7	1.0	1.4	1.7	2.1	2.4
1,500,000.0	0.4	.06	0.9	1.2	1.4	1.7	2.0
2,500,000.0	0.3	0.4	0.7	0.9	1.1	1.3	1.5
5,000,000.0	0.2	0.3	0.5	0.6	0.8	0.9	1.1
7,500,000.0	0.2	0.2	0.4	0.5	0.6	0.8	0.9
10,000,000.0	0.2	0.2	0.3	0.5	0.5	0.7	0.8
15,000,000.0	0.12	0.2	0.3	0.4	0.4	0.5	0.6
25,000,000.0	0.10	0.13	0.2	0.3	0.3	0.4	0.5
50,000,000.0	0.07	0.10	0.15	0.2	0.2	0.3	0.3
75,000,000.0	0.06	0.08	0.12	0.2	0.2	0.2	0.3
100,000,000.0	0.05	0.07	0.10	0.14	0.2	0.2	0.2
150,000,000.0	0.04	0.06	0.09	0.12	0.14	0.2	0.2
250,000,000.0	0.03	0.04	0.07	0.09	0.11	0.13	0.2

Table A3. *Factors for the standard errors of estimates of percentages and values for estimates of standard error means*

State and region	Factor[1]	State and region	Factor[1]
United States	0.974	South – continued	
		South Atlantic – continued	
Northeast	1.000	Virginia	0.948
New England	0.605	West Virginia	0.611
Maine	0.415	North Carolina	1.157
New Hampshire	0.261	South Carolina	0.831
Vermont	0.248	Georgia	1.143
Massachusetts	0.756	Florida	1.198
Rhode Island	0.323		
Connecticut	0.504	East South Central	0.923
		Kentucky	0.915
Middle Atlantic	1.099	Tennessee	0.989
New York	1.282	Alabama	0.944
New Jersey	0.745	Mississippi	0.764
Pennsylvania	0.974		
		West South Central	0.991
North Central	0.817	Arkansas	0.718
East North Central	0.869	Louisiana	0.913
Ohio	0.933	Oklahoma	0.767
Indiana	0.701	Texas	1.094
Illinois	0.966		
Michigan	0.848	West	1.113
Wisconsin	0.699	Mountain	0.519
		Montana	0.303
West North Central	0.672	Idaho	0.247
Minnesota	0.673	Wyoming	0.188
Iowa	0.536	Colorado	0.656
Missouri	0.886	New Mexico	0.463
North Dakota	0.336	Arizona	0.648
South Dakota	0.441	Utah	0.369
Nebraska	0.459	Nevada	0.242
Kansas	0.542		
		Pacific	1.256
South	0.994	Washington	0.629
South Atlantic	1.023	Oregon	0.486
Delaware	0.293	California	1.414
Maryland	0.739	Alaska	0.260
District of Columbia	0.406	Hawaii	0.331

[1] This factor is applied to the standard errors of percentages in table A2 to obtain estimates of standard error for the States, regions, divisions and the United States.

3. Illustration of the computation of the standard error of a difference

We invite the reader to reconsider the data reported in Figure 3.2. The question which we shall ask is whether there is likely to be a real difference in the anglicisation rate of persons 30-40 years of age and those 40-50 years of age. The required data to permit such an analysis are the sizes of the respective subpopulations and the anglicisation rates observed. The anglicisation rate observed for the 30-40 year olds is 70.0%; the population size observed, 479,000; for the 40-50 year olds, 62.3% and 431,000.

The use of Table A2 procedes via linear interpolation. We begin first of all with attempting to estimate appropriate values based on sample sizes between 250,000 and 500,000. Since the percentages observed vary between fifty and seventy-five percent, we shall interpolate values for the last two columns of the table.

Beginning with the figure 479,000, it lies .916 of the distance from 250,000 to 500,000. The estimated standard error for the smaller sample size is 4.2 percent when the observed percentage is 75 percent; 2.9 percent for the larger sample size. By linear interpolation we obtain an estimated value of approximately 3.0 (4.2 - (.916 × 1.3)). Similarly, the standard error estimated for a percentage of 50.0 at a sample size of 479,000 is 3.5 (4.8 - (.916 × 1.4)). Since the observed anglicisation rate is relatively close to seventy percent, the desired standard error of the estimate may be obtained by linear interpolation between the two figures so obtained. This gives us an estimated standard error of 3.1 percent.

Similarly, the figure 431,000 lies .724 of the distance from 250,000 to 500,000. Since the observed percentage once again lies between fifty and seventy-five percent, the same set of base figures must be used. Were the former figure observed, the estimated standard error would be 3.8 percent, while the latter figure would have an estimated standard error of 3.3 percent. Using sixty percent as approximating the actual figure observed for the anglicisation rate of 40-50 year old persons, a linear interpolation yields an estimated standard error of 3.6 percent.

Each of these estimated standard errors must now be adjusted for regional factors and the type of characteristic being examined. This procedure leads to the following results:

$$SE_{30-40} \quad 3.1 \times .974 \times 0.6 = 1.8$$
$$SE_{40-50} \quad 3.6 \times .974 \times 0.6 = 2.1$$

These results are then inserted into an appropriate pooling formula, to obtain the standard error of the difference between these two percentages. Thus, $\sqrt{(1.8)^2+(2.1)^2} = 2.8$. Thus, one standard error of the difference is equal to 2.8 percent. As we have previously noted, if the difference actually observed is greater than two standard errors, the traditional test of significance, $p < .05$, is met. The chances that such an observed sample difference does not really characterize the national population is less than five percent.

The actual difference in anglicisation rates observed between the two age groups is 7.7% (70.0 - 62.3). This difference is superior to 5.6 percent, the figure which represents two standard errors of the difference as calculated. Consequently, we can affirm with confidence that the 30-40 year olds are more anglicized than are the 40-50 year olds, our changes of error being inferior to five percent.

Appendix B:

Design Characteristics of High School and Beyond*

1. Sampling

1.1 *Sample design*. Students were selected through a two-stage probability sample with schools as the first stage units and students within schools as the second stage units. With the exception of special strata (to be described below), schools were selected with probability proportional to estimated enrollment (average of class sizes), and within each school, 36 seniors and 36 sophomores were randomly selected. In those schools with fewer than 36 seniors or 36 sophomores, all eligible students were drawn in the sample. This resulted in a sample that (with the exception of the special strata described below) was approximately self-weighting.

The sampling frame, defined as the universe of high schools in the United States, was obtained from the 1978 list of U.S. elementary and secondary schools of the Curriculum Information Center, a private firm. This was supplemented by the NCES lists of public and private elementary and secondary schools. Any school listed in any of these files which contained either a 10th grade or 12th grade or both was part of the frame. The total number of schools in the sample, as designed was 1,122, from a frame of 26,095 schools with grades 10 or 12 or both. Stratification was as follows:

Special Strata (oversampled)	
Alternative schools	50
Cuban Hispanic (public)	20[a]
Cuban Hispanic (Catholic)	10[a]
Other Hispanic	106[a]
High performance private	12
Other non-Catholic private (stratified by 4 regions)	38
Black Catholic	30[a]

* Reprinted in part from *HSB Information for Users* (1980)

Regular Strata (not oversampled)

Catholic (stratified by 4 regions)	48
Public (stratified by 9 regions; racial composition, enrollment; central-city, suburban, rural)	808
	1,122

a: These schools were defined as those having 30 percent or more of enrollment from the indicated subgroup.

The purpose of the special oversampled strata is to allow a sufficient number of cases for special analysis of sub-groups of students or schools.

1.2 *Sample realization:* Substitution was carried out for schools which refused to participate in the survey, but there was no substitution for students whose parents refused, who themselves refused, or who were absent on survey day and make-up days. Substitution was carried out only within strata, and in certain cases no substitution was possible, because a school was the sole school in a stratum. The realization of the sample by stratum is given in Table B1.

1.3 *Weighting procedures:* Although the sample design specified that students in all but the special strata would be selected with approximately equal probabilities, the probabilities are only approximately equal. In addition, the students in special strata were selected with higher probabilities, in some strata extremely so. The sample as realized also did not equal the sample as drawn, creating further deviations from a self-weighting sample. Weights have been introduced for schools and for students, which give each school or each student a weight equal to the number of schools or students in the universe of schools or students which that school or student represents.

Weights for schools were computed as the product of three factors. Factor one was the inverse of the probability of selection for the school under the assumption that it was part of the initial set of selections. Factor two was the estimated proportion of schools in the stratum which were 'out of scope'. This factor was used in order to compensate for the fact that the design specified that replacement selections were to be made for schools of this type. The final factor involved the ratio of the number of initially selected schools in each stratum to the final 'in sample' schools from the stratum. This factor was

Table B1. *High School and Beyond sample realization*

	Stage 1: Sampling of Schools			
Stratum	Drawn in sample	Original schools	Substituted schools	Total realized
TOTAL	1,122	811	204	1,015
Public, regular	808	585	150	735
Public, alternative	50	41	4	45
Cuban public	20	11	–	11
Other Hispanic public	106	72	30	102
Catholic, regular	48	40	5	45
Catholic, black	30	23	7	30
Cuban Catholic	10	7	2	9
High performance private	12	9	2	11
Other non-Catholic private	38	23	4	27

	Stage 2: Sampling of Students					
	Total drawn in sample	Absent, survey and make-up days	Student refused	Parent refused	Partial materials missing	Surveyed, in file
Number	69,662	8,278	1,579	223	1,132	58,270
Percent	100[2]	12	3	*	2	84

[1] Includes additional selections made when schools were found to be out-of-scope.
[2] The total adds to more than 100 percent because of rounding.

employed to compensate for the differential cooperation rates (at the school level) across the various strata, and to adjust the total sample projections to reflect the total frame rather than only cooperating schools. It should be pointed out that refusals, as well as substitution for schools which refused, introduce some uncertainty into the sample, due to the unknown differences between schools which refused (some of which were substituted for) and the stratum as a whole.

Weights for students consist of the product of the school weight as described above and a within-school student weight. The within-school student weight consists of the number of students in the class represented by this student (the inverse of the probability of being drawn), multiplied by the ratio of the number of students sampled in that school divided by the number for whom questionnaire data was obtained. As in the case of the school weight, the second stage weight involves two underlying factors, compensation for overall and differential selection probabilities with respect to the initially selected sample, and adjustment for bias components induced by differential response rates. It should be noted that the adjustment for bias due to non-participation availability is only partial. What remains is any bias which might be due to overall differences between responders and non-responders.

The student weight described above and contained on the student file is the estimated number of students in grade 10 or 12 of American high schools represented by the student on whose record the weight appears. Since weights differ for students in different schools, it is important that weights be used in estimating any proportion or mean for American sophomores or seniors as a whole, or for any subgroups. Use of weights should lead to correct estimates (within sampling error) of the population of 10th and 12th grade students in United States schools in spring, 1980, and correct estimates of subgroups within it.

1.4 *Sampling errors.* Approximate sampling errors for estimated percentages and test score means may be computed as follows:

Percentages. An approximate standard error for any given percentage calculated from HSB data may be derived by the following equation:

$$SE = Adj \sqrt{P(100-P)/N} \qquad (B.1)$$

where SE is the standard error of the percentage observed, P is the percentage observed, and N indicates the actual (unweighted) sample size for the subclass for which the percentage is developed. Adj represents an adjustment for specific subgroups in the population and for specific subregions. It is formally defined as the square root of the design effect. Since we have not divided our data by subregion of the United States, only two adjustment factors need retain our attention. That for students of Hispanic origin is approximately 1.45 (sophomores = 1.39; seniors = 1.49). We then need to determine an appropriate subgroup for children in the Residual language group. Were we to consider them 'White', an appropriate adjustment factor is approximately 1.50; to be conservative, we can use the estimated adjustment factor for the sample as a whole (approximately 1.62).

For example, we find from Table 5.4 that 33.25 percent of the Spanish language children are unable to speak Spanish with some facility. We may wish to determine the confidence intervals defining the probable population values for this observation. Since we have previously subdivided the population before applying population weights, the newly weighted data presented in our HSB analyses represent relatively well the actual (raw) unweighted numbers of observations. Applying formula B.1 to obtain the standard error:

$$SE = 1.45 \sqrt{33.25 \ (100.00 - 33.25) / 5353} = .93$$

Since two standard errors define the .05 level of confidence desired, we should add 1.86 (.93 × 2) to the observed value to obtain the probable upper limit of the population values. Similarly, we subtract 1.86 to obtain the probable lower limit. Consequently, the probability that a true value of anglicisation (as defined) lies outside the defined range of two standard errors (31.39 to 35.11) is less than five percent.

Once the standard error has been obtained for each of two observed means, the standard error of the difference may be obtained in the same manner as was obtained in the SIE, notably by obtaining a pooled estimate from the equation:

$$SE_{diff} = \sqrt{(SE_1)^2 + (SE_2)^2} \qquad (B.2)$$

where SE_{diff} is the standard error of the difference between the two means, and SE_1 and SE_2 represent the standard error of each mean obtained by applying formula B.1.

Test score means. Standard errors for test scores may be obtained by applying the following equation;

$$SE_{\bar{x}} = Adj \sqrt{S^2 / N} \qquad (B.3)$$

where $SE_{\bar{x}}$ is the standard error of a test score mean and S^2 is the variance computed for the specific subgroup examined. N and Adj are defined as previously. The appropriate adjustment factors are 1.40 for the Spanish sample, 1.90 for the Residual sample.

For example, we found that the mean reading score for all Residual language children was 52.21. The variance was 96.62 and the sample size 3325. Inserting these values into formula B.3,

$$SE_{\bar{x}} = 1.90 \sqrt{96.62 / 3325} = .32$$

Once again, using the criterion of .05, we must set a confidence interval of two standard errors around the mean. Consequently, we may be assured that 95 out of 100 times, the true population mean will fall between 51.57 and 52.85.

2. Field Procedures

The data were collected between February 1 and May 15, 1980. Sophomore and senior groups within each school on a given day met separately, and completed the questionnaires and tests in one session. A field representative was present with each group to explain survey procedures and to answer questions.

The first step for the students was to complete an identification booklet which provided information about how the student might be located if selected for future follow-up. To preserve student confidentiality these booklets were handled, shipped and stored separately from the other student instruments.

At the end of the identification section there was a series of questions designed to locate all students who had some exposure at home to a language other than English. For those students who did have other language exposure there was a special series of questions about that language.

All students then filled out the self-administered questionnaire. When the group had all finished the questionnaire (usually in about an hour) a number of the school staff administered the cognitive tests. While the students were taking the tests, field personnel spot edited the questionnaires for completeness of a subset of key questions. Students were asked to provide any missing key information after they completed the tests. Since both participation in the survey and responding to any particular item were completely voluntary, students were given the option of marking a special oval to indicate that they preferred not to answer a question.

School staff usually conducted a series of make-up days if any sample students were absent on survey day. To preserve the confidentiality of student data these questionnaires were not subject to spot edit.

All student questionnaires and tests were optically scanned. The questionnaire data was machine edited after scanning, and any key items which students had neither answered nor indicated that they preferred not to answer were flagged. Editors attempted to retrieve this flagged information by telephone.

3. *Data Preparation*

The student questionnaires and tests were designed to be optically scanned to eliminate error in the transfer of data from the instruments to machine-readable form and to make the data available to users in the shortest possible time. Checks on data quality were carried out in the data collection procedure, the optical scanning operation, and the telephone follow-up effort.

The editing and response consistency checks were relatively simple because the questions and responses in the student questionnaire were designed so only one explicit skip pattern appears in the senior questionnaire (seniors not going on to college do not complete the last section on college education), and none in the sophomore questionnaire. In the case of two or more related questions, the question(s) following the implicit screening question contains a response appropriate for those respondents 'screened out' by the first question in the series of related questions. No inter-item consistency checks have been carried out for the implicit screener questions.

4. *Further Information*

Further information may be obtained from the Longitudinal Studies Branch National Center for Education Statistics, United States Department of Education or from the principal contractor, the National Opinion Research Center of the University of Chicago.

Appendix C:

Fidelity of Language Reports by HSB Students

One topic which we could not treat in the text itself concerns the extent to which self-reported data by high school students can be accepted as trustworthy. There are a number of opportunities where the responses furnished by a sample of HSB students can be compared to those furnished to identical questions by their parents. One such question is that which asked for the language usually spoken by members of the household. This question is particularly important since the presence of English as the usual home language is associated with anglicisation.

We present in Table C.1 the results of the cross-classification of parent and student responses to the home language question.

Table C.1 *Comparison of parental and child declarations of usual home language by language group, United States, 1980*

Parental declarations	Children's declarations		Total
	English	Minority	
Spanish language group:			
English	371	86	457
Spanish	41	187	228
Total	412	273	685
Residual language group:			
English	412	36	448
Minority	16	56	72
Total	428	92	520

Source: High School and Beyond

The examination of this table reveals first of all that there is considerable disagreement between parents and children as to which language is the principal language of the home. For example, in the Spanish language group there were 127 disagreements regarding the principal home language. In 41 cases the parents said that Spanish was the usual home language, while the child said that English was most frequently used; in 86 cases the reverse was true. The 127 cases represent 18.5 percent of the total. The extent of discordant reporting is lower in the Residual language group where only 52 of the 520 paired comparisons were in disagreement, a rate of 10.0 percent. That the rate is lower is readily explained by the degree of anglicisation which characterizes the Residual language group. Since the use of English is so widespread, there is less cause for disagreement.

If we examine only the discordant cases, it is evident that the reported use of specific languages tends to be biased in a given direction. In the Spanish group, for example, only 41 of the 412 (10.0%) children who declared an English home language were contradicted by their parents, while 86 of the 273 (31.5%) who declared Spanish as usual home language were contradicted by their parents. Similar patterns prevail in the Residual language group. Only 3.7 percent of those declaring an English home language were contradicted by their parents (16 / 421 = .037), while 39.1 percent of those declaring a minority home language were so contradicted (36 / 92 = .391). It appears, then, that perceptions about the extent to which the English language is used vary by generation, the parents being more likely to perceive that the household environment is anglicized, the children more likely to see it as retentive.

While these contradictory reports are partly structured by the extent to which the household is in fact anglicized, they are also structured by the mother tongue of the student. The incidence of discordant reporting is higher among children of minority mother tongue. The relevant data for the children of the Spanish language group are presented in Table C.2.

Examing the children who declared that they had English for their first language, we find that those who declared an English home language were rarely contradicted by their parents. Disagreement is observed in only 3.5 percent of the cases (12 / 348 = .035). However, the child who declared that Spanish was the principal home language was contradicted more than one-half of the time (34 / 63 = .535). The extent of disagreement for these latter pairs raises the total extent of discordance to 11.2 percent of the children of English mother tongue (46 / 411 = .112).

The extent of discordant reporting among the children of Spanish mother tongue is markedly higher, 29.6 percent (81 / 274 = .296). Children reporting either household language were frequently contradicted by their parents. Nearly one-half of those reporting English as household language (29 / 64 = .453) and nearly one-quarter of those reporting Spanish as household language (52 / 211 = .246) were contradicted by their parents. Thus, children of Spanish

Table C.2 *Comparison of parental and child declarations of usual home language by mother tongue, Spanish language group, United States, 1980*

Parental declarations	Children's declarations		
	English	Minority	Total
English mother tongue:			
English	336	34	370
Spanish	12	29	41
Total	348	63	411
Spanish mother tongue:			
English	35	52	87
Spanish	29	158	187
Total	64	211	274

Source: High School and Beyond

mother tongue were less frequently contradicted when they declared Spanish as household language than were those who declared English. A somewhat similar finding was obtained for the English language children, namely that those who declared Spanish as home language were the most often contradicted. These findings suggest that there is a strong association between home language and mother tongue. Children who declare a home language which is different from their mother tongue are more likely to be contradicted by their parents.

In addition, the data presented in Table C.2 reveal that the parents more frequently declared English as usual home language than did the children. This was true for children of both Spanish and English mother tongue. While 90.0 percent (370 / 411 = .900) of the parents of children of English mother tongue declared that English was the usual home language, only 84.7 percent (348 / 411 = .847) of the children declared English home language. Similarly, 31.8 percent (87 / 274 = .318) of the parents of children of Spanish mother tongue declared English as home language as opposed to only 23.4 percent (64 / 274 = .234) of the children. On the whole, there would seem to be some confusion among children in the Spanish language group as to which language is generally spoken in their homes. We should probably conclude that in such cases both languages are spoken with sufficient frequency that children and parents are permitted to diverge in their interpretations of which language is the one most frequently spoken.

Similar data are presented for the children of the Residual language group in Table C.3.

Table C.3 *Comparison of parental and child declarations of usual home language by mother tongue, residual language group, United States, 1980*

Parental declarations	Children's declarations English	Minority	Total
English mother tongue:			
Englsih	359	22	381
Minority	<u>9</u>	<u>3</u>	<u>12</u>
Total	368	25	393
Minority mother tongue:			
English	53	14	67
Minority	<u>7</u>	<u>53</u>	<u>60</u>
Total	60	67	127

Source: High School and Beyond

The extent of discordant reporting is noticeably lower for children of both Residual and English mother tongue than that observed among the children of the Spanish language group. The proportion of discordant reports for children of English mother tongue was only 7.9 percent (31 / 393 = .079), while that for children of minority mother tongue attained 16.5 percent (21 / 127). Children of English mother tongue declaring a minority household language were nearly universally contradicted by their parents, while few of those who declared English as home language were contradicted. This pattern is similar to that observed for the children of Spanish mother tongue. On the other hand, among children of Residual mother tongue, those who claimed that English was the home language were generally supported by their parents, a finding which contradicts the observed pattern in the Spanish language group. Those who claimed that the Residual language was the principal language were as likely to be contradicted as were those claiming the minority language as home language in the Spanish language group. Once again, the parents on the whole were more likely to claim English as usual home language than were the children.

Needless to say, the extent of discordant reporting of usual home language presents problems for the analyst. In the first place, the concept of a principal home language seems relatively unambiguous. Nonetheless, the actual practice of families involved in the language shift process appears to be relatively more ambiguous, sufficiently ambiguous to permit parents and children to interpret their joint interactions somewhat differently. These interpretations seem, nonetheless, relatively well grounded in the different social realities to which parents and children have been exposed, the parents coming from settings in which the minority language was much more dominant (if not the sole language used), the children comparing their experiences most likely to those of their English speaking peers. That is to say, the parents are probably better judges of the extent to which their family environment is anglicized when compared to their language past.

Empirically, these discordant judgments raise a number of further problems, not the least of which is the estimation of the regression coefficients attached to the presence of English as home language. Children living in settings which are described by parents as dominated by English and by children as dominated by the minority language are more anglicized than those living in settings where both parents and children agree that the minority language is dominant. Similarly, children living in settings which they characterize as English dominant but which parents describe as minority dominant are less anglicized than those living in homes where both parents and children agree that the English language is that which is most frequently used. Consequently, when the parental declaration of home language is substituted for the child's declaration of home language, the presence of English as home language is still more strongly related to anglicisation than that estimated in chapter five.

Unfortunately, apart from recognizing the extent and sources of discordant reporting, the analysis presented in this appendix does not permit us to correct the regression estimates presented in the text of chapter five. The sample sizes which contain both parental and child data on the language usually spoken at home are simply too small to permit us to discard the data which do not contain parental reports. Thus, the data presented in the intergenerational analysis of language shift use only the home language data declared by the child, introducing biases in the direction indicated in this appendix.

References

Angel, R. and M. Tienda (1981) 'Household composition and income generation strategies among non-Hispanic Whites, Blacks, and Hispanic origin groups in the U.S.', pp. 92-120 in M. Tienda et al., *Hispanic Origin Workers in the U.S. Labor Market: Comparative Analyses of Employment and Earnings*. Washington: U.S. Department of Labor.

Beck, E.M., P. Horan, and C. Tolbert II (1978), 'Stratification in a Dual Economy: A Sectoral Model of Earnings Determination,' *American Sociological Review* 43: 704-739.

Bowman, Carl (1981), 'Between Cultures: Toward an Understanding of the Cultural Production of Chicanos,' pp. 1-58 in M. Tienda et al., *Socioeconomic Attainment and Ethnicity: Toward an Understanding of the Labor Market Experiences of Chicanos in the U.S.* Washington: U.S. Department of Labor.

Boulet, Jac-André (1979), *L'évolution des disparités linguistiques de revenus de travail dans la zone métropolitaine de Montréal de 1961 à 1977*. Ottawa: Conseil Economique de Canada (# 127).

Brown, George, N. Rosen, S, Hill, and M. Olivas (1980), *The Condition of Education for Hispanic Americans*. Washington: The National Center for Education Statistics.

Cardenas, Gilbert (1976), 'Los Desarraigados: Chicanos in the Midwestern Region of the United States,' *Atzlan* 7: 153-186.

Castonguay, Charles (1976), 'Les transferts linguistiques au foyer,' *Recherches Sociographiques* 17: 341-351.

− (1978), 'La mobilité ethnique au Canada,' *Recherches Sociographiques* 18: 431-450.

− (1979), 'Exogamie et anglicisation chez les minorités canadiennes-françaises,' *Canadian Review of Sociology and Anthropology* 16: 21-31.

− (1979b), 'L'exogamie précoce et la prévision des taux de transfert linguistique,' *Recherches Sociographiques* 20: 403-408.

− (1981), 'Critique,' in C. Veltman (ed), *The Retention of Minority Languages in the United States*. Washington: The National Center for Education Statistics.

Census Bureau, United States (1974), *Accuracy of Data for Selected Population Characteristics as Measured by Reinterviews*. Washington: U.S. Bureau of the Census (PHC(E)-9).

Census Bureau, United States (1975), *Accuracy of Data for Selected Population Characteristics as Measured by the 1970 CPS-Census Match*. Washington: U.S. Bureau of the Census (PHC(E)-11).

DeVries, J. (1974), 'New effects of language shift in Finland, 1951-1960: a demographic analysis,' *Acta Sociologica* 17: 140-149.

DeVries, J. and F. Vallée (1979), *Language Use in Canada*. Ottawa: Statistics Canada (# 99-762E).

Dubois, David (1980), *The Children's English and Services Study: A Methodological Review*. Washington: The National Center for Education Statistics.

Estrada, Léo (1981), 'Critique' in C. Veltman (ed), *op. cit.*

Featherman, David (1971), 'The Socioeconomic Achievement of White Religious Ethnic Subgroups: Social and Psychological Explanations,' *American Sociological Review* 36: 207-222.

Fishman, Joshua, V. Nahirny, J. Hoffman and R. Hayden (1966), *Language Loyalty in the United States*. The Hague: Mouton.

Fishman, J. and John E. Hoffman (1966), 'Mother Tongue and Nativity in the pp. 157-176 in J. Fishman, R. Cooper and R. Ma, *Bilingualism in the Barrio* (2nd ed). Bloomington, Indiana: Indiana University Press.

Fishman, J. and John E. Hoffman (1966) 'Mother Tongue and Nativity in the American Population,' in J. Fishman (ed), *Language Loyalty in the United States*. The Hague: Mouton.

Garcia, Steve (1979), *Language usage and the status attainment of Chicano males*. Unpublished M.A. Thesis, Madison: University of Wisconsin.

Gordon, Milton (1964), *Assimilation in American Life*. New York: Oxford University Press.

Grenier, Gilles (1981), 'An Analysis of the Effect of Language Characteristics on the Wages of Hispanic-American males,' mimeo, Université de Sherbrooke.

Grosjean, François (1982), *Life with Two Languages: An Introduction to Bilingualism*. Cambridge: Harvard Universtiy Press.

Johnson, C. (1974), *Consistency of Reporting of Ethnic Origin in the Current Population Survey*. Washinton: U.S. Bureau of the Census (technical paper 31).

Lachapelle, Réjean (1976), 'Sur la comparaison des données linguistiques canadiennes et américaines,' *Le Devoir*, 23 août 1976, p. 7.

Lachapelle, Réjean and J. Henripin (1980), *La situation démolinguistique au Canada: évolution passée et prospective*. Montréal: Institute for Research on Public Policy.

Lacroix, R. and F. Vaillancourt (1980), *Les disparités de revenu au sein de la main-d'oevre hautement qualifiée du Québec*. Québec: Editeur officiel.

References

Lambert, E. (1980), 'The Social Psychology of Language: a Perspective for the 1980's,' pp. 415-424 in Giles, H., P. Robinson, and P.M. Smith, *Language*. Oxford: Pergamon Press.
Lopez, David (1978), 'Chicano Language Loyalty in an Urban Setting,' *Sociology and Social Research* 62: 267-278.
— (1981), 'Critique,' in C. Veltman (ed), *op. cit.*
Lieberson, S. (1965), 'Bilingualism in Montreal: a demographic analysis,' *American Journal of Sociology* 71: 10-25.
— (1970), *Language and Ethnic Relations in Canada*. Toronto: John Wiley and Sons.
Lussier, Marie-Josée (1978), *Une analyse des disparités de revenu sur le marché de la main-d'oeuvre féminine au Québec*, unpublished master's thesis, Université de Montréal.
McArthur, Edith (1979), *Relative Progress of Children in School: 1976*. Washington: U.S. Bureau of the Census (P-20, 337).
McArthur, Edith (1981), 'Language Information from Censuses and Surveys,' *American Demographics* 3: 28-33.
Mincer, Jacob (1958), 'Investment in human capital and personal income distribution,' *Journal of Political Economy* 66: 281-302.
Peng, S. (1981), 'Critique,' in C. Veltman (ed), *op. cit.*
Pes, Johanne (1979), *L'importance des attributs linguistiques dans la détermination des revenus de travail au Québec, 1971*, unpublished master's thesis, Université de Montréal.
Silverman, Leslie (1978), 'The Educational Disadvantage of Language-Minority Persons in the United States, Spring, 1976,' *Bulletin of the National Center for Education Statistics* (78-B4).
Tienda, M. (1981b) 'Sex, Ethnicity, and Chicano Status Attainment,' pp. 59- Comparative Analyses of Employment and Earnings. Washington: U.S. Department of Labor.
Tienda, M. (1981b) 'Sex Ethnicity, and Chicano Status Attainment,' pp. 59-104 in M. Tienda et al., *Socioeconomic Attainment and Ethnicity: Toward an Understanding of the Labor Market Experiences of Chicanos in the U.S.* Washington: U.S. Department of Labor.
Tolbert, C., P. Horan, and E.M. Beck (1978), 'The Dual Economy in American Industrial Structure: Toward the Specification of Economic Sectors,' mimeo, Department of Sociology, University of Georgia.
Vaillancourt, François (1979a), *The Role of Language in the Determination of the Labour Earnings of Quebec Males in 1970*. Montréal: Département de sciences économiques et CRDI (# 7904).
— (1979b) 'La situation démographique et socio-économique des francophones du Québec: une revue,' *Canadian Public Policy* 5: 542-552.

Veltman, Calvin (1976), 'Les incidences du revenu sur les transferts linguistiques dans la région métropolitaine de Montréal,' *Recherches Sociographiques* 17: 323-339.
- (1977), 'La comparabilité des données linguistiques aux Etats-Unis et au Canada,' *Cahiers québécois de démographie* 6: 69-91.
- (1980a), *Relative Educational Attainments of Minority Language Children, 1976: A Comparison to Black and White English Language Children*. Washington: The National Center for Education Statistics.
- (1980b), *The Role of Language Characteristics in the Socioeconomic Attainment Process of Hispanic Origin Men and Women*. Washington: The National Center for Education Statistics.
- (1981a), 'Anglicisation in the United States: The Importance of Parental Nativity and Language Practice,' *International Journal of the Sociology of Language* 29: 65-84.

Veltman, Calvin (ed.) (1981b), *The Retention of Minority Languages in the United States*. Washington: The National Center for Education Statistics.

Veltman, Calvin and Jac-André Boulet (1980), *L'incidence de la mobilité linguistique sur la situation économique et le rang social des travailleurs montréalais en 1971*. Montréal: Office de la langue française.

Waggoner, Dorothy (1981), 'Language and Demographic Characteristics of the U.S. Population with Potential Need for Bilingual and Other Special Educational Programs,' mimeo, National Center for Education Statistics, U.S. Department of Education.

Contributions to the Sociology of Language
edited by Joshua A. Fishman

This series brings to students, researchers, and practitioners in all of the social and language-related sciences the best book-length publications dealing with sociolinguistic theory, methods, findings and applications.

J. L. Dillard (Editor) Perspectives on American English
vol. 29, 1980, VIII + 468 pp. DM 110,–; US $50.00

Twenty-seven essays providing some essentially historical perspectives for the study of American English, including recent studies on the early influence of nautical terminology on American English as well as the variations used by the Pennsylvania Germans, Yiddish-speaking groups, and those speaking Puerto Rican "Spanglish," Black English, and Pidgin English.

Joshua A. Fishman (Editor) Never Say Die!
A Thousand Years of Yiddish in Jewish Life and Letters
vol. 30, 1981, XVI + 762 pp. DM 95,–; US $43.25

With nearly 800 pages of articles (about half of them written in Yiddish, with English summaries) and illustrations about the role of Yiddish during a thousand years of Jewish life in Eastern Europe, the United States, and Israel, this volume is intended not only for all those who speak the language but also are eager to find out what outstanding writers, cultural spokesmen, political leaders, and religious authorities have long said and written about Yiddish as a great storehouse of Jewish values.

Peter G. Forster The Esperanto Movement
vol. 32, 1982, XIV + 413 pp. DM 120,–; US $54.75

Research monograph examining the history of the Esperanto movement from a sociological and linguistic perspective, from its beginnings in late 19th century Russian Poland to its growth into an international movement. The present volume offers the first in-depth treatment of the movement for those unable to read Esperanto, but curious to explore the movement's tendency to appeal to wider values in support of Esperanto.

The author relies principally on printed documents, supplemented by participant observation and questionnaires to show the variations in the orientation of Esperantists during the history of the organized movement and the difficulties these pose for categorizing the movement sociologically. Consideration is given both to the dynamics of the movement within the broad context of European international relations and in the particular context of British society. Included in the appendices is a summary of the Esperanto-grammar.

Prices are subject to change without notice

mouton publishers
Berlin · New York · Amsterdam

Contributions to the Sociology of Language
edited by Joshua A. Fishman

This series brings to students, researchers, and practitioners in all of the social and language-related sciences the best book-length publications dealing with sociolinguistic theory, methods, findings and applications.

Mary Ritchie Key (Editor) **Nonverbal Communication Today**
Current Research
vol. 33, 1982, XIV+319 pp. DM 105,—; US $35.95

This collection of papers addresses extra-linguistic messages — non-verbal expressions that are part of every communicative/behavioral event. The studies include the areas of animal communication, cognition, infant and child behavior, eye behavior, emotions, communication of the deaf, quantum scattering theory, cerebral specialization, acquisition of language and gestural language.

Juan Cobarrubias and Joshua A. Fishman (Editors) **Progress in Language Planning**
International Perspectives
vol. 31, 1983, 383 pp. DM 122,—; US $49.95

A collective undertaking to update and expand the field of language planning, this volume contains fifteen interdisciplinary essays that cover the areas of decision making in language planning, codification, implementation and evaluation. The approach of the essays is mainly international, including essays that refer to the implementation of language planning in China and the Soviet Union and a special section on language planning in North America. The theoretical framework rests on the distinction between status planning (policy planning) and corpus planning. Thus, some of the essays study the relation between legislative decisions and decisions about language status; others study the ethical implications of decisions about language status; others cover a wide array of issues pertaining to the standardization process, language modernization and models of non-native language varieties; while still others cover the theoretical and practical aspects of language planning implementation and the entire spectrum of evaluation of language planning.

Prices are subject to change without notice

mouton publishers
Berlin · New York · Amsterdam